W9-BNA-404

The Broadband Explosion

Leading Thinkers on the Promise

of a Truly Interactive World

Edited by

Robert D. Austin

and

Stephen P. Bradley

HARVARD BUSINESS SCHOOL PRESS

Boston, Massachusetts

Printed in the United States of America

09 08 07 06 05 5 4 3 2 1

Library of Congress Cataloging-in-Publication Data

The broadband explosion : leading thinkers on the promise of a truly interactive world / edited by Robert D. Austin and Stephen P. Bradley.
    p. cm.
 Includes bibliographical references.
 ISBN 1-59139-670-0
 1. Telecommunication—Technological innovations. 2. Broadband communication systems. 3. Internet industry. I. Bradley, Stephen P., 1941- II. Austin, Robert D. (Robert Daniel), 1962-
  HE7631.B757 2005
  384.3'3—dc22

                                                    2005005507

The paper used in this publication meets the minimum requirements of the American National Standard for Information Sciences—Permanence of Paper for Printed Library Materials, ANSI Z39.48-1992.

Contents

Creating Value in a Broadband World

Capturing the Value of Wireless Broadband

Policy and the Broadband Future

Preface

The Harvard Business School's fourth colloquium on the state of the converging worlds of information technology and telecommunications, "The Bandwidth Explosion: Living and Working in a Broadband World," was held in April 2003, an interesting time for the telecommunications industry—interesting in the sense of the Chinese curse.[1] As was apparent to colloquium participants, the telecommunications industry was then mired in a depression. Large service providers, such as MCI WorldCom and Global Crossing, struggled to emerge from a vast upheaval. A plague of bankruptcy had swept the industry. The optical networking sector, once an investor's darling, lay in near total ruin, despite widespread acknowledgment that its technologies would be a vital part of any infrastructure of the future. Surviving public companies had lost an order of magnitude in their share prices; private companies had abandoned exit strategies for the foreseeable future.

Because so much had changed so quickly, because the ups and downs had come in such a short interval, the spring of 2003 was a difficult time to engage in sense making. Nevertheless, sense making is just what we attempted during those two days in Boston, Massachusetts. The outcomes of our efforts are contained within this book. Contributors to this volume subjected their ideas to debate among a distinguished group of colloquium participants, and subsequently developed the chapters that follow. Despite the challenges inherent in the attempt to see order amid the industry's chaos, the results are, we hope, a significant addition to the tradition of Harvard Business School (HBS) colloquia on the subject.

The Harvard Business School has sponsored a series of colloquia on the converging worlds of information technology and telecommunications. The four colloquia to date are depicted in figure P-1 against the stages of information technology evolution. The initial colloquium, "Future Competition in Telecommunications," was held in 1987, three years after the first breakup of AT&T in response to the Modified Final Judgment issued by the Federal District Court of the District of Columbia. The judgment initiated an era in which telecommunications and computers began to integrate in earnest. Companies began to experience the full impact of Moore's Law, the doubling of computing power (or halving of

FIGURE P-1

HBS IT colloquia, 1987–2003

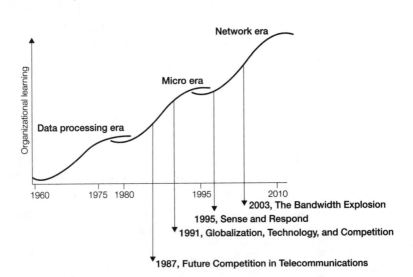

Source: "The Bandwidth Explosion" Colloquium, Harvard Business School, April 2003.

cost) every eighteen months, in combination with similar growth in the availability of network bandwidth.[2]

The second colloquium, "Globalization, Technology, and Competition," held in 1991, focused on "the fusion of computers and telecommunications in the 1990s" and took stock of emerging data and voice communications networks, with a focus on their international aspects. Both the United Kingdom and Japan had privatized their formerly government-run telephone companies; both countries permitted competition in long-distance service. Though restrictions persisted in some countries (such as France and Germany), many other countries allowed broad competition in data services, equipment purchases, and cellular services. The effects, many and complex, laid the groundwork for the emergence a few years later of the commercial Internet.[3]

The 1995 colloquium, "Sense and Respond: Capturing Value in the Network Era," examined the development of the Internet, client/server technologies, and online service providers such as AOL. The strategic paradigm that emerged from the colloquium called for companies to shift from "make and sell" approaches geared to producing goods for inventory—a strategy driven by the annual budget cycle—to a "sense and respond" approach that sought to understand customers' needs and to dynamically redeploy assets—a strategy driven by actual customer demand.[4] But sense-and-respond could not be fully implemented with the technology available in 1995. A shift to the new paradigm had to await the burgeoning commercial Internet, real-time computing, and—most crucially—true interactivity.

As the industry emerges from its present difficulties, we appear to be on the verge of achieving some of the long-awaited successes suggested by the trajectory of earlier colloquia. This book illustrates how the momentum of the industry continues to play out, influenced by business forces and policy decisions; it describes details being worked on to move us toward a broadband world, as well as the many challenges and choices that remain. As the past held numerous surprises, though, so will the future. Participants in the next HBS colloquium, as they consider the outcomes of this one, will no doubt be astounded by what we missed. Maybe (hopefully), they will also be impressed by what we understood and foresaw. Time will tell. For now, perhaps readers will discover here ideas and insights to help navigate through and beyond these interesting times.

Acknowledgments

We owe a great deal of thanks to a large number of people who contributed in one way or another to the creation of this book. We are especially grateful to Dean Kim Clark and the Division of Research of the Harvard Business School for making the time and resources available for this work, including the support for the colloquium "The Bandwidth Explosion: Living and Working in a Broadband World," held on the Harvard Business School campus in April 2003. The colloquium provided a dynamic and provocative forum for discussing the key drivers of the broadband explosion. We are particularly indebted to its engaging and enthusiastic keynote speakers—Clayton Christensen of Harvard Business School, Dr. Douglas Van Houweling of Internet2, Jeffrey Hunker of the H. John Heinz III School of Public Policy and Management, Reed Hundt of McKinsey & Company and former chairman of the Federal Communications Commission (FCC), and Takeshi Natsuno of NTT DoCoMo—for identifying some of the most significant issues.

We thank the distinguished panelists—Salvador Arias of IBM Global Services, Jim Balsille of Research In Motion, Sky Dayton of Boingo and EarthLink, Paul Florack of VeriSign Inc., Rob Glaser of RealNetworks, Jeff Huber of eBay, Darren Huston of Starbucks, Dave Labuda of Portal Software Inc., Bob Meyers of CNBC Ventures, Geoffrey Moore of The Chasm Group and Mohr, Davidow Ventures, Stagg Newman of McKinsey & Company, Rick Rashid of Microsoft, Eric Schmidt of Google, Russell Siegelman of Kleiner Perkins Caulfield & Byers, Kevin Werbach of the Supernova Group, and Jonathan Zittrain of Harvard Law School—who shared their vision, practical experience, and knowledge of the broadband world with the colloquium participants.

We greatly appreciate the contributions of the presenters—Erik Brynjolfsson of MIT; Eric Clemons of the Wharton School of the University of Pennsylvania; John Keane of ArcStream Solutions Inc.; H. T. Kung of Harvard University; and John Deighton, Thomas Eisenmann, and David Upton of Harvard Business School—who have been instrumental in the creation of the book, serving as a foundation for several of the chapters. Thank you to the group of session moderators—Rebecca Henderson of MIT; Charles Nesson of Harvard Law School; and Lynda Applegate, Andrew McAfee, and F. Warren McFarlan of Harvard Business School—who provided thought-provoking questions for the panel discussions. A special appreciation is extended to the colloquium attendees, who, though too numerous to mention by name, nevertheless contributed a great deal to the creative discourse from which the contents of this book ultimately emerged.

There were numerous individuals, often behind the scenes, whose talents, commitment, and creativity during preparation and execution of the colloquium were crucial to its success. In particular, from the Information Technology group of Harvard Business School and Harvard University, Ivan Audoin, Jeff Craddock, John Defriese, Raul Domingo, Leo Donnelly, Joel Frederick, David Habeeb, Ann Marie Henke, Jeff Lee, and Dana Urbach successfully conducted and managed a significant number of technically challenging, real-time, and time-sensitive activities. A special thank-you to Tom Snook, CTO, Howard Herring, CEO, and Chris Wallingford of the New World Symphony, Sara Carter, cellist, Larry Lesser, music coach, and Ted Hanss of Internet2 for their innovativeness and excitement, which made the master cellist lesson (discussed in chapter 1) possible. Thank you to Troy Fernald and Michael Savic of VBrick Systems Inc., who provided live video from Monterey Bay via Internet2, and Vickie Nauman of KEXP online for cutting-edge Internet radio programming. In addition, we acknowledge the valuable work of HBS Executive Education staff members Jessica Dukas and Cheri Mehigan, who provided around-the-clock support to the colloquium participants and ensured a flawless event. We appreciate the skill and creativity of Tammy Dotson and Tyler Hayes of Stolz Design in designing the Web site, and of Robin Panaro in the creation of the promotional material. Our appreciation goes out to Ramsey Stewart for his considerable contributions at the outset of the colloquium.

Many people helped us during the course of manuscript preparation. We owe a great deal of thanks to Ann Goodsell, whose unsurpassed talent and expertise was crucial to bringing together sixteen chapters from more than twenty authors to form a cohesive book. We are thankful for the time and pragmatic feedback from the reviewers of the manuscript. We thank our editor at Harvard Business School Press, Astrid Sandoval, for her valuable assistance. Our appreciation is extended also to our faculty assistants, Kathryn O'Brien and Zoya Omartian.

Finally, we are especially grateful to our research associate, Nancy Bartlett, the talented project manager for both the colloquium and the book.

Nancy tirelessly provided constructive suggestions throughout the project, handled many of the administrative details, and made significant research and drafting inputs, especially to the third part of the book. Without her invaluable assistance, this book would never have been written.

—*Rob Austin and Steve Bradley*

Notes

1. "May you live in interesting times." The origins of this curse are uncertain. Robert F. Kennedy used it in a speech in Cape Town, South Africa, on June 7, 1966. According to http://www.noblenet.org/reference/inter.htm, however, "the popularity of this 'Chinese curse' puzzles Chinese scholars, who have only heard it from Americans." This source goes on to say of the supposed curse that "it may be a paraphrase of a liberal translation from a Chinese source, and therefore unrecognizable when translated back to Chinese."

2. For more details about this colloquium, see Stephen P. Bradley and Jerry A. Hausman, eds., *Future Competition in Telecommunications* (Boston: Harvard Business School Press, 1989).

3. For more details about this colloquium, see Stephen P. Bradley, Jerry A. Hausman, and Richard L. Nolan, eds., *Globalization, Technology, and Competition* (Boston: Harvard Business School Press, 1993).

4. Stephen P. Bradley and Richard L. Nolan, eds., *Sense and Respond* (Boston: Harvard Business School Press, 1998).

The Promise of Broadband

1

The Broadband Explosion

Robert D. Austin and Stephen P. Bradley

The student embraced her cello, bow raised, eyes fixed on a sheet of music, attentive to the teacher's words. The teacher held his own cello, but with bow lowered. The object of their attention: a difficult Bach suite from the "Anna Magdalena" manuscripts. At the teacher's prompting, the student played two passages, from different parts of the suite. As she completed the second, a startled look crossed her face. The teacher noted her change of expression.

"Yes," said the teacher, "they have a parallel structure."

The student nodded, excited.

"Have you noticed that before?"

"No. It's . . . important . . . I see that."

The teacher smiled. The student played again. Moments later, she mused: "It's good. It's very . . ."

"Yes," the teacher agreed, "that Bach—he's a pretty good composer . . ." The student erupted in laughter. The teacher joined in. A moment later, the lesson continued.

A SKILLED TEACHER conveys a subtle lesson in the intense environment of a master class. Exactly the sort of experience, you might think, that music teachers and students have been sharing for centuries. But if that's what you thought, you'd be wrong.

This talented cellist, Sarah Carter, a student at Harvard University, took her lesson not in a practice room at the music school but in a classroom at the business school, before an audience of participants in the fourth Harvard Business School (HBS) Colloquium on the Information Technology and Telecommunications Industries, "The Bandwidth Explosion: Living and Working in a Broadband World." Her audience was rapt.

But the most notable feature of her lesson was that the teacher, Larry Lesser, an experienced professional musician, was at that moment located in a room at the New World Symphony, thousands of miles away in Miami, Florida. Carter was facing not Lesser himself but a full-size, high-resolution video image projected onto a screen. Sound from Miami arrived in Boston via high-fidelity digital sound encoding and decoding technology. Lesser saw and heard Carter in the same way. Communications between student and teacher were transmitted in real time using Internet Protocol (IP) across "Abilene," the high-bandwidth Internet2 backbone network. Data transmission rates were on the order of 10 million bits per second. The resulting qualitative experience was rich enough to convey subtle meaning.

Although clearly not an experience that music teachers and students had been sharing for centuries, this music lesson was far from historic. The New World Symphony, working with Internet2, had conducted many such classes, and continues to experiment with this and other uses of information and telecommunications technology. Typically, the students are located in Miami, and the teachers are performing abroad. Students receive training from masters who would otherwise be geographically inaccessible.

If the event was not itself history-making, however, surely the phenomenon it exemplifies is. Since nearly the dawn of the computer age, people have sought to employ digital technology to bridge distance, in order to enhance work productivity and provide entertainment, and for a variety of other purposes. Almost forty years ago, Internet pioneers J. C. R. Licklider and Bob Taylor described their prescient vision of computerized collaboration in "The Computer as a Communication Device."[1] Today, finally, their vision seems near to being realized. Experiences like the cello master class are still far from commonplace, but communication via computer technologies is increasingly approximating what might reasonably be called "interactivity." As amazing as PCs, e-mail, and the Web are, as greatly as they have transformed our lives, they are not as *interactive* as newer technologies like instant messaging, full-function text pagers, cell phones, and other personal wireless devices. At the heart of the new interactivity, its *sine qua non*, is cheap and abundant bandwidth—the broadband explosion.

This story is not just about the growing capacity of data "pipes." The context of recent progress in telecommunications is complex. The Internet bubble has burst. A period of intense experimentation with information technologies has passed, and its like will not be seen again. But a mature worldwide network has survived—a network with a steadily improving infrastructure to support not just communication and computation but also commerce. Even during the lull after the Internet storm, that period of fiscal conservatism in information technology, people still worked quietly to make the network better: getting pieces to work together more easily, connecting more computing resources and storage capacity, securing transactions, and improving systems of search and retrieval. When the master cellist asked the student whether she had seen an alternative version of the Bach manuscript, she said no. Within minutes, David Croson, a colloquium participant, tracked down the alternative version on the Web and presented it to the cellist in full-screen mode on his wirelessly networked notebook computer. On-the-spot retrieval of an obscure, several-hundred-year-old manuscript may not be historic, but the ease with which Professor Croson accessed a document once consigned to dusty museum archives impressed colloquium participants as another remarkable dimension of a generally remarkable experience.

To be sure, the technology on display in that Harvard classroom had limitations. During the question-and-answer period, a colloquium participant asked whether teacher and student could play together. They tried to but could not. The problem, as one technician put it, was "that speed-of-light thing." The few-millisecond delay between transmittal and receipt of message packets that traversed so many miles, unnoticeable when teacher and student were taking turns, was apparent when they tried to play in unison. Moreover, both rooms were staffed with numerous technical-support people. The session was difficult to initiate and was delayed at the start for troubleshooting. In this and other ways, a substantial gap remains between daily face-to-face interaction and computer-supported communication. Nevertheless, we have—perhaps—turned a significant corner.

In the decade since the last HBS colloquium on this subject, the growth in deployment of telecommunications devices has been impressive. In 1995, there were 235 million personal computer users and 40 million Internet users worldwide. In 2005, PC users topped 700 million, and Internet users—thanks to proliferating means of accessing the network—moved even higher, surpassing 1 billion.[2] More-interactive technologies grew faster. Cellular telephone subscribers, for example, grew from 91 million in 1995 to over 1.3 billion in 2003 (about a quarter of them in China).[3] Instant messaging was virtually unknown in 1995; by 2004 there were more than 600 million instant messaging accounts.[4] Broadband penetration lurks in this story as a subplot. By 2003, more than 16 million U.S. households were connected to the Internet via high-speed lines.[5] Other countries were even more "wired"; South Korea led the way, with more than 70 percent of households connected via broadband at the end of 2003. (Interestingly, the United States does not make the top 10 list when it comes to the proportion of households that are broadband connected; see table 1-1.) Meanwhile, richer media promote interactivity by improving communicative experiences: of the estimated 600 million cell phones sold worldwide in 2004, 150 million included a digital camera, capable of transmitting photos over telecommunications networks.[6] A popular holiday gift at the end of 2004 was a cell phone that could capture and send video. Computer equipment is now routinely sold with low-cost video equipment included. When

TABLE 1-1

Broadband penetration rates by country

Rank	Country	Number of broadband subscribers per 100 inhabitants (Jan. 2004)	Households using broadband as a percentage of total households (end of 2003)	Percentage of population with high-speed Internet access (2002)
1	South Korea	24.0	70.5%	21.3%
2	Hong Kong	17.0	50.3%	14.6%
3	Canada	15.0	36.2%	11.5%
4	Iceland	14.5	na	8.6%
5	Taiwan	12.5	43.2%	9.4%
6	Denmark	12.0	25.7%	8.6%
7	Belgium	11.5	24.7%	8.4%
8	Japan	11.0	28.0%	na
9	Netherlands	11.0	na	6.5%
10	Switzerland	11.0	23.1%	na
13	United States	10.0	22.5%	6.5%

Sources: Data from http://www.itu.int/osg/spu/newslog/2004/09/15.html; International Telecommunications Commission; eMarketer, September 2004; Yesawich, Pepperdine, Brown & Russel, May 2003, http://www.ypbr .com; ETC New Media Review, http://www.etcnewmedia.com.

we look back on this period several years from now—to that day when Sarah Carter took her first (and probably not her last) music lesson over a broadband connection—it may turn out to have been an important inflection point.

The Rise of Interactivity

There are interesting parallels between technology developments in the early twenty-first century and the late 1960s. Then, people struggled to understand Moore's Law, which expressed the exponentially growing power of digital computer technologies. One view held at the time was that the growing power of computers would reach a point of diminishing returns. People who thought of computers as giant calculators, or giant transaction machines, believed that all the most important calculations and transactions would soon be accomplished, leaving only mundane tasks for which such expensive machines were uneconomical. Looking forward to a not-far-distant time of superabundant computation, some asked, "What will we do with all that processing power?" Faced with this question, many had no good answer.

Fortunately, a few imaginations were less limited. A group of computing pioneers, mostly trained as psychologists, mostly interested in perception—Licklider, Taylor, Doug Engelbart, Wesley Clark, and others—had plans for all that processing power. While most people extrapolated in a straight line from the transactional uses of computers that prevailed in the 1960s, this group of visionaries thought laterally. They imagined a use for extra processing power that involved not more of the same kind of computation, but something entirely different: enhancing the experience of using computers, making them more useful and extending human capabilities.

Licklider spelled out the frustrations of working with computers more than forty years ago: "You formulate your problem today. Tomorrow you spend with a programmer. Next week the computer devotes five minutes to assembling your program and 47 seconds calculating the answer to your problem. You get a sheet of paper 20 feet long, full of numbers that, instead of providing a final solution, only suggest a tactic that should be explored by simulation." [7]

The lead times in using computers then were too long; too much time was required between trying something once and trying another variation. Thus, Licklider and his fellow visionaries suggested using the computing

power projected by Moore's Law to shorten the cycle of use—to change
how people and computers could work together. Extra computing power
would be used not to perform additional conventional transactions but to
provide a more natural experience for computer users. Much of this vision
has been realized. It is now commonplace for computing power to be dedicated to friendly interface formats and making sure the computer responds
immediately and helpfully to inputs from the user. Computers have become, in a word, more *interactive*, and human-computer interactivity no
longer strikes us as new or remarkable.

But there is an aspect of interactivity, involving digital devices, that *is*
new since the mid-1990s. Consider this complaint about using communications technologies, a deliberate echo of Licklider's complaint four decades
ago: "You make final adjustments to the proposed deal today and e-mail it.
Tomorrow the other party extracts himself from meetings long enough to
catch up on his e-mail. Next week, when his staff in this area returns from a
business trip, the two of them discuss your proposal for ten minutes, make
three minutes' worth of adjustments to it, and e-mail it back to you. You receive a modified document that, far from closing the deal, brings to mind
another factor you ought to introduce into your negotiations."

The problem here, as in the earlier example, is an absence of interactivity,
but of a different sort. The lead times associated with the communication
medium, e-mail, are too long. Too much time passes between adjustments to
the proposal.

Now imagine the same scenario using the kind of technology available
during the cello lesson. The cycle of proposal and counterproposal that con-
sumed more than a week by e-mail might take five minutes via video teleconference. If that video teleconference could be mounted from wherever
relevant staff might be in the world, we could begin to rely on such short cycles of interaction in communication. There would be no delay while waiting
for a partner to return from a business trip. The interactivity of computing
and communicating would become more ordinary and seamless.

In recent years, some commentators have echoed the skeptics of the
1960s, responding to technology enthusiasts' forecasts of abundant and inexpensive broadband with a resounding "So what?" "What," these pes-
simists ask, "will we do with all that bandwidth? Surely we will soon be able
to send all the information that is of any importance, and extra bandwidth
will be devoted to conveying minutiae or unedifying noise." It is not hard to
find examples of minutiae and noise in broadcast media, such as television,

and even on the Internet. Indeed, the world has undeniably transitioned in the last hundred years from an information environment of relative scarcity to one of overwhelming abundance. And yet the memory of how computing has evolved up until now reminds us of the need for lateral thinking.

What will we do with all that bandwidth? Perhaps something similar to what we did with all that computing power in the 1960s: make the experience of using computers and related technologies still more interactive. High bandwidth is not required for all forms of communicative interactivity—text messaging, for example, is interactive but not bandwidth-hungry. But greater bandwidth greatly enhances the scope of activities that can be undertaken interactively, and the quality of the interactions. If we take our cue from computing pioneers, we should expect that the most exciting uses of cheap and abundant bandwidth will not be more of the same. The most important effects will be of a second or third order. What second- and third-order effects? Or if we cannot envision them in particular, what will be their general nature? What happens when interactivity reaches a new level?

Interactivity and Business Innovation

The business implications of interactivity—especially the enhanced interactivity emerging from the broadband explosion—extend far beyond the productivity-enhancing effects of better human-computer interfaces. One less than obvious implication of interactivity in communication is that it allows innovation in business to become more rapid and less expensive. When computerization dramatically reduces effort and lead time required to, say, arrive at an agreement on the terms of a deal, we can make more adjustments and adjust more often. We are, therefore, more likely to reach a more creative agreement.

When people think about using computers to automate business activities, they typically think of the *efficiency-enhancing* effects. Computers make it possible to perform the same actions over and over rapidly, cheaply, and correctly. Typically, these actions are parts of procedures that have been set up in advance. In making automobiles in a factory, for example, computers might be used to execute process steps already thought out in detail, to ensure efficiency, consistency, and quality.

But the computerized interactivity of a cello master class, or a deal being hammered out at a distance, has effects different from those that arise from efficiency-enhancing technology. The point of a cello lesson or a deal is to move action into *novel* territory. What matters about this kind of automation is not that it enforces consistency but that it enables cheap and rapid adjustment to produce original (not previously thought-out) outcomes. When Professor Croson retrieved the alternative "Anna Magdalena" manuscript, he was using technology to support collaborative activity in a way that no one had anticipated before the master class began. This is the essential characteristic of true interactivity that separates it from the effects of traditional automation technology—that it supports truly novel activity that was not, and perhaps could not have been, thought out in advance.

Interactivity accelerates innovation by making it possible to explore more thoroughly, to try more approaches than you would otherwise have been able to. Two parties negotiating at a distance can do deals that never would have been done otherwise; they can come up with a more creative deal because it is less time-consuming and costly to keep trying new ideas before coming to agreement. Value is created that would not have been created otherwise.

Because interactivity makes adjustments easier and quicker, people who are creating something new (products, strategies, businesses) can substitute experience for planning. They can just try something, rather than planning at length before taking action, because, if it turns out wrong, it will be easy to adjust. They can *prototype* new ideas (see figure 1-1). The pressure to "get it right the first time," born out of fear of costly adjustment and rare opportunity for high-quality interaction, diminishes. You don't have to get it right the first time, because there is ample time and money for a second, third, and fourth time. You can wait longer to "freeze" a contractual relationship, a design, or anything else you might be in the process of creating, because there is less to be feared from additional changes.

Applying computer and communication technologies to enhance interactivity is fundamentally different from using them for consistent and efficient replication of a preprogrammed process. To use these technologies to enhance interactivity is to support ongoing *reconception*—making a thing different and *better* each time you return to it. The power of reconception is magnified when interactivity is qualitatively rich, as in the cello lesson, and when it can occur at a distance and draw on resources that might otherwise be unavailable, such as the master cello teacher. Collaboration at a distance becomes more similar to collaboration in person. This kind of collaboration underpins the most important forms of today's knowledge work, and it is arguably the key to the next level of economic value creation in many areas of commerce.[8]

FIGURE 1-1

An iterative process enabled by interactivity

Conceive agreement, idea, or prototype

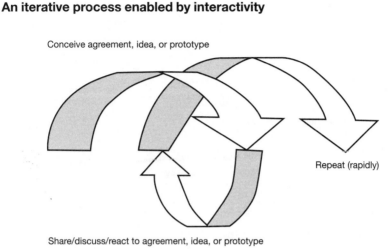

Repeat (rapidly)

Share/discuss/react to agreement, idea, or prototype

Source: Robert Austin and Lee Devin. *Artful Making: What Managers Need to Know about How Artists Work,* 1st ed., © 2003. Reprinted by permission of Pearson Education, Inc., Upper Saddle River, NJ.

The Impacts of Broadband Deployment: A Framework

Figure 1-2 summarizes the forces that can lead to new business innovation and provides a framework for the contents of this book. Massively deployed broadband is a prerequisite for the future we envision. Massive broadband deployment gives rise to real-time interactivity and rich media experiences; together these create the possibility for collaboration at a distance of a quality and reliability similar to what we experience in daily face-to-face interaction. Collaboration of sufficient quality, in turn, generates an explosion of new capabilities, markets, and strategies. Underlying all of this, forming the landscape upon which the potential of broadband will be nurtured or inhibited, resides a layer of hopefully effective public policy.

The first part of this book, "The Promise of Broadband," discusses how massive broadband deployment might come about and explains the forces that combine to create high-quality collaboration at a distance. In chapter 2, "Broadband and Collaboration," Jeremy Allaire and Robert Austin argue that when real-time interactivity combines with rich media experience, we can expect spectacular second- and third-order outcomes. Allaire, a venture capitalist and the former CTO of Macromedia, and Austin, an

FIGURE 1-2

The broadband explosion

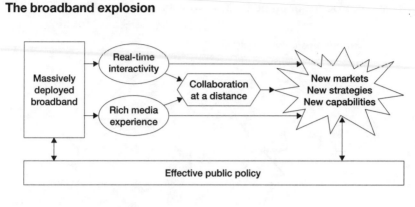

Source: Robert D. Austin and Stephen P. Bradley

HBS professor who studies the processes that underlie innovative knowledge work, combine complementary viewpoints to demonstrate that collaboration at a distance is ready to appear and that its effects on the conduct of business might well be dramatic.

In chapter 3, "Broadband Deployment: From Vision to Reality," Dr. Stagg Newman, a McKinsey & Company consultant and former FCC economist, describes the current state of the overall broadband landscape. This important chapter provides context for every other chapter in the book as it outlines alternative visions of the broadband infrastructure, differing views on how best to deploy that infrastructure, what has been accomplished already, and what remains to be done. A particularly important question Newman raises is whether a market economy can be depended upon to supply the level of broadband deployment that will maximize societal value creation, or whether some form of additional government encouragement (e.g., funding) might be advisable. Some of the interest in this question derives from the fact that countries answer it in different ways. The Republic of Korea, for example, where broadband penetration is highest, has not relied solely on market-based solutions to deploy infrastructure; the United States, in contrast, has taken a much more market-based approach, but also has significantly lower broadband penetration. Whether the additional stimulus provided by Korea has resulted in oversupply, or whether imperfections in the market for broadband services have caused undersupply in the United States can be debated. But if you believe that the effects of broadband deployment are as economically important as chapter 2 suggests, then there can be no debating that this is a high-stakes question.

Chapter 4, "Valuation Bubbles and Broadband Deployment," by HBS professor Thomas Eisenmann, tackles this issue of whether markets will reliably supply appropriate levels of investment in infrastructure by closely examining a related investment phenomenon—the recent Internet "bubble." The boom and bust character of the pattern of investment in Internet companies, beginning with the Netscape IPO in 1995 and continuing to the present day, does not *appear* to be the best way to invest in emerging industry segments. The Internet bubble is often cited, in fact, as a reason why markets alone *cannot* be relied upon to maximize value to society. Bringing to bear data and careful analysis, Eisenmann reaches conclusions that are not entirely consistent with such casual interpretations of recent events.

In the second part of this book, "Creating Value in a Broadband World," we shift our attention to the right side of figure 1-2, from "broadband" and its social effects to the resulting business "explosion." In chapter 5, "Disruption, Disintegration, and the Impact of New Telecommunications Technologies," Clay Christensen and Scott Anthony interpret the recent history of the telecommunications industry through the lens of Christensen's well-known theory of disruptive innovation. Extrapolating the theory into the future, they offer two models for predicting how new technologies will develop, which players will prevail, and how the structure of the industry will shift. Their analysis of causes and effects of industry competition move us into the realm of business strategy, providing detailed insight into the futures of such important technologies as Voice over IP (VoIP) and wireless broadband.

In chapter 6, "Internet2: The Promise of Truly Advanced Broadband," Ted Hanss and Dr. Douglas Van Houweling take us on a tour of the pre-commercial world of advanced broadband applications in university and corporate laboratories. Internet2 is a consortium of universities (more than two hundred) plus industry and government partners with a common interest: to develop and deploy advanced network applications and technologies, thus accelerating the creation of tomorrow's Internet. The idea behind Internet2 is to re-create the same kind of collaboration among academics, industry players, and government agencies that gave us the first version of the Internet, in hopes of creating a next-generation version (i.e., Internet2). Hanss has spent the past several years overseeing the consortium's advanced applications; Van Houweling, the president and CEO, has been responsible for the Internet2 vision; they are, thus, expert guides. It may be difficult to grasp now how high-definition TV over IP or remote sensing of atmospheric conditions in Greenland makes for a compelling business plan, but every one of these impressive applications includes ideas that might grow into business models. In all likelihood, somewhere amid the test beds and experiments described in this chapter lurk the next-generation "killer apps."

If chapters 5 and 6 introduce us to new strategies and capabilities that result from broadband deployment, chapter 7 shows us how broadband-enabled collaboration can create new markets. In "Broadband and Hyper-differentiation: Creating Value by Being *Really* Different," Eric Clemons and several fellow researchers from the Wharton School of the University of Pennsylvania demonstrate how rich media collaboration between geographically dispersed sellers and buyers allow businesses and their customers to realize value that was previously inaccessible. The ability to market highly specialized products focused on very narrow market segments via the Internet and other telecommunications media—products that would not have been viable in earlier markets—completes the cycle of reconceiving described earlier in this chapter. Interactivity allows us to *create* more unique products and services because it makes adjustments to them quicker and easier. But that same interactivity also provides a means to *sell* more unique, highly differentiated products and services by connecting (in rich media environments) sellers and buyers who would not have gotten together without broadband technology intermediation.

Chapter 8, "eChoupal: Revolutionizing Supply Chains in Rural India," by David Upton and Virginia Fuller, both of HBS, presents a case study that demonstrates how information and telecommunications technology can transform markets. The market for soybeans in India's central state of Madhya Pradesh had operated for centuries with inefficiencies that particularly harmed farmers, who were routinely cheated by middle operators who knew more about world commodity prices. These same inefficiencies were a principal reason the agricultural export division of corporate giant ITC underperformed its business targets. To address the problem, ITC launched an ambitious initiative aimed at providing computer and telecommunications technologies, and thus information (commodity prices, weather, growing advice, etc.), to farmers in rural villages. To date, the impact of this program has been substantial, expanding the economic surplus available to be divided among the players, improving the lives of all in the supply chain, and creating secondary markets for agricultural and other products (e.g., insurance, DVD players) that can be sold to the newly affluent farmers and their families. Nearly 2.5 million people have so far benefited from the program.

Arguably the most important technology trend in the broadband world is the expansion of wireless technologies; the nature of business opportunity in the wireless space is the topic of the third part of this book, "Capturing the Value of Wireless Broadband." In chapter 9, "i-mode: Value Chain Strategy in the Wireless Ecosystem," Takeshi Natsuno, the entrepreneurial dynamo behind the strategy for NTT DoCoMo, the most innovative and successful wireless company in the world, explains the logic behind i-mode's extraordinary success. The i-mode strategy was largely built around a contentcentric business model with a very strong consumer-orientated marketing approach. Rather than create its own proprietary standards, DoCoMo adopted the de facto standards of the Internet in order to get the content providers to partner with the company and rapidly create a content-rich set of exciting applications, which in turn drove the explosive growth of the i-mode service. This same approach of creating a *wireless ecosystem* of supporting content suppliers has been carried over to DoCoMo's launch, in October 2001, of the world's first fully commercialized 3G mobile service, which by March 2004 covered 99 percent of the populated areas of Japan. In this chapter, Natsuno extrapolates from his DoCoMo experiences to a set of general strategic principles pertinent to the evolution of wireless broadband.

Chapter 10, "Wi-Fi: Complement or Substitute for 3G?" by HBS professor Stephen Bradley, examines the race between competing Wi-Fi and 3G technologies and asks whether the two might be substitutes rather than complements. In the United States, various forms of Wi-Fi (802.11a, b, g, etc.) have been deployed and are now widely available in private corporate settings and increasingly available in public settings such as airports, hotels, Starbucks, and so forth. Wi-Fi has the benefit of being truly broadband as it operates at 11 megabits per second (or greater) but is not truly mobile in the sense that it currently does not deal with handoffs in automobiles and trains. 3G, on the other hand, is truly mobile but is not really broadband, as it operates at 2 megabits per second at best and more often than not at 386 kilobits per second. Bradley looks at the apparently complementary value propositions of the two technologies and examines whether in fact Wi-Fi undermines the value proposition for rolling out 3G in the United States.

H. T. Kung, a Harvard computer scientist, weighs in on the prospects for Wi-Fi in chapter 11, "Wireless Local Area Networks: Why Integration Is Inevitable," arguing that integration of wireless local area networks (WLANs) into telecommunication systems promises extraordinary benefits for end users. Handset manufacturers, together with ISPs, fixed-wire operators, and WLAN aggregators, should be among the first to move toward integration, with WLAN-enabled handsets as the initial focal point. When such handsets become widespread, Kung suggests, other sectors will rapidly expand as competition emerges between traditional cellular operators and WLAN aggregators.

Ellen Daley, John Keane, and Ali Towle, of ArcStream Solutions Inc., a services firm that develops mobile solutions for vertical markets, offer their vision of the future of the wireless enterprise in chapter 12, "Widespread Adoption of Wireless Enterprise Solutions." The widespread adoption of these emerging technologies is driven, the authors suggest, by three key relatively independent factors: (1) their evolving technical maturity, (2) the availability of proven solutions, and (3) the general business climate. In the case of mobile and wireless technologies today, Daley, Keane, and Towle argue that the technical maturity and proven solutions have been achieved, but that a relatively weak business climate has discouraged widespread adoption. As the business climate continues to improve, they expect that widespread adoption will rapidly result.

In the book's final part, "Policy and the Broadband Future," we turn our attention to the public policy foundations that will influence the magnitude of any broadband explosion. In chapter 13, "The Inevitability of Broadband," Reed Hundt, former head of the FCC and the architect behind the controversial Telecommunications Act of 1996—the first effort in six decades to overhaul U.S. telecommunications law to make it more conducive to competition—draws on his experiences to offer advice and warnings to policy makers. In Hundt's view, the key goal of any regulatory policy is to promote economic growth. He speculates that the benefit of the FCC's promoting real broadband access to all households is to better ensure the competitiveness of the U.S. economy. He concludes that the best way to promote demand is (1) to avoid policies that would cause serious economic harm to cable and/or telephony firms or discourage construction of the broadband physical infrastructure, and (2) to stimulate growth through an efficient universal service policy that would produce economic and social benefits. A broadband infrastructure, he submits, is a platform for innovation and competitiveness.

Jeff Hunker, a Carnegie Mellon University professor of public policy and former senior director for critical infrastructure within the White House in charge of cyber security, offers warnings of his own in chapter 14, "Protecting Telecommunications Infrastructure from Malicious Threats." Hunker provides a comprehensive rundown of the nature and potential severity of threats, and suggests ways we might minimize our risks. His thoughts are, of course, newly relevant in a world of festering geopolitical conflict. No longer can we assume that hackers will be "script kiddies" bent on adolescent exploration; as we enter the twenty-first century, newfound cyber markets and other business activities are increasingly endangered by sophisticated organized criminals and even terrorists.

In chapter 15, "Open Spectrum: The Great Wireless Hope," Kevin Werbach, a professor of legal studies at Wharton with a focus on telecommunications, proposes revisions to the prevailing approach to allocating electromagnetic spectrum for communication. Werbach points out that the old paradigm, which calls for dividing up spectrum into separately owned segments to prevent interference, is obsolete, thanks to new technology. He imagines a world that embraces that fact and redesigns regulatory regimes to match the new reality. This open-spectrum world, Werbach points out, would foster innovative services, reduce prices, foster competition, create new business opportunities, and bring our communications policies in line with our democratic ideals.

Finally, in chapter 16, "The Balkanization of the Broadband Internet," Harvard Law professor Jonathan Zittrain points to a trend that is parallel to the deployment of broadband: the development of technologies that permit information providers to control access based on the location of the person attempting access. There are many legitimate reasons why businesses might want to know where a person accessing its services resides geographically. And yet, as Zittrain shows, there is a dark side to this trend as well. At the same time that the potential for broadband communication is growing, access may well also be compartmentalizing. He describes various means, many invisible, by which business or government interests may intrude into a broadband "world" to control what is accessible and who can access it. Eventually, he worries, states, countries, or entire continents might have very unequal access to the possibilities of a broadband explosion.

Tremendous Promise Yet Unrealized

In the evolving broadband world, much remains unsettled. The technologist's vision of a telecommunications infrastructure delivers vast bandwidth with very high reliability to virtually every conceivable point of access; this version of a broadband future would no doubt make many new things possible, including many that we cannot now imagine. But it would probably require huge up-front investments in optical infrastructure—investments that are unlikely to make sense to individual companies, at least given the constraints of existing technologies. As we have noted, some countries have begun subsidizing this kind of investment and have measurably progressed with their broadband deployment.

U.S. policy makers have taken a different approach, preferring to create a regulatory environment conducive to competition in telecommunications and leave the supply of infrastructure to the market. Although technologists are typically disappointed with the rate of progress so far achieved by this approach, it is too early to say which is the better course. Advantages of the latter approach may reveal themselves in the form of new technologies that create low-cost means of providing high levels of bandwidth, allowing companies to deploy cheap broadband without extensive government subsidies.

As we have argued, though, there is reason to believe that when real-time connectivity and rich media combine to a sufficient degree, when a critical mass of infrastructure deployment has been reached, the result may be something like an explosion. Enthusiasts for high-bandwidth applications foresee a qualitative change beyond a certain level of bandwidth, a point at which "the world changes." At this point, the rate of business innovation improves. New capabilities, new markets, and new strategies become available. Business success would ostensibly follow. Whether and how countries invest in telecommunications infrastructure may turn out to be a matter of national competitiveness. Where in the world will people be able to mount a music lesson over thousands of miles' distance? How much of an advantage will companies that can count on high-quality collaboration at a distance have over those that cannot? High-stakes questions with high-stakes answers. We hope that the chapters that follow will shed some light on at least some of the issues that must be considered in deciding such questions.

Notes

1. J. C. R. Licklider and Bob Taylor, "The Computer as a Communication Device," *Science and Technology*, April 1968.

2. Source: http://www.internetworldstats.com/stats.htm and http://www.clickz.com/stats/.

3. Info Trends Research Group. Available at http://www.infotrends-rgi.com/home/infotrends.html.

4. The Radicati Group. Available at http://www.eos-solutions.com.au/news_2003/news_aug/news_aug1.htm.

5. Federal Communications Commission, "Trends in Telephone Service: Industry Analysis and Technology Division Wireline Competition Bureau," May 2004. Available at http://www.fcc.gov.wcb/stats.

6. Info Trends Research Group. Available at http://www.infotrends-rgi.com/home/infotrends.html.

7. J. C. R. Licklider, "Man-Computer Symbiosis," *IRE Transactions on Human Factors in Electronics*, HFE-1 (March 1960).

8. Some of the ideas in this paragraph are explored in much greater detail in Rob Austin and Lee Devin, *Artful Making* (Upper Saddle River, NJ: Financial Times Prentice Hall, 2003).

2

Broadband and Collaboration

Jeremy Allaire and Robert D. Austin

THE RAPID WORLDWIDE GROWTH of broadband is bringing to collaboration at a distance the same richness and spontaneity we enjoy in face-to-face interaction. The eventual impacts—new uses of computers, networks, and the Internet in commerce, education, entertainment, politics, research, and personal communications—can hardly be predicted.

Broadband is, of course, a mere prerequisite for a new kind of computer-based collaboration; in itself it is not sufficient. Other technologies are converging with broadband to move us toward real-time collaboration at a distance:

- Wireless networks, both cellular networks and Wi-Fi or other 802.11 variants of wireless broadband access

- Non-PC and PC-integrated client devices, including media- and camera-enabled mobile phones and handheld devices, and commodity peripherals like digital video cameras and Webcams

- Real-time peer-to-peer software platforms that enable multiperson interaction on computers without central orchestration

- Rich client runtime platforms that combine audio/video communications, Web services, and collaboration frameworks

Several of these technologies are discussed at greater length in other chapters. Our purpose here is to focus on the emerging possibilities such technologies present for collaboration. First, we will revisit the prescient vision of computer-supported collaboration articulated nearly four decades ago by Internet pioneers J. C. R. Licklider and Robert W. Taylor, an ambitious benchmark for current achievements. Then we will offer a framework for thinking about uses of technology to support collaboration, and for distinguishing collaborative uses from past applications of information technology to business and organizational problems. Finally, we will assess current progress toward the still-unrealized vision of seamless collaboration and describe some notable commercial developments in collaborative technologies.

The Early Vision: Licklider, Taylor, and Other Pioneers in Collaboration

As recently as thirty years ago, computers and software had essentially no role in the everyday lives of consumers and workers. Today, people in industrialized nations use the Internet routinely, to gather and disseminate information, to be entertained, to conduct commerce, and to interact with colleagues, family, and friends. Many twenty-first-century citizens access the Internet as casually as they consult their watches or turn on TVs. Also dramatic is exponential growth in the use of untethered mobile devices, which have progressed beyond voice communication to capture and send photographs and support game playing and other entertainments.

As dramatic and profound as these advances in computing and software infrastructure have been, though, mechanisms and platforms for real-time communication and collaboration have been slow to evolve. Current technology does not, in fact, embody the vision of computer-supported collaboration put forth by J. C. R. Licklider and Robert W. Taylor in the 1960s. When Licklider's influential 1960 paper introduced "Man-Computer Symbiosis," computers were known to the popular imagination primarily as large calculating machines that executed planned transactions with great speed and efficiency. Licklider strove to modify this image of the computer by proposing "cooperative interaction between men and electronic computers":

Present-day [that is, circa 1960] computers are designed primarily to solve preformulated problems or to process data according to predetermined procedures. The course of the computation may be conditional upon results obtained during the computation, but all the alternatives must be foreseen in advance . . . However, many problems that can be thought through in advance are very difficult to think through in advance. They would be easier to solve, and they could be solved faster, through an intuitively guided trial-and-error procedure in which the computer cooperated, turning up flaws in the reasoning or revealing unexpected turns in the solution.[1]

The kind of interactivity that springs free of predetermined procedures to create outcomes not conceived in advance is obviously consistent with collaborative activity; in fact, it is one of the aspects of human collaboration that people value most. But the relationship that Licklider envisions, between a person and a computer, does not yet amount to what most people mean by collaboration, because it does not (necessarily) involve more than one person.

In a 1968 paper coauthored with Robert W. Taylor, "The Computer as a Communication Device," Licklider remedied this shortcoming by examining explicitly how computers could facilitate interactivity among people: "We want to emphasize . . . the increasing significance of the jointly constructive, the mutually reinforcing aspect of communication—the part that transcends 'now we both know a fact that only one of us knew before.' When minds interact, new ideas emerge. We want to talk about the creative aspect of communication."[2]

Licklider and Taylor were intimately involved with computers (Taylor was head of the U.S. Defense Department initiative that created the first four nodes of the Internet, a position Licklider had held earlier in the decade), but both had been trained as psychologists, and they shared an interest in problems of human-computer interaction. They described collaboration as a process in which individuals compare their "mental models" of phenomena or problems that they are jointly experiencing. People begin with individual models, they suggested, and then "externalize" those models as a focus for discussion. Through discussion, individual models are examined, compared, and modified interactively: "When mental models are dissimilar, the achievement of communication might be signaled by changes in the structure of one of the models, or both of them . . . The meeting of many interactive minds is a more complicated process. Suggestions and recommendations may be elicited from all sides. The interplay may produce, not just a solution to the problem, but a new set of rules for solving problems. That, of course, is the essence of creative interaction." The primary appeal of this characterization of collaboration is that it suggests technological approaches to real-time collaboration at a distance. It did not take long for such technological approaches to appear in prototype form.

On December 9, 1968, Douglas Engelbart and seventeen other researchers from the Augmentation Research Center at Stanford Research Institute in Menlo Park, California, presented a ninety-minute live public demonstration of "the OnLine System" (NLS) at the Fall Joint Computer Conference in San Francisco. Engelbart and his team introduced numerous innovations conducive to interactivity and collaboration, including the computer mouse, hypertext, object addressing, and dynamic file linking, as well as a screen that allowed two people at different sites to externalize and interactively modify shared representations.[3] The team received a standing ovation. Since this very promising start, we have continued to search for ways to make computers real substitutes for physical communication and collaboration. But we have largely failed. Things have moved much more slowly than Licklider and Taylor believed they would.

It took nearly twenty years for the personal computer to become a mainstream consumer device. And PCs alone could not solve the collaboration problem, because both their hardware and their software were designed in a way that left them unconnected to other computers. It took almost as long for basic local area networks (LANs) to emerge, providing some of the essentials needed to deliver on the vision of collaboration. But the reach of networked computers was still too limited—the promise of communicating and collaborating inside the walls of an organization was insufficient motivation for a drive toward real-time collaboration. When PC operating systems did evolve to support network-based applications, their thrust was toward basic operations like moving files between machines and accessing remote databases.

In the mid-1990s tens of thousands of LANs connected to the public Internet, creating a foundation for communications and collaboration. Indeed, the primary driver of TCP/IP-based internetworking was communications—in particular, e-mail, public newsgroups, and mailing lists. The drive to collaborate and communicate, even in relatively primitive forms, has consistently motivated the growth and adoption of internetworking. E-mail continues to be the number one use of the Internet and was arguably the primary motive for consumer adoption of dial-up connectivity.

Asynchronous threaded messaging has continued to proliferate in globally distributed newsgroups, mailing lists, and Web-based discussion systems. The past few years has seen rapid adoption of real-time instant messaging over computers and mobile devices, the first massive-scale adoption of real-time communications on computer devices.

We should not underestimate the importance of these advances, but they do not yet support the easy consideration and adjustment of sophisticated ideas and models by people in disparate locations that Licklider and Taylor envisioned. A heated discussion in a newsgroup is a sign of progress, but it is not a rich enough interaction to fulfill their vision. Today's commonplace examples of collaboration remain disappointingly rudimentary in comparison and should not be viewed as demonstrations of what is ultimately possible. More promising technologies are emerging. But before we look at recent developments, let us consider a framework—an elaboration on the ideas of Licklider and Taylor—for comparing how information technologies have supported productive activities in the past and how they will be used to support innovative collaboration in the future.

Using Technology to Support Reconceiving

Repetition is a fundamental feature of productive work; much of what we do when we create value must be done again and again. Moreover, information technologies have been particularly useful in performing the repetition required for useful actions. "Automating" a manufacturing plant, for example, typically means applying technology to make repeated processes more consistent and efficient. When people try to solve a problem interactively, they also employ repetition, using trial and error or experimentation to learn more about the problem and its possible solutions. In a problem-solving context, you might not repeat exactly the same motions, as in a manufacturing plant, but you are still usually trying something again and again, iterating through a process that is recognizably similar from repetition to repetition.

For purposes of understanding computer-supported collaboration, it will be useful to introduce some nuance into our concept of repetition and our view of how technology supports repetition. Specifically, we wish to distinguish between *replicating* and *reconceiving*, two forms of repetitive productive activity.[4] The repetition embodied in what Licklider and Taylor call "intuitively guided trial and error" and "creative interaction" is of a different nature than repetition in a manufacturing plant. Reconceiving and replicating differ in many ways, but the most important resides in their objectives.

We will deal first with replicating because it is more familiar in technological contexts. Replicating aspires to outcomes that conform as exactly as possible to an objective or a specification defined in advance. An automobile assembly line, for instance, might replicate Ford Taurus LXs with standard options in a spruce-green clear-coat metallic finish. The company intends to make all such vehicles identical (even if it makes that particular product permutation only rarely). What constitutes both a good car and a good process for making a car is known in detail in advance. Technology helps the automakers make certain that what they actually make conforms to what they conceived in advance. Or consider the interactive voice response (IVR) system that you interact with when you call your bank: it replicates the service of providing balance information. The bank intends to respond to every balance inquiry in exactly the same way (except for the actual dollar amounts retrieved). If the outcomes of replication are not identical when they are intended to be, we say we have a "quality problem." Much of the conceptual and physical machinery of industrial production is intended to perfect replication, to enhance efficiency, and avoid quality problems.

Reconceiving, by contrast, never tries to produce an outcome precisely defined in advance. People who are engaged in reconceiving may cycle repeatedly through a series of stages, such as brainstorming, problem definition/reformulation, experimentation and analysis, evaluation, and discussion. But this kind of repetition does not seek conformity to preconceptions of process or outcome. Often, reconceiving seeks the opposite: freedom from preconceptions and other constraints on creative thinking. Reconceiving takes conflicting circumstances, materials, and outcomes, and makes from them a new set of circumstances, materials, and outcomes. The new set tends to be more valuable than its precursors, but not always. Some repetitions "regress," producing outcomes that don't work as well as earlier ones. Progress tends to be incremental, but now and then reconceiving yields innovative leaps that surprise everyone. Reconceiving is the approach we usually use when we seek a new solution to a problem, a new product or service, or a new point of view on a familiar situation. It is also the process we typically often adopt when we collaborate.

Table 2-1 specifies differences between replicating and reconceiving as they apply to a variety of activities. In reconceiving, one often "discovers" an outcome—a strategy or a plan, say—while creating it. The sequence of activities involved in reconceiving may tend to converge in some degree of regularity in outcomes—subsequent strategies or designs generated by a reconceiving process may resemble each other—but the iterations never converge completely, nor do those who engage in this kind of activity aspire to complete convergence. Because reconceiving does not involve prespecification of an objective, it is capable of an infinite number of subtle variations in outcome, as opposed to a finite number of prespecified ones. And there is a further difference: replication processes are often managed to protect against uncertainty in inputs, demand, and environmental conditions, whereas reconception processes treat uncertainty as fuel for adaptation and innovation. Such a process, which is unconstrained by a specification, and which leaves itself open to environmental variation, retains a significant ability to adapt, to make anew. When people are reconceiving, the goal of production shifts from "getting it right the first time"

TABLE 2–1

Replicating versus reconceiving

Replicating	Reconceiving
Prespecified outcomes	Outcomes that are not prespecified
Design and manufacturing that are separate, sequential phases: the process for producing the prespecified desired outcome is also designed in advance	Design and manufacturing that are inseparable: the process that produces a desired outcome is the same process by which the desired outcome is discovered
A finite and discrete number of outcomes (such as a car in red, green, or blue)	An infinite number of unique outcomes, including "in-between" outcomes (such as a car that is "a little darker green than that")
Processes that are buffered against variation	Processes that seek out and are driven by variation
Well-defined notion of final outcome	Ongoing adjustment of outcome; notion of a "final product" problematic

Source: Robert Austin and Lee Devin, *Artful Making: What Managers Need to Know about How Artists Work*, 1st ed., © 2003. Reprinted by permission of Pearson Education, Inc., Upper Saddle River, NJ.

to "making it great before the deadline"—which more accurately describes what is needed in many collaborative situations.

This nuanced view of repetition has important implications for how technology should be deployed: technology should be used very differently to support reconceiving than in support of replicating. This point needs emphasis because the use of information technology to support replicating has been so pervasive and successful. When people think about applying information technology to work processes, they typically think of end-to-end automation, which imposes uniformity. Indeed, uniformity is often equated with quality and is often the very point of automation. But this is not a suitable approach when we are seeking to produce rich, real-time collaborative technologies.

Technologies useful in reconceiving must support trying things again and again, but in different ways each time. The objective is not to enforce uniformity but to support ongoing innovation and change. Whereas information technology has been used successfully to reduce costs and improve quality by standardizing, streamlining, and reducing variation, the technology used to support collaboration will need to accommodate creating something new with each try. Such a process may be more likely to yield value in revenue enhancement—creation of new products, expansion of markets, development of new strategies—than in cost reduction. Such technologies will need to be flexible, and rapidly and cheaply reconfigurable, if they are to support tasks that cannot be known in advance, because valuable outcomes must be discovered during the process. And they must support human-human interaction that evolves rapidly with a richness that resembles that of physically proximate interaction.

That today's primarily text-based communication technologies (such as instant messaging) fall short is clear when we look at even the most commonplace example of physically proximate collaboration. Consider a familiar classroom setting. Perhaps twenty students gather, able to see and hear each other. They can freely communicate and perceive each other's emotions. They have on hand contextual materials like handouts, slides, and whiteboards with which they can view and comment on ideas and representations of models. They may have their own tools for writing and capturing ideas, such as a pencil and paper or laptop computer. As they work together, they progress through phases of inventing, examining, and evaluating, sometimes in varying order. They draw on their contextual materials and tools in different and rarely preconceived ways to serve the needs of the collaboration.

Text-based technologies are unable to creditably approximate such real-world situations. One could argue that it is too difficult to render the details of a rich interaction on a computer, or that people don't want to use computers this way, or that computer-supported collaboration is an unnatural approximation of something best left to happen in a natural way. Let the physical world be the physical world, and let the digital world do what it does best. Our position is the opposite: that rendering the most important aspects of the physical and social world in computer-supported environments is possible and desirable, and that the real constraints have been technical and experiential. Human experiences with computers have thus far been so limited that even the most innovative software engineers have yet to fully accommodate social interaction in their designs.

The technical constraints have been real. Until quite recently, bandwidth available to the majority of computer users has been limited. Workplace connectivity has been reasonably high-speed, but consumer connectivity has not. Bandwidth is a bottleneck that governs what we perceive as the richness of communications, real-time interaction, and data sharing. Moreover, software runtime models, especially the interfaces that allow software packages to work with other software packages—the application program interfaces, or APIs, of operating systems and software platforms—have not addressed real-time interaction in a significant way. APIs exist for sending messages between software applications, but the kinds and levels of abstraction that would enable software developers to build applications that incorporate real-time communications and collaboration are virtually nonexistent.

Experiential constraints may also have slowed the emergence of computer-based collaboration. The number of people connected via computers, and therefore the overall social value of collaborating via computers, has been limited. The vast majority of people in the world—more than 5.5 billion out of a total of 6 billion—are not online. Of those who are online, only a small proportion have even basic real-time communications tools like instant messaging. Computer-based communications and collaboration must be widely, if not universally, available if they are to be counted on as substitutes for physical-world interaction. Likewise, communication needs to be untethered from location. If it works from where you are this week, but might not work from where you will be next week, you will not form the habit of using it. Mobile phones have become popular, but only recently have such devices become capable of richer communications and integration into broader data networks, and they still do not work in many places. Even advanced networked PCs have only recently become able to be untethered in a meaningful way.

Understanding Real-World Communication and Collaboration

Given the stunning successes of replication-based applications, it is not surprising that the software industry has yet to fully address how to incorporate real-time communications technology into its applications. This is not the only way that we fall technologically short of true computer-supported collaboration, but it might be the most significant. To remedy this situation, we will need to understand the basic building blocks of successful real-world collaboration and to unpack them in a way that submits to technological solution.

Effective collaboration typically involves four key components: emotion, context, action, and location.

Emotion

One of the most valuable and gratifying aspects of human-to-human interaction is our ability to share emotions and experience others' personalities and sensibilities. Seeing reactions, hearing tones of voice, and perceiving other expressions of temperament and feeling are all crucial aspects of meaningful collaboration. Text-embedded "emoticons" such as :) or >:-< are not a substitute for the emotional richness we derive from seeing and listening to other people.

Context

Context adds information and interest to a collaborative undertaking. Our human interactions do not happen in a vacuum; most occur in a physical context with which we are also interacting and about which we are communicating. In a traditional classroom, the context might include desks, whiteboards, handouts, and other students. In a store, it might include products and product displays; in a meeting, a form or a report. Instant messaging and e-mail essentially "stovepipe" communications, stripping away context;

we can share a document, but not the surroundings that may also convey meaning and importance.

Action

Many real-time interactions are intended to culminate in an end-action. In the classroom, the end-action might be taking a test; in a store, it might be purchasing a product; with an insurance agent, filling out a form; with a friend, playing a game. Current computer-based, communications tools cannot be attached usefully to end-actions, because they have been designed to work within self-contained environments rather than to integrate with action-oriented applications. In reconceiving activities, furthermore, it is impossible to anticipate all the ways that we might want to attach communications to end-actions. Hence, a framework that integrates communication tools and action-oriented applications would need to be very flexible.

Location

Most collaboration in business, education, industry, and commerce occurs while the participants are in the same physical location. This scenario has both benefits and limitations. On the one hand, proximity facilitates the first three components of successful collaboration: emotion, context, and action. On the other hand, the requirement of proximity restricts the who, the how, the what, and the when of interactions. People today range farther and wider in the normal course of their lives than ever before in human history. As they do so, they want to feel certain that if they need to accomplish a task, they can find a suitable location to do so. General-purpose collaboration on a broad scale over the Internet calls for individuals to be able to participate freely from any location.

As we enter into a new world of broadband collaboration, we must aim to capture these dimensions of human interaction in our real-time collaborations. Too many companies have attempted to build "collaboration environments," without recognizing the importance of emotion, context, action, and location.

Convergent Forces Fill the Gap

The good news is that many technical limitations are disappearing as new innovations help us introduce fundamental aspects of human interaction into computer-supported experiences more successfully.

TABLE 2-2

Progress in incorporating human interaction in computer-supported settings

	The problem	Emerging solutions
Emotion	Primarily text-based communication technologies are unable to convey the emotional dimensions of human interaction.	Commodity audio and video equipment and widespread broadband access
Context	Current technologies strip away context that imparts meaning to work, its materials, and products.	Software with real-time APIs that support shared workspaces and artifacts
Action	Communication technologies are often self-contained, not linked to end-actions that are accomplished with software applications.	Convergent software APIs and Web services that allow impromptu integration of communication and end-actions
Location	Computer-based collaboration cannot be counted on, because it is not available everywhere.	Wireless broadband technologies that support collaboration technologies in many more locales

Source: Robert D. Austin.

Emotion

The most significant development in this realm is commodity audio and video equipment, which allow collaborators to share tones of voice or facial expressions. Most computer installations now routinely include this equipment (or can attach it at low cost). Broadband data volumes, multimedia PCs, commodity video cameras, and new software tools that support real-time audio/video are coalescing to enable much improved (and continually improving) communications.

Context

Increasingly advanced client software platforms are making possible real-time communication APIs that allow data-sharing between users. Gradually, these capabilities are generating virtual versions of the documents, whiteboards, and other physical artifacts that collectively constitute shared context.

Action

Advanced client software platforms are also converging with Web services to enable people to create actionable user interfaces in shared contexts.

For example, one might design an online store where a real-time salesperson would guide a user through the process of browsing and purchasing. Or you might be able to bring a friend with you to the online store to get the benefit of her opinion about a purchase you are considering. Your communication with her would take place in context, and that context could culminate in a transaction or another action.

Location

Powerful mobile handsets, smartphones, and wireless Wi-Fi broadband are making applications more location-independent. Increasingly, smartphones and laptops incorporate broadband wireless as a standard feature, enabling richer interaction with places that were previously inaccessible.

Table 2-2 summarizes recent progress toward incorporating these four dimensions of human interaction in a computer-supported setting.

Collaboration Platforms Today and Tomorrow

Dozens of companies are creating software and other technology to support communication and collaboration over the Internet. We will focus here on two companies, Microsoft and Macromedia, that are approaching the problem of computer-supported interaction in ways that appear likely to yield real collaboration. Both companies have been assembling software platforms as collections of building blocks that others can build on to customize collaborative capabilities.

Microsoft's Real-Time Collaboration Platform

For a decade Microsoft has been building a comprehensive platform for communications and collaboration in Windows. Its efforts have recently accelerated, and the company has publicly identified collaboration as a crucial next wave in PC use. Many initiatives promote collaboration, but three are particularly important.

Windows/MSN Messenger

Windows Messenger and its sister, MSN Messenger, have evolved from simple text-based instant messaging clients into full-featured applications offering real-time audio and video communications and document sharing. Today Windows Messenger is an application, but in the future it will be a generic building block that other independent software vendors and application developers can incorporate into their own applications.

PlaceWare

In 2003, Microsoft acquired a Web-conferencing software company, PlaceWare, which offers a best-of-breed online meeting system. On its own, PlaceWare is a powerful application for creating shared meeting spaces where multiple users can view a screen or PowerPoint presentation in real time. PlaceWare's foundation, however, is a deeper framework for real-time applications. As Microsoft integrates these functions into its operating system, and combines them with the real-time communications functions of Windows Messenger, we can foresee the emergence of a set of building blocks for creating customized collaborative applications.

Peer-to-Peer APIs

Microsoft has also released a set of APIs that enable Windows developers to build peer-to-peer (P2P) applications. P2P is an approach to software construction that allows applications on one computer to communicate easily and directly with applications on another computer without central orchestration. Exchanges between computers are point-to-point rather than through a hub or another form of centralized node. Used as yet another building block in collaboration environments, P2P APIs can help developers enable rich real-time interactions.

Microsoft has committed significant resources to the problem of collaboration. Company leaders have articulated a road map to future operating systems that will make real-time communication and collaboration a potential capability of any software application delivered on Windows.

Macromedia

In the past few years, Macromedia has gradually concentrated its capabilities, market positioning, and suite of technologies around a product and technology called Flash. With the introduction of its Flash MX suite, the company transformed Flash into a rich client for delivering Internet applications that also supports real-time collaboration and communications.[5] What began as a powerful graphics technology evolved into a ubiquitous runtime client; it has become the most widely available real-time communications client on the Internet, with over 90 percent of the Internet's 500 million-plus users having Flash Player 6, the version that provides communications and collaboration facilities. Designed in anticipation of a new generation of Internet applications that combine media, communication, and software functionality, the Macromedia Flash client provides a simple integrated cross-platform runtime environment to deliver collaborative experiences to users.

Flash Communications Capabilities

Flash MX incorporates a broad set of APIs useful in building broadband communications experiences:

- *Multiway text, audio, and video messaging.* With these APIs, customers can add real-time one-to-one, one-to-many, or many-to-many audio and video communications to any custom application.

- *Real-time collaboration.* Through a technology called SharedObjects, this set of APIs enables a customer to share any data or user-interface element with any number of connected clients. For example, a graph or a shopping cart could be shared across multiple user computers; changes entered on one computer would appear on all the other computers.

- *Web services.* Using Web services technology, Flash Player allows shared collaboration and communication applications to integrate very easily with transactional back-end systems (such as customer-service systems) and databases, enabling context and action-oriented collaboration.

All of this functionality is offered as an open set of cross-platform APIs that customers can use to craft their own experiences and applications, in pursuit of the deeper, more fluid, and more spontaneous forms of collaboration that reconceiving processes require. Figure 2-1 is an example of an application built on a Macromedia platform.

A New Communications Device

Since Macromedia released Flash Player 6 (which contains these new runtime capabilities) in early 2002, hundreds of millions of copies have been downloaded and installed; no client software in the history of computing has been adopted so widely and so quickly. The revolutionary

FIGURE 2-1

Home page of DateCam.com

A real-time application of the Macromedia Flash Communications platform

Source: Reprinted with permission from One World Media LLC.

aspect of this rapid diffusion resides in the fact that these broadband-ready, real-time communications devices are waiting to be leveraged and used by customers around the world.

Macromedia is taking advantage of its wide penetration of its client by introducing packaged software, called Breeze Live, that allows corporate customers to create their own rich multimedia shared conferencing spaces. Another company, Convoq, is applying this technology to create a powerful new instant messaging and real-time communications application tailored to individuals and corporations.[6] Because these building blocks can be taken up and used by others in varying configurations, the collective efforts of many developers, working with the fabric of a well-integrated software infrastructure, will surely bring us closer to rich real-time collaboration than we have ever been.

A Broadband Collaboration Future

The industry has turned a corner. The next few years promise greater innovation and wider adoption. Microsoft's forthcoming operating systems are certain to include communication and collaboration features that leverage broadband connectivity. Macromedia has adopted an aggressive agenda for its broadband-enabled communications applications and next-generation rich-client technology in Flash. Also emerging are designs for broadband-equipped wireless video devices that support 3G and Wi-Fi standards, enabling emotive, contextual, and location-independent broadband video communications. Standards like Session Initiation Protocol (SIP) and Voice over IP (VoIP) for broadband multimedia communications, and H.263 for video, are transforming the entire communications industry.

Whatever standards and platforms emerge, collaborative broadband applications will continue to drive the convergence of our physical and social lives with the digital world. Licklider and Taylor pointed out the characteristics of interactive communication that make them susceptible to computerization:

> Creative, interactive communication requires a plastic or moldable medium that can be modeled, a dynamic medium in which premises will flow into consequences, and above all a common medium that can be contributed to and experimented with by all . . . Such a medium is at hand—the programmed digital computer. Its presence can change the nature and value of communications even more profoundly than did the printing press and the picture tube, for, as we shall show, a well-programmed computer can provide direct access both to informational resources and to the *processes* for making use of the resources.[7]

These observations and optimistic claims speak eloquently to our situation today. Perhaps it is not premature to reissue the assertion that these Internet pioneers articulated nearly forty years ago: "In a few years, men will be able to communicate more effectively through a machine than face to face."[8]

Notes

1. J. C. R. Licklider, "Man-Computer Symbiosis," *IRE Transactions on Human Factors in Electronics*, HFE-1 (March 1960): 4–11.

2. J. C. R. Licklider and Robert W. Taylor, "The Computer as a Communication Device," *Science and Technology*, April 1968, 21–43.

3. The original ninety-minute video of this event is part of the Engelbart Collection in Special Collections of Stanford University. A downloadable video is available at http://sloan.stanford.edu/mousesite/1968Demo.html.

4. See Rob Austin and Lee Devin, *Artful Making: What Managers Need to Know About How Artists Work* (Upper Saddle River, NJ: Financial Times Prentice Hall, 2003).

5. One of us, Jeremy Allaire, was involved in this strategy as Macromedia's chief technology officer.

6. One of us, Jeremy Allaire, sits on the board of directors of Convoq.

7. Licklider and Taylor, "The Computer as a Communication Device."

8. Ibid.

3

Broadband Deployment

From Vision to Reality

Dr. Stagg Newman

Since the Internet revolution of the 1990s, prognosticators, technologists, and policy makers have invoked the coming "broadband world"—a communications utopia of practically unlimited bandwidth, an anywhere-anytime world in which we all communicate via a seamless high-speed network. In testimony to the U.S. Congress, Chairman Michael Powell of the U.S. Federal Communications Commission (FCC) declared that "broadband deployment is the central communications policy objective in America today . . ., [and] the primary challenge facing policy makers today is to show we can drive the enormous investment required to turn the promises of broadband into reality."[1]

That large economic benefits would ensue from widespread deployment of such a broadband infrastructure is widely believed. Crandall and Jackson estimate the net present value to the U.S. economy of widespread adoption to be as much as $500 billion.[2] The bursting of the telecom-and-tech bubble put a damper on the business plans of companies that had hoped to rapidly realize the dream, but many policy makers and pundits still consider its ultimate realization critical to U.S. telecommunications development. According to one knowledgeable estimate, deploying a gigabit network—a ubiquitous network offering one gigabit per second in the first mile—would generate $376 billion for the incremental gross state product in the year 2010 of California alone and could create 2 million jobs by the year 2010 in that state alone.[3]

Alternative Visions of U.S. Broadband Deployment

There are two prevailing visions of broadband deployment. The vision invoked by the high-tech community would feature a bandwidth-rich, deep-fiber, open-IP network employing "future proof" network architecture that enables users to obtain ever-increasing performance with only moderate incremental new capital expenditures. Network interconnection and network access would be open to other network operators, applications service providers, content providers, and end users. The network would offer availability, reliability, and quality of service comparable or superior to that of a public-switched telephony network (PSTN) of today. This approach would provide for vastly more bandwidth than we have today and stimulate the growth of the information, communications, and technology (ITC) industry. The consumer would enjoy a services-rich, always-on network supporting many multimegabits in each direction. The closest approximation of such a network today is the experimental Internet2, which connects numerous universities.[4] This vision is espoused by Intel, the One Gigabit or Bust Initiative, and the Fiber-to-the-Home (FTTH) Council, among others.[5] Advocates of this vision favor fiber—because of its tremendous bandwidth or transmission capacity—and an open-IP network as critical components of a future-proof architecture that could reignite growth in the information technology industry.

The alternative vision, which FCC policy makers have been citing for several years, might be less bandwidth-rich but would offer consumers a choice of several competing access providers:

- Incumbent local exchange carriers (ILECs) using digital subscriber loop technology over twisted copper pairs or fiber to the premises

- Competitive local exchange carriers (CLECs) using unbundled loops from the incumbent and/or overbuilding with a fiber and/or wireless technology

- Cable TV operators with their hybrid fiber/coaxial cable networks

- Power line communications operators transmitting information over electrical power lines connected to a backbone fiber network

- Terrestrial licensed or unlicensed wireless operators using wireless access technologies connected to a high-speed fiber backbone

- Satellite operators

This scenario would deploy high-speed networking in a market-driven, competitive manner consistent with the goals of the 1996 Telecom Act: "to promote competition and reduce regulation in order to secure lower prices and higher-quality services for American telecommunications consumers and encourage the rapid deployment of new telecommunications technologies."[6] Truly competitive access of this kind would eliminate the need for regulation of competition except in "legacy" situations—for instance, interconnection to today's PSTN. Even this kind of regulation could be eliminated over time as the legacy networks are supplanted, as shown in figure 3-1. This vision is the one that FCC policy makers have been citing for several years.[7]

FIGURE 3-1

Deregulators' dream: circa 2005, freedom of choice

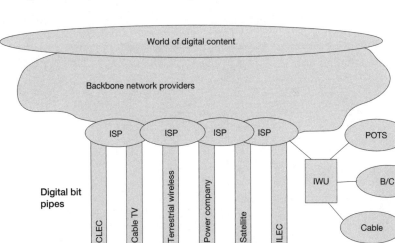

Note: CLEC (competitive local exchange carrier); ILEC (incumbent local exchange carrier); IWU (interworking unit); POTS (plain old telephone service); B/C (broadcast)

Source: Stagg Newman speech to National Association of Counties, October 29, 1999.

These two versions of the future are not necessarily mutually exclusive—that is, one or more of the digital pipes could be a deep, fiber-based infrastructure.

The Realities of Broadband Deployment Today

Several Asian countries are progressing faster than the United States toward building a widespread high-bandwidth infrastructure, as figure 3-2 shows. Over 70 percent of homes in Korea now have broadband access, as compared to U.S. penetration of about 25 percent. Japan, which had only one-third as many broadband subscribers as the United States in mid-2001, has probably overtaken the United States since then. Figure 3-2 does not show Canada and Taiwan, which have both surpassed 40 percent penetration.

Moreover, subscribers in other countries are enjoying far more "bandwidth for the buck," as figure 3-3 shows. The average Korean or Japanese

FIGURE 3-2

Comparative national broadband penetration rates, 2003

	Total number of households (millions)	Households with BB connection (millions)	2003 broadband penetration (Percentage of all households)
South Korea	15.3	11.3	74%
Hong Kong*	2.2	0.9	42%
United States	110.8	26.3	24%
Japan	49.3	11.44	23%
Singapore*	1.2	0.2	16%
Sweden**	4.7	0.7	15%
Germany	38.7	4.3	11%
France	23.9	1.7	7%
China*	348.0	2.5	1%

*2002 data
**Other Scandinavian countries have similar penetration rates
Source: IDC 2002; Merrill Lynch: Broadband Dashboard; MIC.

broadband subscriber is typically getting at least ten times the speed available in the United States—and at lower cost. In Japan, for example, subscribers can get 20 megabits per second (Mbps) for about $25 per month, whereas the typical U.S. digital subscriber line (DSL) subscriber pays at least $30 per month for a few hundred kilobits per second (Kbps) access.

FIGURE 3-3

Broadband value delivered, 2003

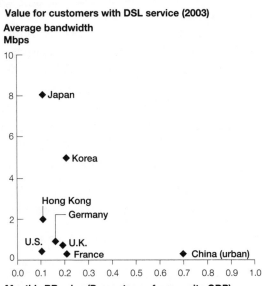

Value for customers with DSL service (2003)
Average bandwidth
Mbps

Monthly BB price (Percentage of per capita GDP)

Penetration by connection type
Percentage of all households

	U.S.	Sweden	Japan	Korea
Narrowband (dial-up)	34	52	40	4
Middleband (up to 2 Mbps)	24	9	5	65
Broadband (more than 2 Mbps)	<1	6	19	8

Sources: Pyramid Research; Forrester; NTT-X; MIC; KT; Hanaro Telecom; Broadband Dashboard, 2003 Texas Instruments report; KT, Acca Networks; NTT.

The good news in the United States is that the core inner-city IP-based broadband infrastructure has been built and even overbuilt. Most large enterprises have direct high-speed, fiber-based access to the broadband core, and many have a choice of fiber providers. The bad news is that fewer than 10 percent of business locations and virtually no residences are directly linked to this broadband fiber network.[8] Therefore, these consumers must obtain broadband access from another technology platform—or new deep-fiber networks must be built. Because of the shared media nature of the cable infrastructure, U.S. cable companies typically offer customers only a few hundred kilobits per second in the upstream direction (to the network) and 1 to 2 Mbps per second in the downstream direction (toward the user). Cable systems can be upgraded to provide more bandwidth but at a capital cost.[9] DSL in the U.S. residential market offers similarly limited upstream and downstream speeds. One key reason is that DSL speeds are very sensitive to the length of the copper loop serving the customer, and impairments like splices. The United States on average is characterized by much longer copper loops and more impairments than Korea, Japan, Taiwan, or even Canada, due to the low linear density of housing and how the telephone network was designed. Thus, these questions are critical for policy makers:

- Will U.S. mass-market access to the broadband IP network of networks be adequate in terms of price and performance?

- Will broadband access be available to all Americans?

The FCC's Broadband Working Group

The FCC's goal, in response to Chairman Powell's challenge "to show we can drive the enormous investment required to turn the promises of broadband into reality," is to establish appropriate policy for broadband access, the so-called first-mile services (the connections between customers' premises and providers' networks).[10] To achieve this goal, the FCC must first determine whether this market can be fully competitive, a simple duopoly, or even a natural monopoly in certain locales. The FCC must then either decide how much to regulate, or—if it believes that robust competition will occur without its intervention—could choose to minimize or eliminate regulation and let market forces rule.[11]

As input to the FCC's deliberations, the Broadband Working Group of the FCC's Technological Advisory Council was asked to address the question of intermodal competition (competition among enterprises using different technology platforms) for mass-market broadband access. (The FCC Technological Advisory Council is a group of outside industry experts that provides technology advice to the FCC.)[12] The goal of the Broadband Working Group was to describe the factors affecting the economic and technical capability of all available broadband access platforms to provide the three services—cable, telephony, and high-speed Internet access—that consumers spend substantive money for today, and to analyze the suitability of different platforms to provide those services. A key objective was to help the FCC distinguish between promised technology—that may or may not materialize in the future—and reality. By making such distinctions in a clear-eyed way, the FCC can avoid a frequent failing of public policy: decision making based on technological promises that never come to fruition in the marketplace.

Alternative Technology Platforms

The two leading technologies providing high-speed Internet access in the United States today are cable modem service from cable providers and DSL service from telephone companies. Cable currently competes in a small way with telephone companies in the voice market, but it has the potential to do so on a much larger scale in the future. There is already considerable competition between cable and satellite for video services.

Meanwhile, nine other technology platforms could potentially be used to provide broadband access to the mass market: very high speed digital subscriber line (VDSL), fiber-to-the-premises (FTTP), power-line communications (PLC), satellite, local multipoint distribution system (LMDS), low-GHz licensed wireless systems (below 6 GHz), unlicensed wireless systems (e.g., Wi-Fi), stratospheric platforms, and third-generation (3G) cellular systems. In 2002, the FCC Technological Advisory Council produced a series of presentations on these platforms, to which the reader is referred for detailed descriptions of each technology and obstacles to its deployment.[13]

The rest of this chapter describes the Broadband Working Group's methodology for assessing the suitability of alternative broadband access platforms to deliver services, characterizes the services to be delivered in more detail, and then enumerates the key economic factors that determine the suitability of a platform to deliver such services. The incremental economics of delivering high-speed Internet access using cable modems or DSL provides a baseline for assessing suitability. Nine alternative technology platforms are compared with the baseline.

Methodology for Assessing the Suitability of Alternative Broadband Platforms

The working group's methodology proceeded in three parts. First, they identified the services that can be offered over a broadband platform that customers purchase today: voice, multiprogramming video services, and high-speed Internet access. Speculative services that may or may not gain market share in the future were not included. For each service, the group defined the key features that customers expect.

Second, the working group defined the key economic factors that determine the suitability of given technology platforms to offer the set of services specified earlier. The typical incremental economics of either cable operators or incumbent telephone companies offering high-speed Internet access via either cable modem or DSL were used as a frame of reference.

Finally, the group analyzed the technical capability of each platform to deliver each of the services, followed by an analysis of suitability. The *suitability* of each platform is a function of its technical feasibility, state of development and deployment, and ability to compete with the economics of the existing alternatives. This evaluation took into account such factors as deployment status, deployment roadblocks, platform feasibility, and our qualitative assessment of each platform's economics. The assessment focused on competition in the one- to five-year time frame and particularly the one- to three-year time frame. This time frame seemed appropriate given that the market for broadband access will probably be reaching maturity within three years. Entrants into the market after then will be battling to take market share from entrenched incumbents, a much more daunting proposition than fighting for market share by winning new subscribers.

Services over Broadband Platforms

Customers have demonstrated willingness to pay for three services currently provided via broadband technology platforms:

- Voice

- High-speed Internet access

- Multichannel video services

Voice Services

There are two types of voice service: primary-line and secondary-line.

Primary-Line Service

Primary-line service assumes consistent, high-quality voice signals ("toll quality" voice) and rare service outages—perhaps only one a year. Primary-line services are also expected to include features like call waiting, three-way calling, and call forwarding, which customers take for granted. All of a subscriber's extension lines should continue to function as they do today. A less obvious but high-value feature is the ability of 911 emergency-service providers, such as the police, to identify the caller's address; some of the alternative phone services on the market today do not offer this capability. Another feature is operator services, including the opportunity to be listed in a directory or to request an unlisted telephone number. Many customers will be unwilling to change service providers for their primary line unless they can port their telephone number to the new service provider. The primary line also typically provides "lifeline" service in that it does not require electricity from the commercial power grid to function and is thus available even when power lines are cut. Few customers realize that their voice service offers this feature, but if new market entrants offerings do not include lifeline service, the incumbent will almost certainly promote it to generate awareness and retain customers. Yet another feature of primary-line service is adherence to the Communications Assistance for Law Enforcement Act (CALEA), which specifies that law-enforcement personnel be able to perform a legal wiretap on a primary phone line and to obtain information about the calls made on a given line from the telephone company. If CALEA is made applicable to new offerings, such as Voice over Internet Protocol (VoIP), it could impose significant costs on the companies offering those services.

Customer Local Area Signaling Services (CLASS) and custom calling are sets of features, such as call forwarding and caller ID, that are integral to the primary-line offering. A feature of primary-line service that is taken for granted is the seamless way that multiple telephone extensions work together allowing more than one party to speak with a caller simultaneously, no matter what type of phone is in use (cordless, touch-tone, rotary dial). Customers are likely to expect all extension phones to continue to work seamlessly without rewiring or the purchase of new handsets. Any technology platform that offers primary-line services must provide all of these capabilities or a similar set that customers and regulators find acceptable.

Secondary-Line Service

Secondary-line service refers to a secondary voice connection that is not relied on for the same quality, security, and flexibility as a primary line. A wireless phone service may be considered a secondary line, as might a second phone line for dial-up Internet service. It is important to distinguish between primary and secondary lines because several alternative voice technologies will be eminently able to provide a secondary line but will struggle to provide the quality and range of services inherent in primary-line service.[14]

High-Speed Internet Access

The Broadband Working Group defined high-speed Internet access as broadband service that is at least as fast as DSL and cable—potentially several hundred kilobits per second upstream and a megabit or more per second downstream, though the lowest-priced offering today is often slightly slower.[15] High-speed Internet service should also feature low latency—*latency* is the amount of time it takes information to travel through a network. Both the application used and the network size contribute to latency. On a phone call overseas using a satellite link, for example, communication is delayed for about half a second, which is perceptible and annoying to the customer. Low latency is particularly important for two-way real-time communications, such as voice, videoconferencing, and interactive high-speed gaming.

Multichannel Video Services

Multichannel video services are today's cable and satellite TV programming services, typically featuring about two dozen basic channels, including local and national over-the-air broadcast networks, subscription services typically sold as premium packages, and pay-per-view.[16]

Economic Factors in the Viability of Broadband Access Platforms

Several key economic factors determine the viability of broadband access platforms:

- Revenue-generating services supported
- Costs of customer acquisition, equipment, and installation
- Operations, billing, and customer care
- Network access and transport

Revenue-Generating Ability

Many of the costs associated with serving customers, such as billing, do not increase much as a provider adds services. Thus, a company that offers only a single service—and captures only a single revenue stream—faces a significant market disadvantage. It cannot apportion fixed costs among several services to capture economies of scope, particularly in customer acquisition, marketing, and SG&A (selling, general, and administrative) costs. Furthermore, its customers are more likely to defect to other providers. A user who purchases both telephone and high-speed Internet service from the same provider, for example, is less likely to switch to a new provider because of the inconvenience of multiple changes at once, including, for example, her e-mail address, her user interface to the Internet, and possibly even her phone number.

High market penetration, or take rate, for revenue-generating services is another important factor. Most network providers experience heavy fixed costs to implement service to a specific locale, such as a particular street. They therefore need to serve as many users in that locale as possible, with as many products as possible, if they are to allocate their costs efficiently. Providers of technologies that are appropriate platforms for all three services—voice, high-speed Internet access, and multichannel video—can potentially capture multiple revenue streams. Other technologies, such as satellite, are best suited to a single service and are therefore less feasible competitors outside of their current niche.

Customer Acquisition

The second major factor in a platform's economics is customer acquisition, including the costs of customer equipment and installation. For example, primary-line telephony requires a piece of equipment at the customer's premises called a network interface device (NID). In a modern digital network with digital service to the home, the NID translates the signals between the incoming line and the end user's equipment, such as the touch-tone and off-hook signals sent by the user's phones. A competitor that wishes to offer an equivalent service must replace the NID with a "smart NID," which can translate signals between a customer's current equipment and the packet language of the provider's network.

Similarly, digital video services require set-top boxes, usually one per TV. These devices translate the incoming digital video signal into the analog signal that most TVs use today.

Installation costs for telephony also include interior wiring at a customer's home to connect to the smart NID or its equivalent. Because few customers wish to perform this installation task themselves, providers of primary-line telephony send technicians on a "truck roll," or visit, to the customer's location. For high-speed Internet access, PCs must be connected to the provider's network, which can be a rather complex operation. If a cable modem is being installed, for instance, and the cable outlet is not near the PC, the household must be rewired. Installation of wireless services can also be complex; the operator must determine whether it can extend a wireless signal to a given customer. Some wireless technologies require line-of-sight visibility from the transmission point to the customer premises; in its absence, the provider must either expand its network or lose the customer.

Operations, Billing, and Customer Care

It is typically very expensive for companies to develop support systems to perform the functions of operations, billing, and customer care. Having developed such a system, furthermore, a provider must be prepared to modify it to add the new services and features that this rapidly changing market will mandate. A company with limited market share, and thus few customers to share this expense, would be in a highly unfavorable position. Many CLECs underestimated this expense during the telecom bubble of the late 1990s.

Such support systems must also be scalable. For example, it is fairly easy for a provider to build a system that can accommodate a small number of customers. A company with few users and a single service representative who performs all order entries on a PC could build a simple, effective system easily and cheaply. But such a system clearly would not be appropriate for a company that employs many service representatives serving millions of customers. These large systems, for example, must allow many representatives to update large master databases in parallel, requiring more complex database management systems that can handle concurrent updates without conflicts. As a result, acquiring and operating large, robust, scalable operating systems adds significantly to the cost.

Network-Access and Transport Costs

Network-access and transport costs include the cost of adding new customers to the network, physical construction costs such as trenching for fiber-optic lines, the cost of rights of way (RoWs) or antenna sites, the cost of concentrating or backhauling signals—a traffic-management technique used to reduce expenses—and the cost of resolving other network issues. One possible issue of this kind is the need to install more bandwidth or better network capabilities to alleviate the slow download times that cable modem users experience when a few customers dominate bandwidth usage.

The Cost Structure of High-Speed Internet Access for the Incumbents

The attractive cost structure of high-speed Internet access service over cable and DSL presents a formidable challenge to potential competitors. In 80 percent or more of the U.S. market, customers have access to high-speed Internet service from at least one provider. Thus, any new technology must compete with at least one incumbent player. In most areas, furthermore, the incumbent company provides high-speed Internet access as an incremental accompaniment to other services: cable companies offer high-speed Internet access as an adjunct to multichannel video; telephone companies offer DSL in addition to their bread-and-butter telephone services.

Table 3-1 presents current estimated monthly costs per subscriber of providing high-speed Internet access, via DSL for an incumbent telephone company and via cable modem for a cable-system operator. It is noteworthy that only a small portion of these costs is related to the technology deployed: network transport costs only $3 per month, and depreciation of the new technology is only $7 and $3, respectively, for DSL and cable.[17] Marketing, customer-acquisition, and provisioning costs represented by far the largest component of the cost structure of both types of service. Thus, a new competitor entering the broadband market—even if it could deliver service of comparable quality, which is not a given for wireless or power-line players—would be hard-pressed to compete against incumbent

TABLE 3-1

Cost structure of incumbent high-speed Internet providers[a]

Average broadband costs per subscriber per month, 2005E (in dollars)[b]

	DSL (incumbent local exchange carrier)[c]	Cable
Network transport	3.0	3.0
ISP costs	2.0	2.0
Marketing, acquisition, and provisioning	10.0	6.0
Maintenance	2.0	1.0
Installation	2.0	5.0
Customer service/billing	8.0	4.0
Depreciation[d]	7.0	3.0
Total costs, estimated, 2005	$34	$24

[a]Detailed comparisons depend on many modeling assumptions, including which services are bundled, financial policies, underlying labor costs, maturity of market, % customers self-install, etc.

[b]Costs depicted include all periodic costs averaged over existing subscribers (P&L view of per-sub economics).

[c]Competitive local exchange carriers, which lease the UNE loop from the incumbent local exchange carrier that has the physical copper pair to the customer, would have to pay an additional $2–$20 per month for line-shared UNE loop or entire UNE loop.

[d]Depreciation includes costs for CPE, incremental variable capex per subscriber, and additional high-speed data outside plant build and maintenance.

Source: Adapted from *Broadband 2001,* a report by JP Morgan and McKinsey & Company.

operators, given the latter's attractive cost structures and established customer base. Even if its technology costs were essentially zero, a newcomer would have difficulty building a new network, acquiring customers, and servicing those customers in a competitive way. Marketing, customer-acquisition, and servicing costs, though treated here as monthly costs, are the costs incurred for adding customers and thus are actually recurring costs driven by growth and churn. These costs are likely to be higher for a new entrant, who must convince existing customers to leave their current supplier. Moreover, unlike the telephone company or the cable provider, the new entrant may not have an existing customer relationship to leverage in selling and in billing and customer service.

Comparison of Broadband Access Platforms

The Broadband Working Group's comparison of broadband access platforms was presented to the FCC and later to the Telecommunications Policy Research Conference (TPRC).[18] The presentation used a Harvey ball (or phase-of-the-moon) format to summarize the suitability of each broadband technology as a platform for each of the three services discussed. Figure 3-4 summarizes those findings. (To reiterate, *suitability* is a measure of the capability of a given platform to provide the service in question, such as the ability of cable to provide primary-line voice, including consideration of the comparative economics.) For a given platform/service combination, a full moon indicates that at least one provider now offers it and that its quality and features are comparable to the prevailing standard for that service.

The size of the smaller sphere to the right of each moon indicates availability. A large sphere indicates that the service is currently available on the platform in question. A medium-size sphere indicates that it is in the early stages of rollout and has not yet been deployed for the mass market. The smallest sphere signifies that the service is not yet available but is potentially deployable on a large scale within a three- to five-year time frame. It normally takes three to five years for such new services to proceed from initial trials to widespread deployment, despite providers' or technology vendors' claims to the contrary; the time from laboratory prototypes to widespread deployment is typically closer to ten years. For example, early prototype trials of both cable modem and DSL technology began in the early 1990s. Even Internet technology, which exploded in the 1990s, dated back to the 1970s.

Now let us look more closely at the suitability of each of the platforms to deliver the services in question.

Cable

Cable-operator networks today are capable of providing multiprogramming video services, high-speed Internet access and—at relatively little additional cost—voice service by VoIP without deploying fiber deeper into their networks.[19] VoIP can be offered via the packet cable service defined by Cable Labs, the technical specification setting organization for the cable industry, or by third-party providers such as Vonage, with its VoIP product.[20] To deploy primary-line voice, a cable operator must provide a network interface device,

FIGURE 3-4

Broadband access platform suitability

The analysis focused on the costs of serving existing homes and small businesses, not the build-out of new developments.

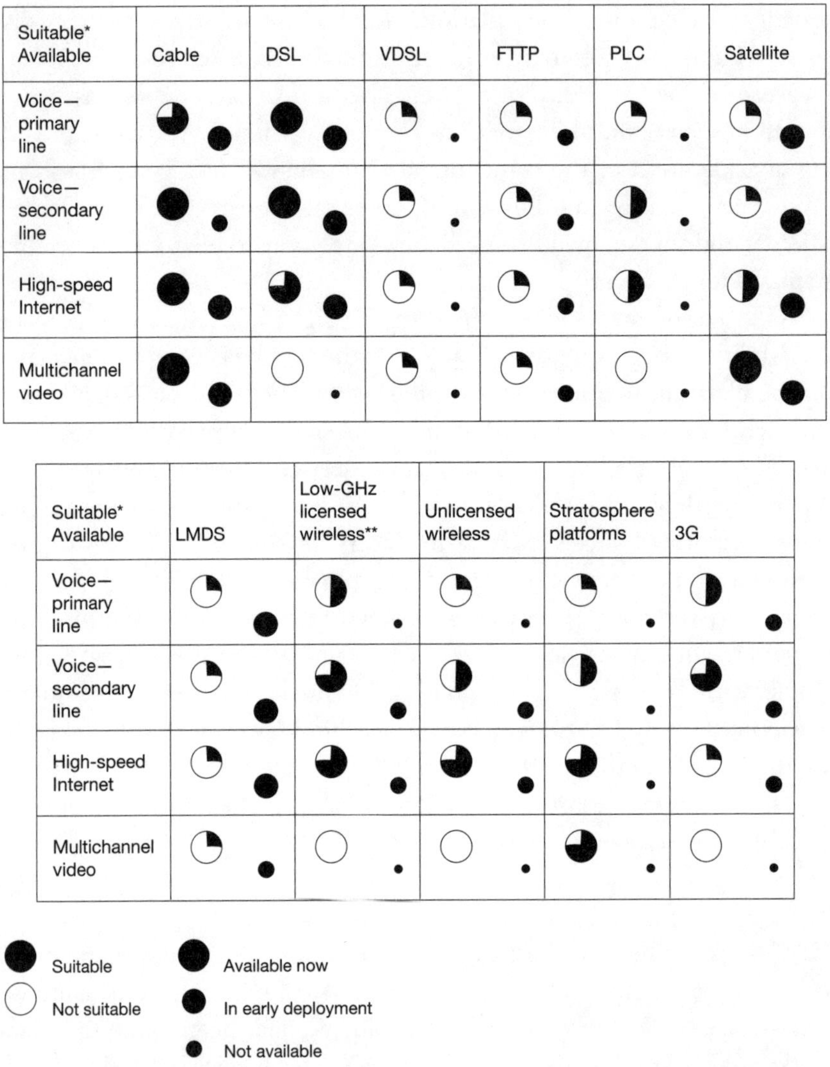

Suitable* Available	Cable	DSL	VDSL	FTTP	PLC	Satellite
Voice—primary line						
Voice—secondary line						
High-speed Internet						
Multichannel video						

Suitable* Available	LMDS	Low-GHz licensed wireless**	Unlicensed wireless	Stratosphere platforms	3G
Voice—primary line					
Voice—secondary line					
High-speed Internet					
Multichannel video					

Suitable   Available now

Not suitable   In early deployment

Not available

*Suitable refers to the technical and economic ability to deliver desired services.

**Low-GHz wireless refers to portable and fixed wireless systems using licensed frequency below 4 GHz.

Source: Adapted from Stagg Newman, "Broadband Access Platforms for the Mass Market: An Assessment," presentation to the Telecommunications Policy Research Conference, September 20, 2003.

which may require rewiring a customer's facilities to connect the phones to the cable box, as discussed earlier. To deploy a primary-line service comparable to that of telephone companies, moreover, cable providers would have to deliver lifeline voice services. To do so, an operator would have to implement some type of backup power solution, an additional expense.[21]

Cox and part of Comcast Corporation's network offer the equivalent of the primary-line service offered by telcos, including powering when commercial power fails. Other cable companies have not designed their networks to provide this level of service, and upgrading to do so will add significant expense.

DSL

DSL was designed to piggyback on standard telephone service. Most providers can currently offer high-speed Internet access only within about three miles of their central offices on their copper loops, which takes in around 60 percent of their customer base. To offer DSL to the remainder of their customers, they would need to extend fiber lines to more branches of their network and to deploy remote terminals. This can be an expensive proposition if the fiber is not already in place, as it is not in the case of approximately half of the remaining customers; the up-front capital cost could be over $1,000 per customer. Even if the fiber to a remote terminal is in place, and the remote terminal can accommodate DSL plug-ins, such a DSL installation is more expensive because an extra truck roll is necessary to the remote terminal. As for video services, the inherent design of DSL networks and the platform's technical specifications, particularly the limited bandwidth available for multiprogramming video services, make this technology unsuitable to compete with cable or satellite.

VDSL

VDSL could provide all three services, but cost issues appear prohibitive— VDSL equipment is considerably more expensive than DSL equipment. Moreover, at the speeds necessary to support multiple video channels, including at least one high-definition TV channel, telcos can only provide VDSL to customers situated within about three thousand feet of their central offices, or only about 20 percent of the total telco customer base in the United States. (This estimate assumes the telephone companies continue to deploy technology that complies with published standards.) To serve more customers using VDSL than they do currently, telephone companies would need to extend fiber near to more customers' homes, install costly electronics, and spread the expense of this equipment among what could be a small user base. It would cost telephone companies about $2,000 to $3,000 per user to provide VDSL to the remaining 80 percent of their customers.[22]

FTTP

FTTP is a fiber-optic connection from the provider's central office to the end user. Fiber is an extremely capable medium, and once installed, it can effectively deliver all three services (although offering video would require a complex piece of equipment to convert the signal, adding significantly to cost). But according to data submitted to the FCC by AT&T, it would cost approximately $800 per home passed to install fiber in a typical residential area, and optimistically at least another $600 per home served.[23] At 100 percent market penetration, this estimate represents over $1,400 per home served; at a more realistic 35 percent market penetration, it represents a cost of over $2,900 per home served.

Fiber could be a feasible option in situations where incremental construction costs are minimal, such as a new suburban development in which many new services must be installed at once. Fiber cable could be installed when trenches are dug to install electrical wires, thus spreading construction costs among services and eliminating a barrier to the feasibility of fiber as a broadband platform. Fiber could also be attractive in dense residential areas with an aerial plant.

PLC

PLC transmits broadband signals over the electric grid. Though the fundamental concept dates back to the 1800s, the platform is still relatively unproven and has several significant disadvantages. It does not have enough bandwidth for full multichannel video services, nor as much bandwidth as cable or DSL for high-speed Internet access over a typical serving area. Its unproven nature also makes its cost structure unclear. Clearly, professional installation would be required for any equipment on the commercial power grid. The nature of the U.S. power grid—typically only four to eight customers on the low-voltage side of the transformer—means that the cost of fairly expensive equipment and installation would be shared among a very few users, particularly given realistic predictions about market share among high-speed Internet users. New hybrid approaches using PLC on the medium-voltage network for distribution to a neighborhood and Wi-Fi for the last few hundred feet to the customer could address part of this problem (see the discussion of Wi-Fi later in this chapter for issues related to its deployment).[24] PC-based primary-line telephony would be unlikely to include lifeline services, since the lines would probably not function in the event of a power outage.

Widespread deployment of this technology raises radio frequency (RF) interference issues under consideration in a pending FCC Notice of Proposed Rulemaking.[25] This rulemaking is quite contentious, which could lead to regulatory delays and market uncertainty.[26]

Satellite

Satellite technology is clearly a viable platform for video services. It is a suboptimal conduit for high-speed Internet access, however, for cost reasons and because of the latency problems inherent in transmitting a signal to a satellite and back. Latency is not apparent to a user performing tasks like Web browsing, but it is problematic when doing anything highly interactive, such as online gaming or videoconferencing. Latency is also an issue in transmitting voice, because the perceptible delay between speaking and being heard necessitates pauses between speaker and listener. DIRECTV's withdrawal from the consumer Internet-access market attests to satellite's unsuitability in that market.[27]

LMDS

LMDS is a high-speed, high-frequency wireless technology—typically in the 24–38 GHz range—that appeared highly promising a decade ago, but its promise has not been realized. The primary issue is cost, but LMDS also requires a clear line of sight to work well. Wet trees and heavy rain, for instance, destroy an LMDS signal. Furthermore, this platform only allows transmission over distances of a few kilometers. Thus, it requires a fairly expensive network, including numerous base stations and expensive backhaul, to transmit effectively; the customer premises equipment is also relatively expensive.

Low-GHz Licensed Wireless

Low-GHz licensed wireless includes several low-bandwidth platforms that could use multichannel multipoint distribution system (MMDS), at around 2.1–2.6 GHz, or personal communications services (PCS), at around 1.9 GHz, or newly available spectrum such as the UHF TV spectrum (around 700 MHz) that is being returned to the government for auction as part of the conversion to digital TV. Many companies have been experimenting with low-GHz technologies and testing them in the market. Incumbent telcos, such as BellSouth, and competitors like Clearwire have announced deployment of such platforms. None has enough bandwidth, however, to deliver video. They all appear to be capable platforms for high-speed Internet access, though most require reasonably clear line of sight or proximity to the tower. For wireless technologies, customer qualification (determining which customers can receive a good enough signal to be served) and adequate RF engineering can add substantially to costs. Moreover, wireless signals lose considerable strength when passing into buildings; installation of an outside antenna plus cabling to the customer's inside wiring also adds considerable cost. For secondary-line voice, low-GHz services would probably rely on VoIP technology. Primary-line voice, comparable to wireline telephony, again calls for installing and connecting a smart NID and power backup.

Unlicensed Wireless

Unlicensed wireless, particularly the technology known as Wi-Fi, presents the same issues as low-GHz licensed wireless. Some even argue that because it uses a low-power signal and is unlicensed, it could be even more impractical. One significant advantage of this technology, however, is its steep growth curve; an enormous amount of capital is backing its development for other markets. Corporations are increasingly employing Wi-Fi for enterprise LANs and campus applications, and many consumers are using it for home networking. The rapid deployment of Wi-Fi clients means that the customer end of the connection is quite inexpensive. On the other hand, Wi-Fi still has relatively short range, requiring many base stations and substantial backhaul costs. Various efforts are afoot to tackle this problem, but it is too soon to know how effective they will be. Wi-Fi was not originally designed to provide voice, and there could be voice-quality problems. At the same time, recent developments suggest that Wi-Fi using VoIP might be a capable medium for voice.

There are many unanswered questions about the cost of a Wi-Fi rollout in a typical urban/suburban area. Within a given "footprint" or coverage area, for instance, what portion of potential customers can be served? If the signal is only strong enough to provide service to half the homes in the footprint, the provider's expenses per subscriber will increase dramatically without expensive RF engineering. Furthermore, the company will not normally be able to identify which potential customers would receive an acceptably strong signal and which would not. Wi-Fi also sometimes requires an outdoor antenna and a cable connection to the inside wiring, as do the licensed technologies discussed earlier.

Stratospheric Platforms

Stratospheric platforms would involve stationing an antenna on an unmanned aircraft, such as a blimp, above a metropolis high enough to reach a large area, but low enough to avoid latency issues. Such a platform could potentially provide video, high-speed Internet access, and voice (using VoIP). A stratospheric venture involves substantial risk, however, particularly aeronautical risks. This proposition has not progressed beyond the venture stage.

3G

3G is a specification for the third generation of mobile communications technology. It promises increased bandwidth, ranging from 128 Kbps in an automobile to 2 Mbps in fixed applications. 3G was originally designed as a voice technology, and as a platform for high-speed Internet access, it has been subject to an inordinate amount of hype. This technology clearly does not offer enough bandwidth for multichannel video, and our analysis found that it is unlikely to be able to provide high-speed Internet access comparable to cable modem or DSL for very many users. Mobile services like 3G could substitute for primary-line voice service, essentially replacing the wireline phone. The voice quality of current offerings is inferior to traditional standards, however, and the need for battery power prevents this technology from offering lifeline service.

Conclusion and Questions for Policy Makers

In broadband deployment, the United States is lagging behind other leading countries, particular in Asia, in terms of both penetration of the mass market and performance available at a given price.

Various technology platforms can deliver broadband access. In most markets, however, any new technology platform will be hard pressed to compete with hybrid fiber coax from a cable company or DSL from an incumbent telephone company for delivery of high-speed Internet access. Among the alternatives to cable and DSL, terrestrial wireless—using either licensed spectrum below 6 GHz or unlicensed—represents the best option. But even service providers using these technologies will have trouble competing broadly for high-speed Internet access customers since their customer-acquisition and other nontechnology costs will substantially exceed the technology costs.

In areas served by neither cable nor DSL—which is about 10 percent of American homes today—new technology platforms may well provide a means of extending the reach of the broadband network into otherwise unserved locales.

These are the key questions that policy makers should ask:

1. Does the United States need a high-speed, mass-market infrastructure comparable to that of the leading Asian nations in order to have a world-class information technology infrastructure?

2. If the answer to question 1 is yes, must that network be based on a deep-fiber architecture? Or can the likely evolution of today's cable and DSL networks—perhaps supplemented by wireless technology—meet the need?[28]

3. Do current public policies provide the necessary incentives for network modernization by incumbents and new network deployment by attackers?

4. If a deep-fiber-based infrastructure is needed for the mass market, is the infrastructure a natural monopoly in the economic sense?

5. If the needed new infrastructure is a natural monopoly, should policy makers encourage the construction of this infrastructure through methods that differ radically from today's competition policy? Such approaches include:

   • Building municipal networks

   • Authorizing franchised monopolies for mass-market broadband access, similar to the monopolies responsible for distribution of natural gas and electricity and the construction of the original telephone infrastructure

   • Allowing cable and telephone operators to share and jointly modernize a "first mile" infrastructure

   In any of the preceding scenarios, what incentives and safeguards are needed to guarantee continuing investment in and access to an evolving high-bandwidth broadband infrastructure?

6. Do new technologies on the horizon, such as new wireless technologies, offer an alternative to deep-fiber infrastructure? If so, what policies, including spectrum policies, are necessary to nurture these technologies and foster their deployment?

Acknowledgments

The author sincerely thanks the members of the FCC Technology Advisory Council and of the Broadband Working Group for the wealth of information and insight presented to the FCC and incorporated into this chapter.[29] The author also appreciates the support of Jeff Goldthorp and Behzad Ghaffari of the FCC, who sponsored this work and provided excellent guidance. The author also thanks his many McKinsey colleagues throughout the world who have contributed to the understanding of broadband deployment.

Notes

1. Michael K. Powell, "Written Statement of Chairman Michael K. Powell, Federal Communications Commission, on Competition Issues in the Telecommunications Industry," to the Committee on Commerce, Science, and Transportation, U.S. Senate, January 14, 2003. Available at http://www.wga.org/pr/fcc.html.

2. Robert J. Crandall and Charles L. Jackson, "The $500 Billion Opportunity: The Potential Economic Benefits of Widespread Diffusion of Broadband Access," Criterion Economics LLC, July 2001. Available at http://www.criterioneconomics.com/pubs/articles_crandall.php.

3. CENIC (Corporation for Education Network Initiatives in California) and Gartner Inc., "One Gigabit or Bust Initiative—A Broadband Vision for California," May 2003. Available at http://www.cenic.org/GB/gartner/index.htm.

4. More information on Internet2 is available at http://www.internet2.edu/about/aboutinternet2.html.

5. Sriram Viswanathan, "Future View of Broadband Demand" (presentation to the FCC TAC, April 17, 2003), available at http://www.fcc.gov/oet/tac/meetings_2003-2002.html; CENIC and Gartner Inc., "One Gigabit"; information is available at http://www.ftthcouncil.org.

6. Preamble to the Telecommunications Act of 1996, Pub. LA. No. 104-104, 110 Stat. 56 (1996).

7. Powell, "Written Statement."

8. Stagg Newman, "Lowering Barriers to Fiber Deployment," *Report of the 2nd Meeting of FCC Technological Advisory Council II*," November 5, 2001. Available at http://www.fcc.gov/oet/tac/meetings_2001-1999.html.

9. David Reed, "Copper Evolution" (presentation to the FCC TAC, April 17, 2003). Available at http://www.fcc.oet.tac_III_04_17_03/Copper_Evolution.ppt.

10. Powell, "Written Statement."

11. There are numerous ongoing proceedings in front of the FCC dealing with various aspects of broadband regulation, including the recently overturned UNE (Unbundled Network Element) Triennial Review rulemaking, which determines what elements of an ILEC network must be made available at what rates to competitors; the Wireline Broadband Item,

which determines what broadband services are subject to traditional common carrier regulation; the Second Cable Modem Service Order, which addresses the question of how broadband access over cable facilities should be regulated; and the Dominant/Non-Dominant Carrier Proceedings, which raises the question of when ILEC broadband access should be subject to broadband.

12. The FCC Technological Advisory Council's membership working papers, presentations, and meetings notes are all available at http://www.fcc.oet.tac

13. See the April 26, 2002, and December 4, 2002, meetings of the FCC Technological Advisory Council. Available at http://www.fcc.oet.tac/meetings_2003-2002.html.

14. For good discussions of the difference between primary line and secondary line, and the implications of offering primary line over VoIP, see Ralph Brown, "Primary Versus Secondary Line Telephony Service," available at http://www.fcc.gov/oet/tac/meetings_2003-2002.html, and Cox Communications, "Whitepaper: Preparing for the Promise of Voice over Internet Protocol (VoIP)," available at http://www.cox.com.

15. Neil Ransom, "DSL-Cable Modem Comparison." Available at http://www.fcc.gov/oet/tac/meetings_2003-2002.html.

16. Barry Singer, "Broadband Access for Multiprogramming Video/Audio Services." Available at http://www.fcc.gov/oet/tac/meetings_2003-2002.html.

17. These cost estimates are from *Broadband 2001*, a report by J. P. Morgan and McKinsey & Company; they thus need updating. The basic points about the challenges facing new entrants with new technology platforms are nevertheless still valid. McKinsey & Company and J. P. Morgan H&Q, *Broadband 2001: A Comprehensive Analysis of Demand, Supply, Economics, and Industry Dynamics in the U.S. Broadband Market* (New York: April 2001).

18. Stagg Newman, "Broadband Access Platforms for the Mass Market: An Assessment" (read-out of a report by the Broadband Working Group of the FCC Technological Advisory Council, presented to the FCC TAC on December 4, 2002). Available at http://www.fcc.gov/oet/tac/meetings_2003-2002.html. Also see Stagg Newman, "Broadband Access Platforms for the Mass Market: An Assessment" (presentation to the Telecommunications Policy Research Conference 2003, September 20, 2003). Available at http://www.tprc.org/tprc03/Sat830Sess03.htm#broadband.

19. Cox Communications, "Whitepaper: Preparing for the Promise of Voice over Internet Protocol (VoIP)."

20. Vonage's service offerings are described at http://www.vonage.com.

21. Cox Communications, "Whitepaper: Preparing for the Promise of Voice over Internet Protocol (VoIP)."

22. Stagg Newman, Very High Speed DSL, FCC TAC Broadband Working Group reports (meeting of the FCC Technological Advisory Council, December 4, 2002). Available at http://www.fcc.oet.tac/meetings_2003-2002.html.

23. Nicholas J. Frigo, "Whatever Happened to Fiber to the Home?" (presentation to the FCC TAC, April 17, 2003). Available at http://ftp.fcc.gov/oet/tac/TAC_III_04_17_03/fiber_to_the_home.ppt - 512.0KB .

24. Amperion Inc., "Powerline Communications, An Overview" (presentation to the FCC TAC, April 17, 2003). Available at http://www.fcc.gov/oet/tac/meetings1.html.

25. FCC 04-29 NPRM, "Carrier Current Systems Including Broadband over Power Line Systems, Amendment of Part 15 Regarding New Requirements and Measurement Guidelines for Access Broadband over Power Line Systems," http://www.fcc.gov.

26. The reader is referred to Rahul Tongia, "Promises and False Promises of Power-Line Carrier (PLC) Broadband Communications—A Techno-Economic Analysis" (presentation to the Telecommunications Policy Research Conference 2003, September 21, 2003), for a good explanation of the challenging economics facing this technology in most markets. Available at http://www.tprc.org/tprc03/Sun1040Sess03.htm.

27. Michael Liedtke, "Failure of DirecTV Broadband Narrows Consumer Choice," Associated Press newswire, January 30, 2003.

28. See David Reed, "Copper Evolution," and John Ryan, "Broadband Wireless" (presentation to the FCC TAC, April 17, 2003). Available at http://www.fcc.gov/oet/tac/meetings1.html.

29. Dr. Newman, of McKinsey & Company, served as chair of the FCC TAC Broadband Working Group. This chapter represents his perspective on the work of the Broadband Working Group and not that of McKinsey & Company.

4

Valuation Bubbles and Broadband Deployment

Thomas R. Eisenmann

THE WIDESPREAD DEPLOYMENT of broadband networks will require enormous investments in both new infrastructure and new applications. In the wake of the millennium bubble, which saw the valuations of
Internet, technology, and telecommunications stocks skyrocket and then
plummet between 1998 and 2001, can we trust investors to deliver the capital
that will be required for broadband's development? Could we see a replay of
the dynamics that fueled the millennium bubble, in which irrationally exu-
berant investors provided either too much or too little capital as sentiment
shifted? Put another way, is it possible that our supposedly efficient capital
markets pose a barrier to broadband deployment?

Skeptics might contend that the mistakes that characterized the recent
bubble are unlikely to be repeated soon, because huge losses have surely
taught investors and managers some powerful lessons. History, however,
suggests otherwise. The millennium bubble, though noteworthy for its
magnitude, was by no means unique: boom-bust valuation cycles often ac-
company the adoption of important new technologies, in particular, networked infrastructure businesses. Consider, for example, the bubbles in
railroads in the nineteenth century and in PC hardware and software in the
early 1980s.[1] Furthermore, valuation bubbles sometimes recur in rapid

succession within the same industrial sector. In England, for example, speculation in railroad stocks peaked in 1836, 1847, and 1857.[2] Once burned, U.K. railroad investors were by no means twice shy.

In fact, boom-bust dynamics have already resurfaced in several technology sectors since the crash of Internet stocks began in March 2000. Valuation "minibooms" have occurred in wireless networking, XML-based software, optical network equipment, peer-to-peer services, and storage network hardware and services. In view of these patterns, it seems safe to bet that companies that deploy and leverage broadband networks will be subject to sharp swings in investor sentiment over the next ten years.

To assess how capital markets might affect the pace of broadband deployment, this chapter will examine the causes and consequences of the boom-bust valuation cycle for Internet companies. The decision to focus on dot-coms rather than other subsets of the millennium bubble, such as telecommunications, is based on two premises. First, we assume that the pace of broadband network deployment will be determined by the rate of growth in bandwidth *demand*, rather than constraints that limit bandwidth *supply*. If this assumption is correct, valuation bubbles should have a greater impact on application providers than on infrastructure companies. Second, we assume that the millennium bubble's impact on narrowband Internet application providers—dot-coms—serves as a model for how future boom-bust valuation cycles might influence the development of broadband applications.

These assumptions warrant amplification. With respect to bandwidth demand, uncertainty still prevails about adoption rates for broadband applications, including business and residential video telephony, media streaming and downloads, multiplayer games, and peer-to-peer file-sharing services. Most of these applications exhibit strong network effects, high customer switching costs, and static scale economies based on high fixed costs. These structural attributes tend to engender "winners take most" outcomes, in which a few players quickly dominate the market. Winners-take-most (and the corollary that losers get little) encourages companies to race for first-mover advantages.[3] Such markets call for heavy capital investments in the face of uncertainty about customer demand and business-model viability. The prospect of big payoffs prompts investors to supply this capital by placing speculative bets. When speculation gets overheated, valuation bubbles may ensue.

In their early stages, narrowband Internet markets were subject to similar dynamics. Uncertainty prevailed about demand for dot-coms' services. Furthermore, many narrowband Internet businesses—including B2B exchanges, mass-market portals, auction and recruitment Web sites, and on-line brokerage businesses that facilitated home and car buying—exhibited strong network effects, high switching costs, and static scale economies.[4] In these segments, racing strategies were commonplace, and "winners took most." For these reasons, narrowband Internet markets should represent a reliable template for how broadband applications will evolve.

With respect to bandwidth supply, there is enormous excess capacity in long-haul fiber networks, and end users in most areas can now readily secure "last mile" broadband connections. Cable operators and local phone companies have completed major network upgrades; they have invested the risk capital required to supply broadband. Looking ahead, success capital will represent a greater share of their total investments. *Risk capital*, in the parlance of venture capitalists, is fixed up-front spending required to deliver a new service. In the case of cable operators, for example, expenditures for installation of fiber-optic trunk lines represent risk capital. By definition, risk capital must be committed before demand for a new service is certain. By contrast, *success capital* is variable in nature; it consists of incremental investments incurred to acquire and serve additional customers after an enterprise is launched. An example is the provision of cable modems or DSL line cards. Since projects that employ success capital yield quick and predictable payoffs, markets that mobilize such capital are unlikely to be prone to bubbles.

This chapter asserts that supplying bandwidth will require a great deal of success capital but comparatively modest amounts of risk capital. Two massive broadband infrastructure projects could conceivably reverse the proportions of risk and success capital required: the widespread rollout of fiber-to-the-home and 3G cellular technologies. We will assume, however, that these highly ambitious and risky projects will be deferred for many years. In the meantime, most residential and mobile users will continue to rely on cable modem, DSL, or 2.5G technologies for broadband connectivity. For these technologies, little additional risk capital will be required.

The balance of this chapter consists of three sections. The first addresses the question, *Did irrational exuberance fuel the Internet stock bubble?* Managers and investors with relevant experience may consider it self-evident that the answer to this question is "Yes!" For economists, however, this question is complicated by a different definition of the term *irrational*. In economic theory, *irrational* is a provocative label signifying that investors failed to act in their own self-interest. An alternative explanation for a bubble's upward and downward price movements conceptualizes investors' decision making as rational. According to this alternative hypothesis, investors make rational decisions to buy based on the best information available to them and then make rational decisions to sell based on new information.

For our purposes, it is important to determine whether the Internet bubble was caused by lapses in rational behavior. We will be especially concerned with the possibility that managers recognize that their equity is mispriced, and then deliberately skew their investment decisions to cater to investor sentiment. Specifically, do managers knowingly overinvest when they believe their equity to be overvalued, and underinvest when they perceive their stock to be undervalued? Overinvestment and underinvestment are serious problems from several perspectives. For society at large, they imply a diversion of resources from their most productive use and thus an erosion of social welfare. For shareholders, overinvestment will almost certainly depress long-term returns. For managers, overinvestment will boost the odds of their firm's failure, with attendant career consequences.

The actions posited in the preceding paragraph *deliberately* diverge from management's perception of the firm's long-term value-maximizing strategy. Shareholders or policy makers might be able to devise alternative governance or incentive-compensation arrangements to prevent such actions. There is not much scope for productive intervention, however, if over- or underinvestment is unintentional—that is, if managers make fully informed investment decisions seeking to maximize long-term value, but these investments yield poor returns due to unforeseeable or uncontrollable events. The second section of this chapter will ask, *Did the Internet stock bubble lead managers to overinvest deliberately?*

In light of this review of the causes and consequences of the Internet stock bubble, the concluding section will ask, *How might future bubbles affect broadband deployment?* We will also discuss the implications for managers who must make investment decisions in the belief that investors have mispriced their equity.

Did Irrational Exuberance Fuel the Internet Stock Bubble?

To help answer this question, let's first consider what bubbles are.

Bubbles: Their Nature and Causes

Webster's New World Dictionary defines a bubble as "any idea, scheme, etc. that seems plausible at first but quickly shows itself to be worthless or misleading." This definition ignores a central question about bubbles: do they reflect serious and widespread deviations from individually rational behavior? In one view, sharp swings in asset prices reflect the rational reactions of traders to new information: a market's potential may look highly promising at first, but investors appropriately revise their expectations—and sell—after bad news arrives.

Another thesis holds that bubbles are flagrant episodes of *mispricing*. Mispricing occurs when an asset's price cannot be explained by rational analysis of business fundamentals. More specifically, mispricing represents a departure from *fundamental value*, defined as the discounted present value of future cash flows expected to accrue to a long-term investor pursuing a "buy and hold" strategy. The view that bubbles are caused by mispricing is at odds with classic financial theories about market efficiency.[5] These theories hold that trading by well-informed arbitrageurs should prevent prices from persistently deviating from fundamental value.

Mispricing due to lapses in individual rationality should be distinguished from price movements resulting from asymmetric information. Classic financial theories recognize that certain individuals may possess private information that yields different beliefs regarding an asset's fundamental value, and may profit by trading on that information. Moreover, if asset prices do not immediately adjust to reflect relevant private information, an investor might rationally engage in "informed speculation"—that is, buy stock at a price he or she believes to exceed fundamental value. The speculator expects to "flip" the stock to a less well-informed investor—a "greater fool"—who assesses the stock's intrinsic worth more favorably.

Since the late 1970s, a growing body of research has challenged the presumption that asset markets are efficiently priced.[6] This research has proceeded on three fronts. The first seeks empirical evidence of mispricing. Since it would be extremely difficult to collect extensive real-time data on current and prospective investors' private beliefs about an asset's future cash flows, researchers have relied instead on analysis of pricing anomalies that should not persist in efficient markets. When corporations spin off business units, for example, they often retain an equity stake in the newly created public company. Whether a share of such stock is owned by its parent corporation or by a third-party investor, it should have the same intrinsic value. During the late 1990s, however, the high valuations of many Internet spin-offs were not fully reflected in their parent corporations' stock prices.[7] These anomalies often lasted for months. In some cases, valuing the parent's equity stake at the spin-off's market price actually implied a negative valuation of the parent corporation's non-Internet businesses.

In an efficient market, such pricing anomalies would be corrected quickly by arbitrageurs. This points to the second front in research on mispricing. Scholars have argued that arbitrage that involves shorting an overvalued stock can be both *risky* (when mispricing worsens before a correction occurs) and *costly* (when the supply of shares available for shorting is limited).[8] Consequently, mispricing may persist far longer than efficient market theories would predict.

Behavioral economics, the third front for research on mispricing, draws on social psychology to explain why individuals might be prone to lapses in rationality.[9] Behavioral economists have amassed evidence of several pervasive biases in decision making:

- *Overconfidence.* Individuals consistently overestimate their odds of success in a risky situation, especially when they believe they have personal control over the outcome.

- *Conservatism and representativeness.* When decision makers lack a model for the situation they are evaluating, they tend to *underweight* relevant data; they adjust their prior beliefs based on new information, but to an insufficient degree. However, when decision makers determine that a situation is representative of a familiar model, they tend to *overweight* data and disregard base rate probabilities. For example, investors who conclude that stock trading patterns conform to their model of a bull market are likely to overweight evidence that stock prices will continue to appreciate and to neglect historic data on the infrequency of sustained bull markets.[10]

Behavioral economists have hypothesized different mechanisms through which these and other decision-making biases can fuel bubbles:

- In a model developed by Barberis, Shleifer, and Vishny, a conservative initial reaction to positive public news—such as an unexpectedly strong earnings report for a new company—gives way to a pattern of strong stock-price gains as investors gradually recalibrate their expectations.[11] This pattern of stock-price gains is reinforced by the representativeness bias when investors conclude, after several quarters of steady appreciation, that the company fits their model of a growth stock. Prices then rise beyond fundamental value, and a correction inevitably follows.

- Daniel, Hirshleifer, and Subrahmanyam present a model in which certain traders are overconfident in private information they happen to possess.[12] They edit out public information that might contradict beliefs based on their private data, and consequently drive asset prices beyond fundamental values until a correction ensues.

- Hong and Stein posit the existence of two types of investors.[13] *News traders* act only on private information; *momentum traders* buy and sell stocks in response only to recent price movements. The slow diffusion of private information between news traders yields a pattern of price gains. Momentum traders respond to this pattern and then underreact to public information indicating that prices have exceeded fundamental value.

Evidence on Mispricing of Internet Stocks

The Internet sector experienced a spectacular valuation bubble between 1998 and 2001. The ISDEX, Wall Street Research Net's index of 50 Internet stocks, rose from 100 in January 1998 to a peak of 1,132 in March 2000, then declined sharply to a low of 106 in September 2001. The ISDEX recovered to 183 by year-end 2001, then traded between 72 and 205 during 2002.

Do these dramatic price movements reflect mispricing or the rational response of investors to news about the rapidly evolving Internet sector? Using several different analytical methods, researchers have found considerable evidence that Internet stocks were mispriced. One line of inquiry calculates the earnings growth rates required to justify the valuations that Internet companies enjoyed at the bubble's peak. Amazon.com has been the subject of several studies employing this approach. Two studies completed before the Internet bubble burst determined that Amazon.com's projected cash flows would warrant a market capitalization in the range of $5 billion, and thus concluded that the company was substantially overvalued during 1999.[14] A third study was able to justify the company's $23 billion valuation in October 1999, citing strong growth opportunities beyond the marketing of books.[15] Parenthetically, Amazon.com's market capitalization was $20 billion in September 2003. The company's stock price had cycled from a $113 high in December 1999 to a $6 low in October 2001, and stood at $46 at the beginning of September 2003.

Writing after the dot-com crash, Ofek and Richardson examined 50 e-commerce companies with an aggregate market capitalization of $73 billion in February 2000.[16] To justify this valuation, Ofek and Richardson showed the companies would need to earn returns 41 percent in excess of their 16 percent weighted average cost of capital for a period of ten years. Since such performance would be extraordinary for any individual company, it seems inconceivable that an entire sector—particularly one characterized by low entry barriers—could earn supernormal returns of this magnitude.

A second body of research on the pricing of Internet equities focuses on the value relevance of traditional accounting information.[17] The issue of mispricing is most directly addressed by Hand, who found that economic fundamentals (such as earnings growth forecasts) are strongly predictive of equity market values.[18] For business-to-consumer Internet companies, however, Hand observed that equity supply-and-demand factors (such as short interest, public float, and institutional holdings as a percentage of total shares outstanding) are also correlated with market values. Consistent with traditional asset-pricing theory, these factors did not predict market value for a sample of non-Internet companies.

A third set of studies examines event-driven pricing anomalies to make the case for mispricing of Internet equities.[19] As we have seen, the relative valuations of Internet spin-offs and their parent corporations offer strong evidence of mispricing. Ofek and Richardson also describe an anomaly for Internet companies related to the expiration of "lockup" provisions precluding equity sales by insiders and venture capital (VC) firms, usually for a period of 180 days following a firm's IPO. Ofek and Richardson found cumulative abnormal stock returns (price changes that cannot be explained using conventional capital-asset pricing models) equal to negative 4.5 percent over the five-day period surrounding lockup expiration. Since the expiration date is public knowledge, efficient-market theories predict that a pricing anomaly of this magnitude should not occur.

Finally, several studies have examined constraints on arbitrageurs who traded Internet equities.[20] These studies show that short sales as a percentage of total shares outstanding were very high for Internet companies as compared to non-Internet stocks. In the face of this strong demand, however, it was difficult to find enough investors willing to lend their shares to short sellers. Due to lockup provisions, the public floatation of Internet stocks was often small relative to total shares outstanding, and an unusually large portion of the public float was held by retail investors—who tend to be less willing than institutions to lend their shares to short sellers. As a result, Ofek and Richardson concluded, short selling was often difficult and expensive for Internet equities.[21]

Did the Internet Stock Bubble Lead Firms to Overinvest?

First, let's examine whether a correlation exists between overvaluation and overinvestment.

Past Research on the Link Between Overvaluation and Overinvestment

Scholars debate whether asset-market mispricing influences firms' investment policies.[22] In this debate, the distinction between *correlation* and *causality* is crucial. If managers and investors are both vulnerable to lapses in individual rationality, then overvaluation and overinvestment might be correlated, but it does not necessarily follow that overvaluation causes overinvestment. This possibility is illustrated in cell 1d in figure 4-1, which summarizes factors that may encourage under- and overinvestment.

As we saw earlier, overconfidence tends to be more severe when individuals believe they have influence over the outcomes of risky decisions. Social psychologists have also shown that decision makers are prone to overoptimism, especially when they are emotionally invested in an outcome (for instance, a bet on one's hometown sports team).[23] Managers—entrepreneurs, in particular—are likely to feel a strong affiliation with their own firms and to perceive that they have control over the outcomes of their investment decisions. Consequently, managers may be overconfident and overoptimistic about prospective payoffs from their investment decisions, and thus may tend to overinvest.[24]

Overinvestment and overvaluation would be correlated if investors and managers had similar information and were subject to the same decision-making biases in assessing the prospective payoffs of their actions. In this scenario, however, overinvestment would not be motivated by overvaluation

FIGURE 4-1

Factors that may encourage under- and overinvestment

Panel 1
Impact of investor and managerial rationality on investment outcomes

		Do current asset prices reflect fundamental value?	
		Yes	No
Do managers forecast ROI accurately?	Yes	**Cell 1a** Investments are more likely to be consistent with maximization of fundamental value	**Cell 1b** Outcome depends on firm's equity dependence and managers' time horizon
	No	**Cell 1c** Under/overinvestment is possible (but less likely if managers have short-term orientation and/or equity dependence is high)	**Cell 1d** Under/overinvestment is likely (but not *caused* by under/overvaluation)

Panel 2
Impact of equity dependence and managerial time horizon when managers forecast more rationally than investors (as in cell 1b)

		Equity dependence	
		Low	High
Managers cater to . . .	Long-term investors	**Cell 2a** Investments are more likely to be consistent with maximization of fundamental value	**Cell 2b** Underinvestment is likely; overinvestment is possible
	Short-term investors	**Cell 2c** Under/overinvestment is likely	**Cell 2d** Under/overinvestment is very likely

Source: Thomas R. Eisenmann.

of the company's equity, and flawed investment decisions would be unintentional. Managers—like investors—would believe they were pursuing a long-term value-maximizing strategy.

Theories that focus on asymmetric information examine the possibility that asset-market mispricing might cause managers to *deliberately* make investment decisions that they expect will fail to maximize fundamental value.[25] These theories assume that managers, as insiders, have better information about their firms' prospects than do investors, and thus have a reliable sense for when equity markets are too bullish or bearish on their firm's stock. (This assumption corresponds to cells 1a and 1b in figure 4-1). Management's ability and willingness to convey this information to investors may be constrained by its inherent complexity, by credibility issues (when managers assert that their stock is undervalued), and by personal costs (when managers' equity holdings or options would be worth less after "talking down" an overvalued stock).

Of course, managers may believe that their equity is mispriced, yet still make investment decisions that they expect will maximize fundamental value (that is, they may find themselves in cell 1b in figure 4-1). Reflecting on this possibility, Morck, Shleifer, and Vishny raised the question, Does the stock market really matter, or is it a sideshow?[26] Stein argued that mispricing is most likely to encourage deliberate managerial investment decisions that fail to maximize fundamental value when (1) managers favor the preferences of short-term shareholders over those with a long-term horizon, and (2) firms are dependent on external equity markets for financing.[27] These contingencies are illustrated in panel 2 in figure 4-1.

Agency conflicts might lead managers to favor the interests of short-term investors. For example, short-term stock price declines could increase the odds of a hostile takeover that would put top managers' jobs at risk.[28] Likewise, if managers are willing and able to sell stock or exercise options (*able* implies lapsed lockup or vesting restrictions), they have an incentive to try to boost the company's short-term stock price. To maximize their personal incomes, therefore, managers may be inclined to avoid investments when they believe their equity is undervalued. Under these conditions, investors believe—incorrectly, in management's view—that the firm's investment opportunities are not attractive. Presumably, if the firm were to pursue an aggressive investment strategy, these investors would sell, driving down the stock price further.

When managers believe their company's stock is undervalued relative to fundamentals, dependence on external equity markets may also reinforce their propensity to underinvest. A firm is dependent on external equity markets when its cash balances and internal cash flow are insufficient to fund all attractive investment projects, and when it cannot borrow. Lenders may be reluctant to deal with a firm that lacks a record of reliable earnings or tangible assets that can serve as collateral. If managers believe their stock is undervalued and wish to maximize returns to long-term shareholders, they may forego positive net present value (NPV) projects rather than issue dilutive new equity at what equates to a very high cost of capital.

The impact of *overvalued* equity on firms' investment policies is less clear-cut. When managers who are focused on short-term personal priorities recognize that their stock is overvalued, they may have an incentive to overinvest—that is, to fund what they believe will be negative-NPV projects—to meet investors' inflated growth expectations. An alternative would be to issue additional equity while the company's stock price is overvalued, and then to fund only positive-NPV projects, banking any leftover proceeds from the equity offering.[29] By earning interest on these funds rather than squandering them on negative-NPV projects, managers could conceivably maximize the firm's short- *and* longer-term valuation. However, overoptimistic investors might only be willing to commit fresh capital when a firm articulates specific—and aggressive—investment plans. Reneging on those plans and diverting funds to a bank account might damage management's reputation and undermine the company's stock price or its ability to raise funds in the future.

If a firm must raise new equity to fund ongoing operations, and overoptimistic investors will accept nothing less than an aggressive growth strategy, managers who wish to maximize returns to long-term shareholders may be obliged to overinvest. Under these conditions, managers would be forced to weigh the long-term value consequences of issuing no new equity—which at the extreme might jeopardize the company's survival—against the impact of raising and spending too much capital.

Only a few empirical studies have explored whether firms' investment policies are correlated with asset-market mispricing. These large-sample econometric studies have predicted investment growth rates using measures of (1) fundamental economic performance (e.g., earnings growth rates) and (2) investor sentiment (e.g., lagged stock returns).

This research has yielded mixed findings. For a diverse sample of publicly traded corporations, Morck, Shleifer, and Vishny observed that growth in investment is correlated with investor sentiment (measured as lagged stock returns), but concluded that the stock market "is not a dominant force in explaining why some firms invest and others do not" when compared to the impact of fundamentals.[30] Blanchard, Rhee, and Summers derived similar results using *Tobin's q*—the ratio of a firm's market

value to the replacement cost of its assets—as a measure of investor sentiment.[31] In contrast, examining the growth rate for real fixed, nonresiden-
tial, private domestic investment, Barro found that lagged stock returns
had significant predictive power after controlling for fundamentals.[32]

More recent empirical studies have examined conditions seen by theorists as likely to skew firms' investment policies (the contingencies explored
in panel 2 in figure 4-1). Consistent with predictions, Baker, Stein, and
Wurgler found that after controlling for fundamentals, investment growth
rates are much more sensitive to measures of mispricing for firms that are
highly dependent on external equity financing.[33] Polk and Sapienza speculated that managers might feel stronger pressure to favor the preferences of
short-term investors over those of long-term shareholders when short-
term investors control a large share of a firm's equity.[34] Consistent with
their theoretical predictions, Polk and Sapienza found a substantially
stronger relationship between investment growth rates and their proxies
for mispricing when firms had a high proportion of short-term investors
(measured by daily turnover relative to total shares outstanding).

Evidence on Overinvestment by Internet Companies

As we have seen, scholars have amassed considerable evidence that Internet
stocks were overvalued during the millennium bubble. Did overvaluation
lead Internet companies to overinvest, as conventional wisdom asserts? In
the popular view of the Internet gold rush, callow entrepreneurs goaded by
greedy venture capitalists and investment bankers overcrowded the sector
with "me too" business plans. In this view, entrepreneurs overspent on "get
big fast" strategies to satisfy the expectations of foolish speculators.[35]

Drawing on the research cited earlier, we might also posit that overvaluation led to overinvestment by Internet companies, subject as they were to
conditions that theorists believe may increase managers' propensity to cater
to short-term investor sentiment. First, most Internet start-ups were highly
dependent on external equity markets: nearly all had negative cash flow, and
few had material debt balances.[36] Second, share-turnover rates were two to
four times higher for Internet companies than for non-Internet firms.[37]
Following the logic of Polk and Sapienza, this situation may have increased
the pressure on managers to favor the preferences of short-term investors.[38]

This section will present some evidence on long-term returns on investments in Internet companies. Briefly, the evidence indicates that (1) at
the firm level, Internet companies tended to invest in IPO-year marketing

at levels close to those that, observed after the fact, would have maximized long-term value; and (2) at the sector level, long-term returns on the aggregate pool of capital invested in Internet companies were positive. One interpretation of this evidence is that managers in Internet companies made investment decisions with the goal of maximizing fundamental value, and that they were largely successful. If this interpretation is correct, then contrary to both conventional wisdom and theory-based prediction, overvaluation did not lead to overinvestment in Internet companies. However, caution must be exercised in drawing this inference, because the evidence is also consistent with a second interpretation. Perhaps managers in Internet companies, catering to investor sentiment, deliberately made what they believed would be negative-NPV investment decisions, but were later surprised by stronger-than-expected payoffs. Occam's razor favors the simpler first explanation—that is, that managers followed long-term value-maximizing norms. Lacking data on managers' beliefs and intentions, however, we cannot rule out other interpretations.

Marketing Investments

A cross-sectional econometric analysis of a sample of 117 publicly traded firms employed a two-step analytical approach to determine whether Internet companies invested in marketing at levels that maximized long-term value.[39]

In the first step, IPO-year marketing expenditures were estimated using only variables apparent to managers as they made IPO-year investment decisions. These variables included a company's status as a first or late mover; whether its business model exhibited strong network effects, switching costs, and static scale economies; and several controls, including the company's IPO-year sales and cash balance.

A firm's commitment to an accelerated growth strategy was measured using the residual of this first-step marketing equation, which fit the data reasonably well ($R^2 = 0.51$). A positive residual indicated that a company invested more heavily in growth than would be predicted, after controlling for firm and market characteristics.

In the second step, the marketing residual and other variables apparent to managers as they made IPO-year investment decisions (e.g., first-mover status, IPO-year sales) were used to estimate long-term returns. Long-term rates of return on invested capital (ROIC) were defined as the ratio of a company's post-bubble (year-end 2001) market value to the total amount of capital it had raised historically.

As expected, an inverted-U relationship was observed between long-term returns and departures from predicted IPO-year marketing spending. Firms with IPO-year marketing spending substantially above or below predicted levels earned lower long-term returns. On the basis of these results, the analysis concluded that the sample companies tended to invest in marketing, prospectively, at levels close to those that would have maximized long-term returns, observed after the fact.[40]

Aggregate Returns to Investors

The evidence to this point suggests that publicly traded Internet companies were overvalued but, despite mispricing, typically invested in IPO-year marketing at levels close to those that would have maximized fundamental value. Beyond the caveats raised earlier about inference testing, our ability to generalize from these results is restricted by two factors. First, the preceding analysis focuses only on marketing, ignoring investments in, for example, mergers or technology development. Second, the apparently rational behavior of publicly traded companies may reflect a selection bias: perhaps firms only managed to complete IPOs if their management teams were smart enough to avoid gross overinvestment.

To address these concerns, we examined the aggregate long-term return on all the capital ever committed by professional investors—both private and public—to Internet companies, including firms that eventually failed, merged, or survived but never went public. As table 4-1 shows, the combined market value of U.S.-based Internet companies is estimated as $98.6 billion at year-end 2001. Consistent with a winners-take-most payoff structure, just a few firms realized a large share of this value. Specifically, five stocks accounted for $41.2 billion of market value: eBay, Yahoo!, Amazon, E*TRADE, and WebMD. In total, about $85 billion was invested in 2,121 Internet companies from their inception through 2001. These estimates of market value and aggregate capital investment imply a sector-level pretax internal rate of return (IRR) of 9 percent.[41]

Of course, focusing on sector-level aggregate results may mask serious overinvestment in individual markets, such as online pet-supply retailing. But, if the Internet sector had been subject to grossly excessive rates of entry and investment, as conventional wisdom holds, we would have expected a significant sector-level capital loss rather than a somewhat disappointing—relative to the risk borne by investors—but still positive long-term payoff.

TABLE 4-1

Aggregate enterprise value versus total capital raised, all U.S.-based Internet companies

	Number of firms	Enterprise value, year-end 2001 (in $billions)	Total capital raised, 1995–2001 (in $billions)
Private firms			
Active	1,650	$24.0	$35.3
Failed	99	0	6.0
Merged into non-Internet companies	183	5.2	6.1
Merged into other Internet companies	50	Included in totals for acquiring companies	
Total	1,982	$29.2	$47.4
Public firms			
Active	77	$66.5	$29.6
Failed	22	0	5.2
Merged into non-Internet companies	23	2.9	2.8
Merged into other Internet companies	17	Included in totals for acquiring companies	
Total	139	$69.4	$37.6
All firms			
Active	1,727	$90.5	$64.9
Failed	121	0	11.2
Merged into non-Internet companies	206	8.1	8.9
Merged into other Internet companies	67	Included in totals for acquiring companies	
Total	2,121	$98.6	$85.0

Source: See the appendix for definitions, assumptions, and data sources.

In summary, conventional wisdom probably exaggerates the economic damage wrought by what some have labeled "the dot-com debacle." When we consider the economic impact of valuation bubbles, it is important to distinguish stock market gains and losses—transfers of wealth between traders—from poor long-term returns on the capital invested directly in companies. It is also important not to conflate high business-failure rates resulting from excessive rates of entry with the high failure rates we would normally expect to observe in new markets—like those targeted by many Internet companies—with winners-take-most potential and low entry barriers. Given lottery-like payoffs in such markets, high rates of entry and failure may be fully consistent with rational economic behavior.

How Might Future Bubbles Affect Broadband Deployment?

The evidence reported earlier suggests (subject to the caveats already noted) that Internet equities were significantly overvalued, but that this state of affairs did not lead managers to deliberately overinvest. If this interpretation is correct, and if broadband-application markets are likely to replicate the patterns that prevailed for narrowband Internet businesses, we might reasonably conclude that future bubbles should not have much impact on broadband's development.

This sanguine "stock market as sideshow" view is based largely on analysis of the economic consequences of *overvaluation*. Before we embrace this view, however, let us consider the potential consequences for broadband deployment of *undervaluation*.

Incumbency and the Impact of Undervaluation

Economic historians observe that bubbles often end with an overcorrection, during which investors shun promising opportunities; Kindleberger calls this the bubble's "revulsion" phase.[42] When firms are dependent on external equity markets, as we have seen, undervaluation may force managers to underinvest. Consequently, future bubbles could slow broadband's development relative to rates that would maximize social welfare and firms' fundamental values.

Firms with strong internal cash flow might invest more aggressively during the revulsion phase to capture attractive market opportunities that would otherwise lie fallow due to a shortage of external equity. The companies best positioned to pursue these opportunities—in terms of their access to relevant skills and resources, including relationships with prospective customers—are likely to be industry incumbents. In the case of broadband, these incumbents would include cable TV system operators, phone companies, and leading providers of offline and narrowband online content and transaction services. Some of these incumbents might be inclined to invest heavily to exploit growth opportunities in new broadband markets. However, industrial-organization economics suggests that, absent a threat of competition, incumbents who dominate an established market may have an incentive to delay the development of new products and services that would cannibalize that market and render past investments obsolete.[43] If incumbents are sheltered during a future bubble's revulsion phase from equity-dependent start-ups, broadband deployment could conceivably stall.

Choices Confronting Managers During Bubbles

At the beginning of this chapter, we predicted that firms that deploy or leverage broadband technologies are likely to experience valuation bubbles over the next several years. How should managers respond when they perceive their equity to be under- or overvalued?

As we have just seen, managers' options in the face of undervaluation will depend on whether or not their firm is dependent on external equity markets. Options will be limited when companies confront severe capital constraints: they can try to "talk up" their stock price, but if this fails, the firm may not be able to raise enough new equity to fund all positive-NPV projects. When companies do have strong internal cash flow or ample cash balances, managers must decide whether to approve the full roster of attractive projects. If they do, bearish investors might drive their stock price down further, at least over the short term. If managers do not approve the full roster of positive-NPV projects, however, they will fail to maximize their firm's long-term value.

In this situation, should managers cater to the interests of shareholders with a short-term investment horizon or of those who prefer to "buy and hold" for the long term? From society's perspective, the answer is clear: maximizing fundamental value would put resources to their most productive use. As we saw earlier, however, managers may have a powerful personal incentive to sacrifice fundamental value for short-term performance; doing so may prevent a hostile takeover and thereby preserve their jobs. From the perspective of long-term shareholders in firms vulnerable to undervaluation, this scenario argues for the adoption of poison-pill defenses and "golden parachute" employment contracts. From society's perspective, the risk of underinvestment due to undervaluation could conceivably justify government intervention to stimulate spending, or even direct government subsidization. This rationale for government intervention would only hold, however, if government policy makers were immune to the decision-making biases that caused capital providers to misprice attractive investment opportunities.

When they perceive their equity to be overvalued, managers must also decide whether to cater to the preferences of short- or long-term investors.[44] A short-term focus implies aggressively raising and spending new capital to satisfy speculators' expectations for growth. By following this approach, managers might maximize stock option gains. Likewise, if lockup provisions have lapsed, venture capital investors might support an aggressive growth strategy. However, social welfare would suffer if management deliberately approved negative-NPV projects. Consequently, from a policy perspective, this scenario argues for a long holding period for any management equity incentives in firms vulnerable to overvaluation, and for truly independent boards of directors. When large shareholders who are able and eager to liquidate their overvalued holdings dominate boards, management may be pressured to take actions that boost the firm's short-term share price at the expense of long-term value.

Appendix: Analysis of Internet Sector Returns

This appendix describes the data sources and methodology employed in calculating aggregate return on investments in Internet companies as presented in table 4-1.

Data sources and definitions. U.S.-based Internet companies that raised capital from professional investors were identified using data compiled by Venture Economics, Morgan Stanley Dean Witter Internet Research (May 2, 2000), and Wall Street Research Net (WSRN.com, which was purchased by Internet.com). *Internet companies* were defined as firms that rely on the World Wide Web as their principal channel for delivering products, services, or information to consumers or businesses. This definition excludes (1) companies that earn most of their revenue by providing professional services, software, or hardware to Internet companies; (2) firms that provide Internet access or Web site hosting services; and (3) the online units of established brick-and-mortar corporations. *Professional investors* were defined as venture capital firms (including corporate venture funds) and institutions that purchase public equity and debt securities. Firms funded exclusively by "angels" or by strategic investments from non-Internet companies were excluded from the analysis, although strategic investments were included in estimates of total capital raised by VC-backed firms.

Valuation approach. Enterprise values were estimated as of December 31, 2001. By that date, the Internet valuation bubble had subsided, according to analysis of the ISDEX. Valuations for VC-backed Internet companies that remained private reflect only the market value of equity. Data was not available on the total amount of debt raised by these companies, but case studies suggest that most privately held Internet companies had little or no debt. Enterprise values for publicly traded firms reflect the market value of their equity as of year-end 2001, plus the book value of any debt.

Valuation of active privately held firms. For active privately held Internet companies that raised funds during 2001, year-end 2001 equity market value was assumed to equal 98 percent of total capital raised historically, based on analysis of Venture Economics data on post-round valuations for funding transactions completed by this group during the second half of 2001. For active private firms that did not raise funds during 2001, prior-round valuation figures were inflated due to the Internet bubble and thus do not accurately reflect year-end 2001 market values. Instead, year-end 2001 equity market value for these firms was assumed to equal 49 percent of total capital raised historically, based on analysis of Venture Economics data on average total returns, as of year-end 2002, for all VC funds launched during 1999 (April 21, 2003, press release). These returns, which averaged 62 percent of capital raised, can be used to estimate the performance of Internet companies, because 82 percent of all venture capital investments during 1999–2000 were allocated to Internet businesses, according to VentureOne and PricewaterhouseCoopers.[45]

Valuation of merged firms. Valuation estimates for merged firms are intended to reflect their contribution to the market values of the companies that acquired them, rather than proceeds actually realized by the merged firms' shareholders. For transactions completed during 2001, these figures were presumed to be the same, implying that sellers captured 100 percent of the value created by the merger. Specifically, for private firms merged into non-Internet companies during 2001, year-end 2001 market value was assumed to equal the announced merger transaction proceeds, which averaged 76 percent of total equity capital raised historically by the acquired companies.

For firms acquired by non-Internet companies prior to 2001, merger transaction values were skewed by the Internet bubble and thus do not accurately indicate their contribution to the acquiring entities' year-end 2001 market valuations. Instead, year-end 2001 market value for these firms was conservatively assumed to equal the total capital they raised historically. Returns actually realized by shareholders of the acquired companies were typically higher, because bubble-inflated transaction proceeds were paid in the form of cash or equity in non-Internet companies, which, on average, declined in value less sharply than did equity in Internet companies after the spring of 2000.

For mergers involving two Internet companies, the acquired company's value need not be separately estimated: it is already included in the acquiring company's year-end 2001 market capitalization. However, the capital raised by the acquired company is added to the capital raised by the acquiring firm to indicate total investment in the combined entity.

Accuracy of IRR calculation. The estimated 9 percent IRR on aggregate investments in U.S.-based Internet companies is overstated to the extent that (1) founding equity diluted the collective ownership stake of capital investors and (2) private firms raised debt and then failed. However, the IRR estimate is understated to the extent that proceeds paid to shareholders of Internet companies merged prior to 2001 exceeded the appraised year-end 2001 value of such companies to the acquiring entities.

Notes

1. W. Sahlman and H. Stevenson, "Capital Market Myopia," *Journal of Business Venturing* 1 (1985): 7–30; and C. Kindleberger, *Manias, Panics, and Crashes: A History of Financial Crisis* (New York: Wiley, 2000).

2. Kindleberger, *Manias, Panics, and Crashes*, Appendix B.

3. T. Eisenmann, "A Note on Racing to Acquire Customers," note 9-803-103 (Boston: Harvard Business School, 2003).

4. T. Eisenmann, ed., *Internet Business Models: Text and Cases* (New York: McGraw-Hill, 2002).

5. N. Barberis and R. Thaler, "A Survey of Behavioral Finance," working paper 9222, National Bureau of Economic Research, Cambridge, MA, 2002; also in N. Constantinide, M. Harris, and R. Stulz, eds., *Handbook of the Economics of Finance* (Amsterdam: North-Holland, 2004).

6. For summaries, see E. Fama, "Market Efficiency, Long-Term Returns, and Behavioral Finance," *Journal of Financial Economics* 49 (1998): 283–306; and Barberis and Thaler, "A Survey of Behavioral Finance."

7. E. Ofek and M. Richardson, "The Valuation and Market Rationality of Internet Stock Prices," *Oxford Review of Economic Policy* 18 (2002): 265–287.

8. A. Shleifer and R. Vishny, "The Limits of Arbitrage," *Journal of Finance* 52 (1997): 35–55.

9. For a literature survey, see Barberis and Thaler, "A Survey of Behavioral Finance."

10. R. Shiller, "Bubbles, Human Judgment, and Expert Opinion," discussion paper 1303, Cowles Foundation, New Haven, CT, 2001, available through http://cowls.econ.yale.edu/P/cd/dy2001.htm.

11. N. Barberis, A. Shleifer, and R. Vishny, "A Model of Investor Sentiment," *Journal of Financial Economics* 49 (1998): 307–343.

12. K. Daniel, D. Hirshleifer, and A. Subrahmanyam, "Investor Psychology and Security Market Under- and Overreactions," *Journal of Finance* 53 (1998): 1,839–1,885.

13. H. Hong and J. Stein, "A Unified Theory of Underreaction, Momentum Trading, and Overreaction in Asset Markets," *Journal of Finance* 54 (1999): 2,143–2,184.

14. A. Perkins and M. Perkins, *The Internet Bubble: Inside the Overvalued World of High-Tech Stocks* (New York: HarperCollins, 1999); and E. Schwartz and M. Moon, "Rational Pricing of Internet Companies," *Financial Analysts Journal* 56 (2000): 62–75.

15. D. Desmet, T. Francis, A. Hu, T. Koller, and G. Riedel, "Valuing Dot-coms," *McKinsey Quarterly* no. 1 (2000): 148–157.

16. Ofek and Richardson, "The Valuation and Market Rationality of Internet Stock Prices."

17. For instance, B. Trueman, T. Wong, and X. Zhang, "The Eyeballs Have It: Searching for the Value in Internet Stocks," *Journal of Accounting Research* 38 (Supplement 2000): 137–162; S. Rajgopal, S. Kotha, and M. Venkatachalam, "The Value Relevance of Network Advantages: The Case of E-commerce Firms," *Journal of Accounting Research* 41 (2003): 135–162; and J. Core, W. Guay, and A. Van Buskirk, "Market Valuations in the New Economy: An Investigation of What Has Changed," *Journal of Accounting and Economics* 34 (2003): 43–67.

18. J. Hand, "The Role of Economic Fundamentals, Web Traffic, and Supply and Demand in the Pricing of U.S. Internet Stocks," working paper, Kenan-Flager Business School, University of North Carolina, Chapel Hill, 2000, available through Social Science Research Network (SSRN), http://www.ssrn.com.

19. For a summary, see Ofek and Richardson, "The Valuation and Market Rationality of Internet Stock Prices."

20. See, for instance, Hand, "The Role of Economic Fundamentals," and Ofek and Richardson, "The Valuation and Market Rationality of Internet Stock Prices."

21. Ofek and Richardson, "The Valuation and Market Rationality of Internet Stock Prices."

22. R. Barro, "The Stock Market and Investment," *Review of Financial Studies* 3, no. 1 (1990): 115–131; R. Morck, A. Shleifer, and R. Vishny, "The Stock Market and Investment: Is the Market a Sideshow?" *Brookings Papers on Economic Activity* 2 (1990): 157–215; and O. Blanchard, C. Rhee, and L. Summers, "The Stock Market, Profit, and Investment," *Quarterly Journal of Economics* 108 (1993): 115–136.

23. E. Babad, "Wishful Thinking and Objectivity Among Sports Fans," *Social Behavior: An International Journal of Applied Social Psychology* 4 (1987): 231–240.

24. A. Cooper, C. Woo, and W. Dunkelberg, "Entrepreneurs' Perceived Chances for Success," *Journal of Business Venturing* 3 (1988): 97–108; L. Busenitz and J. Barney, "Differences Between Entrepreneurs and Managers in Large Organizations: Biases and Heuristics in Decision Making," *Journal of Business Venturing* 12 (1997): 9–30; J. Heaton, "Managerial Optimism and Corporate Finance," *Financial Management* 31 (2002): 33–45; and for empirical research that supports this hypothesis, see U. Malmendier and G. Tate, "CEO Overconfidence and Corporate Investment" (paper presented at the AFA meetings, Washington, DC, October 13, 2003), manuscript available through SSRN.

25. Morck, Shleifer, and Vishny, "The Stock Market and Investment;" and J. Stein, "Rational Capital Budgeting in an Irrational World," *Journal of Business* 69 (1996): 429–455.

26. Morck, Shleifer, and Vishny, "The Stock Market and Investment."

27. Stein, "Rational Capital Budgeting in an Irrational World."

28. Morck, Shleifer, and Vishny, "The Stock Market and Investment."

29. Blanchard, Rhee, and Summers, "The Stock Market, Profit, and Investment."

30. Morck, Shleifer, and Vishny, "The Stock Market and Investment," 31.

31. Blanchard, Rhee, and Summers, "The Stock Market, Profit, and Investment."

32. Barro, "The Stock Market and Investment."

33. M. Baker, J. Stein and J. Wurgler, "When Does the Market Matter? Stock Prices and the Investment of Equity-Dependent Firms," *Quarterly Journal of Economics* 118 (2003): 969–1,005.

34. C. Polk and P. Sapienza, "The Real Effects of Investor Sentiment," working paper, Northwestern University, Evanston, IL, 2002, available through SSRN.

35. See, for example, J. Madrick, "The Business Media and the New Economy," research paper R-24, Kennedy School Shorenstein Center, Harvard University, Cambridge, MA, 2001, and M. Lewis, "In Defense of the Boom," *New York Times Sunday Magazine*, October 27, 2002, 44.

36. T. Eisenmann, "Internet Companies' Growth Strategies: Determinants of Investment Intensity and Long-Term Performance," working paper 03-110, Harvard Business School, Boston, 2003.

37. Ofek and Richardson, "The Valuation and Market Rationality of Internet Stock Prices."

38. Polk and Sapienza, "The Real Effects of Investor Sentiment."

39. Eisenmann, "Internet Companies' Growth Strategies."

40. Ibid.

41. See the appendix for a description of data sources and assumptions; also see E. Fama and K. French, "The Corporate Cost of Capital and the Return on Corporate Investment," *Journal of Finance* 54 (1999): 1,939–1,967, who used a similar methodology to calculate the IRR of investments across the entire U.S. nonfinancial corporate sector.

42. Kindleberger, *Manias, Panics, and Crashes.*

43. D. Fudenberg and J. Tirole, *Dynamic Models of Oligopoly* (Chur, Switzerland: Harwood, 1986).

44. J. Fuller and M. Jensen, "Just Say No to Wall Street," working paper 02-01, Amos Tuck School of Business, Hanover, NH, 2002, available through SSRN.

45. P. Buckley and S. Montes, "The Evolving Online Environment," Chapter 2 in *Digital Economy 2002*, U.S. Department of Commerce, Economics and Statistics Adminstration, February 2002, 11.

Creating Value in a Broadband World

5

Disruption, Disintegration, and the Impact of New Telecommunications Technologies

Clayton M. Christensen and Scott D. Anthony

T HROUGHOUT MUCH of the 1800s, the U.S. telecommunications industry was dominated by a single integrated firm, Western Union, which was ultimately disrupted by a fragmented horde of telephone companies. By the 1920s, another monopolist, AT&T, had come to dominate the industry—but its dominance was undone between 1970 and 1995 by another group of less integrated companies. The decade 1994–2004 witnessed a swing back toward dominance by a few increasingly integrated companies. But new technologies like Voice over Internet Protocol (VoIP), 3G, Wi-Fi, cable telephony, and instant messaging all threaten to alter the structure of the industry once again—possibly bringing new companies to prominence and hastening the demise of others.

This chapter will present two models that explain how technological progress interacts with customers' abilities to utilize that progress, and show how that interaction affects the fortunes of entrant and incumbent companies and the structure of industries. We will use key developments in the history of telecommunications to illustrate the explanatory power of the models, and then apply the models to predict how new technologies are likely to impact the telecommunications industry.

The Models of Disruption and Disintegration

The likely impact of new technologies on incumbent companies can be assessed using the model of disruptive innovation, whose conceptual foundation is the well-recognized phenomenon that the pace of technological progress almost always outstrips customers' ability to utilize that progress.[1] Figure 5-1 depicts this phenomenon. The gentle upward slope of the dotted line signifies the gradual rate of improvement that customers in every market can utilize. Consider the auto industry: automotive engineers keep giving us new and improved engines, but we can't utilize all the performance they make available under the hood; safety concerns and speed limits constrain how much performance we can use. There are many tiers of customers in a market. Those in the most demanding tiers may be unsatisfied even with the best-performing products, and those in the least demanding tiers can be oversatisfied with very little.[2]

The topmost arrow in the model represents the trajectory of technical progress that innovating companies achieve as they introduce new and improved products. This pace almost always outstrips the absorptive abil-

FIGURE 5-1

The model of disruption

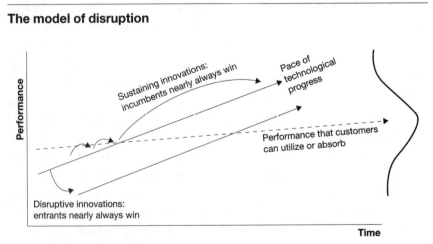

Source: Adapted with permission from Clayton M. Christensen and Michael E. Raynor, *The Innovator's Solution* (Boston: Harvard Business School Press, 2003), 33.

ity of customers in any tier of the market. Thus, a company whose products are not yet adequate to address mainstream customers' needs at a given point is likely to overshoot what those customers will be able to utilize in the future. This happens because companies keep striving to make better products that they can sell for higher profit margins to not-yet-satisfied customers in more demanding tiers of the market. For instance, in 1983–1984, when people first started using personal computers for word processing, they often had to stop typing to let the Intel 286 chip catch up; the technology was not good enough even for a simple application like word processing. But today's processors offer much more speed than customers using mainstream applications can use—while still unsatisfied customers using the most demanding applications continue to need even-faster chips.

The innovations that propel firms up this trajectory are called *sustaining innovations*; some are incremental improvements, and others are breakthrough technologies. The incumbent leaders in an industry almost always triumph over new entrants in battles of sustaining technology, no matter how radical the technology is. The evidence is overwhelming that when an innovation helps industry leaders make better products that they can sell for higher profit margins to their best customers, they invest resolutely and remain atop their industries.

But there is another type of innovation, which we have termed *disruptive innovation*, in which entrants rather than established leaders typically emerge victorious. Disruptive innovators' products perform less well than established products—and thus the best customers of the established industry leaders initially ignore disruptive products. Profit dollars per unit sold are typically much lower for disruptive products than leaders earn selling their best products to their best customers. Leaders who listen to their best customers and focus their resources where profit margins are most attractive are not motivated to pursue disruptive innovations aggressively. That is why entrants almost always seize the lead in disruptive innovation. Ultimately, the entrant firms outstrip the prior leaders when their products' performance becomes good enough.

Most of today's giant companies entered their industries and supplanted the prior leaders on the strength of disruptive innovation—not by bringing better products to established markets but by bringing simpler, more affordable products to customers who had previously lacked the money and skill to own and use them. Such companies include Wal-Mart, Cisco, Intel, Microsoft, Dell, Charles Schwab, Oracle, Southwest Airlines, Sony, Nucor, and Toyota.

Terminology

For readers unfamiliar with these models, we will define some terms here. A product's *architecture* specifies its constituent components and subsystems, and how they must interact to achieve the targeted functionality. The junction where any two components fit together is called an *interface*. Interfaces can exist within a product and between stages in the value-added chain.

An architecture is *interdependent* at an interface if one part cannot be created independently of the other—if how one is designed and made depends on how the other is designed and made. When an interface is characterized by unpredictable interdependencies, the same organization must simultaneously develop *both* of the components if it hopes to develop *either* component. Interdependent architectures tend to optimize *performance*, defined as the functionality and reliability of the product. Interdependent architectures also tend to be proprietary because competitors optimize performance differently.

In contrast, a *modular* interface is characterized by such fully understood interactions that there are no unpredictable interdependencies across components of a product or stages of the value chain. Modular components can be designed by independent work groups or different companies working at arms' length because complete specifications within a *modular architecture* define how the components must function and fit together. The specified parameters are measurable. Modular architectures optimize *flexibility* to upgrade or interchange one piece of a system without redesigning the entire product system. But because they require complete and standardized specification, modular architectures give engineers less freedom in design. As a result, modular flexibility sacrifices some of performance.

Pure modularity and interdependence are ends of a spectrum; most products fall somewhere between these extremes. Companies are more likely to succeed when they match product architecture to their competitive circumstances. Their investments bear fruit if they develop complete systems with interdependent architectures when the product system's performance is not yet good enough. When system performance is more than good enough, by contrast, developing and selling modular performance-defining components, materials, and subsystems earns the most attractive profits.

Two Types of Disruption

As figure 5-2 illustrates, there are two types of disruption. The first type, shown in the rear plane, is a *low-end disruption*. Low-end disruptors bring inexpensive but good enough products into tiers of an existing market whose customers have been overserved by the functionality of prevailing products. Steel minimills and discount retailing are examples of low-end disruptions. Low-end disruptors stymie established competitors by employing a business model that is unattractive to incumbents—entailing lower gross margin percentages made possible by lower overhead costs and higher asset turns.

The second type of disruption, depicted in the foreground plane, is a *new-market disruption*. New-market disruptors bring products that are so simple and affordable that a whole new population of customers who had

FIGURE 5-2

Two types of disruption

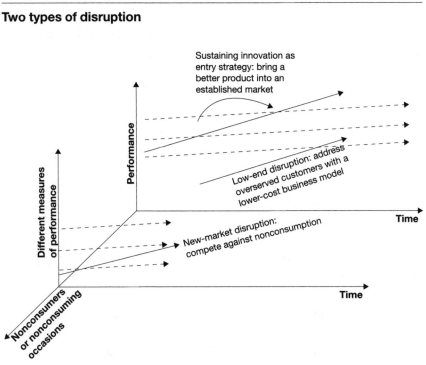

Source: Adapted with permission from Clayton M. Christensen and Michael E. Raynor, *The Innovator's Solution* (Boston: Harvard Business School Press, 2003), 44.

previously lacked the money and skill to do so can begin owning and using them. Incumbent leaders typically ignore new-market disruptions because the markets are small at the outset, and profit dollars per unit sold are lower than they can earn by pursuing sustaining innovations in established markets. New-market disruptions create entirely new markets, and their performance improves in the new plane of competition: when their products ultimately become good enough, customers abandon the original plane in favor of the new one, attracted by the affordability and convenience of the disruptive products. Personal computers, routers, and relational database software are examples of new-market disruptions.[3]

Incumbent companies frequently invest in disruptive technologies, but because the established market in the original plane of competition is so much larger and apparently more attractive, they often try to "cram" the disruption into the mainstream market rather than deploying it in a new application whose primary competition is nonconsumption. Cramming obligates them to spend enormous sums to make the disruptive technology better than existing technology, and they nearly always fail. Companies that have tried to supplant computer-based word processing with voice-recognition technology and companies that have sought to make solar energy good enough to supplant centrally generated power in North American and European markets have dissipated billions of dollars pitting a potentially disruptive technology's performance against that of established technologies in existing markets. These technological concepts could be deployed as disruption—and they *are*, by entrant companies. But the leaders in the industries try to cram them as sustaining technologies into established markets. Because new markets are initially small, incumbent companies typically leave them to new entrants with simple, affordable products. The technologies often fail commercially in the hands of the incumbents, in other words, not because they lack valuable potential. Rather, they fail because incumbents target the technologies at large but complicated, rather than simple, market applications.

Technologies that have promised wireless access to the Internet have witnessed a replay of this tendency. Incumbent telecommunications providers and some start-ups backed by growth-thirsty venture investors dissipated billions of dollars attempting to develop and deploy 3G technologies as a sustaining innovation. The companies that have gotten traction are those whose strategies are new-market disruptions, targeting new customers or simple applications. Examples are NTT DoCoMo's deployment of i-mode, and Research In Motion's (RIM) BlackBerry.

A Model of Integration and Disintegration

When there is a performance gap—when product functionality and reliability are not yet good enough to fulfill the needs of customers in a given tier of the market (represented by the upper-left domain of figure 5-1)—companies must compete by making the best possible products. In the race to do so, firms that build their products around proprietary, interdependent architectures enjoy an important competitive advantage. The reason: when the best products' performance is inadequate, competitive forces compel engineers to fit the pieces of their systems together in ever-more-efficient ways in each new product generation in order to wring the maximum performance out of the available technology. When firms must compete by making the best possible products, they cannot simply assemble standardized components. Standardization of interfaces (meaning fewer degrees of design freedom) would force them to back away from the frontier of what is technologically possible. When the product is not good enough, backing off from the best that can be done means that you will fall behind.

Companies that compete with interdependent architectures *must* be integrated: they must control the design and manufacture of *every* critical component of the system in order to make *any* piece of the system. During the early days of the mainframe computer industry, for instance, an independent manufacturer of mainframes was an impossibility because there was no clean interface between design and manufacturing: the way the machines were designed depended on the art that was used in manufacturing and vice versa. By the same token, there could be no such thing as an independent supplier of operating systems, core memory, or logic circuitry to the mainframe industry because these key subsystems had to be interdependently designed too.

As a result, IBM—the integrated giant—dominated its industry at this stage. For the same reasons, Ford and General Motors, the most integrated companies, were the dominant competitors during the automobile industry's not-good-enough era. RCA, Xerox, Standard Oil, and U.S. Steel likewise dominated their industries at comparable stages because they were similarly integrated, with proprietary, interdependent product and process architectures. Their market dominance was an outgrowth of the not-good-enough circumstance, which mandated interdependent product or value-chain architectures and vertical integration. Their proprietary architectures and the high fixed costs that characterize integrated companies conferred strong performance and cost advantages on them. This is why they enjoyed near-monopoly power during that era in their histories.

This stage rarely lasts, however, because the pace of improvement in functionality and reliability eventually outstrips customers' ability to utilize it. Companies then find themselves on the right-hand side of the disruption model, which is characterized by a performance surplus. Customers confronted with a performance surplus tend to be happy to *accept* improved products but unwilling to pay a premium price for them. This shift is depicted in figure 5-3.

FIGURE 5-3

Circumstances in which interdependent and modular architectures predominate

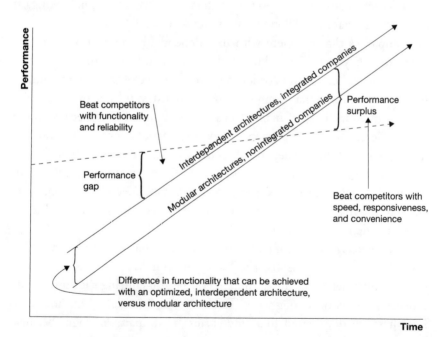

Source: Adapted with permission from Clayton M. Christensen and Michael E. Raynor, *The Innovator's Solution* (Boston: Harvard Business School Press, 2003), 127.

Overshooting does not mean that customers will no longer pay for improvements. It means that the *type* of improvement for which they will pay a premium price will change. Once their requirements for functionality and reliability have been met, customers redefine what is not good enough: what becomes not good enough is that they can't get exactly what they need when they need it, as conveniently as possible. Customers become willing to pay premium prices for improved performance along this new trajectory of innovation in speed, responsiveness, and convenience. When this happens, we say that the *basis of competition* in a given tier of the market has changed.

The pressure of competing along this new trajectory forces a gradual evolution in product architecture away from the interdependent architectures of the not-good-enough era toward *modular* designs, which enjoy competitive advantage in an era of performance surplus, as depicted in figure 5-3. Modular architectures help companies compete on the dimensions that matter in the lower-right quadrant of the disruption model. They can introduce new products faster because they can upgrade individual subsystems without having to redesign everything. Although standard modular interfaces invariably impose compromise on system performance (represented by the parallel, lower-performing trajectory of improvement for modular architectures), firms have the slack to trade away some performance with these customers because functionality is more than good enough.

Modularity has a profound impact on industry structure because it enables independent, nonintegrated organizations to sell, buy, and assemble components and subsystems. Whereas in the interdependent era firms had to make all of the key elements of a system in order to make any of them, in a modular world they can prosper by outsourcing or by supplying just one element. Ultimately, the specifications for modular interfaces coalesce as industry standards, allowing firms to mix and match components from the best suppliers in order to respond flexibly to the specific needs of individual customers.

When technological innovators get this wrong—attempting modular architectures built on industry standards when their industry is in the upper-left domain of the disruption model, or clinging to proprietary architectures long after the industry has transitioned to the overserved phase represented by the lower-right portion of that model—their innovations frequently fail.

Examining the Past and Future of Telecommunications

These models can help us understand many of the most important technological and competitive transitions in the history of telecommunications.
This section will examine five incidents: Bell Telephone's disruption of
Western Union; the emergence of AT&T as a vertically integrated monopolist; the industry's "dis-integration" as specialist firms like MCI became
successful; the failure of the competitive local exchange carriers (CLECs);
and the disruptive router of Cisco.

Bell's Disruption of Western Union

Why did Western Union, the dominant telecommunications giant of the
late nineteenth century, ignore the telephone and get toppled by Bell Telephone? Bell's telephone was a new-market disruption relative to the telegraph. Because Bell's early telephone could carry its signal only a few miles,
Western Union—whose business focused exclusively on long-distance
communications—saw no use for it. Its major customers were railroads and
financial institutions, which used telegraphy to transmit data over long distances. A product that transmitted personal messages was largely irrelevant
to the purposes for which these customers used the telegraph.

When Alexander Graham Bell realized that he lacked the capital to
roll his innovation across the United States ahead of would-be competitors, he began to license his technology to other entrepreneurs. It was one
of these entrepreneurs who first launched voice telephony in New Haven,
Connecticut, in 1878 by creating a new market: local telecommunication.
In a new plane of competition quite different from long-distance telegraphy, businesses with multiple offices a few miles apart began stringing
point-to-point wires so their employees could communicate in real time
without needing the services of telegraphers who had mastered Morse
code. Soon the advent of the central switching office enabled anyone with
a telephone to talk to anyone else with a telephone in New Haven.

Between 1894 and 1904, more than 6,000 independent telephone companies went into business in the United States. Little by little, in pursuit of
better customer service and improved profit, these companies, many of
which were Bell licensees, stretched the distance over which their signals
would carry—and little by little drew all of Western Union's customers
into their new telephonecentric plane of competition.

Why Integration Won

In 1881, the Bell Company took steps to become more vertically integrated by purchasing a leading telecommunications equipment provider, Western Electric, and in 1885 reorganized as AT&T. Under the stewardship of Theodore Vail, AT&T began acquiring independent local telephone companies. There were solid reasons why Vail's strategy of vertical and horizontal integration gave it a huge competitive edge. Bell's licensing model had led to the creation of thousands of local operators and numerous equipment suppliers. This hodgepodge of suppliers and providers created overwhelming management challenges. Coordination was difficult because modular interfaces hadn't been—and couldn't be—clearly defined. Engineers often didn't know what parameters needed to be specified. Even if they knew what to specify, they often couldn't measure or verify whether the spec had been met. And there often were unpredictable interdependencies between the way one component of the system was designed and built, and the way other elements of the system had to be designed and built. Network monitoring was next to impossible, and service quality suffered because it was often difficult to pinpoint responsibility for a problem.

Only integration could solve such problems, and integration gave AT&T crucial advantages over nonintegrated competitors. For example, owning its equipment supplier, Western Electric, enabled the Bell Company to ensure the interoperability of every piece of equipment on its network, improving the predictability of equipment interactions and increasing the network's reliability. Theodore Vail's fully integrated system solved many of the problems that had beset the loosely coupled Bell network, which can be collectively characterized as inadequate functionality and reliability (occupying the upper-left quadrant of the disruption model).[4] Vail was responding to the same mandate that led U.S. Steel, RCA, IBM, Intel, and Microsoft to become dominant, integrated companies at similar junctures in their respective industries' histories. The reliability of Vail's integrated solution became so competing that he was ultimately able to convince the U.S. government to confer a regulated monopoly status upon AT&T, in exchange for AT&T's agreeing that it would provide universal service.

The Creep of Disintegration

Why did AT&T lose its dominant position as an integrated monopoly? The conventional explanation is that regulators broke up the company. In fact, regulators have never been able to achieve a result that competitive conditions and the technology itself did not mandate. Disintegration of AT&T's integrated monopoly began when interfaces became modular. This is how competition emerged in the customer premises equipment (CPE) market. In the 1950s, Western Electric (AT&T's equipment arm) controlled the residential CPE market. CPE is any device a customer plugs into the network, such as a standard telephone. Western Electric produced a phone that was indestructible and available in any color you wanted—as long as you wanted black or beige. Efforts to sell non–Western Electric CPE were restricted, because plugging in nonsanctioned equipment might unexpectedly undermine the entire network's reliability.[5]

In the late 1950s, entrepreneur Tom Carter introduced the "Carterfone."[6] Resembling a walkie-talkie, the Carterfone transmitted a voice signal from a remote device to a speaker placed next to the phone; farmers could use their telephones when they were in the field. Because the Carterfone had a direct electrical connection to AT&T's network, AT&T cut off service to any subscriber it discovered using the device. After an FCC decision in 1968 sanctioning the use of the Carterfone, and a protracted legal battle that eventually reached the Supreme Court, regulators decided that consumers could attach to the edge of the network devices that met a set of specifications and that did not cause performance problems elsewhere in the system. In other words, when there was a modular interface between the device and the rest of the network, there was no reason to insist on integration.

When regulators had responded to the emergence of a modular interface, the floodgates opened. New specialist companies offering a wide variety of devices entered the CPE market and stole substantial share from Western Electric. Competition eventually led to innovative types of CPE that created booming new market segments, like the fax machine, the modem, and the private branch exchange (PBX). Specialist companies arose and captured these new markets.

MCI was a low-end disrupter. It not only disrupted AT&T but also accelerated the disintegration of the industry by decoupling it at the local–long-distance interface. MCI began not by incubating its business in an unattractive new market, as AT&T had done against Western Union, but by attacking the core long-distance market from its low end—by targeting price-sensitive customers who did not need all the functionality offered by AT&T.[7] MCI's Execunet service, introduced in the 1970s, allowed business users to pay lower prices if they were willing to dial a twenty-two-digit code to connect to MCI's network. MCI built its own long-distance network and relied on AT&T's local lines for call origination and completion. Although AT&T predictably protested the obligation to allow its competitor to use its local network, MCI could plug its equipment into AT&T's switches relatively easily. The modular interface between local and long-distance systems within AT&T existed because regulations required long-distance rates to subsidize low local rates, in order to ensure affordable universal service. This necessitated separate, clean billing systems for local and long-distance calls. MCI enjoyed a price umbrella just like other low-end disruptors in regulated and unregulated industries. The entrant had a business model enabling it to earn profit at low prices. The incumbent was faced with the difficult decision of cutting prices across the board on huge volumes of business just to respond to a tiny entrant. Doing so did not make sense for many years, until the entrant had become huge and there was no choice.

Although MCI did not (and could not) offer all the advanced features that AT&T's customers enjoyed, its prices were much lower than AT&T's. Regulation prevented AT&T from dropping its prices without appealing to the local regulatory commission.[8] Exploiting this price discrepancy, MCI began to build a large customer base by reaching price-sensitive business customers with its low-price offering.[9] MCI's customers tolerated lower functionality in exchange for lower prices.

The Failure of the CLECs

Buoyed by the success of deregulatory efforts to encourage competition in long-distance (with consequent improvements in pricing and performance), the government turned in the 1990s to what it perceived as the last refuge of the old AT&T monopoly—the Regional Bell Operating Companies (RBOCs). The complicated 1996 Telecommunications Reform Act chipped away at some remaining barriers to competition in the local market by forcing the RBOCs to share their lines with competitive local exchange carriers. Most CLECs failed, some quite spectacularly.

Digital subscriber line (DSL), a primary product offered by many CLECs, occupied the not-good-enough realm of functionality and reliability at the time. In contrast to MCI's modular, low-end disruption, DSL was a radical *sustaining* innovation, and thus the CLECs had to integrate their technology with proprietary network architectures riddled with interdependencies left over from decades of monopoly control. And because it was a better product targeted at the best existing customers in the market, the telephone-network operators were highly motivated to pursue the same prize.[10]

This was the critical difference between MCI and the CLECs. MCI had created a disruptive business model relative to AT&T. More importantly, MCI built its own network and connected to the rest of the network at a modular interface that was specifiable, measurable, and predictable—three tests of modularity. Egged on by naive deregulators and venture investors who misapplied the nonintegrated business models of successful companies like Dell, Cisco, and MCI to a circumstance where they would not work, CLECs did not build their own networks and tried to enter at a point that was still rife with legacy interdependencies.[11] Just because a company has the *legal* ability to do something does not mean that it has the *technological* or *operational* ability.

The Disruptive Router of Cisco Systems

The rise of data networking is a classic story of new-market disruption in which entrants like Cisco captured most of the growth. Data networks facilitated the creation of new forms of communication, such as e-mail—and, as we shall see, this wave of disruption is continuing its upmarket advance into VoIP.

In the 1980s, users began connecting personal computers to share information, using rudimentary networks with local area network (LAN) technology as the key connector. Early LANs had a shortcoming: every piece of equipment on a LAN was connected to every other piece of equipment. This setup worked fine in small settings but was very inefficient as LANs grew to include more users.

Cisco's multiprotocol router solved this problem. The router "spoke" the varied "dialects" (AppleTalk, Ethernet, etc.) of the LAN, translated them into Internet Protocol (IP)—the open, connectionless "best effort" protocol—and layered on intelligence that forwarded packets toward their ultimate destination. The router acted as the traffic cop for emerging LANs. It was cheap, and—because IP is the ultimate modular interface—it was flexible and scalable. Easily added to any network, routers enabled companies to interconnect LANs while minimizing network degradation and maximizing network efficiency.

Cisco's sales grew dramatically. It then looked at the mission-critical data-transport market, dominated by IBM and its System Network Architecture (SNA), where most of the *real* networking money was made. IBM created its proprietary networking technology when the functionality and reliability of enterprise data networks were not yet good enough. At the time, centralized mainframes dominated enterprise computing. Companies reserved these large, expensive machines for tasks critical to day-to-day operations, such as transaction processing. The sprawling private data networks found throughout major enterprises contained high-quality, point-to-point, circuit-switched connections; those connections were expensive to install, provision, and maintain. IBM dominated this market with an overwhelming share of the mainframe, data application development, and data-transport markets. At the core of every system was SNA—a highly reliable, proprietary computing language.

So Cisco added to its multiprotocol router the capability to transmit SNA—thus modularizing it. Instead of traveling over dedicated circuits, SNA data traffic could be split into IP packets, routed over a private data network, and reassembled at its destination. This setup lacked the reliability and security of a point-to-point connection provided by SNA over dedicated leased lines. But as it improved, increasingly sensitive and demanding applications began to be pulled into Cisco's plane of competition as it became apparent that they could be accomplished in a simpler and inexpensive way.

IBM tried to respond to Cisco's disruption with its own line of internetworking products. But the multiprotocol router had characteristics that made response all but impossible. It was not a matter of technological capability—IBM had plenty of that. But the only way IBM could sell routers was to sell to a completely different set of customers who, one by one, appeared to be decidedly less profitable than those that had valued IBM's proprietary technology in the circuit-switched world.

In September 1999, IBM arranged to sell its entire internetworking business to Cisco for $2 billion. IBM shifted its focus to what it described as "higher margin sales support and service opportunities."

The Probable Market Impacts of New Telecommunications Technologies

Now let us use the models of disruption and modularity-interdependence to assess when, where, and why certain new technologies are likely to take root in telecommunications—and the impact they are likely to have on the structure of the industry and on competitors within it.

Voice over Internet Protocol

VoIP has all the hallmarks of a classic new-market disruption that took root nearly two decades ago, when data-routing technology entered a new plane of competition relative to voice technology. In that new plane, the router and LAN made it possible for a new population of nonexperts with limited budgets to build and operate networks for themselves. Because the LAN competed against nonconsumption, its customers were delighted even with its limited functionality and reliability—their alternative was no data network at all.

Figure 5-2 offers a suitable model for visualizing how IP might affect voice telephony now that IP-based packet-switching technology has become capable and mature in the new plane of competition. One possibility is for companies to bring the technology to the existing market, represented by the rear plane of the model, as low-end disruptors. When early companies like Net2Phone and Dialpad Communications Inc. attempted to do so, latency delays initially made the technology unattractive for all but the most price-sensitive customers.[12] Now that latency delays have been shortened, companies like Vonage are invading the voice market with VoIP service that seems good enough for less-demanding customers.

The other possibility for VoIP is for companies to draw customers and applications from the circuit-switched plane of competition, at the rear of figure 5-2, into the packet-switched foreground plane. The first serious implementations of this scenario have been within enterprises, because users can only reap all the benefits of VoIP, such as unified messaging, within a self-contained system. Companies like Avaya, a Lucent Technologies spin-off, have used their IP-PBX equipment to begin layering voice onto other LAN applications.

A wrinkle in this story, however, leads us to predict that the incumbent telephone companies, not the entrants, will emerge as the survivors of the across-enterprise VoIP battle. We will base our prediction on a phenomenon that is best explained by analogy: failed disruptions in the airline industry.

Disruptors succeed by creating a situation in which the established competitors are motivated to flee upmarket where profit margins are higher, rather than fighting to retain the less profitable low-end business that the disruptors are targeting. When steel minimills attacked the low end of the steel-products market (rebar, angle iron, bars, and rods), for example, the integrated mills were happy to abandon those products in favor of more attractive, high-margin business at the high end (structural and sheet steel). Similarly, when discount retailers like Wal-Mart attacked the low end of the merchandise mix (branded hard goods), the full-service department stores were happy to focus instead on higher-margin apparel and cosmetics.

The economics of some industries, however, make it impossible for incumbent companies to forsake the low end. These are fixed-cost-intensive industries in which the volume at the low end is critical to capacity utilization and profitability. Airlines are one such industry. Southwest Airlines entered as a new-market disruptor, explicitly using its discounted fares to compete against cars, buses, and nontravel. Southwest served small, out-of-the-way airports, and for years eschewed competing directly against the major airlines in high-volume, major-city routes. It has been very successful. Other discount airlines, however, have adhered to a low-end disruption model, and their mortality rate has been very high. Why? The heavy-fixed-cost structure of the major airlines makes it impossible for them to walk away from the volume at the low end of their fare structures in pursuit of higher-margin business. The industry is eminently disruptible because entry is easy. And once the discounters begin to take significant share, the majors must turn around and swat the discounters down: their cost structure forces them to continue to compete at the low end, to fight rather than flee.

We suspect that similar economics will drive network telephone-service operators' response to VoIP. Once the entrant VoIP competitors begin to take significant volume at the price-sensitive end of the market, the major telephone companies will be forced to fight rather than flee because, given their high-fixed-cost structure, they cannot afford to lose the volume at the low end of their markets. The symbiotic relationship between data networks and voice networks gives incumbents an easy response mechanism to VoIP, because the two planes of competition have significant points of overlap. Furthermore, across-enterprise VoIP won't operate in a self-contained plane of competition: except possibly in the case of an eventual freestanding Wi-Fi network. As we shall see, Internet Protocol voice will need to be ported onto last-mile twisted-pair copper telephone lines. This scenario is another reason that VoIP is likely to be very much on the radar screen of the telephone companies.

Hence consumers and businesses are likely to be the sole beneficiaries of VoIP's low cost and features flexibility. The voice-telephony business is likely to begin resembling the major airlines' business, whose managers and investors are grateful to earn subsistence profits.

As a modular addition to Internet service, VoIP will enable the decoupling of network operations from service provision (a very different situation from the provision of DSL, which entailed unfathomable interdependencies).[13] Hence it is easy for entrants to enter by offering unlimited local and long-distance calling for a very low flat fee per month. Over time, pressures to become cost-competitive service providers in the VoIP world might force the network operators to decouple or divest their network-operations business from the telephony service business. Decoupling the industry at this point would create opportunities for new horizontal business models—focusing on 800 services, call-center management, and so on—to emerge where incumbents previously erected impenetrable barriers.

In summary, these models would lead us to predict that the disruptive impact of VoIP on the incumbent telcos will be to collapse pricing, but not lead to the failure of the leading providers. Probably the most powerful impact of VoIP is that it will facilitate further disintegration of the industries, enabling more and more focused players to thrive, providing pieces of a system within which more interfaces become more modular.

Wireless Broadband: 3G Versus Wi-Fi

For a decade or more, telecommunications technologists have sensed that the ability to transmit data wirelessly would someday create a splendid growth opportunity. Some have wasted significant capital, and others have generated significant returns, in pursuit of this opportunity, for reasons that these models can explain. For example, wireless-telephony providers in Europe and North America negotiated a Wireless Application Protocol (WAP), which specified how components made by focused suppliers should interface in a system that would provide Internet access over mobile phones. They envisioned that WAP devices would enable mobile-phone users to do pretty much anything they could do with wireline Internet access—including trading stocks, shopping, and making travel arrangements. Their efforts were a miserable, expensive failure, for two reasons. First, wireless access to the Internet occupied the not-good-enough domain represented by the upper-left quadrant of figure 5-3, where interdependent proprietary architectures, not WAP-standard modularity, were required to maximize functionality and reliability. Second, in marketing the technology to utilize existing applications where the wireline Internet set a demanding performance standard, these companies were "cramming" a disruptive technology into the established market.

In contrast, the Japanese mobile-telephony providers NTT DoCoMo and J-Phone built their systems with optimized, proprietary architectures that required much more extensive integration. And instead of cramming, they disruptively competed against nonconsumption by helping teenage girls have fun doing simple new things like downloading ringtones, wallpaper, and "Hello Kitty" characters. They log billions in profitable revenues.[14] As of September 2003, DoCoMo had more than 40 million delighted i-mode customers enjoying rich graphical experiences.[15]

Even before the failure of WAP Internet access, many North American and European mobile-service providers had paid their respective governments billions to purchase licenses to "third generation" (3G) technology—a technology that promised to broaden the bandwidth of wireless devices. Our prediction is that these investments will fail too, because they still are driven by the logic of cramming: if we can only provide enough bandwidth, customers will begin to do on their wireless phones what they already do on the wireline Internet. Interestingly, North American and European teenagers have begun using their mobile phones for simple asynchronous play with their friends using short-text-messaging services, just like their counterparts in Japan. But they still use the wireline Internet for activities that require its screen size and bandwidth—and they will continue doing so until a wireless alternative is good enough.

Just such an alternative wireless data technology, dubbed Wi-Fi (for Wireless Fidelity), uses the 802.11 protocol and its successors. An important advantage of Wi-Fi-based products is that, unlike 3G, Wi-Fi does not require obtaining scarce licenses from national governments. It operates in the so-called unlicensed spectrum, set aside by the government to encourage experimentation and innovation.[16] Wi-Fi is much more likely to succeed because the firms that are commercializing it are following strategies of new-market disruption. Though Wi-Fi has extraordinary bandwidth and can handle large amounts of data at high speeds, its signal can carry only three hundred feet or so from the node, or transmitter. It is thus deployed at present only in homes and at "hotspot" access points like Starbucks coffeehouses and airport waiting lounges. Some office-building managers are installing wireless local area networks (WLANs) by distributing Wi-Fi access points throughout their buildings; tenants can connect to the Internet from anywhere in the building without finding a broadband plug. Ultimately, as VoIP is incorporated in these WLANs, users will be able to carry their telephone numbers with them temporarily to conference rooms and permanently when they switch offices, without needing expensive technicians to reroute the telephone wires. We expect that innovators will gradually figure out how to extend the reach of individual Wi-Fi nodes and create linked networks of nodes from building to building, perhaps by installing nodes in public telephone boxes or attaching them to utility poles, automobiles, and the like. Such a high-bandwidth network would be independent of the telephone companies' wireline and wireless telephony networks, thus offering the opportunity for new entrants to disrupt established companies.

Whether incumbent leaders or entrants seize this opportunity depends upon whether the incumbents follow the prescription of setting up an autonomous organization that can hone a business model that is tuned to this application. Of course, these wireless data providers must connect to a wired network at some point. But this interaction occurs at a true point of modularity; everything beyond that point can be largely independent. Unless they disrupt themselves with this technology, this new-market disruption would thus leave incumbent network providers with an important backbone role, but they could largely lose control of the customer and become significantly less important industry players.[17]

Cable Companies: How to Create Asymmetries

The 1996 Telecommunications Reform Act granted cable operators permission to offer voice and data services with relatively minor upgrades to their existing infrastructure. What threat, if any, do cable companies (now redefined as multiple service operators, or MSOs) pose to incumbent telephony suppliers?

The MSOs must make two critical strategic decisions: their choice of delivery technology and their target application. Should they use existing, highly reliable circuit-switched technologies over their cable networks, or deploy relatively less reliable IP-based technologies? Should they go after the primary-line market, where most of the voice money is today? Or should they target the smaller secondary-line market or try to introduce communications into a new context?

Most MSOs that offer cable telephony have chosen to use circuit-switched technology to target the primary-line market, opting for a head-to-head sustaining-technology battle against the incumbents. A few, however, have begun deploying IP-based packet-switching systems, creating a cost position from which a disruptive strategy could be launched.

The two decisions are interdependent. Circuit-switched technology costs a lot of money to deploy. MSOs have to invest in switching equipment at the cable-head end and at the customer premises. They need to send a technician to the customer's premises to install specialized equipment. Regulation forces them to invest in "line powering" technology to ensure service during a power outage. Analysts estimate total incremental costs of up to $600 per customer.[18] And those costs do not include the hefty costs that cable companies were already shouldering to upgrade their networks to accommodate digital cable and video on demand. Given these high costs, an MSO that chose to use circuit-switched technology would logically target the primary-line market, where prevailing pricing promises the best possible returns. In response, some telephone service providers are counterattacking, investing in broader-band technology to offer downloadable video entertainment over DSL lines.

Entrants typically lose out to incumbents when they choose sustaining-innovation fights, because the incumbents have more to lose than the entrants have to gain, and are thus very motivated to fight back. If history is any guide, the unlikely result of the MSOs' and telcos' choosing these respective strategies is that the telcos will retain telephony and MSOs will retain video, but they will have ruined each other's businesses. If only some industry visionary had articulated a doctrine of mutually ensured destruction to preserve détente!

The MSOs' hopes for competitive advantage seem to rest on a bundling strategy, enticing consumers with the convenience of a single bill and lower prices for combining services they had bought separately. Will the bundle truly be lower-cost? No. Bundling adds value when stitching the bundle together requires resolving unpredictable interdependencies between bundled components. If there are *interdependencies in production or provision*, an integrated firm can create an offering that a collection of focused specialists cannot match. If there are no interdependencies, however, a bundled service is not inherently better or cheaper than two separate services.

Second, will consumers value the bundle? Consumers value bundles when they consume the components of a bundled offering simultaneously or in an interrelated manner. This *interdependence in purchase or consumption* means that customers see unique value in bundled pricing only when buying the components together. From this perspective, there would seem to be few benefits in bundling circuit-switched telephony and cable television.

The savings to the customer is a first-class stamp each month, and even that savings disappears with online bill payment.

The Road Not Taken: Cable IP as a Second-Line Replacement

Some MSOs have waited on the sidelines of telephony. If they choose to enter, they could adopt IP as a low-cost disruption to telephony. Deploying IP telephony is relatively straightforward, and IP-based solutions could cost hundreds of dollars less to upgrade and install. What market application should they target? The best way to attack incumbents would be to offer overserved customers a good enough product at a lower price. Although VoIP may not yet be reliable enough for primary-line replacements, cable companies could offer IP for cheap second lines where reliability is less critical and customers' price elasticity might be higher. This approach—a lower-cost business model targeted at the incumbent's most overserved customers—appears to have real potential.

Targeting the second line might take advantage of asymmetries of motivation. By 2004, the secondary-line market was already shrinking; parents bought wireless phones for teenagers, and DSL eliminated the need for a dedicated line for modem connections. Given more profitable investment opportunities on their plates, RBOCs might not be motivated to fight to retain this shrinking market.[19]

A cable company could use this approach to both learn about the telephone service market and increase the slope of the technology's improvement trajectory. Improving technology could eventually convince customers to use IP for primary-line service. MSOs could add new converged services, such as unified messaging. This strategy would allow them to build the skills necessary to win in a full-on attack. In this scenario, furthermore, there is a cogent argument for a bundled price: because the MSO can use the same infrastructure it uses to deliver high-speed access to the Internet, it appears to be genuine interdependence in production in the provision of IP-based telephony over a cable wire. Hence, a bundle consisting of IP-based telephony and high-speed access to the Internet could provide a real cost advantage that an RBOC would be unable to match.

Instant Messaging: Toy or Disruptive Platform?

Millions of teenagers worldwide spend hours communicating with each other via instant messaging (IM) services while their parents think they are doing homework. The free applications offered by IM's big three—AOL, Yahoo!, and Microsoft—have been downloaded onto millions of computers around the globe. Users can type a message—often littered with IM-acronyms like LOL, TTYL, and AAMOF—press Enter, and almost instantly transmit the message to a friend's computer or portable device.[20] IM allows users to gossip in real time to their hearts' content without fear that parents or others will hear a telltale snippet of conversation.

This is disruptive growth. IM is relentlessly improving, and adults are adopting it. Colleagues on different continents can jointly create and edit a PowerPoint presentation. People can use IM on mobile devices. Users can press the talk button and broadcast their voices across the Internet to their friends. Teenagers can purchase a cheap Web camera, connect it to a PC, press the Web Cam button, and voilà—a simple videoconference. IM also has presence-management capability: a user's contacts know whether she is online or offline.

Telecommunications service-provider executives might scoff at the relatively poor quality of these services, but they work and they are free. Users are delighted. Executives ought to pay attention, because companies that play in the IM market could develop business models that just do not make sense to telecommunications companies. Companies that offer IM do not expect to directly monetize usage of IM; communications itself is not their raison d'être. Their goal is to use IM to bolster the relevance and usage of their core products and service. These companies are solving problems and creating skills around software development and entertainment that bear little resemblance to incumbent service-provider skills related to building and operating complicated telecommunications networks. IM could be the ultimate decoupled service, teeming with asymmetries. Whether or not IM really heralds changes to the telecommunications industry remains to be seen. But watching its upmarket advance will tell us whether it portends peril for existing providers.

Summary

The pace of technological progress tends to outstrip the ability of customers to utilize that progress, and new technology thus sets in motion a sequence of changes that can affect an industry's structure and competitive balance. In general, when the effect of a new technology is to sustain the trajectory of performance improvement, and when implementation of the technology entails unpredictable interdependencies with other elements of the system, incumbent integrated firms are likely to stay entrenched at the top of their industry. Entrants have the upper hand, by contrast, when the technology can be commercialized disruptively and when modularity enables the entrant's product to interface with other elements of the system in specifiable, measurable, and predictable ways. These principles can explain key turning points in the history of the telecommunications industry. Likewise, the models based on them can help us assess the probable impact of new technologies on the competitive structure of the telecommunications industry.

VoIP is a disruptive innovation that is intrinsically modular—a scenario in which we would normally expect entrant firms to thrive. Entry will indeed be relatively easy, but we anticipate that the RBOCs' high-fixed-cost economics will force them to fight to retain even their most price-sensitive customers—creating a situation in which entrants and incumbents vie to offer more and more IP-enabled services, along with unlimited local and long-distance calling, at fixed per-month prices that yield only subsistence profits to providers that aggressively cut costs. Entrant companies in the within-enterprise plane of competition enjoy a strong advantage in commercializing another disruptive technology. Deutsche Telecom's T-Mobile unit has likewise used Wi-Fi as its disruptive entrée into the U.S. market, with its hotspot strategy. Technologies that forward Wi-Fi signals from one enterprise to the next, or one hotspot to the next, have powerful disruptive potential because they could create a freestanding data network capable of carrying digitized voice signals. Our models suggest that 3G investments are less likely to prove profitable. Whether cable telephony creates growth opportunities for its providers depends on whether they pursue a sustaining or a disruptive strategy (for instance, IP-based and targeted at nonconsumption, such as inexpensive second lines). Instant messaging may ultimately prove to be the strongest disruptive platform of any of the technologies we've examined. Its power lies not in any direct threat it poses to established applications, but in the fact that it does not pose a direct threat—it is a new-market disruption that will undergo significant new growth before it begins to pull current applications into its plane of competition.

Whenever we attempt to see into the future, we consciously or subconsciously employ a theory or model of cause and effect. We hope that our offer in this chapter to examine the past and peer into the future of telecommunications through the lenses of such theories will persuade our readers not just to see the world as we see it but also to become more aware of the theories of cause and effect they use when looking ahead.

Notes

1. The model of disruption is developed in Clayton M. Christensen, *The Innovator's Dilemma* (Boston: Harvard Business School Press, 1997). Its applications are further explored in Clayton M. Christensen and Michael E. Raynor, *The Innovator's Solution* (Boston: Harvard Business School Press, 2003).

2. For consistency, we will use the term *product* when explaining these models, but they apply with equal validity to service businesses, in both regulated and unregulated industries.

3. In other writings, we have used the term *value networks*. We call them *planes of competition* in this chapter to prevent readers from confusing this concept with other uses of the term *network* in telecommunications.

4. Many historians suggest that a monopoly had to emerge because the telephone system is a natural monopoly. A *natural monopoly* is commonly defined as a market situation wherein a single producer is able to obtain an average cost per unit of production low enough to make it inefficient for any other producer to supply that product or service. Natural monopolies typically occur in markets characterized by a large fixed capital component coupled with steadily declining average marginal production costs, allowing one supplier to attain unmatchable production advantages. However, the fact that independent phone companies outnumbered Bell-controlled companies in 1903 raises doubt about whether the telephone system is indeed a natural monopoly. In fact, dual service was available in about 60 percent of American cities with populations larger than 5,000; it was common to observe multiple sets of telephone wires strung between buildings in dense urban areas.

For more on natural monopolies and their implications, see Stephen G. Breyer, *Regulation and Its Reform* (Cambridge, MA: Harvard University Press, 1982); Thomas J. Dusterberg and Kenneth Gordon, *Competition and Deregulation in Telecommunications: The Case for New Paradigm* (Indianapolis: Hudson Institute, 1997); Alfred E. Kahn, *The Economics of Regulation: Principles and Institutions* (New York: Wiley, 1970); Richard A. Posner, *Natural Monopoly and Its Regulation* (Washington, DC: Cato Institute, 1999); William W. Sharkey, *The Theory of Natural Monopoly* (New York: Cambridge University Press, 1982); and John T. Wenders, *The Economics of Telecommunications: Theory and Policy* (Cambridge, MA: Ballinger, 1987).

5. Nonsanctioned equipment (anything not made by Western Electric) was known as a "foreign attachment." Published tariffs—lists of rates and services with obligations and restrictions on service use—subjected customers using foreign attachments to fines.

6. Three years before the Carterfone's introduction, the courts decided to allow customers to use a simple snap-on device introduced by the Hush-a-Phone Corporation. Essentially a rubber cup, the seemingly innocuous invention caused an incredible stir. AT&T's managers took legal action and approached the FCC. After careful consideration, the FCC decided in 1955 that the device would be "deleterious to the telephone system and injure the service rendered by it." The courts overturned the FCC decision in 1956 and established the ability of subscribers to use the telephone in "ways which are privately beneficial without being publicly detrimental." See Kevin D. Wilson, *Telecommunications: U.S. and Canadian Telecommunications*, 1840–1997 (Lanham, MD: Rowan & Littlefield, 2000) (Introduction, footnote 9) p. 111 and 420, quotes from *Hush-a-Phone Corp. v. United States*, 238 F.2d 266 (D.C. Cir. 1956).

Theory explains why AT&T presciently protested the (seemingly innocuous) Hush-a-Phone rubber cup, even if its efforts were ultimately fruitless. AT&T probably realized full well that there were other places in its network where competitors could enter without interfering with the rest of the network. At these "modular" interfaces, any third-party device that met a set of specifications could "plug into" the network without causing harm, thus taking business away from AT&T. AT&T didn't want to let that door open even a crack.

7. The erosion of AT&T's long-distance monopoly began innocently enough with a 1959 FCC decision that became known as the "Above 890" decision. The decision allowed firms to use microwave frequencies above 890 megahertz for their private communications. In 1963, MCI petitioned the FCC to allow it to build a shared private network between Chicago and St. Louis using microwave technology originally developed for military purposes. The private network would only be used for firm-to-firm traffic; it was "shared" because multiple firms would use the same network. The FCC decided in the late 1960s to "allow a little competition at the fringes of the long-distance market," never intending its decision to lead to the breakup of AT&T's monopoly. AT&T again challenged MCI in the courts, but, drawing on the FCC's original ruling, a judge decided that MCI could compete with AT&T, opening the door to true competition in long-distance services. See Philip L. Cantelon, *The History of MCI 1968–1988: The Early Years* (Dallas: Heritage Press, 1993); Steve Coll, *The Deal of the Century: The Breakup of AT&T* (New York: Athenaeum, 1986); and Lorraine Spurge, *Failure Is Not an Option: How MCI Invented Competition in Telecommunications* (Encino, CA: Spurge Ink!, 1998).

8. It is unclear that AT&T, as a profit-maximizing monopolist, would even want to lower its prices. Monopolists seek to maximize profits; firms in perfectly competitive environments seek to maximize revenue.

9. It is noteworthy that MCI did not initially intend to compete in a low-end disruptive manner. Its intention was to compete head-to-head with AT&T. The only way it could enter the market, however, was to take on characteristics that made it look like a low-end disruptive innovation. In its early days, MCI gave an underperforming product to price-sensitive customers. Once the government lifted constraints, MCI quickly moved to replicate AT&T's business model.

10. Plain old local telephone service, not just DSL, was served through a very complicated, unpredictably interdependent architecture as well, making it all the more difficult for a nonintegrated competitor to plug into the local network.

11. Theoretically, the local network should have consisted of highly mature and easily modularized technologies. But the absence of cost-based competition—the primary driver of the shift from interdependence to modularity—had allowed the RBOCs to maintain highly interdependent systems. Without competition, an incumbent has little incentive to standardize any aspect of its operations. The shield that protects monopolists from competitive forces allows it to continue to squeeze out additional profitability by solving problems in an interdependent way. Stories abound of Bell System workers coming up with novel solutions; their knowledge of the subtle intricacies of the telecommunications network enabled them to solve problems that an outsider could not.

12. We are drawing a distinction between delivering packets over any-to-any systems and over connection-oriented systems. Frame relay, Asynchronous Transfer Mode, and multiprotocol label switching (MPLS) all allow companies to send packets over point-to-point technologies. This affords them greater reliability, but obviates the flexibility and low-cost benefits of an any-to-any solution. The lost packets that have historically plagued packet-switched systems lead to two problems in a voice application: latency and jitter. *Latency* is delay whose duration equals the time it takes for a bit of data to travel from its origin to its destination. *Jitter* is variation in the quality of the voice signal resulting from the out-of-sequence arrival of a stream of packets. Public networks with low (or no) quality of service do not guarantee the arrival of packets in the order they were sent, which can create

distortions in voice transmissions. Other explanations range from network congestion to more complex routing and translation challenges.

13. A key enabler of VoIP within enterprises was the introduction of IP-based private branch exchanges (IP-PBXs). IP-PBXs are software solutions that run on off-the-shelf servers. IP-PBXs sold by companies like Cisco, Mitel Networks, and Avaya (a Lucent spin-off) let companies run both voice and data traffic over a single network. IP-PBXs compete against traditional PBXs, sold by industry heavyweights like Lucent Technologies, Nortel, Alcatel, and Siemens. These systems are expensive and complex. They handle end-to-end digital transmission of voice throughout an enterprise, as well as related services like voice mail and three-way calling.

14. We found Professor Jeffrey Funk from Kobe University in Japan to be a particularly knowledgeable source about i-mode's history. For example, see Jeffrey Funk, "The Interaction Between Path Dependencies, Disruptive Technologies, and Network Externalities: Implications for Theories of Technological Change," unpublished working paper. More of Professor Funk's astute work is available at http://www.rieb.kobe-u.ac.jp/~funk/.

15. Robert Budden, "i-mode Getting Through," *Financial Times*, September 16, 2003. Some academics discount i-mode's success and argue that its commercialization path was largely a historical accident resulting from the unique nature of the Japanese market. Low activation charges and no roaming fees, they argue, inexorably lead companies to try to meet the needs of the mass consumer market, while European and American firms gravitate toward the business markets. Unlike in the United States, where traveling business customers are highly coveted, the consumer market is equally important and a source of tremendous innovation in Japan. Also, the Japanese population is highly concentrated, making it less complex to provide reliable coverage. The smaller geographic footprint of this comparatively dense population has ruled out the need for roaming agreements and elevated the appeal of the mass consumer market.

16. That spectrum is in the 2.4 or 5 gigahertz range.

17. Deutsche Telecom's U.S.-based mobile telephony company, T-Mobile, has been aggressively deploying Wi-Fi hotspots—disrupting other providers, not itself—and other wireline companies such as Verizon are contemplating ventures with this technology.

18. Yankee Group estimates the cost to deliver circuit-switched telephony at $500–$625 per subscriber, in addition to the already significant cost of upgrading the cable plant to allow digital video, video on demand, and two-way data transmission for Internet service. See Imran Kahn, "Cable Telephony: Still Far from Threatening ILECs?" *Yankee Group Report* 1, no. 6, March 2002.

19. Aggressively pricing a secondary line as a cheap add-on to data service would present some challenges. Since dial-up Internet access is one of the primary drivers of traditional second-line purchasers, cable companies packaging the second line with broadband technologies (which eliminate the need for a second line) will have to creatively target high-speed consumers to drive adoption. Bundling voice as part of a data offering and positioning it as a relatively inexpensive second line will require creative marketing tactics to convert existing multiple-line owners or create new ones. Second lines have recently been used for faxes and dial-up modems, but an inexpensive line might expose a new and untapped additive opportunity.

20. For the uninitiated, these are acronyms for "laugh out loud," "talk to you later," and "as a matter of fact."

6

Internet2

The Promise of Truly Advanced Broadband

Ted Hanss and Dr. Douglas Van Houweling

INTERNET2 IS a U.S. higher-education-led partnership of universities, government, and industry working to develop and deploy advanced network applications and technologies to accelerate creation of tomorrow's Internet. Established in 1996, with headquarters in Ann Arbor, Michigan, Internet2 is higher education's commitment to further the development of Internet technologies in teaching, learning, research, and clinical activities.

As of spring 2004, Internet2 had 205 university members. These members are primarily the major U.S. research universities, but liberal-arts institutions committed to innovative applications are also key participants. Over sixty corporate members—both vendors and technology end users—share the objectives of exploration and knowledge transfer. The nearly forty affiliate members represent government laboratories, regional networking organizations, and non-research-oriented educational institutions. The leadership and vision of several federal agencies has been critical, particularly the National Science Foundation, the National Institutes of Health and its National Library of Medicine, the Department of Energy, and NASA.

The global scope of Internet2 collaborations is represented by over forty international partners with which Internet2 has signed cooperate agreements. These agreements have led to the physical interconnection of nearly thirty countries, creating a truly global community of advanced Internet development.

Internet2 has five main principles:

- *Address the advanced networking needs and interests of the research and education community.* As a university-led organization, Internet2 is keenly aware that progress in nearly every scientific discipline, notably including genomics, astronomy, and high-energy physics, increasingly relies on access to networking capabilities that exceed those available through the commercial Internet. Advanced networking is a key enabling technology for academic collaboration and new modes of teaching and learning. Internet2 aims to meet the research and education community's leading-edge need for new networking capabilities by fostering their development and deployment.

- *Provide leadership in the evolution of the global Internet.* Just as today's commercial Internet evolved from the early successes of an academic-led effort, a primary goal of Internet2 is to serve as a model for future Internet development. By serving as both a test bed for, and large-scale proof of concept of, new network technologies and uses, the Internet2 community functions much as early Internet users did for technologies like TCP/IP (the underlying network protocols for the Internet), the domain-name system, e-mail, and the Web. In this role, Internet2 is an advocate for principles, such as end-to-end architecture, that have been critical to the Internet's sustained growth and record of spurring innovation. *End-to-end architecture* refers to the consistent and unimpeded ability of any Internet device to connect to any another, without firewalls, caches, and network address translation being inserted in the communications path and thus potentially interfering with the applications performance.

- *Implement a systems approach to a scalable and vertically integrated advanced networking infrastructure.*[1] Because of its broad membership and focus on qualitatively new capabilities, Internet2 is able to address holistically the challenges facing today's Internet, such as end-to-end performance and security that require integrated approaches. Methods developed by the Internet2 community to address these challenges preserve the Internet's foundational principles while ensuring its continued growth and innovation.

- *Leverage strategic relationships among academia, industry, and government.* Today's commercial Internet was fostered in its infancy by a partnership among academia, industry, and government. Internet2 continues that partnership by providing a framework within which organizations and individuals from these sectors can work together on new networking technology and advanced applications. The Internet has evolved into a critical underpinning not only for research and education but also for national and international commerce and communication. Internet2 fosters partnerships that address the complex interests at stake in the evolution of the Internet.

- *Catalyze activities that cannot be accomplished by individual organizations.* Internet2 serves as a focal point and framework for increasing the effectiveness of its members' collective efforts. It does so by supporting working groups and initiatives, convening workshops and meetings, and providing an operational home for projects that serve the entire Internet2 community. As an organization, Internet2 focuses on deployable, scalable, and sustainable technologies and solutions.

The Internet development spiral illustrated in figure 6-1 begins with a research-and-development focus and moves through successive phases of partnerships, privatization, and finally commercialization. The R&D phase is concentrated within university, government, and industry laboratories. In the partnership phase, promising research efforts are translated into leading-edge production uses for the education community. Privatization occurs when successful technologies are transformed into the offerings that make up the commercial Internet of today. One goal of Internet2 is to identify the research efforts that are ready for early adopters and to facilitate technology transfer to the commercial Internet when appropriate.

The Internet has come a long way from its research origins in the 1960s, through the NSFnet era of the mid-1980s to mid-1990s that laid the groundwork for the commercial Internet, and the boom and bust of the last decade. But that, however, did not mean that development of the Internet

FIGURE 6-1

The Internet development spiral

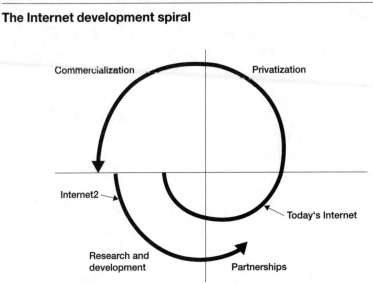

Source: Adapted from a presentation by Ivan Moura Campos to UCAID, August 1996. Adapted with permission.

stopped. In fact, investment has increased within the higher-education community over the past several years. The result is a robust leading-edge infrastructure that has spurred the development of new applications.

As a further spur to progress, Internet2 has established the "Internet2 Land Speed" competition to recognize innovation in moving information quickly across advanced Internet links.[2] The Internet2 Land Speed Record is now published in *The Guinness Book of World Records*. A team of scientists from the California Institute of Technology and the European Organization for Nuclear Research (CERN) holds the current record: the team transferred 1.1 terabytes of data from Geneva, Switzerland, to Chicago, Illinois, in less than thirty minutes. This is a data transfer rate of 5.44 gigabits per second, over twenty thousand times faster than a typical data transfer over a home broadband connection.

Innovations like these rely on global deployment of research-and-education networks. Within the United States, Internet2 operates the Abilene Network, illustrated in figure 6-2, as a nationwide high-performance backbone service on behalf of its members.[3] Abilene is a partnership of Internet2,

FIGURE 6-2

The Abilene Network

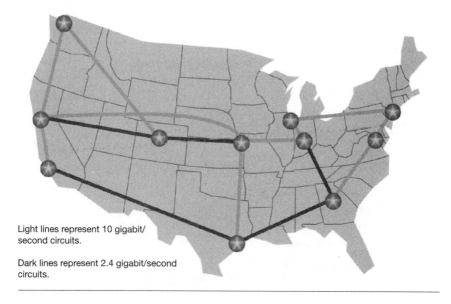

Light lines represent 10 gigabit/second circuits.

Dark lines represent 2.4 gigabit/second circuits.

Indiana University, Juniper Networks, Cisco Systems, Nortel Networks, and Qwest Communications. First deployed in 1999, Abilene provides connections in all fifty states, the District of Columbia, and Puerto Rico. The Abilene Network was upgraded in 2003 to run at 10 gigabits per second. The more than 220 connectors to Abilene send data through regional aggregation networks at speeds up to the full rate of 10 gigabits per second.

Abilene's goals are to support:

- Cutting-edge applications developed with innovative, experimental techniques that require high-performance network services unavailable on commercial networks

- Deployment and testing of advanced services—including multicast, IPv6, measurement, and security—rarely possible on the commercial Internet

- Connectivity to other research and education networks throughout the world and peering with federal research networks, enabling the international research community to collaborate in new ways[4]

- Access for researchers to a rich set of network-characterization data collected in a high-performance networking environment supporting innovative applications

Beyond Broadband

Internet2 focuses on the needs of the higher-education community, but the evolution of the commercial Internet is also a very important part of its mandate. The term *broadband* is commonly used to describe Internet connectivity faster than that of dial-up modems, typically data rates of 300–1,000 kilobits per second for cable modems and phone-company-provided digital subscriber lines (DSL). The Internet2 community is looking beyond these first steps in broadband deployment to anticipate "advanced broadband," the next generation in networking.

Advanced broadband is based on communications services offering multi-megabit-per-second data flows in both directions, to and from a personal computer or other networked device. With always-on and always-available connectivity, whether at home, at work, or traveling, users will no longer think about *connecting to the Internet*; its applications and services will be continuously accessible. It's also a services-rich environment, supporting IP multicast, the next-generation Internet protocol called IPv6, network performance measurement, and advanced service monitoring.[5]

Commercial broadband services are deploying quickly, so we have a good start toward the advanced broadband future. The United States may have led the way in development of the Internet, but deployment of broadband has reached higher penetration levels in other countries. According to the International Telecommunications Union, the United States is not even in the top ten in per-capita deployment of broadband services.[6] Within the United States, though, the pace is quickening, with regional and state-level efforts to leap beyond traditional broadband through community fiber projects. In California, for example, the One Gigabit or Bust Initiative is investigating the technical, policy, and financial challenges to bringing gigabit connectivity to all Californians by 2010.[7] Several other states also have significant fiber projects, including initiatives in Utah and Illinois with notable government, industry, and education involvement.

We can be confident of the benefits of advanced broadband because its environment already exists today on Internet2 networks. Drawing on what we have learned, we believe the commercial Internet will provide comparable jumps in functionality and performance over the next few years. We can anticipate those changes by looking at Internet2 as a time machine that offers a glimpse of the Internet of the future.

Advanced Broadband in Action

The best way to understand the potential of advanced broadband is to look closely at specific applications in education, large corporate environments, small and medium enterprises, and the home. What is already operational within the Internet2 community will someday be commonplace on the commercial Internet. Advanced video-streaming applications, including operation of remote scientific instruments, will roll out within the next five years—perhaps run from TV-attached game devices. Some of the more immersive virtual-reality environments, by contrast, rely on data-transfer rates and wall-sized displays unlikely to be affordable for ten or more years.

This section will look at some examples of applications in use today on Internet2. Dozens more applications are documented at the Internet2 Web site.[8]

Public Television's Next-Generation Interconnection Pilot

Public television stations are currently connected to each other by a one-way satellite system. The Public Broadcasting Service (PBS) stations at the University of Wisconsin and Washington State University, along with a consortium of other university-based public TV stations, are using the Internet2 network to develop new applications for their next-generation interconnection system. Using broadband IP video connections, the project members are testing station-to-station broadcast-quality (MPEG-2) video streaming, server-based broadcast video on demand, video segment search and fulfillment at MPEG-2 levels, and collaborative program editing. The goal is to demonstrate how the television production process can become more efficient and to provide greater viewing options for PBS audiences.

High-Definition Television

Several projects are distributing high-definition (HD) television across Internet2 networks. The ResearchChannel consortium, based at the University of Washington, is pushing the boundaries of high-definition video over advanced networks with a variety of projects, including uncompressed extreme-quality HD at 1.5 gigabits per second; editable studio-quality HD at 270 megabits per second; production house–quality HD at 45 megabits per second; and viewer-quality HD-to-the-desktop at 19.2 megabits per second.[9] Rather than using multiple means of distribution, such as tape by courier, satellite, and multiday commercial-Internet transfers, these different formats can be simultaneously delivered in real time via Internet2.

Theater-Quality Film Transmission

A collaboration of Nippon Telegraph and Telephone Corporation (NTT), the University of Illinois at Chicago (UIC), and the University of Southern California (USC) has shown that true theater-quality experiences are possible across advanced networks. This partnership successfully transported a super-high-definition (SHD) stream over the Abilene Network to the Fall 2002 Internet2 Member Meeting. An NTT system at the UIC Electronic Visualization Laboratory in Chicago sent SHD to the Robert Zemeckis Center for Digital Arts at the USC School of Cinema-Television in Los Angeles. Super-high-definition scientific visualizations and student films—at four times the resolution of high-definition TV—were compressed to 200–400 megabit-per-second streams using an experimental video encoder, stored, sent over Abilene to an NTT real-time decoder, and displayed in a theater via an 8 megapixel projector to an audience of technologists and film industry experts.

The Space Physics and Aeronomy Research Collaboratory

If anything can be described as the "killer app" for Internet2, it might be distance-independent collaboration. In education, collaboration can range from remote lectures and master classes to researchers working together from dispersed locations. An example is the University of Michigan's Space Physics and Aeronomy Research Collaboratory (SPARC). No longer compelled to travel to Greenland and other remote locations, upper-atmospheric scientists can use SPARC collaboration tools to provide a "better than being there" environment that delivers real-time access to scientific instruments and data resources. (See figure 6-3.) A second-order effect of this National Science Foundation–supported project is its dominant use by students, enriching the education of the next generation

FIGURE 6-3

Space Physics and Aeronomy Research Collaboratory

Research facilities in Greenland

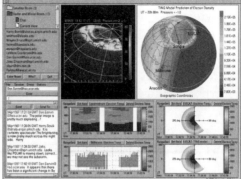

Web-based tool for remote instrument control and collaboration

Source: Reprinted with the permission of the University of Michigan; photo by Craig Heinselman.

of scientists. These students have, for example, developed mentoring relationships with faculty and researchers at other institutions.

The NEPTUNE Project

Collaboration isn't limited to university-level education. NEPTUNE is an international, multi-institutional project that is part of a larger worldwide effort to develop regional, coastal, and global ocean observatories.[10] NEPTUNE's 3,000-kilometer network of seafloor fiber-optic and power cables will encircle and cross the Juan de Fuca tectonic plate in the northeast Pacific Ocean. A series of experimental sites will be equipped with instruments to collect data from the tops of waves to below the seafloor. Hardwired to advanced telecommunications, NEPTUNE will extend the Internet to the ocean and seafloor: real-time data will flow to land-based laboratories, classrooms, and science exhibits around the world, and commands to instruments will flow from shore to ocean. Remotely operated and autonomous underwater vehicles will reside at depth, recharge at nodes on the cable, and offer command-and-control capabilities to remote users.

NEPTUNE will be used by a wide variety of audiences, including earth and ocean scientists, university students, K–12 students, informal science learners, and decision makers. Live video images from the seafloor and ocean can be streamed into a classroom or exhibit space and turned into a 3-D virtual-reality world of seafloor and ocean. Teachers will be able to take students on a virtual field trip to spaces they otherwise could never explore. They will use remotely operated video cameras to observe the environment, thermometers to "feel" the temperature of the water, and robot samplers to collect and analyze *extremophiles* (the heat- and chemical-loving microbes that live at undersea volcanic vents). Collaborative applications will allow scientists to guide observations and experiments without ever leaving the laboratory. Students will be able to move through time as well as space by consulting NEPTUNE's data archives, which will serve as a rich and lasting resource for exploration of the oceans. (See figure 6-4.)

The California Orthopaedic Research Network

A very active health-sciences community is working across Internet2 networks to address opportunities in clinical practice, medical and related

FIGURE 6-4

NEPTUNE ocean observatory

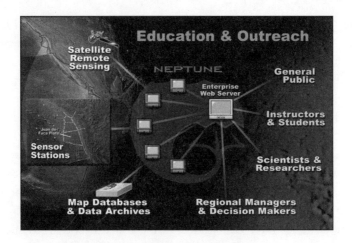

Source: Reprinted with the permission of the University of Washington.

biological research, and public education and health awareness. The California Orthopaedic Research Network (CORN), launched at the Fall 2002 Internet2 Member Meeting, has since then grown internationally, enabling surgeons and medical students in different countries to remotely observe surgical procedures and interact with each other using high-bandwidth videoconferencing. Networked surgical simulation tools allow remote participants to practice techniques subsequently used by the operating room–based surgeons.

Real-Time Collaboration

With advanced networks, location is no longer a barrier to collaboration. With TV-quality or better videoconferencing, interaction with a distant colleague can be as natural as sitting together in the same room. With remote device control, of manufacturing equipment or scientific instruments, you can easily share access to expensive or rare resources. And with distributed databases, advanced data mining facilitates obtaining data from disparate sources, allowing for real-time and interactive access that increases information flow.

Increased information flow can in turn provide strategic advantage to corporations. Real-time analysis, discovery, and dialogue among collaborators increases productivity. Facilitated by Internet2 advanced networks, Internet2 member Johnson & Johnson is researching the integration of devices such as laser capture microscopes and other scientific instrumentation into the collaborative space via the Access Grid, a network of distributed computation, application, and collaboration resources.[11] This initiative will allow numerous scientists to share the output from a given scientific instrument. The benefits include real-time high-quality collaboration among individuals, teams, or large groups, and enhanced productivity in the drug-discovery process.

Taking advantage of advanced broadband networks doesn't just mean doing things faster—it can also facilitate new business processes. Advanced applications strengthen partnerships within a distributed organization and with partners, and can contribute to new discoveries. Corporations, government labs, and universities connected to Internet2 networks are demonstrating this today. As the commercial Internet continues to mature, these capabilities will become far more widely available.

Middleware

What will it take for the commercial Internet to be capable of providing the advanced broadband services we have described? The short answer is investment and cooperation. Investment is needed in infrastructure, particularly the "last mile"—that is, the local connection to homes and office buildings. Realizing the full potential of that infrastructure will also require cooperation on end-to-end performance. End-to-end performance is related to, but distinct from, the end-to-end architecture of the Internet. End-to-end performance is focused on ensuring that the endpoints involved in a data transfer on the Internet get the full benefit of the capacity available on the links between them. For example, tuning the local area network may greatly increase the performance of applications by removing the sole bottleneck that limited the capacity of the entire network path. Network providers must ensure that applications are working reliably and have full access to the available network capacity.

Infrastructure does not just mean copper wires and fiber-optic cables. It also encompasses provision of a secure environment for applications. *Middleware* is the umbrella term for the layer of software between applications and the network. Within Internet2, our focus has been on software that provides the components of security, privacy, and trust necessary for deploying a wide range of applications. In the advanced environment of Internet2, federations of enterprises are cooperating on these issues to facilitate consumer access to resources and to promote business-to-business collaborations. Consensus on optimal middleware approaches is necessary for deploying applications and is achieved through alliances of vendor and user communities, such as the partnerships within Internet2.

Security and privacy technology developed by Internet2 is now available for academic and commercial use. During 2003, Internet2 released new versions of Shibboleth, an open-source package that supports interinstitutional sharing of Web resources subject to access controls. The Shibboleth project is also developing a policy framework that will allow interoperation across the higher-education community. The following concepts are fundamental to Shibboleth's policy framework:

- *Federated administration.* The origin campus (home to the browser user) provides attribute assertions about that user to the target site. The trust fabric that exists between campuses allows each site to identify the other user and to assign a trust level. That trust, or co-ordinated set of security policies, is what constitutes the federation. A single technical solution, or centralized approach, is not feasible, as local control of local resources must be maintained. Origin sites are responsible for authenticating their own users, but can use any reliable means to do so.

- *Access control based on attributes.* Access-control decisions are made using the attribute assertions provided by the user's origin site. These assertions might include identity, but many situations will not require identity (when accessing a resource licensed for use by all members of the campus community, for example, individual information need not be shared). Shibboleth has defined a standard set of attributes. The first set is based on the eduPerson object class, which includes attributes widely used in higher education.[12]

- *Active management of privacy.* The origin site and the browser user control the information released to the target. A typical default is merely "member of community." Individuals can manage attribute release via a Web-based user interface. Users are no longer at the mercy of the target's privacy policy.

- *Reliance on standards.* Shibboleth will use the industry's de facto standard, OpenSAML, for the message and assertion formats and protocol bindings, which are based on the Security Assertion Markup Language (SAML) developed by the OASIS Security Services Technical Committee.[13]

- *A framework for multiple, scalable trust and policy sets (clubs).* Shibboleth uses the concept of a *club* to specify a set of parties who have agreed to a common set of policies. A given site can belong to multiple clubs. This arrangement expands the trust framework beyond bilateral agreements, and provides for flexibility when different situations require different policy sets.

Internet2's middleware efforts are founded on an enterprisecentric view of the world: the enterprise provides basic authentication, authorization, and attributes for its users, and brokers the release of that information to other enterprises within the federation on behalf of the user.

As an illustration, consider the applicability of this approach to a collaboration among members of a supply chain. Purchasers and suppliers may have their own authentication methods (password, public key encryption, token, etc.). They agree, though, to a common approach to attribute-based access controls—such as permitting anyone to request a price quote, but

FIGURE 6-5

Example of a federated enterprise

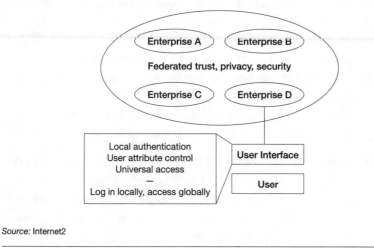

Source: Internet2

"purchasing managers" are the only ones who can actually buy something. This shared trust environment is illustrated in figure 6-5. Federation has been the basic paradigm for higher education in general and for Internet technology as well. This federated administration approach is now gaining acceptance in the corporate sector as well, as the Liberty Alliance demonstrates in its consortium activity of over one hundred fifty companies defining standards for secure and interoperable federations.[14] Internet2 is a member of the Liberty Alliance, working to effect knowledge transfer between higher education and industry.

Federated trust environments benefit the end user. He or she enjoys more uniform access to networked resources when a single sign-on is extended to a set of external partners within the federation. The user's local authentication is used to authenticate access to remote resources through established trust federations. The user also has control over his or her attributes, deciding which should be released. Authorization, for example, may be more appropriately based on membership in a group (university faculty) than on personal information (such as the user's name).

A Systems Approach to Internet Architecture

Applying a systems approach to Internet2's development enables applications, middleware, network services, and the physical network to be viewed as a whole. In addition, the system consists not just of the technology but also of users and policy. The systems approach allows improvement in any one area to be leveraged for greater overall gain in user satisfaction. For example, although the simplicity of the Internet architecture allows users to run applications without awareness of the physical network, if the PC operating system knows how the underlying network is operating, it can enhance application performance and thus improve the user experience. As innovations occur in the network layer, such as IP multicast and IPv6, new services are made available for applications use. This is a continuous cycle for Internet2, in which applications motivate network service enhancements, and new network services enable new applications, as illustrated in figure 6-6. Furthermore, end-to-end performance improvements and security enhancements cannot be achieved unless simultaneous attention is given to each component of the system.

With a systems approach, it is not just backbone networks that are important to realizing the vision of the advanced broadband Internet. The objective of reaching the home and small business is often more challenging than building super-high-speed nationwide connections. The payoff of deploying advanced broadband services and applications for large enterprises and universities may be obvious, but what would result from gigabit networking to the home? The answer is quite simple. On the Internet, the end user is the innovator. Individuals at personal computers with Internet access are creating new services and applications. Consider,

FIGURE 6-6

Internet2 systems approach

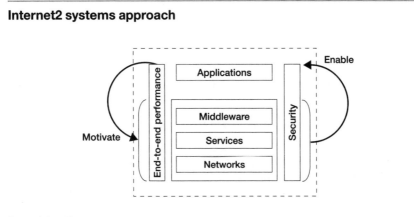

Source: Internet2.

for example, recent trends in blogs, or personal Web diaries, a grassroots phenomenon. These personal publishers are now expanding from text to video documentation of their lives and interests, with a corresponding increase in bandwidth consumption.

What can one do to realize the vision of widely available advanced broadband? First, by becoming an early adopter, you can live in the future today—and help to define the next-generation Internet. Access is available at the national level through Internet2 membership and at the local level through school and community projects. Second, by participating in the definition and development of middleware technology, particularly for security, privacy, and trust, we can more quickly deploy advanced applications that provide value for consumers, business, government, and education. Cooperation is key to facilitating knowledge and technology transfer from early adopters to the broad Internet community.

Academia, industry, and government fostered the Internet in its beginning—Internet2 continues that partnership by providing a framework for organizations and individuals from each of these sectors to work together on new networking technology and advanced applications. As a result of these collaborations, universities are better able to fulfill their missions in teaching, learning, research, clinical practice, and outreach, while corporations are positioned to test and deploy the next generation of services and applications.

Notes

1. Any innovations proposed for the Internet must be scalable. That is, the design of the Internet infrastructure must support potentially billions of devices. Any enhancement, thus, must not be constrained to a subset of the current, or future, Internet community. The current Internet layers, such as the network layer, the transport protocols, or the applications, operate independently of one another. Vertical integration is intended to enhance the performance of the Internet by, for example, allowing applications to be more aware of the status of the underlying network and adapting as necessary. One example might be automatically switching video compression methods, depending on the amount of congestion on a network link.

2. For more information, see http://lsr.internet2.edu.

3. A *backbone* comprises a very high performance network to which regional networks are often attached to provide connectivity among them and subsequently the customers the regional networks serve. For more information, see http://abilene.internet2.edu/.

4. *Peering* is the arrangement of traffic exchange between Internet service providers.

5. *IP multicast* is the efficient delivery of data from a server to multiple destinations simultaneously, without requiring a separate packet of information being sent to each re-

ceiver, thus relieving both servers and the network of extra load. Extensive use of multicast for large-scale group communications should improve the performance of all applications.

Advanced service monitoring refers to a yet-to-be-achieved Internet management environment that comprises all aspects of network, middleware, and application performance and availability with an automated analysis of the interplay among the different components, leading to a more reliable Internet experience.

6. The International Telecommunications Union Web site can be found at http://www.itu.int.

7. For more information on the One Gigabit or Bust Initiative from CENIC (Corporation for Education Network Initiatives in California), see their Web site at http://www.cenic.org/NGI/index.html.

8. See http://www.internet2.edu.

9. For more information, visit their Web site at http://www.researchchannel.org/.

10. For more information, visit their Web site at http://www.neptune.washington.edu/.

11. The Access Grid is an ensemble of resources including multimedia large-format displays, presentation and interactive environments, and interfaces to Grid middleware and to visualization environments. More information is available at http://www.accessgrid.org.

12. For more information, visit http://www.educause.edu/eduperson.

13. More information on the implementation of OpenSAML (Open Source Security Assertion Markup Language) is available at http://www.opensaml.org. For more information on the OASIS Security Services Technical Committee, visit http://www.oasis-open.org/committees/tc_home.php?wg_abbrev=security.

14. For more information, visit http://www.projectliberty.org.

7

Broadband and Hyperdifferentiation

Creating Value by Being Really *Different*

Eric K. Clemons, Rick Spitler, Bin Gu,
and Panos Markopoulos

I N ONE SENSE, altering the information available to firms and to their customers changes nothing: a consumer packaged-goods manufacturer still needs to determine what customers want to buy, what competitors have on offer, what to offer that both meets customer demand and differs from competitors' offerings, and how to price the product given its own costs and competitors' prices. An airline still needs to figure out how to attract the best mix of discount travelers, full-fare coach business travelers, and premium first-class passengers, in the face of price pressure from corporate travel managers and competition from other airlines.

And yet, in another sense, information availability changes everything.[1] The cost of identifying customer preferences may be lower than before. The cost of communicating with customers is sure to be lower, because of customers' use of online search mechanisms and online rating services and the firm's use of direct e-mail. In many industries the cost of tailoring products and services to customer preferences is significantly lower as well, because of the availability of information needed for precise targeting, and because the product's high information content facilitates targeting. Each of these trends suggests that the value of being different has increased, since differentiation is more easily achieved and more easily communicated. Meanwhile, the competitive pressure on highly standardized commodity offerings has greatly increased. Thus, the value of producing differentiated products and services has grown, and the cost of failing to do so has grown as well.

We use the term *hyperdifferentiation* to capture the increased value of being truly different. Hyperdifferentiation can be described as *the art of reducing the importance of price as the principal determinant of customers' selection among alternative goods and services*. Specifically, hyperdifferentiation encourages customers to select goods and services based on deep delight, delight that provides value sufficient to distinguish one offering from all of its competitors, and thus to make the purchaser less concerned with price differences between the selected product and its competitors. This phenomenon does not mean that all consumers will select the same product, or that one product is better or more valuable than the others; it simply means that each consumer will have a distinct preference, based on the specific product attributes that contribute to his or her delight.

Hyperdifferentiation is increasingly *important* in a high-bandwidth world, since information availability increases price competition among products that are seen as interchangeable. Fortunately, hyperdifferentiation is also increasingly *possible* in a high-bandwidth world, since firms have better information endowments with which to make differentiation decisions, and better mechanisms for communicating their differentiation strategy and their value proposition to existing and potential customers. The idea of differentiation is not new; it is as old as marketing and quite possibly as old as commerce. What is new is the degree of differentiation now possible and the motivation to pursue it. The value of differentiation has risen, as has the penalty for failure to differentiate.

In a market characterized by hyperdifferentiation, the customer need not compromise but can get precisely what he or she wants from a product. That does not mean buying a Rolls-Royce convertible or a professional photographer's Nikon digital camera. It means that for the particular category of family sedan or point-and-shoot digital camera he is seeking, the customer gets what he wants. In an automobile, this may consist of a specific combination of brand and image, color and styling, handling and acceleration, fuel economy and safety. In a camera, it may be a specific configuration of size and weight, ease of use, range of zoom, number of pixels, and quality of lens. When a customer is making no compromise, willingness to pay approaches what the customer would be willing to pay for his or her ideal product. I am willing to pay whatever I would pay for a perfect midsize family sedan or a perfectly convenient consumer point-and-shoot digital camera. The product being considered has no effective competition, and thus its price is determined by its *value to the customer* rather than by the best competitor's *cost to produce*. As we know from experience, this scenario rarely applies to cars or cameras, but the concept of matching the consumer's ideal remains useful as a target and as a metric for assessing how close a product, or a category, comes to exhibiting hyperdifferentiation.

Not all product categories are equally amenable to new hyperdifferentiation strategies. Some industries, like cosmetics, have probably maintained hyperdifferentiation strategies for decades. Others, like intercity scheduled bus service, have little scope for hyperdifferentiation; the budget constraints of most bus customers ensure that price alone will be the basis of competition. Between these two extremes—industries that already exhibit a high degree of hyperdifferentiation and industries in which little hyperdifferentiation is possible—lie the industries and products we will explore here. Many are consumer packaged-goods products, such as beer and ice cream, or experience goods like hotels and resorts. It will be more complex to implement hyperdifferentiation strategies in durable goods like automobiles and appliances, but we believe that this will occur as well. Any product that can be made in numerous varieties, and sold to consumers who do not all value the same features equally, has the potential for hyperdifferentiation. Though consumers will not all respond identically to hyperdifferentiation in all categories, all consumers appear to respond to *something* in *some categories*. And from iced tea to ice cream, from Pop-Tarts to PowerBars, all categories seem to attract some truly passionate consumers.

Motivation for Hyperdifferentiation Research

Three hypotheses have interacted to motivate hyperdifferentiation research. First, the *efficient-electronic-market hypothesis* suggests that the cost of failure to differentiate will become greater and greater, and thus potentially catastrophic to producers of undifferentiated goods and services.[2]

Efficient-Electronic-Market Hypothesis

Transparency refers to the ease of finding information. Originally used to describe the ease of finding prices in a securities market or a stock exchange, the term can now refer to the ease of finding almost any information about a product or service before purchase. The Internet and high-bandwidth communications have actually had a far greater impact on transparency than on the volume of sales that have moved to new online distribution channels. As transparency reduces search costs, making consumers better informed about prices available in the marketplace, competition increases and margins on commodity products and services will drop to zero.

As an extreme example, consider the selling of J. K. Rowling's third Harry Potter novel, *Harry Potter and the Prisoner of Azkaban*, on the Internet. Both Amazon and Barnes & Noble offered the book for advance purchase at a 50 percent discount, which means that they were selling the book at precisely their own cost. When Barnes & Noble decided to ship the book to customers via overnight delivery without additional charge—easily done from their array of local bookshops and distribution centers—Amazon had to offer free overnight delivery as well, which entailed free Federal Express shipment to customers throughout the United States. Zero-profit pricing with free FedEx delivery is a nightmare example of what undifferentiated service offerings will imply in the future.

The *winner-take-all hypothesis* suggests that, for many goods and services, we will all get what we want, and the rewards will flow to those who can persuade customers that they are best. The source of this hypothesis is entertainment: digital media allow entire markets to watch the best athletes and performers, and the rewards for the best tenors, NBA guards, and popular vocalists have never been greater.[3]

In contrast to the winner-take-all hypothesis, the *hyperdifferentiation hypothesis* suggests that we will not all want to listen to Luciano Pavarotti sing, or watch Allen Iverson shoot, or sit through a Britney Spears video, but that we will pay for whatever it is that we do want, and that those who offer something that people do not truly want will be unable to sell it.[4]

The Winner-Take-All Hypothesis

Once, the number of people who could see a sporting event or hear a concert was limited by the size of the stadium or concert hall; now electronic recording, broadcasting, and replication make the best of everything available to anyone who can pay to enjoy it. Moreover, there is a pronounced electronic bandwagon effect, as music groups and other performers win the attention of the media and surge to national or international prominence. Thus, electronic media can both amplify the audience and amplify the performer's reputation. As electronic distribution and electronic reputational effects increase, all profits tend to flow to the best. Consumers only watch what they really want to see.

The Hyperdifferentiation Hypothesis

As transparency increases, it informs service providers and manufacturers as well as customers. As transparency reduces consumers' search costs, they will be able to find what they want. Since all customers will be able to find what they truly want, service providers will have to offer what their customers want. Service providers who wish to compete effectively will need to tailor their offerings, and there will be something in the marketplace for every taste. In the end, we will all pay for what we want and only for what we want.

This doesn't mean that what is made will be in any absolute sense *better or more expensive*; it simply means that we will offer a better fit for each customer's preferences. Nor does it mean that we will try to delight every customer, or even every frequent customer; we will delight those customers willing to pay for what we produce. In short, hyperdifferentiation is not about generosity or virtue, although it may indeed be both virtuous and good for consumers. Hyperdifferentiation is about profit!

Information and Hyperdifferentiation

Delight is personal; we do not all love the same things. Consequently, information profoundly increases the degree of differentiation that is possible and that firms will consider desirable, by increasing their ability to match customers' preferences by differentiating their offerings and customers' ability to locate the offerings they value the most.

The efficient-electronic-market hypothesis implies that, given easy search and easy comparison, those who provide identical offerings (such as online booksellers selling Harry Potter novels at zero margins) will earn very little. In contrast, the winner-take-all hypothesis asserts that the rewards for truly differentiated offerings have never been greater, as an ever-increasing number of customers can locate what they want. Our example was artists and entertainers, such as J. K. Rowling, who has been very well rewarded for writing the Harry Potter novels. The hyperdifferentiation hypothesis contradicts only part of the winner-take-all hypothesis, concurring that consumers will purchase only what they truly want, but asserting that we will not all want the same thing. This hypothesis suggests that the ability to market hyperdifferentiated offerings has never been greater, which also implies that the rewards for being different will in general be less dramatic for all producers than they are for mass-market entertainers. Nonetheless, both hypotheses make the same basic argument that the potential rewards for providing differentiated offerings are indeed larger than ever before.[5] Two simple examples will help explain.

Why be different if nobody can find you? Walter Kunitake is a third-generation coffee grower in Kona on the Big Island of Hawaii. His coffee is highly regarded in Hawaii, and coffee fanciers consider it among the finest in the world. Before the advent of the Internet, Walter sold his coffee to blenders and retailers in Kona, and the price he got was determined by the local market price for coffee. Walter can now easily be found by searching the Internet, and, like other top growers, he uses the Internet to offer his coffee directly to consumers throughout the world. He now enjoys much higher prices for his superior coffees; likewise, his customers now enjoy much better coffee. Everyone is better off, but none of this would be possible without the Internet or some equivalent form of low-cost search and direct distribution. In summary, there is no advantage to being different if no one can find you, but it has never been easier to make sure you can be found.

Why be different if no one knows the difference? Victory Brewing Company brews beers that differ significantly from the mass-market beers of its largest competitors. Victory's beers are also significantly more expensive to produce and thus sell at higher prices to consumers. The Big Three brewers—Anheuser-Busch (the maker of Budweiser), Coors, and Miller—grabbed the center of the beer market and clustered their offerings around the mass-market middle. Rather than differentiating their products in a real sense, which might have limited their appeal to some consumers or increased production costs, they attempted to differentiate largely through advertising. Reliance on advertising had the added advantage of creating real economies of scale, since only the largest brewers could mount effective ad campaigns. Indeed, it is widely accepted that the massive consolidation of the U.S. beer industry between the 1960s and the 1980s, in which three companies accounted for almost all domestic production, is in part explained directly by this phenomenon.

It is noteworthy that the trend toward world consolidation was initially halted and then reversed in the last few years, precisely when greater information availability to producers and consumers would have created pressure for hyperdifferentiation strategies in the U.S. beer market. A causal relationship has not been demonstrated, but all of the following phenomena have been observed:

- Brewers have *plugged the gaps*, producing beers that are strikingly different from existing beers. Victory HopDevil Ale, for instance, has a greater concentration of hops and a higher degree of bitterness than were available from other American brewers at the time of its introduction.

- Brewers have *spaced themselves out in product-attribute space*. Flying Fish has carefully avoided making a pale ale like Sierra Nevada Pale Ale, or competing head-to-head with its geographic neighbor Victory. There are plenty of ways to be different. Why be different in the same way your competitors have chosen and thus create a price war with them, when you have carefully avoided a price war with Anheuser-Busch or Coors?

- Brewers have found a way to inform the customer about the beers they offer. Victory cannot create an effective ad campaign for each of its dozens of beers. Nor can Boston Beer Company (the maker of Samuel Adams), or Sierra Nevada, or any of the smaller microbreweries mount a promotional campaign to compete with the $500 million that Anheuser-Busch spends on advertising. Fortunately, it is not necessary for them to do so, since the detailed value proposition of each of their beers can readily be located by potential customers using one of several popular rating services. For example, customers can go to RateBeer.com to learn what other beer drinkers think about almost thirty thousand beers, based on more than three hundred thousand ratings. Consumers can compare the ratings of similar beers from different producers and can search for beers similar to beers they have enjoyed. Ratings are signed (with coded names) so that users can identify raters whose taste is similar to their own. Over time, users develop a sense of whether or not they will enjoy a beer simply by reading the ratings posted on the Web site.

With a hyperdifferentiated product, having customers love you is the ultimate goal. Victory is delighted when a reviewer gives HopDevil a perfect 5.0 rating and declares that it is what an India Pale Ale (IPA) is supposed to taste like. Of course, with a hyperdifferentiated offering, customers will hate you as well. Some customers will rate Victory products at or near the bottom of the scale, and some will use words like *gross* and *horrid* to describe them. Unlike traditional mass marketers, who want their products to be acceptable to the largest number of customers, producers following a hyperdifferentiation strategy are not dismayed when their product is hated, since a product that is sufficiently mainstream to be liked by all is no better than a product that is hated by all. In a hyperdifferentiated marketplace, liking a product is not sufficient reason to buy it; a customer must actually love it before he or she will select it over its competitors and pay the higher price that hyperdifferentiated offerings command.

Victory learned the importance of being loved rather than liked very early in its company history. Among the first three beers it introduced were the differentiated and apparently risky HopDevil and the mainstream and apparently safe Victory Lager. HopDevil was like nothing else on the market, and it succeeded beyond its brewers' expectations; it now accounts for over two-thirds of Victory's sales. Victory Lager was merely a lager done well; it can be thought of as a perfect Budweiser. Perfect or not, Victory Lager is also a marketplace failure; customers like it, but not enough to pay the significant price premium relative to Bud.

In a differentiated market, it is better to delight some people than merely to please everyone. So the strategy is to avoid the middle, stake out a vacant position, and let a newly efficient market produce your rewards.

What Do We *Actually* Know About the Effect of Information on Sales?

What do we actually know? Experience with music CDs suggests that more readily available information does indeed increase consumers' purchase of music CDs. The effect is measurable and statistically significant, and it varies among different consumer groups.

Anecdotally, this makes sense. A consumer is more likely to buy unusual and unfamiliar music if he or she can sample it first. Discs like *A Feather on the Breath of God*, by Abbess Hildegard of Bingen, and unfamiliar musical styles like klezmer (traditional eastern European Jewish) and gamelan (traditional Javanese and Balinese), are easier to sell if consumers can listen to them before they buy. The more the customer actually knows about the music—the more certain he or she is about what is on the disc, how it will sound, and how he or she will feel about it—the more likely the customer is to buy it. Conversely, the greater the customer's uncertainty about the music before buying it, and thus the greater the chance that he or she will dislike the music, the less the customer will be willing to pay for it.

Availability of information does not affect all groups of consumers equally, as illustrated by the study whose results are presented in table 7-1. The base population of the study—college-age single females who listened to music an average of ten times a week and lacked ready online access to information about music—bought an average of 6.95 CDs every six months. When given access to high-speed Internet for music-product research, the base group's purchases of the study rose on average by 1.75 CDs each six months, for an increase of 25 percent. Access to online information has less impact, however, on more music-oriented consumers: for a similar group of college-age single females who listened to music twenty times a week (about three times a day), online information only increased purchases by 0.85 CDs. Thus, the increase in purchases was greatest not among those who already listened to music most actively, but among those who experienced the greatest increase in their information endowment. The consumers who were already the best informed—those who had done the bulk of their music purchasing by mail order before the Internet

TABLE 7-1

The incremental impact of high-speed Internet access on the semiannual CD purchases of various consumer groups

	Demand without Internet access (CDs purchased semiannually)	Demand with high-speed Internet access (CDs purchased semiannually)	Change in demand	Change in demand (%)
College-age females who listen to music 10 times a week	6.95	8.70	1.75	25%
College-age females who listen to music 20 times a week	8.35	9.20	0.85	10%
College-age females who order music by mail	13.25	13.18	-0.07	-1%
30+ females who listen to music 10 times a week	5.21	7.58	2.27	45%
30+ females who listen to music 20 times a week	6.61	8.08	1.47	22%
30+ females who order music by mail	11.51	12.06	0.55	5%
40+ females who listen to music 10 times a week	4.85	7.47	2.62	54%
40+ females who listen to music 20 times a week	6.25	7.97	1.72	28%
40+ females who order music by mail	11.15	11.95	0.80	7%

Source: Bin Gu, "Does Product Information Increase Consumer Demand? An Empirical Investigation" (PhD diss., University of Pennsylvania, 2002).

was available—exhibited the smallest change. When high-speed Internet access was provided, the semiannual purchases of this group actually decreased by 0.07 CDs, indicating that on average increasing their access to information has no impact on their purchases. Similar effects were observed in the behavior of older (and presumably more affluent) consumers. When groups of consumers in their thirties and forties were studied, the largest increases again occurred among those who were previously least well informed. In sum, table 7-1 shows that ready availability of information has a bigger impact on consumers who would otherwise have limited access to product information. Consumers who are more familiar with the products in question appear, unsurprisingly, to gain less from online information and consequently to be less influenced by it.[6]

The fact that consumer groups are not equally affected by an increase in available information suggests that retailers and distributors might need to reconsider their marketing strategies. Traditionally, firms have targeted promotions at their best customers (those who bought the most of their products). But table 7-1 indicates that, in all three age groups, the best customers are most likely to be well informed already, and are less likely to learn from or be influenced by a marketing campaign aimed at providing them with more information; a campaign aimed at these consumers is unlikely to provide a large increase in sales. Instead of targeting their biggest customers, therefore, retailers would gain more new sales by targeting consumers who lack easy access to product information. Figure 7-1 illustrates this idea. The y-axis represents the relative ease with which a particular consumer group can already access online information. The x-axis represents the additional purchases a particular consumer group can be expected to make after receiving additional information. The group that is the optimal target of an informational marketing campaign lies on the upper-right corner of the figure.

We also know that manufacturers are actually diversifying their product offerings. Though we do not yet know why, their behavior is consistent with knowing what competitors are offering and seeking to maintain some distance between their own offerings and those of their competitors. For example, PC games became more dissimilar, effectively reducing competition, when it became more feasible to provide downloadable demos online due to a sharp increase in household broadband connections after the year 2000. The increased ease with which consumers could download game demos and decide among products clearly increased consumers' information about PC

FIGURE 7-1

The values of different targeting strategies

Providing more information to customers who purchase the most will increase sales. So will providing more information to customers who value information but are less likely to search for it themselves. Thus, the optimal strategy to achieve the greatest increase in total sales is to target information at customers who represent a balance between size of expected purchases and incremental impact on purchases of additional information.

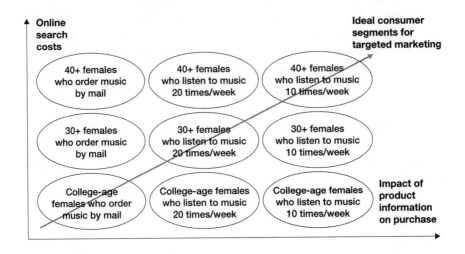

Source: Bin Gu, "Does Product Information Increase Consumer Demand? An Empirical Investigation" (PhD diss., University of Pennsylvania, 2002).

games—but it also increased game developers' information about consumer preferences. Game developers could better observe how the sampling of different products actually led to different purchase decisions.

Games really have become more differentiated. The idea of measuring conceptual distance between games initially sounds quite abstract, but it is really quite simple. Just as we can measure the distance between two points on a line (width) or a sheet of paper (width and depth), or in a box (width, depth, and height), we can measure the distance between two games. Instead of width, depth, and height, we use a set of four dimensions: the quality of the *graphics*, the quality of the *sound*, the quality of the *gameplay* (user interface and speed of response), and the game's longevity, or the amount of time it takes a player to experience most of the game, which we refer to as *value*. Game developers have to make trade-offs between these parame-

ters, either because being better than all other competitors on all parameters is economically infeasible, or because the parameters themselves conflict to a certain degree. For example, endowing a game with spectacular
graphics will slow down the game speed on most consumers' PCs, degrad-
ing the quality of gameplay. Game developers' choices on each of the four
parameters are carefully measured by expert game testers, who post their
opinions on popular PC-game Web sites. Each game receives a score from
the experts on its various attributes, and these scores can be viewed as the
game's coordinates in a four-dimensional space called the *product space*. If
two different game developers make radically different choices about their
games' product attributes, the two games would appear very far from each
other in the product space.

If we could see a four-dimensional product space in which each game is
represented by a point, we would immediately observe that games are moving farther apart, and that the average distance between games increases as

FIGURE 7-2

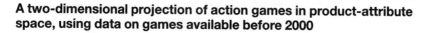

**A two-dimensional projection of action games in product-attribute
space, using data on games available before 2000**

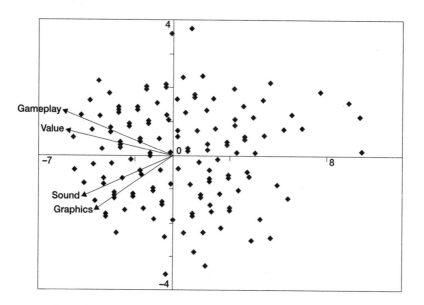

Source: Adapted from GameSpot.com.

game developers make more complicated choices regarding their games' qualities along the different product attributes. The average distance between games increased by 8 percent before and after 2000; if we compare only 1998–2000 and 2001–2003, the average distance has actually increased by 19.5 percent. This increase in differentiation occurred at precisely the same time that game developers were becoming better informed about competitors' offerings and better able to communicate the attributes of their games to potential buyers.

Fortunately, just as we can see our three-dimensional world on our two-dimensional TV screens, a mathematical technique called *principal component analysis*, or PCA, allows us to project multidimensional spaces in two dimensions. The importance of this technique is that it chooses a point of view that maximizes the amount of information that is projected in two dimensions. Thus, if games appear farther apart in their two-dimensional projection, it is because they are indeed farther apart (more

FIGURE 7-3

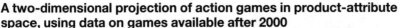

A two-dimensional projection of action games in product-attribute space, using data on games available after 2000

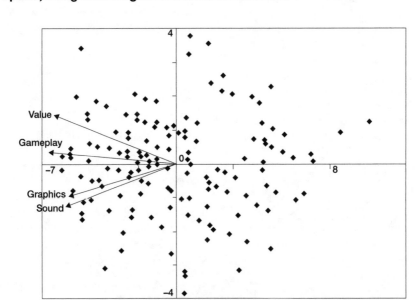

Source: Adapted from GameSpot.com.

differentiated) in their four-dimensional product space. Two-dimensional projections of the product space for action PC games before and after the year 2000 are depicted in figures 7-2 and 7-3, respectively, using data and reviews collected by GameSpot.com. PCA projected the original four product dimensions, which appear in the figures as arrows, to two new axes, having chosen two slightly different points of view for each projection (hence the small shift in their positions from one figure to the next).

What Do We *Think* We Know About the Effect of Information on Sales?

Amazon.com's book-sales Web site has exhibited a clear progression in complexity, first adding book reviews by customers, then online sample pages and even sample chapters. Clearly, this elaboration was not motivated by competition among books, since Amazon cares more about how much you buy than which books you buy. So Amazon executives must believe that providing more information increases Amazon's sale of books. Likewise, Amazon added customers' reviews of music CDs, and then sample MP3 cuts, to the Web site. Once again, executives must believe that providing more information to consumers will increase Amazon's sales of CDs. Online music samples had to wait for more bandwidth to be available to consumers. Amazon currently provides customers reviews of videos, CDs, and DVDs; if precedent is a good guide, when more customers have even more bandwidth, Amazon will provide online MPEG clips. This pattern suggests that when consumers have more information, their purchases increase.

Can more and better information increase sales of experience goods more generally? Hard data is not yet available, but the proliferation of Webcams at luxury hotels suggests that leisure-property owners and managers believe that it can.

It is appropriate at this point to ask whether reducing uncertainty can ever actually *decrease* sales of any products and services. That is, can providing the customer a more accurate assessment of a specific product, and exactly where it lies in its product-attribute space, ever reduce customers' willingness to buy the product? It appears that it can, but again our experience is more anecdotal than statistically significant. Think of a product with a spectacular upside if it really works as you hope it will, such as a putter that will align your putts correctly or a driver that will add thirty yards to your drive while keeping you on the fairway. These products may actually deliver as promised for some golfers, but they will probably not work for the average golfer who cannot read the greens correctly, or who lacks the swing speed to benefit from the new clubface technology. These customers may buy the products in hopes of improving their game; with better information, they would not do so, because they would know that the products will not work for them. In other words, more information—information that distinguishes between hope and reality—could actually reduce sales of these products.

Two Propositions to Explain the Impact of Information on Sales

A pair of propositions help explain our claims about what we know and think we know. Both propositions address the impact of decreasing the customer's *range of uncertainty*—that is, shrinking the area in product space in which the customer believes that a product might be found. To say that we have increased the customer's certainty about where in the product space a particular product lies is identical to saying that we have reduced the customer's range of uncertainty. The two propositions differ in the location of the range of uncertainty relative to the customer's ideal product. The first proposition pertains to products that the customer views as near-ideal—or to put it another way, products for which the customer's range of uncertainty about their expected location spans his or her ideal point. If a customer wants a beer that is light and hoppy like a German lager, and he is considering a beer he expects to resemble a Heineken, his range of uncertainty about the lager he is considering will almost cer-

---

Proposition 1

Increasing the amount of information available to a customer increases the customer's willingness to pay for a product that approaches his or her ideal.

Assumption: a customer's willingness to pay decreases with the distance between a product and the customer's ideal.

---

tainly span his ideal point. If he wants something light and hoppy, but is considering something dark and thick like a Guinness Stout, his range of uncertainty is unlikely to span his ideal point.

Figure 7-4 shows a customer's valuation of a specific product—a single beer, or camera, or hotel, or SUV—whose characteristics he is uncertain about. The length of the x-axis represents the product-attribute space, or the full range of beers, cameras, hotels, or SUVs that could be produced.[7] Each point along the x-axis represents a single instance of the set of possibilities (a single possible beer, camera, hotel, or SUV). The height of the V line above each point represents the value a given customer assigns to

FIGURE 7-4

A customer's valuation of a product with a high degree of uncertainty, where the product's range of locations in its product-attribute space spans the customer's ideal point

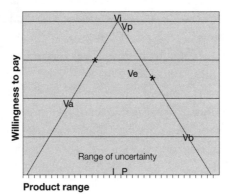

Key

I = ideal product for *this* given customer

P = actual product

V = value of product to customer

Va = the value the customer places on the products associated with the beginning point of range of uncertainty

Vb = the value the customer places on the products associated with the ending point of range of uncertainty

Ve = expected value of the customer's willingness to pay, computed over the range of uncertainty

Vi = highest value that this customer will pay

V = customer's willingness to pay *for that product*

* = average of range between Va and Vi or between Vb and Vi

Source: Eric K. Clemons.

the specific product corresponding to that point, or, in other words, the customer's willingness to pay for that product. The curve is highest corresponding to the customer's preferred, or ideal, product. In figure 7-4, the customer is uncertain about where the specific product he is considering will actually be located, and thus uncertain about its actual *value* to him. He knows the range of possible product characteristics this product might have, and thus he knows the average location that he can expect the product to occupy in some product-attribute space. Unfortunately, there is a broad range of possible locations for the product in this space, and hence a broad range of possible product value to him. The location of the customer's *ideal point*—the collection of product attributes he would value most—is on the left side of the range, about one-third of the way into the product range. As the figure shows, the customer would realize the highest value, Vi, from products near his ideal point; the greater the distance from this ideal point in either direction, the less value the product has for him. At the left end of the range of uncertainty, the value is reduced to Va; at the right end of the range, the value is reduced to Vb. The average of the left side of the range is the asterisk between Va and Vi, and the average of the right side of the range is the asterisk between Vi and Vb. The expected value of the product is Ve. The customer's expected value from purchasing this product is significantly less than his ideal value, because the endpoints of the range—far from the ideal—have significantly less value to him than would his ideal product. Thus, the customer's willingness to pay, based as it is on expected value, is constrained by this large uncertainty.

To provide a concrete example, suppose the customer is booking a hotel in Hyderabad, and he knows that it is within ten miles of his 9 a.m. meeting location, which may mean that it is either too close to the airport or too far beyond the center of town in the other direction; since both possibilities can represent a commute of an hour or more during the morning rush hour, this range of uncertainty significantly reduces the value of the hotel to him. Other examples of ranges of uncertainty might include the amounts of salt, fat, and sugar in a specific menu item at a fast-food restaurant, how a given model of a cell phone from a wireless service provider will feel when you use it, or the hoppy bitterness of a given beer. With too much salt and sugar, you will not want your child to eat the food; with too little, your child may refuse to eat it. A phone that is too large and heavy is inconvenient to use; a phone that is too small and light may feel flimsy and cheap, and its keys may be too close together. A beer like Corona (below 20 on a bitterness scale) may strike you as bland and boring, and one like Rogues's Old Crustacean (well over 100 on the scale) may be impossible for you to drink. Clearly, not all consumers feel the same way about these products; neither Corona nor Old Crustacean is objectively superior, and there are consumers for whom each represents an ideal purchase. We are interested in consumers who have an ideal purchase point—perhaps a Victory HopDevil (about 65)—but who are considering making a purchase in the presence of a high degree of uncertainty.

Now consider the implications of reducing the customer's uncertainty about the actual range of locations that can be occupied by the product's attributes. For instance, the customer now knows that the hotel is within five miles of his meeting. Alternatively, the customer now knows more about how the phone will feel in his hands, or about the salt and sugar content of the restaurant menu item, or about the hoppy bitterness of a specific beer. Compared to figure 7-4, the range of uncertainty in figure 7-5 is considerably narrower. It is important to emphasize that reducing uncertainty about the range does not reposition the center of the range, or the expected location of the product in its product-attribute space. But we significantly improve the product's expected fit with the customer's desires by shortening the tails and eliminating the least attractive of the previously possible product-attribute locations—precisely the locations that most significantly reduce the value of the product to the consumer. The new expected values to the customer of products on the left and right sides of the range are once again represented by Va and Vb. However, if we compare the locations of Va and Vb in figure 7-4 to their values in figure 7-5, it is clear that the values are higher in the latter figure. Moreover, and most importantly, the expected value of the product the consumer is contemplating, Ve, is higher as well. Thus, we see that reducing the customer's uncertainty does not alter the expected *location* of the product, but does increase its expected *value* to the customer.

The principal implication of comparing these two figures is that greater access to information reduces uncertainty, and that reducing uncertainty increases the customer's willingness to pay for offerings that approach his or her ideal point. Thus, more information and less uncertainty increase the value of differentiation strategies for the producers of these goods and services.

Our second proposition pertains to products that the customer believes to be remote from his or her ideal point—that is, products about

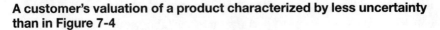

FIGURE 7-5

A customer's valuation of a product characterized by less uncertainty than in Figure 7-4

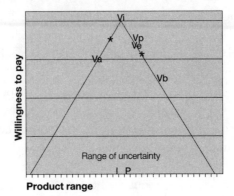

Key

I = ideal product for *this* given customer

P = actual product

V = value of product to customer

Va = the value the customer places on the products associated with the beginning point of range of uncertainty

Vb = the value the customer places on the products associated with the ending point of range of uncertainty

Ve = expected value of the customer's willingness to pay, computed over the range of uncertainty

Vi = highest value that this customer will pay

V = customer's willingness to pay *for that product*

* = average of range between Va and Vi or between Vb and Vi

Source: Eric K. Clemons.

whose attributes the customer's range of uncertainty does not span his or her ideal point.

Consider the product-choice situation represented in figure 7-6. The consumer's range of uncertainty about the location of the specific product in its product-attribute space is extremely wide. And, significantly, unlike in figures 7-4 and 7-5, the possible range of locations for the offering being considered, designated as the range of uncertainty, does not span the consumer's ideal point, I. Moreover, this is assumed to be a hyperdifferentiated market; many products are available, and at least some of them should come close to each consumer's ideal point. In such a hyperdifferentiated market, the consumer's postpurchase regret for less-than-ideal products will be quite high because of the associated opportunity cost. In

Proposition 2

In a hyperdifferentiated marketplace, increased access to information decreases the customer's willingness to pay for a product that is far from his or her ideal.

Assumption: with many choices available, a customer's willingness to pay for a product or service falls off quickly as the fit between such an offering and his or her ideal decreases. The customer's preference curves actually change shape, as shown in figures 7-6 and 7-7.

fact, any product sufficiently far from the consumer's ideal will have no value at all; it will be a beer that is not drunk, a driver or putter that is not used, a video game or music CD that is used only once. The speed with which a specific product offering loses value to a consumer is very different from that illustrated in figures 7-4 and 7-5. Products that are close to the ideal lose value very slowly, but value drops very quickly as the product offering becomes more remote from the ideal. Once the product reaches a certain distance from the customer's ideal point, it retains only slightly negative value, the cost of disposal. Once again, the values at the ends of the ranges are Va and Vb, and once again the expected value of the specific offering is Ve. However, because of the shape of the curve of values for willingness to pay, the expected value, Ve, is significantly less than the average of Va and Vb.

Now consider the product-choice situation represented by figure 7-7, in which the expected location is again remote from the customer's ideal product location. Once again, we are assuming that the customer is facing a hyperdifferentiated market characterized by numerous choices, some of which should be quite close to each consumer's ideal point. Uncertainty has been reduced relative to figure 7-6. As in figure 7-6, we assume that product valuation drops off very quickly as the product becomes more distant from the customer's ideal, and that it rapidly reaches a steady low valuation, that of its cost of disposal. The expected value of purchasing such a product is still significantly less than the customer's ideal value; the reduced willingness to pay derives, of course, not from the uncertainty but from how remote the specific product offering truly is from the consumer's ideal, I. Va, the value at the left end of the range of uncertainty, is not high,

FIGURE 7-6

A customer's valuation of a product selection characterized by a high degree of uncertainty

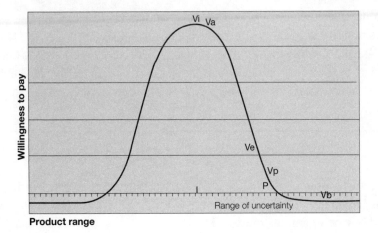

Key

I   = ideal product for *this* given customer

P = actual product

V = value of product to customer

Va = the value the customer places on the products associated with the beginning point of range of uncertainty

Vb = the value the customer places on the products associated with the ending point of range of uncertainty

Ve = expected value of the customer's willingness to pay, computed over the range of uncertainty

Vi = highest value that this customer will pay

V = customer's willingness to pay *for that product*

* = average of range between Va and Vi or between Vb and Vi

Source: Eric K. Clemons.

because the product is remote from I. Vb, the value at the right end, is actually less than zero because of the product's distance from I. Comparing this figure to figure 7-6, we see that the value on the left has dropped even lower here, because the best location that the consumer can expect for the product has moved farther from I. We see that the value on the right has not moved higher to compensate for the drop on the left; this is a function of the shape of the willingness-to-pay curve in this hyperdifferentiated environment. Consequently, Ve is less in the reduced-uncertainty case than in the high-uncertainty case. In this hyperdifferentiated environment, reducing uncertainty does not improve customers' willingness to pay for product

FIGURE 7-7

A customer's valuation of a product selection characterized by a low degree of uncertainty, where the range of uncertainty does not span the customer's ideal product location

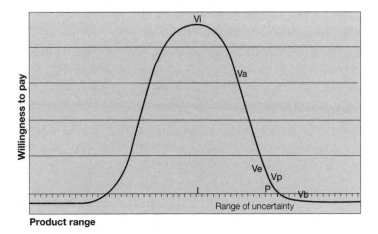

Product range

Key

I = ideal product for *this* given customer

P = actual product

V = value of product to customer

Va = the value the customer places on the products associated with the beginning point of range of uncertainty

Vb = the value the customer places on the products associated with the ending point of range of uncertainty

Ve = expected value of the customer's willingness to pay, computed over the range of uncertainty

Vi = highest value that this customer will pay

V = customer's willingness to pay *for that product*

* = average of range between Va and Vi or between Vb and Vi

Source: Eric K. Clemons.

offerings that are far from their ideal; rather, decreasing uncertainty further constricts the customer's willingness to pay.

The principal implication of comparing figures 7-6 and 7-7 is that when other producers have already differentiated their offerings, increasing the amount and accuracy of information available to consumers increases the pressure on producers to further differentiate, or even hyperdifferentiate, their offerings. The reasoning is clear: as we have seen, increasing the information available to consumers constricts their willingness to pay for goods and services that do not precisely fit their needs or desires.

Comparing figures 7-6 and 7-7 to figures 7-4 and 7-5, we see that when products are close to the consumer's ideal, reducing uncertainty increases willingness to pay; when products are far from consumers' ideal, however, reducing uncertainty has the reverse effect.

In summary, propositions 1 and 2 tell us the following:

- Increasing the information available to consumers and thus reducing their uncertainty *increases* their willingness to pay for products that are *near* their ideal points. Thus, increasing information increases consumers' willingness to pay for differentiated goods and services and *increases the value of hyperdifferentiation strategies.*

- Increasing the information available to consumers and thus reducing their uncertainty *decreases* their willingness to pay for products that are *not near* their ideal points. Thus, increasing information decreases consumers' willingness to pay for undifferentiated goods and services and *increases the penalty for failing to implement hyperdifferentiation strategies.*

The Limitations, Real and Apparent, of Hyperdifferentiation

Not all industries will exhibit the hyperdifferentiation phenomenon that we describe here. In some industries, like pharmaceuticals, hyperdifferentiation has always been desirable, but greater information availability is not likely to have a profound impact. Pharmaceutical firms have always wanted to produce wonder drugs and to distinguish their offerings from lower-priced generics. But the principal cost of developing pharmaceutical products remains biological and medical research, not advertising. More information on consumer preferences will not change the way drugs are developed; the search for AIDS/HIV drugs and SARS drugs is not contingent on Web-related customer research. Just as importantly, most patients' decisions about prescription drugs are determined by their physicians and by the FDA, not by Web-based rating services or other consumer-focused information services. Even so, the number of industries whose customers are willing to accept advice passively from experts is shrinking: self-directed consumers are taking charge of their investment management, their travel planning, and their health care. This shift is attested to by the prevalence of advertisements for new drugs targeted at consumers rather than physicians. Thus, the number of industries that represent exceptions may be decreasing.

In other industries, like automobile manufacturing, the cost of designing and manufacturing the product is also a significant factor. Economies of scale might initially appear to preclude hyperdifferentiation strategies. But customization and microsegmentation are more feasible than in the past and are more plausible than custom-tailored drugs in the near term. Moreover, Net-based marketing efforts enable purchasers to determine precisely which cars are targeted at them and would be most attractive to them. Almost every consumer durable good has similarly high fixed costs of development. On the other hand, most consumer durable goods have experienced drops in the cost of informing consumers about new products and similar reductions in the cost of managing large product portfolios. Consequently, in products as diverse as dishwashers, microwave ovens, SUVs, and cameras, there has been a proliferation of more finely tuned product offerings.

In still other industries, increases in information availability will represent a source of competitive advantage for incumbents. Service providers who enjoy ongoing relationships with customers will know better than their competitors what to offer each customer; this advantage will be especially decisive in industries whose products have a low emotive content or excitement value, like banking services, and those whose customers may have strong preferences but are unlikely to be aware of them or to search out competing offerings. An incumbent who delights a customer can earn more, while a challenger would have little idea what to offer. The key to profitability here is to give the customer those amenities that matter most to him or her, while earning profits from the same customers elsewhere. If some customers care more about fees than interest rates, give them lower fees but not lower interest rates; if others care more about interest than fees, the reverse strategy will please them while ensuring profits. This is the advantage that comes from knowing *how* to delight.

Equally important is knowing *whom* to delight. Hyperdifferentiation is not about delighting all customers equally or despite the expense. Hyperdifferentiation is about delivering delight to some customers in order to maximize the firm's profits. Anecdotal evidence suggests that American Express Concierge, a service for the most demanding customers and most frequent travelers, and American Airlines frequent-flier programs have done a good job of deciding whom to delight. Guessing wrong, or implementing an egalitarian strategy, is likely to result in *winners' curse*, the dilemma of becoming invested in delighting low-profit customers whom no one else wishes to retain.

Summary and Conclusions

Differentiation is not new, but hyperdifferentiation is. Firms have always wanted to achieve the greatest possible degree of differentiation, to discourage direct comparisons and thus to avoid pure price competition. Without differentiation, products are purchased largely on the basis of price; with hyperdifferentiation, each product approaches a monopoly, and purchases are based on value and willingness to pay, rather than competitors' costs. If firms have always wanted to achieve monopoly profits, and to implement and sustain differentiation strategies, why should we expect to see an increase in differentiation strategies today? We have proposed two answers:

- *Because now firms have to.* In accordance with the efficient-electronic-market hypothesis, the pressure created by transparent electronic marketplaces will shrink profits for firms that fail to differentiate their offerings and will do so to an extent that is unprecedented. The failures of many e-businesses, and the systemic lack of profitability of entire e-industries like securities trading, attest to this hypothesis.

- *Because now firms can.* Information available to producers enables them to determine where in product-attribute space competitors have clustered and what product locations are still unoccupied. It also allows them to determine what consumers want—that is, which unoccupied locations would actually attract buyers. And today's information technology allows producers to let each consumer know what they have on offer, reduce the consumer's uncertainty, and increase the consumer's willingness to pay for a product that is precisely what he or she wants.

In other words, information availability creates both the pressure to differentiate and the capability to do so. The pressure to differentiate arises from three sources. (1) Direct comparison will destroy the profit potential of commodities, prompting the move to hyperdifferentiation. Moreover, (2) once consumers become accustomed to getting what they truly want, their dissatisfaction with products that fail to meet their requirements will increase, and their willingness to pay for such products will be greatly reduced. (3) Only products that approach some consumers' ideal points and have communicated this fit to those consumers will earn significant profits. Likewise, the capability to differentiate has three sources: firms can now determine more quickly (1) what competitors are producing and (2) what consumers want, and (3) they can communicate their value propositions more easily.

We predict that this move to hyperdifferentiation will increase product diversity and that it will increase producer prices, profits, and consumer satisfaction. The informed customer will pay more for what he or she wants; the informed customer will also experience greater delight. Informed firms will earn more, and thus margins will increase for incumbents, who are better positioned to design offerings for customers whose preferences they already know.

Notes

1. The concept of *information availability*—effortless access to information on the part of firms and their customers as a result of our inevitable transition to a high-bandwidth world—is so fundamental that we will use the term *information endowment* to describe it throughout the document. The critical concept is that firms and consumers now simply *have* such information and no longer require special effort to acquire it.

2. The efficient-electronic-market hypothesis appears not to have a single identifiable source. The first author to publish on the impact of search costs on the efficiency of consumer markets may have been Yannis Bakos. See Y. Bakos, "Reducing Buyer Search Costs: Implications for Electronic Marketplaces," *Management Science* 43, no. 12 (December 1997): 1,676–1,693; and Y. Bakos, "Towards Friction-Free Markets: The Emerging Role of Electronic Marketplaces on the Internet," *Communications of the ACM* 41, no. 8 (August 1998): 35–42.

3. The concept of the winner-take-all society was popularized by R. H. Frank and P. J. Cook, *The Winner-Take-All Society: Why the Few at the Top Get So Much More Than the Rest of Us* (New York: Penguin USA, 1996).

4. In relating a product's position in an attribute space to customers' willingness to pay for it, the hyperdifferentiation hypothesis draws heavily on work by Hotelling and Salop. See H. Hotelling, "Stability in Competition," *Economic Journal* 39 (1929): 41–57; and S. Salop, "Monopolistic Competition with Outside Goods," *Bell Journal of Economics* 10 (1979): 141–156.

5. That digital word of mouth (or word of mouse) may be more powerful than advertising has been reported in the business press, and the theoretical implications have been explored by Dellarocas. See S. Hansell, "Amazon Decides to Go for a Powerful Form of Advertising: Lower Prices and Word of Mouth," *New York Times*, February 10, 2003, C8; and Nicholas Thompson, "More Companies Pay Heed to Their 'Word of Mouse' Reputation," *New York Times*, June 23, 2003, 4. Also see C. Dellarocas, "The Digitization of Word-

of-Mouth: Promise and Challenges of Online Feedback Mechanisms," *Management Science* 49, no. 10 (October 2003): 1,407–1,417.

6. Bin Gu, "Does Product Information Increase Consumer Demand? An Empirical Investigation" (PhD diss., University of Pennsylvania, 2002).

7. A *product-attribute space* represents the range of all possible products, and two products that customers consider similar would be close to each other in the product attribute space. Such space can indeed be physical, as when two hotels are considered similar because they are physically close together. More typically, the product-attribute space does not actually represent physical space. Examples of products that may be close in product-attribute space without having a physical relationship are two United Airlines flights between New York and Chicago that differ only in their times of departure and arrival; or two recordings of the same movie, one on DVD and another on VHS; two American lager beers; or two pinstripe suits from the same manufacturer, in the same size and style, but in slightly different shades of blue.

8

eChoupal

Revolutionizing Supply Chains in Rural India

David M. Upton and Virginia A. Fuller

I N 1999, Y. C. Deveshwar, chairman of the Indian conglomerate ITC, challenged S. Sivakumar, head of the company's agricultural commodities export business, to generate a plan for improving his division's performance. Parity with ITC's other divisions would require a 400 percent increase in revenue. Sivakumar knew the only way to achieve this was to redesign the supply chain through which soybeans were procured from Indian farmers. The solution that emerged—ITC's *eChoupal*—achieved the company's business goals and brought sweeping change to the soy fields of India.

Drawing on a deep understanding of technology, sociology, and the incentives of the various players involved, the eChoupal provided farmers with effective methods of price discovery, honest trading, and information sharing to the benefit of all. It demonstrated how clever implementation of computer and telecommunication technologies can transform markets and create new economic value. What began in 1999 as a mere experiment with one or two villages in the central state of Madhya Pradesh, by 2004 affected 2.4 million farmers in twenty-one thousand villages across India.

The Old System: From Field to Factory

Farmers traditionally sold their soybeans at ineffective and frequently dishonest physical marketplaces (*mandi*). After the soybean harvest, farmers hauled their produce thirty to fifty kilometers to the closest mandi and waited for the crop to be auctioned. The auction began when a government-appointed bidder valued the produce and set the initial bid. Government-licensed buyers called commission agents (CAs) then bid until the crop was sold.

ITC contracted with a specific CA in each mandi to bid on behalf of the company. Prices were authorized by ITC's office in Bhopal, where a team of traders followed the global market. Nothing prevented the CA from buying at a much lower price than ITC would pay, selling to ITC at market price, and pocketing the difference.

Once a CA won an auction, the farmer brought his produce to that CA's shop and waited for the produce to be weighed on a manually operated balance scale that accommodated only small increments of the lot. The weight was often manipulated because of the inaccuracy of the crude beam scales; the farmer could expect to lose about 0.5 percent of the value of his original lot. By law, CAs were supposed to pay the farmer immediately, but some CAs would simply tell the farmer to return in a few days for the money.

On any given day, at least one thousand farmers might be trying to sell their produce at the market. Some had to wait two or three days just to get in. Farmers suffered from the delay: their product was perishable, and they were dependent on timely cash flow for subsistence. Thus, farmers were in no position to turn down a CA's offer. Furthermore, they rarely had access to storage facilities for a crop that had not yet been sold.

Typically poor and often illiterate, farmers had very limited access to information and education on farming techniques. Limited technological resources constrained the dissemination of know-how in rural communities. Farmers did not have access to quality inputs, like sowing seeds, herbicides, and pesticides, or to information, such as accurate weather reports, that would help them improve their crop and the process of bringing it to market. In fact, farmers were losing 60–70 percent of the potential value of their crop, and agricultural yields were only one-quarter to one-third of global standards. An average farmer, with about nine acres of land, could expect an annual net income of approximately $443 from soybeans and wheat.[1] Inefficiency drastically increased transaction costs and slashed potential profits for the farmer.

Farmers had limited capacity for risk and therefore tended to minimize their investment in crops lest inclement weather or pests destroy that investment. This practice resulted in a lower-value crop, which translated into slim margins for both the farmer *and* ITC. With such risk aversion, farmers were loath to experiment with new farming methods. It was a cycle that continued unabated.

A Seed Is Planted

In an effort to reevaluate the supply chain, Sivakumar studied the farmers' villages and the mandis to identify areas that could be improved upon. He was particularly inspired by the choupals taking place each night in the villages. *Choupal* is a Hindi word meaning a gathering or meeting place. At the end of the workday, before retiring, farmers traditionally congregated in the home of one of their neighbors to relax and share stories from the day. In this staple of village life, debates were sparked, opinions were voiced, and knowledge was shared before farmers went in for the night. In the absence of telecommunications, however, news was limited to the boundaries of the villages. Oral communication from the closest city could take days to reach an outlying farming village. Furthermore, the farmers were isolated from the market trends that were affecting the prices of their soybeans. They had no reference points for pricing other than word-of-mouth reports of the previous day's numbers.

Sivakumar knew that the price trends of soybeans could be forecast and that they generally followed the agriculture futures market on the Chicago Board of Trade and the Kuala Lumpur Commodity Exchange. He felt that with some understanding of the market, farmers would be able to plan their activities with more confidence and grasp the global context of their livelihood.

The eChoupal Concept

When a computer was added to the nightly choupals in the villages, they became known as "eChoupals." Conversations were no longer limited to stories and gossip. Farmers were able to access the World Wide Web through a site dedicated specifically to them, ITC's http://www.soyachoupal.com.

The initiative called for ITC to supply each village with a computer kit with the following components:

1. A PC with a Windows/Intel platform, multimedia kit, and connectivity interface

2. Connection lines, either telephone (with a bit rate of 28.8–36 Kbps) or VSAT (used in 75 percent of villages; providing 64 Kbps inbound, 1 Mbps outbound) [2]

3. A power supply consisting of an uninterruptible power supply (UPS) and a solar-powered battery backup

4. A dot-matrix printer

The total set-up cost to ITC was $3,762 per choupal. Another $2,213 was spent on staff, travel, communication, software, and training. [3] Although ITC incurred some overhead cost from this, Chairman Deveshwar was motivated by a desire to "do something good for India" and believed the company would earn the money back when non-value-added steps in the supply chain were eliminated.

Connecting the Farmers

The http://www.soyachoupal.com Web site, regularly updated by the ITC Bhopal office, contained useful information previously unavailable to farmers in Madhya Pradesh.

The site opened by welcoming farmers into the "community" of the eChoupal. The site offered eight links to key information: weather, best practices, crop information, market information, FAQs, news, feedback, and information about ITC. The feature set had been developed in collaboration with the farmers who were to use the system.

- *The weather page.* Before the eChoupal, weather forecasts were rarely communicated to remote villages. Those that did reach the villages did not report local conditions. ITC negotiated with the national weather service to get forecasts for local districts, allowing a farmer to see a localized forecast. This knowledge helped farmers time the application of herbicides and fertilizers, and, more importantly, the harvest. Ill-timed rains could degrade the value of a soybean crop irrespective of the amount of money spent on it at sowing time. Thus, ignorance of weather trends had created a disincentive for a farmer to spend extra money for higher-quality seed; farmers tended to err on the side of frugality. The ability to predict rain patterns would therefore affect the quality of soybeans sown by the farmers. The eChoupal reduced farmers' weather-based risks and took the guesswork out of timing the harvest.

- *The best-practices page.* On this page a farmer could compare the actual practices of farmers with similar acreage and crop volume to the ideal practices described on the page. For example, eighteen-inch spacing was considered "best practice"; many farmers had been spacing their seed rows nine inches apart, which meant that their crops did not receive proper ventilation and light. This information was presented in the local Hindi vernacular.

- *The crop-information page.* This page contained instructional material, such as "How to take a good soil sample" and suggestions for actions to take in response to soil-test results.

- *Market information.* Links on this page enabled farmers to explore world demand, world production, mandi trading volume, and mandi price lists. The farmer could learn prices (lows and highs) at a given mandi, the number of bags that had arrived at the mandi to date, and estimated daily arrivals. The farmer could thus assess demand for his produce at a particular mandi. This information had previously been available only from research institutions or corporations; now it was being provided directly to the farmer. The site also contained a link to the Chicago Board of Trade, where farmers could find a seven- to ten-day market outlook and track global soybean price trends. One of ITC's strengths was its ability to communicate daily with the global markets. "If we had access to this information," Sivakumar reasoned, "why not translate this into another context and share it with the farmers?"

- *The Q+A forum (FAQs).* Through this interactive feature, a farmer could pose a question to a virtual "panel" of experts. Other farmers with relevant experience could also respond. Weather-related questions were routed to the meteorological department; crop questions went to four or five agriscientists. One farmer asked, for example, "Should we do soil testing before harvest or after?" The answer was posted to the forum soon after: "You can do soil testing anytime but preferably before the rains." Questions from all of the eChoupals were stored in a central database so farmers in other locations could access them. The computer's storage ability represented a significant advantage over television or radio, both of which had been considered as methods of knowledge dissemination.

- *The news page.* This page presented relevant news, such as governmental decisions on subsidies or minimum support prices (MSPs) and innovations in other countries' farming systems. If a farmer did something that was particularly successful or innovative, that news was posted as well. This recognition provided an incentive for farmers to try new things.

- *Suggestions.* Finally, the site solicited suggestions. One advantage of the system was that the site could be continually tailored to the needs of the farmers. ITC had relied on their input from the start, and it was important that the farmers continue to be involved in its improvement.

The eChoupal's purpose shifted across the changing seasons. At harvest time, for example, farmers were most concerned about prices; at sowing time, they were more concerned about weather forecasts. But the eChoupal initiative was based primarily on the belief that the farmer needed an alternative to the mandi system. As we shall see, the eChoupal network offered farmers new channels through which they could sell directly to ITC, eliminating the cost inflation and cheating associated with middlemen.

The Sanchalak

In each village, ITC selected a lead farmer to become the caretaker of the equipment and a liaison between ITC and the farmers. This farmer, designated *sanchalak*, was most often the individual whose home was already being used for nightly choupals. In other words, the sanchalak was a respected and trusted figure in the social fabric of the village.

The sanchalak received basic IT training and instruction in effective methods of communication. On evenings when fifteen to twenty people showed up at the sanchalak's home for their usual choupal gathering, the ITC computer setup offered a new spin on the usual discussions. In addition to the regular chatter, the sanchalak would access http://www.soyachoupal. com and demonstrate the interactive features of the site. Other farmers could then navigate the site themselves. The log-in feature made it possible to offer customized content based on the log-in location; if, in the future, the content were to evolve in a more personalized direction, individual farmers could log in themselves. Until then, the sanchalak, distinguished for his literacy and communication skills, served as liaison.

Weather forecasts and mandi transactions were printed out and posted on a notice board at the sanchalak's house. This way the sanchalak did not need to open the Web site with the arrival of each visitor; farmers could read the printed information at any time. If a farmer was unable to read, he could ask the sanchalak's advice. It was in the sanchalak's best interest to advise farmers correctly, for better-quality produce from each farmer would fetch a higher price from ITC and thus a higher commission for the sanchalak. Sound advice also reinforced his reputation as an honest broker.

Farmers also brought samples of their crop to the sanchalak's home, where he had moisture meters and other tools from ITC to assess the quality of the beans. The company provided each sanchalak with best-quality "control samples" with which to perform a quality comparison, and trained him in quality assessment. The Web site listed prices for best-quality beans, so when farmers brought their samples to the sanchalak, he priced them based on their degree of variance from the best-quality control samples. Using the samples, he could show the farmers: if you grow it like this, you will get a better price. In the words of ITC's trading manager, D. V. R. Kumar: "Visiting the eChoupal is not an extra job; this is part of [the farmer's] routine. Their routine is their agriculture. Before, if they wanted information, they had to go to town and ask somebody. Now, we are bringing the information into the village, into the home. It's natural for them."

Reorganizing the Supply Chain

The eChoupal kiosks facilitated a new kind of supply chain, whose crux was technology. Trading outside the mandi, for example, had been very difficult before the eChoupal. First, the mandi provided the only means of price discovery, and farmers reasonably assumed that they would fare best in open auction. Second, transactions outside the mandi were officially prohibited by the Agricultural Produce Marketing Act. The government had restricted agricultural transactions to the mandis to protect farmers from exploitation by unscrupulous buyers; open auctions were considered the best safeguard. With the advent of the eChoupal, however, ITC convinced the government of its potential benefits to farmers and to the economy, and the government amended the act to legalize purchases of beans (and other agricultural commodities) outside the mandi. The transparency of the eChoupal—the fact that the Web site was accessible to anyone, including the government, to cross-check ITC's prices at any time—facilitated governmental acceptance of the initiative.

Web technology brought price discovery to the village level and changed the way farmers did business. First, empowered with knowledge of the price he would get at an ITC hub (see the next section) and of prices at nearby mandis, the farmer could make an informed decision about where to sell his beans. From the eChoupal computer, he could determine whether he would get a better deal through the open auction at the mandi or at an ITC hub, all before leaving the village. Given the guarantee of the ITC's published prices, and the reimbursement for transport cost, farmers began regularly defecting from the uncertainty of the mandis and choosing ITC.

By following real-time prices on the Web site, furthermore, farmers could decide when to sell. Knowing the price in advance meant that the farmer could go to an ITC hub (assuming he was happy with ITC's price) on his own schedule.

A third distinguishing feature of the eChoupal was its transparency. It is arguable that prices could be communicated to farmers by other means, such as telephone or radio broadcast. These methods, however, still relied on the spoken word. The ability to see prices offered in writing on a computer screen (despite the illiteracy of some of the farmers) was instrumental in establishing the trustworthiness that made the eChoupal effective. The Web model was also more scalable, since one kiosk could serve hundreds of farmers.

The ITC Hubs

ITC had five processing units and thirty-nine warehouses in Madhya Pradesh, a total of forty-four hubs to which a farmer could bring his soybeans. By contrast, there were fifty-one large soybean-based mandis in the state. Farmers traveled an average of twenty kilometers to reach a hub, approximately the same distance a farmer would travel to reach a mandi. The eChoupal model called for a Web kiosk within walking distance (less than five kilometers) and a hub within driving distance (less than thirty kilometers) of every targeted farmer.

Once a farmer arrived at one of ITC's hubs, his beans were weighed on a computerized weighbridge, and the weight was multiplied by ITC's published price. The farmer then received cash on delivery. ITC maintained enough cash at each hub to pay farmers immediately, and they were also reimbursed for transport costs.

The processing facility also included a soil-testing lab, where scientists offered recommendations for fertilizers or additives based on the chemical composition of a farmer's sample. The ITC scientists did not recommend a specific brand of fertilizer; freedom of choice was an important principle of the eChoupal concept.

For his role in the ITC procurement process, ITC paid the sanchalak a 0.5 percent commission on the sale of soybeans. He was, after all, effectively doing ITC's buying—buying that would otherwise have taken place at the mandi. The eChoupal system effectively turned the sanchalak into an entrepreneur, for he also earned a 2–3 percent commission on orders placed for items like herbicides, sowing seeds, fertilizers, gas lanterns, and edible oil from ITC. With the help of commissions from edible soybean oil sales, Kamal Chand Jain earned about $775 during the 2002 soybean season. "That's a good amount of money for him," said Kumar.

The Samyojak

But what of the middlemen, the commission agents of mandi life? All of ITC's CAs were kept on with a new title: *samyojak*. In this role, former CAs were given additional money-making opportunities within the eChoupal system. The samyojak role was threefold: (1) setting up the eChoupals, (2) facilitating ITC's purchasing transactions, and (3) helping with ITC's selling transactions. The samyojak assisted ITC teams in selecting the sanchalak, acted as a liaison between villagers and ITC, and helped villagers understand the potential for the new system to be more efficient and profitable for all parties. Samyojaks also managed warehousing hubs attached to the processing facilities that stored bought soybeans, assisted in the logistics of cash disbursements to farmers, and helped facilitate transportation for farmers who could not reach the ITC processing facility on their own.

It was estimated that ITC saved $5 per ton on freight costs when farmers began taking their crops directly to the ITC processing facility. ITC reimbursed farmers from these funds for the time it took to travel to the ITC facility. Farmers, in turn, earned an average of $8 per ton more than they had under the traditional system.

In the words of ITC chairman Y. C. Deveshwar, "By creatively reorganizing the roles of traditional intermediaries who deliver critical value in tasks like logistic management at very low costs in a weak infrastructure economy like India, the eChoupal plows back a larger share of consumer price to the farmer. Besides providing an alternative marketing channel, this model engenders efficiency in the functioning of mandis through competition and serves to conserve public resources that would otherwise be needed to upgrade the mandi infrastructure to handle higher volumes of agri output."

Principles of the eChoupal

The eChoupal depended strongly on trust. The Web site was simply a medium for human interaction. Farmers were not obligated to sell to ITC once they used the Web site. ITC did not ask for commitment; the farmer was free to do as he wished. In fact, a farmer could use the eChoupal's facilities, absorb all the information, and still choose to take his crop to the mandi.

ITC's bet was that once given these tools, farmers would realize on their own that selling directly to ITC was the best alternative to the mandi. "We feel that this is how we can win people in the long run, by giving them the tools. Communication and information are developing; mobile phones are here, the Internet is here; we must use these things for education, and let there be no question of hiding information," explained Rajnikant Rai, vice president of trading in ITC's International Business Division (IBD). "We let the farmers understand and let them decide who is best in an open, competitive market scenario. They are the judges." To ensure the sanchalak's integrity, he took an oath before the entire village, when he received the computer equipment, to uphold ITC's high standards not to use the computer for wrongful purposes and to maintain the ethics, image, and concept that ITC had created through the soyachoupal.com site. The ITC logo was also painted on the front of the sanchalak's home, identifying the sanchalak as a liaison of ITC. If a sanchalak were to act dishonestly, it would create an uproar in the village, and ITC would be able to take immediate action. Because the role was viewed as an honor, nearly all sanchalaks treated their duties with the utmost pride and seriousness. In fact, since the eChoupal's inception, not one of the three thousand computers deployed has been lost, stolen, or vandalized.

ITC too realized important benefits by buying directly from farmers. ITC had more control over the quality of the product it sourced: direct contact with farmers enabled knowledge sharing about sowing, irrigation, and harvesting. Higher-quality produce, in turn, enabled more competitive pricing in the international market.

Hunting for Growth in Other Commodities

Soon after the soybean eChoupal started showing promise, ITC set up pilot eChoupals in three other crops in regions of India that differed as much as possible: coffee in Karnataka, seafood in Andhra Pradesh, and wheat in Uttar Pradesh. These pilot projects, which were expected to help the company scale up to a national level, shared a common management approach: first, pilot test the concept in a small number of villages; make changes based on the lessons of the pilot phase and validate them in a larger number of villages; and grow the project to reach as many villages as possible and saturate the region. ITC called this approach "Roll Out, Fix It, Scale Up."

As in the case of soybeans, margins could be generated in other commodities by eliminating non-value-added activities between the farm and the factory. Sivakumar wondered, however, if such savings were sustainable over time, benchmarked as they were against an inefficient market. He reasoned that ITC could generate value via three other primary mechanisms: traceability (accountability for the quality of the product vis-à-vis its source), matching farmer production to consumer demand, and facilitation of an electronic marketplace.

The three new eChoupal models were essentially a validation of these mechanisms. With seafood, traceability presented an opportunity for ITC to generate value (and additional revenue) through the eChoupal. If ITC was able to tell customers where a given commodity came from and how it was produced (with or without antibiotics), significant gains would be possible. By controlling the source, ITC could guarantee the safety of the product and thus receive higher prices.

The wheat market was similar. Wheat varies greatly in chemical composition and physical appearance; through the eChoupal, farmers learned to recognize the physical characteristics that represented certain chemical compositions, such as gluten, protein, and starch content. The ability to analyze the crop before purchase, at the farm level, and then to purchase and store it by chemical-composition category, represented an opportunity for cost savings; it was expensive to separate wheat after purchase. The farmer too benefited from this education: by identifying his high- and low-quality wheat, he could price different varieties appropriately. He could command a higher price for high-quality wheat and offer low-quality wheat at a reasonable price for animal feed. He no longer had to charge one low price for an amalgam of wheat of disparate quality.

Coffee presented a different challenge. Coffee is an estate crop, grown by a large number of small-scale farmers. ITC had a deep knowledge of coffee farm practices; much research had already been done on the industry. The price volatility of coffee was high; variance from the base price could reach 40 percent (compared with 20 percent volatility in the soybean market), and buyers would routinely renege on contracts if prices shifted beyond tolerance. Market participants were savvy speculators. An agent was of paramount importance in coffee transactions, and effective price discovery was often the critical part of a deal. By introducing an electronic-trading platform, called Tradersnet, ITC improved real-time price discovery by hosting anonymous trades and letting the prevailing selling prices be known. Information sharing carried over to ITC's customers as well. "The task of adapting the eChoupal concept for different crops and regions continues to test ITC's entrepreneurial capabilities," says Chairman Deveshwar.

eChoupal as a Marketing Channel

As Sivakumar pondered the potential for eChoupal in each of the four commodities, he also contemplated the long-term future of a wired rural India: might marketing and distribution to the 60 percent of India's workforce who live in rural areas be the real growth engine for ITC? ITC's vision for marketing via the eChoupal had three main features: superior product and functional benefits, process benefits (simplified transactions between buyer and seller), and relationship benefits (farmers' willingness to reveal their purchasing behavior). ITC believed that certain input items could be made available to farmers through the eChoupal, thus increasing the value of the farmer's product and generating additional revenue for ITC. Deveshwar called this philosophy "a commitment beyond the market."

Fertilizers

Though Indian farmers spent an average of $5.7 billion annually on urea, diammonium phosphate (DAP), and muriate of potash (MOP), they could not easily access the fertilizers they needed. Thirty-five percent of DAP and 100 percent of MOP were imported. Furthermore, fertilizers were unavailable at many rural markets because of fragmented or nonexistent distribution channels.

Agrichemicals

Indian farmers also spent $774.5 million per year on insecticides, herbicides, and fungicides. The agrichemical market was highly fragmented among multinational corporations such as DuPont, Novartis, and Cyanamid. New chemicals were introduced frequently, but their life cycles in the market were only two or three years; given the short product cycle, big companies needed immediate market access. Farmers too suffered when they could not access these products: the high cost of labor made herbicides preferable to weeding.

Seeds

Only 4 percent of Indian farms used commercial seed; government-promoted seed corporations made seeds available though cooperatives. Multinational companies had entered the market with better-quality material, but it could take as long as three years for new seed varieties to become available to rural farmers.

Insurance

Indians were collectively paying $11 billion in yearly life-insurance premiums, and the market was expected to reach $33 billion by 2010.[4] Life Insurance Corporation (LIC) of India, a government-run insurance provider, derived 16 percent of its portfolio from rural markets by 2003. Meanwhile, new companies were seeking to compete with LIC in rural India. But rural markets remained largely untapped because of a lack of trustworthy intermediaries. ITC believed that it could create a relationship of trust and help farmers understand the rules and benefits of insurance plans. ITC envisioned offering the eChoupal infrastructure to LIC agents for a fee or setting up its own insurance brokerage company. An opportunity also existed to sell fire, marine, motor, and workmen's compensation insurance. Insurers had been biased toward larger accounts, leaving less prosperous farmers unable to participate. Insurers lacked quality data on the risks and parameters of farm life and were hesitant to insure rural customers. With ITC as a liaison, however, data on rural farmers could be delivered to insurance companies, demystifying and opening up the rural market.

Credit

A national survey in 2001 had revealed that Indians saved about 30 percent of their annual incomes, though not through financial institutions. Farmers avoided banks because they lacked a customer-friendly approach and because savings accounts were often linked to crop loans: if a farmer saved at the same bank he had borrowed from, the bank could demand that he use his savings to pay back the loan. Many farmers would prefer to defer the loan and save their cash at home, unbeknownst to the bank. ITC believed that a system of trust promoted by the sanchalak would facilitate financial transactions. It could channel rural farmers toward mutual funds and earn a commission from banks on farmers' investments, using the technology of the eChoupal.

Conclusion

ITC's eChoupal initiative transformed the downstream supply chain for soybeans and also provided a wide range of marketing and purchasing options to reach previously isolated rural communities. In 2003, for example, the products ITC sold to farmers included motorcycles and DVD players. A skeptical observer might suggest that the primary motive for ITC's wiring of the farms was its potential profitability. Sivakumar is quick to point out that the initiative had an equally important set of social goals: increasing the competitiveness of the Indian farmer, minimizing the adverse effects of cheating on those farmers, and fostering a sense of community among a dispersed population of people who share similar challenges. ITC delivered growth to its IBD business unit; at the same time, it improved the quality of its source materials, established direct contact with its suppliers (and, increasingly, customers), and—in essence—built a platform for access to the rural community. The goals of profitability and social benefit were congruent.

What made this effort successful when so many initiatives to exploit the Internet in developing countries have been disappointing? A sample of one cannot deliver a definitive answer, but the principles to which ITC adhered may help to explain the initial and continuing success of the initiative.

Build on Existing Trust

ITC took pains to ensure that all its actions would enhance existing mutual trust between ITC and the farming community. This trust relationship assuaged farmers' fear that ITC would cheat them and instilled confidence in the promise of a new and unfamiliar technology.

Grow Incrementally

The system was set up to be extended by one village at a time. This model allowed ITC to learn with each step and to make adjustments as it learned, thus avoiding many of the pitfalls of a "big bang" implementation.

Offer Choice

Nothing was mandatory. Farmers were free to continue to use the traditional system, and even to free ride by using the soyachoupal.com Web site to glean information while continuing to sell at the mandi. ITC thus had a motive to continue to offer farmers better selling options, and not to rely on "lock-in" to retain farmers' participation.

Provide Clear Value at Each Step

Rather than merely promising value after a long implementation phase, ITC began to deliver value as soon as farmers became connected. Even the most cursorily trained sanchalaks could access the weather page immediately; later they progressed to more complex activities like sales transactions. The immediate benefit was self-evident, encouraging the village to become invested in the new system and excited about its potential.

Build on Existing Social Structures and Ways of Working

Use of the computer was introduced as a "natural" extension of farmers' traditional practices: the eChoupal built on the existing institution of the choupal. Similarities between existing ways of working and the Internet-enabled approach reduced the magnitude of the conceptual leap the farmers had to make and of their perceived risk. ITC wanted to work with the existing cultural infrastructure in the villages rather than owning or controlling the entire value chain from top to bottom.

Avoid Creating Losers

ITC's approach did not simply freeze out the middlemen. Indeed, the company took great care to ensure that the commission agent's role was enhanced so that he could create more value for himself and for the channel as a whole. CAs could reap some margin from sales to farmers, and they also acted as ITC's eyes and ears in the mandis.

Keep It Simple

ITC worked to keep the systems in the villages as simple as possible. Through experimentation, the company determined the bare-bones requirements for connectivity, power, and the PC itself. This approach kept costs down and also enhanced reliability.

Adherence to these principles enabled ITC to overcome obstacles that might have caused its initiative to fail or fade: entrenched practices, farmers' lack of understanding of the new model, middlemen's fears, illiteracy, suspicion of being cheated in a new way, and even existing legislation. Probably the most important feature of the system was that it made everyone involved better off. In industrialized countries, efforts to reengineer supply chains often fail because of disagreements about how to share the "pie" of benefits that results. In the parts of India affected by the eChoupal, however, the supply chain inefficiencies and the benefits reaped by removing them were so vast that all parties accrued significant gains. The fledgling marketing channel created novel business opportunities for ITC and others. Farmers had unprecedented access to goods and services. This clever implementation of computer technology and communications bandwidth, the eChoupal initiative, has facilitated economic growth and improved the well-being of millions of the world's poorest people.

Notes

1. Farmers typically raised more than one type of crop to take advantage of the varying seasons. The soybean season, for example, was from June to September. From October to May, most soybean farmers grew wheat.

2. Very Small Aperture Terminal. Traditionally, VSATs had a few disadvantages: VSAT bandwidth was not very high and was restricted to a few hundred kilobits per second. There was also a certain amount of latency (the time between initiating a request for data and the beginning of the actual data transfer) between nodes. But these limitations have been overcome to a large extent due to advancement in technology. VSAT providers in India offered up to 52.5 Mbps outroute (from hub to VSAT) and 307.2 Kbps inroute (from VSAT to hub) data rates, with 270 millisecond latency (*Network Magazine* India).

3. The company believed it would be able to recover the cost and make a profit within three years of the initial eChoupal rollout.

4. Company information.

Capturing the Value of Wireless Broadband

9

i-mode

Value Chain Strategy in the Wireless Ecosystem

Takeshi Natsuno

N EARLY THREE-FOURTHS of Japan's population, from school-age children to the elderly, own mobile phones. The number of cell phone users in Japan increased roughly ninefold between 1996 and 2002, from about 8 million to 78 million users.[1] A significant factor in this massive adoption of mobile phones was i-mode, a revolutionary service that allowed users to access information from the Internet, use e-mail, take and send digital photos, conduct e-commerce and financial transactions, and play games on their mobile phones.

NTT DoCoMo, a leading mobile telecommunications company, launched i-mode in Japan in early 1999. Within six months of launching, there were 1 million i-mode subscribers; just eighteen months later, the subscriber base exceeded 10 million. As of early 2004, there were more than 40 million active users, two thousand three hundred vendors offering over four thousand sites, and seventy-three thousand voluntary Web sites registered in a search engine. How did DoCoMo and i-mode radically change the role of the mobile phone and achieve such rapid success?

Internet Revolution in Japan

Following regulatory liberalization of the cell phone market in Japan in 1994, competition was fierce, and cell phone usage and wireless coverage exploded. By early 1999, the penetration rate of wireless had reached 37.7 percent.[2] At the time, Japan's cellular market represented a variety of technological standards. DoCoMo had developed the country's first nationwide network using a second-generation technology called Personal Digital Cellular (PDC), whose structure resembled American TDMA (Time Division Multiple Access); rapid growth in the number of cellular subscribers within the limited spectrum caused congestion and reduced quality of service in parts of metropolitan Tokyo at peak periods. Another company, DDI/IDO (the precursor to KDDI Corporation), operated both PDC and cdmaOne (Code Division Multiple Access) systems in the 800 MHz band and PHS (Personal Handyphone System) in the 1,900 MHz band.

Competition and further deregulation promoted consolidation of the cell phone market, and by 2000 three major players remained: NTT DoCoMo, KDDI, and J-Phone.[3] That year the number of wireless phone subscribers surpassed the number of fixed-line subscribers, and DoCoMo had a 57 percent market share. While the cellular market was booming, however, Japan's Internet penetration rate had barely surpassed 10 percent of its population in 1998.[4] By comparison, 14 percent of North Americans and 12 percent of western Europeans were online.[5] The reasons for this low usage were multiple: lack of interest, low computer penetration in Japan, and the high incremental costs of local phone calls (inhibiting dial-up Internet access). However, Japanese consumers had a well-known fondness for personal electronic devices, the same appetite that fed the growing migration to cellular phones; coupled with low Internet usage, this propensity presented DoCoMo with an enormous untapped opportunity to introduce the Japanese to the addictive power of the Internet.

I-mode's Operating Strategy

I-mode was born out of a sense of crisis at DoCoMo: it was obvious that the mobile phone subscriber growth rate could not be sustained. Thus, rather than engage in a battle over the diminishing number of new phone subscribers, the company could create a new market—data communications. Revenues could continue to grow even if the number of subscribers did not, because revenue would flow from the new data communications services and not just from voice services. Increasing subscribers' mobile phone usage would require a pioneering service that would generate data traffic. This new service was i-mode.

Since i-mode was going to be radically different from existing voice communication services, it was critical to the development, introduction, and ongoing management of i-mode that DoCoMo adopt a nontelecommunications way of thinking about the business. From the outset, the i-mode project team thought of itself as operating in the Internet space rather than the telecommunications industry. Seven key strategic facets differentiated i-mode from traditional telecommunications services:

- De facto standards

- Contentcentric business model

- Consumer-oriented marketing

- Digital content market

- Value chain

- Ecosystem

- Seamless and continuous evolution

De Facto Standards

I-mode designers made several decisions that differentiated the technology from that of competing wireless services and ensured i-mode's popularity with consumers. Traditionally, telecommunications companies developed and marketed products in a voice communication environment consisting of the provider of the service and the subscribers. This environment allowed providers to create their own standards, including specifications for handsets and networks. The introduction of data communication, however, added complexity and new constituents to the mix, including content/service providers. Convinced that "standardization in a telecom way" would discourage service and content providers' participation in i-mode, DoCoMo elected instead to adopt or license established technologies. This decision provided an incentive for technology developers to continue to improve their products and for content developers to build new applications and services utilizing these readily accessible technologies.

The second critical design decision concerned i-mode's system network. Because i-mode was conceived at a time when DoCoMo's cellular network faced congestion problems due to the popularity of voice services, an additional data network had to be built for a wireless web to be feasible. DoCoMo decided to use the existing packet communications service network and combine it with the existing voice transmission PDC system. (Packets are the application data units sent across the network.) The packet network provided "always on" connectivity to the Internet, allowing users to receive e-mail and customized news updates seamlessly throughout the day.

The packet network infrastructure has allowed for a unique packet-usage pricing structure. Subscribers pay a monthly subscription fee, plus a per-packet transmission charge to access content from premium i-mode sites. (There is no per-packet charge for nonpremium sites.) Packet rates were based on the volume of data received and sent, rather than time online; this approach differed from the traditional model of charging users for the time they spend logged in to a service, whether or not they were active. The packet pricing structure was possible only because the parallel data network allows mobile phones to transfer data without taking up space on the voice network.

Contentcentric Business Model

As the number of i-mode subscribers increased, a corollary increase was anticipated in the number of applications developed for mobile phones. An expanding selection of content offerings would create a competitive environment motivating developers to continue to improve the quality of their content. The improving quantity and quality of applications would in turn attract new users to i-mode and increase usage by existing subscribers. As usage rates rise, the cycle continues: the mobile phone content market becomes increasingly attractive to Internet content providers, so they migrate services over, helping to increase the subscriber base and subscriber usage rates, which feeds back into the cycle. (See figure 9-1.)

To maintain this "positive feedback" loop—more customers attract better content, attracting even more customers, ad infinitum—the business model focused on attracting content providers. The three key aspects of the business model that best supported content providers and in turn generated the most positive feedback from subscribers were identified as technology, service design, and business model.

FIGURE 9-1

Seamless and continuous evolution

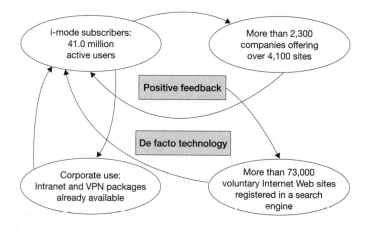

Source: Adapted from "Value Chain Strategy in the Wireless Eco-System," presentation by Takeshi Natsuno at "The Bandwidth Explosion," HBS colloquium, April 2003.

Technology

In keeping with DoCoMo's Internet-focused perspective and decision to use de facto technology, technology is selected that best meets the needs of content providers and that arises naturally from the Internet space. The latter criterion is a significant differentiating factor for i-mode. Legacy telecom, perhaps feeling threatened by Internet providers, developed technologies specific to the wireless industry, such as Wireless Application Protocol (WAP). This approach has been unsuccessful, largely because its focus has been to make the network more efficient rather than to support the content part of the business.

The rapid pace at which content sites have become available to i-mode subscribers is largely attributable to DoCoMo's use of Internet technologies. Because Internet content providers could adapt their Internet-based applications to the mobile handset and wireless environment, rather than having to create applications from scratch using new and unproven technologies, they were able to convert their content quickly. In mid-2000, i-mode boasted over six hundred information providers offering content through DoCoMo's i-mode menu, and over twenty thousand additional "autonomous" information providers. By April 2003, over two thousand three hundred companies offered over three thousand four hundred sites. The technology currently used in i-mode service applications and handsets includes:

- i-mode HTML (iHTML): a subset of computer-based HTML programming language for developing dynamic Internet content

- Musical Instrument Digital Interface (MIDI): a protocol for recording and playing back music

- Java: a Sun Microsystems programming language

Service Design and Business Model

Like technology selection, i-mode's business model and service design (including handset specifications) were intended to be attractive to content providers, not just to telecom operators or wireless vendors. The service design and business model also needed to support DoCoMo's focus on traffic volume—both the number of users and packet transmission volume. The traffic focus played an important role in two aspects of i-mode's business model.

The first is its *small-payments system*. DoCoMo provided a billing and collection platform for content providers of i-mode services. By 2003, the i-mode center processed seventy-five thousand data transmissions per second, or about 800 million transactions per day, thus achieving sufficient economy of scale and scope to make fee-based online delivery of information a profitable business. A typical i-mode premium-service provider received up to three hundred yen a month per subscriber of their service and paid 9 percent of this to DoCoMo.[6] (Some U.S. and European vendors, by contrast, collected a 40–50 percent commission.) This small-payments system provided an incentive for content providers to improve their services. It also allowed DoCoMo to be selective about what content was available on i-mode and where, and ensured that subscribers had access to services that provided them with sufficient value for their money. DoCoMo's billing service was attractive to subscribers as well. By consolidating information fees in one place, the billing service made it easy for customers to buy the content without having to enter credit card information or receive multiple bills.

Secondly, DoCoMo did not receive any commissions for e-commerce conducted over i-mode. Consumers conducting PC-based e-commerce, such as purchasing airline tickets, did not incur additional charges to cover commissions. Nor did i-mode receive a commission from the service provider; this additional cost would be passed on to consumers, making the transaction more expensive over i-mode and thus making a PC-based purchase more appealing. As of 2003, 25 percent of airline e-tickets sold in Japan were sold via i-mode, supporting the content providers and ensuring robust traffic volume.

In the telecommunications industry, traditionally, as a carrier's subscriber base increases, average packet usage per subscriber decreases. Early adopters of any new technology, product, or service are eager to use the new service/product and are typically high-volume users. Subsequent subscribers tend to be less enthusiastic users, thus decreasing average usage volume. But DoCoMo has not experienced this pattern of decreasing activity with i-mode. Instead, i-mode's average daily packet usage has remained consistent over time, and with each new technological offering has been accompanied by a temporary but dramatic packet usage increase. For example, Java-enabled handsets, which allow subscribers to download complex applications, brought about an increase in packet usage. In late 2002, the average daily packet usage of non-Java handsets, Java handsets, and enhanced Java handsets was two hundred, three hundred, and six hundred packets, respectively. (See figure 9-2.)

The increased usage of voice and data communications via i-mode was also reflected in DoCoMo's revenue. In 1998, prior to the launch of i-mode, DoCoMo's annual packet communications revenue (data transmission) was 200 million yen ($1.61 million). In 1999, after twelve months of i-mode revenue contributions, DoCoMo's packet communications revenue surged to over 38 billion yen. With the introduction of each new i-mode phone or enhanced i-mode service, there would be a temporary spike in usage equating to an increase in the average revenue per user (ARPU). Over time, i-mode revenue accounted for an increasing percentage of the total ARPU, up to 20 percent by the end of 2003. Packet usage has grown so dramatically, due to the increased number and complexity of applications and increased overall usage by subscribers, that DoCoMo continually asks content providers to design their sites and applications to optimize the application size.

FIGURE 9-2

Packet-rate usage boosted by Java

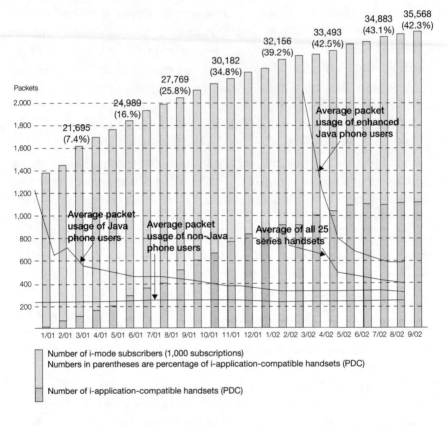

Source: Adapted from "Value Chain Strategy in the Wireless Eco-System," presentation by Takeshi Natsuno at "The Bandwidth Explosion," HBS colloquium, April 2003.

Consumer-Oriented Marketing

People have been using the telephone for voice communication since its invention in 1876. Throughout the decades, telecommunications providers had traditionally marketed the technological features and improvements to their product or service when selling to consumers. As DoCoMo expanded beyond voice communications, it required that users change their behavior and use their mobile phones to conduct data transactions to utilize the full spectrum of i-mode services. This in turn required that DoCoMo's marketing reach an array of potential subscribers including computer users and nonusers and mobile phone users and nonusers. The challenge was to reach people with varying levels of technology knowledge and experience in a way that would communicate clearly to them the advantages of i-mode. Thus, in its marketing and advertising materials, DoCoMo emphasized the benefits of having a mobile phone—the content, services, and applications—and avoided technical jargon like Java, Internet browser, SSL, and the like. This consumer-oriented marketing has proven successful even in reaching the traditional nonsubscriber base (for instance, the elderly).

Digital Content Market

During initial development, it was determined that content available via i-mode had to meet four criteria: freshness, depth, continuity, and clear benefit to the subscriber. Each site has to have new and updated content on a regular basis; the information must be concise, given that it will be displayed on a small screen; its continuity must be evident so that users will access the site on a regular basis; and subscribers should find the site useful, fun, and cool.

The current content portfolio contains e-commerce sites (bookstores, banks), information (weather, maps), databases (dictionary, train routes), and entertainment (services offering standby screen images, ringtones, and online games). The size of the digital content market (subscriber fees for premium content) on i-mode continues to expand, reaching more than $1 billion in fiscal year 2002. The total market for content rose from 314 units of content available to subscribers in 1999 to over 9,900 units of content in 2002. The percentage of users who paid for at least some content also rose dramatically over this same period, from 34 percent in 1999 to over 50 percent by the end of 2002. (See figure 9-3.)

The i-mode Value Chain

From the outset, the i-mode project team created the service in keeping with a specific and thorough vision, the *value chain*. The value chain continues to exemplify the concept that i-mode does not consist of handsets, content, or a network, but the totality of seven critical components, each of which contributes to the i-mode value chain. The i-mode value chain includes content, marketing, business model, server, network, handset, and user.

FIGURE 9-3

Size of the digital content market

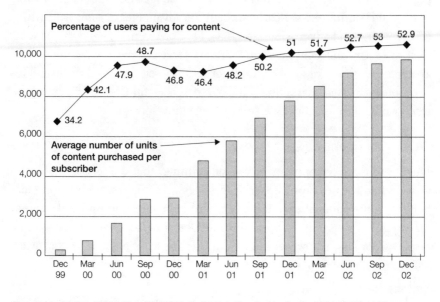

Source: Adapted from "Value Chain Strategy in the Wireless Eco-System," presentation by Takeshi Natsuno at "The Bandwidth Explosion," HBS colloquium, April 2003.

DoCoMo's strategy of forming alliances with various constituents within the value chain and ensuring that i-mode provides value to all participants in return continues. Current alliance partners include phone manufacturers, content providers, and technology developers. (See table 9-1.) Each alliance needs to be a symbiotic *win-win* relationship, generating value for both DoCoMo and the alliance partner. The three categories of alliance partnerships include *technology alliances* that promote the development of mobile phones and mobile phone services; *content alliances* that promote the development of portals operated by DoCoMo; and *platform alliances* that expand the range of times, places, and occasions hospitable to mobile phones. Over time, technology and content alliances have evolved vertically, while platform alliances increase the convenience and utility of i-mode horizontally by creating links with other platforms.

TABLE 9-1

I-mode value chain alliances

		INITIAL VALUE CHAIN ALLIANCES
1999	March	Memorandum of intent with Sun Microsystems concerning co-operation in use of Java technology
2000	March	Investment in Playstation.co.jp
		Investment in Web-based banker Japan Net Bank, Limited
	April	Investment in online payment service Payment First
	June	Establishment of D2 Communications joint venture with Dentsu Inc.
	August	Memorandum of intent to cooperate with Sony Computer Entertainment Inc. in technology development
	September	Contract with America Online (AOL) to develop and provide new Internet services
	October	Establishment of i-Convenience Inc., a joint venture with Lawson Inc., Matsushita, and Mitsubishi Corporation

Source: Takeshi Natsuno, *i-mode Strategy* (New York: John Wiley & Sons, 2003), 70.

Example: A Critical Technology Alliance

In 1997, two months before the introduction of i-mode, DoCoMo approached Sun Microsystems regarding embedding its Java technology in i-mode phones, having identified Java as a de facto Internet content technology standard. This conversation occurred before any programs were developed or handsets were available to handle Java-based applications. Two years later, the first i-mode handset embedded with Java technology was launched. As DoCoMo expected—having selected a Java technology because it supports content developers and because a number of PC-based applications were already in use—it did not take long for developers to adapt their applications to i-mode phones. The marketing of the first Java handset did not mention the technology; it focused on the application's usability. Nevertheless, the success of the positive-feedback strategy model (technology, business model, and consumer-oriented marketing) is such that there are now 17.4 million i-mode subscribers using Java on their small handheld mobile phones; even people who do not consider themselves technology-savvy are downloading Java-based programs (such as games like Sim City) —a theoretically complex process—every day.

The i-mode Ecosystem

DoCoMo encouraged the members of the value chain to view themselves as a community of interactive constituents working together as a unit or an ecosystem. For an ecosystem to remain viable and healthy, a balance must be maintained such that no single member or segment of the system becomes dominant. Within the i-mode ecosystem, this principle called for an appropriate balance among the seven segments of the value chain and DoCoMo itself. (See figure 9-4.) To remain functional, i-mode's ecosystem must provide incentives and value creation for all participants. (See figure 9-5.) Thus, while i-mode's strategy emphasized meeting the needs of the content providers, the same strategy benefits phone manufacturers, in that mobile communications services and handset technology are tightly linked: when new services are made available, mobile phones capable of utilizing the new functionalities are needed. This synchronous develop-

FIGURE 9-4

I-mode's value chain contentcentric coordination

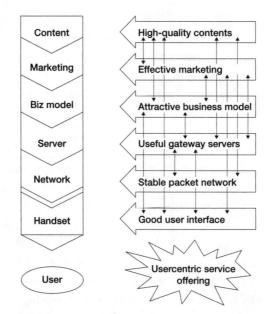

Source: Adapted from "Value Chain Strategy in the Wireless Eco-System," presentation by Takeshi Natsuno at "The Bandwidth Explosion," HBS colloquium, April 2003.

FIGURE 9-5

The i-mode ecosystem

No player or segment can dominate

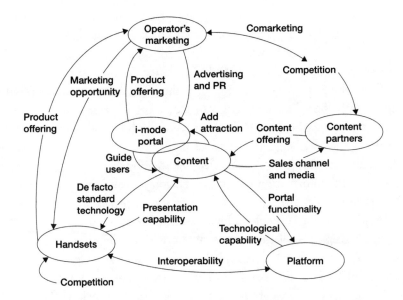

Source: Adapted from "Value Chain Strategy in the Wireless Eco-System," presentation by Takeshi Natsuno at "The Bandwidth Explosion," HBS colloquium, April 2003.

ment of services and hardware was evident in the evolution of i-mode phones.

Example: The Evolution of i-mode Phones

One of DoCoMo's initial technology alliances was with phone manufacturers. From the beginning, the strategy was to promote mass customization of phones—to create an open platform that enabled users to customize a phone by selecting images and applications that fit their personal interests. Thus, it was imperative that the evolution of the phone device be synchronized with the introduction and development of i-mode services. This simultaneous development created demand among users who wanted the new services, new phones, or both.

In early 1999, in conjunction with the launch of the i-mode service, DoCoMo introduced its 501i-series phones, which added packet data transmission and an HTML browser to the conventional voice features of mobile phones, making it possible to browse the Web and to send and receive e-mail. The 502i series, introduced later that year, enabled users to download ringtone melodies by adding MIDI sound-processing features. By the second half of 2000, color displays became a standard feature on all i-mode phones. The 503i series, launched in late 2000, was equipped for Java programming and thus for an abundance of new applications.

From the 501i to the 502i and then the 503i series, i-mode handset development adhered to the strategy of increasing programming openness in support of increasing personalization. With each new phone series, for example, the subscriber gained greater ability to customize the display and phone functionality. Users could select the standby screen (a screen saver–like function), the information they wanted displayed, and the ringtone melody. The radical breakthrough was the 503i series, provision of space on the phone's memory to download Java-based software applications, a first step in the convergence of the mobile phone with a computer. Today, i-mode phones featuring many more high-level capabilities are offered by such vendors as NEC, Sony Ericsson, Panasonic, Mitsubishi, and Fujitsu.

Technology features of i-mode 505i series handsets include the following:

- Java JAR 30K + 100K Scratchpad with HTTP and HTTPS connectivity (enabling more data to be downloaded at one time)

- Java application standby mode (screen saver–like function)

- End-to-end Secure Socket Layer (SSL) for high-level transaction security

- TFT/TFD colored LCD (65K colors) display screen

- 28.8 Kbps packet-network speed (PDC-P)

- Embedded camera (up to 1.3 megapixels)

- IrMC (Infrared Mobile Communications) embedded (can be used for basic operation of electronic devices such as a TV or VCR)

- Flash (for rich content applications with highly fluid animation)

- QVGA LCD (superior display for vivid color)

- Memory stick or Secure Digital (SD) memory capability (for data storage and data exchange with other similarly equipped devices)

- Fingerprint authentication

Seamless and Continuous Evolution

The final facet of DoCoMo's Internet-perspective strategy was the seamless and continuous evolution of i-mode services. It continues to be critical to synchronize the pace of development/improvement among the various components of the i-mode value chain. For example, the evolution of the handset must be synchronized with that of the applications and technology. And more importantly, DoCoMo must always be cognizant of the evolution of the user's experience and state of knowledge. Using a positive-feedback strategy (technology, business model, marketing), DoCoMo's i-mode pursues the seamless and continuous evolution of the handsets, network, content, and user experience.

The Future and 3G

In October 2001, DoCoMo launched FOMA (Freedom of Mobile Multimedia Access), the world's first fully commercialized 3G mobile service based upon IMT-2000-compliant Wideband Code Division Multiple Access (W-CDMA). By March 2004, coverage had extended to 99 percent of the populated areas of Japan.

DoCoMo, like other telecommunications companies around the world, had been working on commercialization of 3G mobile phone technology for a number of years. Before introducing FOMA, however, it was necessary to have success in 2G phones, services, and applications: the operating principle was that high-quality, relevant, and useful content must be in place before migrating applications to 3G. Following successful experiments on high-speed data transmissions using W-CDMA in 1996, DoCoMo began actively promoting W-CDMA as a global standard while refining its related technologies. These efforts led to the decision by the International Telecommunication Union (ITU) in May 2000 to make W-CDMA a global standard. Through its active involvement and initiative, DoCoMo has gained a significant competitive advantage.

Completely unlike 1G and 2G networks, DoCoMo's 3G network utilizes ATM technology that manages packet switching and circuit switching on the same network node, enabling various traffic types. Asymmetric communications with differing characteristics for uplink and downlink are also supported. Terminals have evolved to handle the increasing versatility of 3G technologies.

FOMA terminals are nearly as compact and lightweight as conventional mobile communications terminals, yet offer speeds of up to 64 Kbps of data communications and packet transmissions with reception rates of up to 384 Kbps. Various models allow the transmission and display of still and moving images, e-mail attached image and movie files, and video distribution. Third-generation technology FOMA videophones are enabled to handle international videophone calls and 64 Kbps transmissions to the United Kingdom and between Hong Kong and Japan. All models are compatible with PCs and PDAs and offer the ability to download software and access i-mode services.

I-mode service has become even more advanced with the use of FOMA 3G technologies. FOMA's high-speed packet transmission makes i-mode service significantly faster and able to handle greater volumes of data: e-mail messages of up to ten thousand characters, the ability to attach files of melodies and still images, and an increased data capacity of up to 200 KB.

In May 2004, DoCoMo launched the FOMA international roaming-in service in Japan. This service enables subscribers of foreign mobile phone operators that are part of an international roaming alliance with DoCoMo to make and receive calls using the FOMA's 3G networks in Japan.[7] (See figure 9-6.)

By adopting and adapting an Internet mind-set (with content and consumer marketing among the critical components) and a continued emphasis on the interdependency of the value chain, DoCoMo has achieved industry-leading results. Maintaining this perspective, DoCoMo will continue to build on its 3G network. In addition to introducing sophisticated new terminal functions and expanding its service area, future plans include the reduction of terminal weight to less than 100 g and the extension of terminal battery life to more than three hundred hours. DoCoMo's record of extraordinary innovation and market success has come from pursuing a vision of a twenty-first-century wireless service provider, by abandoning the traditional telecom way of thinking and focusing on an Internet way of thinking.

FIGURE 9-6

FOMA evolution

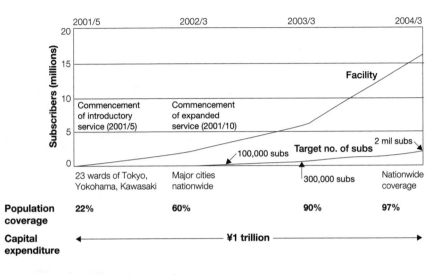

Population coverage	22%	60%	90%	97%

Capital expenditure ←———————— ¥1 trillion ————————→

Source: Adapted from "Value Chain Strategy in the Wireless Eco-System," presentation by Takeshi Natsuno at "The Bandwidth Explosion," HBS colloquium, April 2003.

Notes

1. Ministry of Public Management, Home Affairs, Posts and Telecommunications, available at http://www.stat.go.jp/english/data/handbook/c08cont.htm#cha8_1.

2. Stephen P. Bradley, "NTT DoCoMo (A): The Future of Wireless Internet?" Case 701-013 (Boston: Harvard Business School, 2002).

3. Ibid.

4. Irene Kunii, "Amazing DoCoMo," *Business Week* (International Edition), January 17, 2000.

5. InfoTech Trends, "Forecast Number of Internet Users, by Region, Worldwide," September 22, 2000, http://www.infotechtrends.com.

6. In 2004 U.S. dollars, this equates to $2.65 monthly revenue and a 23¢ commission per service subscriber.

7. For additional information on the FOMA rollout plan, see the NTT DoCoMo Web site at http://www.nttdocomo.com.

10

Wi-Fi

Complement or Substitute for 3G?

Stephen P. Bradley

E VEN BEFORE Wi-Fi's business value has been fully defined, its entry into the wireless market has revived enthusiasm for wireless broadband. Wi-Fi seized the attention of the telecommunications industry when the rollout of third-generation (3G) cellular technology was being stymied by regulatory hurdles, delays in spectrum availability, heavy capital expenditures, and worsening economic conditions. Though those problems persist, U.S. cellular carriers are continuing to assert that 3G will be deployed. In the meantime, however, they are also pursuing the promise of Wi-Fi.

Both Wi-Fi and 3G offer "always on" mobile Internet access, but the fundamental differences between the two technologies raise the question, as yet unanswered, of whether the wireless market has room for two independent services. Wi-Fi—wireless fidelity, also known as 802.11—provides wireless Internet access, typically via laptop or PDA, to multiple users simultaneously within three hundred feet of a base station or *hotspot*.[1] (Hotspots are access points at which the wireless network connects to the Internet via DSL, cable, Ethernet, or T1 line.) Designed to allow for a network of PCs and other devices to share resources, Wi-Fi is speedy, inexpensive to set up, and ready to deploy. However, it has shortcomings, including its limited ability to support the high-speed handoff needed by mobile users and its potential security risk. Third-generation technology, on the other hand, was not originally designed for data services; it is handset-based, having evolved from a voice communications model.[2] It offers secure and highly mobile communication across a wide geographic area, along with built-in digital cameras, games, and advanced Java-based programming capabilities. It represents a migration from the circuit-switched mobile environment of 2.5G to a packet-switched environment. In packet-switched networks, rather than following a fixed route, the message is broken into packets (a piece of the message and the destination address), each of which can take a different route to the destination, where the packets are recombined into the original message. The packet-switched architecture for 3G makes for more cost-efficient network utilization, but it requires significant financial investment on the part of the carriers as it needs entirely new bandwidth. The most notable distinction between the two technologies is that Wi-Fi is truly broadband, operating at 10 megabits per second (and up to 54 megabits per second for 802.11a and g); 3G is only marginally broadband, operating at 2 megabits per second at best (and often at only 386 kilobits per second).

Cellular carriers' initial embrace of Wi-Fi has been cautious and could be characterized as essentially defensive: while reducing capital expenditures to offset the rising costs of 2.5G and 3G deployments, they have continued to debate Wi-Fi's ultimate role and value within their array of service offerings. The basic questions thus still remain to be answered: How will Wi-Fi ultimately be deployed, and by whom? What is its relationship to cellular? Will Wi-Fi be a stand-alone service or a component of a broader bundle of wireless services?

The Cellular World

The cellular telecommunications industry is highly competitive: the top six nationwide U.S. carriers accounted for more than 82 percent of the subscribers and 95 percent of the $87.6 billion service revenue generated by the industry in 2003. The industry's average revenue per user (ARPU) had been declining since 1995, reflecting heavy competition and pricing cuts. However, in 2003 ARPU stabilized as enhanced data services and increased minutes (minutes rose 35 and 30 percent, respectively, in 2002 and 2003) offset the decline in basic voice revenue. (See table 10-1.) The U.S.

TABLE 10-1

Performance of top six U.S. wireless carriers, 2002–2003

Carrier	Subscribers 2003 (2002) (in millions)	Growth in subscribers, 2002–2003 (%)	Market share (%)	Average revenue per user (ARPU) 1Q04 (1Q03) ($)	Revenue 2003 (2002) (in $billions)	Revenue growth (%)	Churn rate 4Q03 (4Q02)
Verizon Wireless	35.5 (32.5)	9.2%	25.7%	$47.98 ($47.20)	$22.5 (19.3)	16.6%	1.70 (2.10)
Cingular	24.0 (21.9)	9.5%	16.4%	$48.76 ($50.65)	$15.5 (14.7)	5.4%	2.8 (2.7)
AT&T Wireless	21.9 (20.9)	4.7%	14.9%	$57.18 ($59.41)	$15.7 (15.6)	1.0%	3.3 (2.4)
Sprint PCS	20.3 (14.8)	37.2%	13.9%	$63.46 ($60.10)	$12.7 (12.1)	5.0%	2.7 (3.5)
T-Mobile	13.1 (9.9)	32.3%	9.0%	$54.31 ($50.67)	$7.2 (5.0)	44.0%	2.7 (2.45)
Nextel	12.9 (10.6)	21.6%	8.8%	$70.53 ($67.88)	$9.9 (8.7)	13.88%	1.5 (1.6)
Other carriers	31.0 (36)	(14.0%)	11.2%	$54.99 ($53.63)	$4.1(1.1)	370.0%	
Total	158.7 (146.6)	14.0%	100%	$53.46 ($53.48) average all carriers	$87.6[a] (76.5)	-14.5%	2.22 (2.31) average for all

[a]Of the $87.6 billion, $3.8 billion was from roaming revenue—fees paid to a local carrier when a subscriber travels outside his or her carrier's area.

Sources: IDC, SG Cowen (March 2003), Standard & Poor's, J.P. Morgan Chase.

market penetration for wireless subscribers was more than 50 percent, reaching 158.7 million subscribers by the end of 2003 (the number of subscribers rose 17.1 percent in 2001, 9.7 percent in 2002, and 12.7 percent in 2003). (See table 10-2.) The 2003 increase has been attributed to an improving U.S. economy, better service quality, greater affordability of wireless services, advanced new handsets with cameras, and other enhanced wireless services. As the number of subscribers begins to approach saturation, the carriers are finding it harder to find new customers. Coupled with the fact that the cost of signing up a subscriber is higher than servicing an existing one, carriers have focused on their *churn rate* (the percentage of subscribers that terminate wireless services in any given month). To keep their churn rates low, carriers must offer customer plans that allow for an increasing number of minutes available and excellent network coverage backed by superior customer service.[3] To lower churn and increase ARPU, the carriers looked toward data services (in 2002 data accounted for only 1–2 percent of the average revenue per user), which required the deployment of their 2.5 and 3G networks.[4] The opportunity for growth in wireless usage will be from nonvoice traffic (e-mailing, text messaging, downloading ringtones, interactive gaming, and so forth) in the future. Although wireless carriers have been planning to upgrade their networks

TABLE 10-2

U.S. wireless industry statistics

	1996	1997	1998	1999	2000	2001	2002	2003	2004E
Total service revenue ($billion)	$23.6	$27.5	$33.1	$40.0	$52.5	$65.0	$76.5	$87.6	$99.9
Subscribers (in millions)	44.0	55.3	69.2	86.0	109.5	128.4	140.8	158.7	178.5
Subscriber growth (%)	30.4%	25.6%	25.1%	24.3%	27.2%	17.3%	9.7%	12.7%	12.2%
Cumulative capital investment ($million)	$32.6	$46.1	$60.5	$71.3	$89.6	$105.0	$126.9	$145.9	$165.6

Source: Adapted from *Standard & Poor's Industry Survey:* "Telecommunications: Wireless," May 2004.

to 3G, as the carriers assessed the high costs of deploying 3G services, spectrum allocation impediments, technical difficulties with the 3G handset, and network infrastructure readiness, many planned to leverage their 2.5G networks as short-term drivers for wireless data revenue over the next few years.[5]

Intense competition, price reductions, and unfavorable revenue projections jointly portend further consolidation among the top U.S. providers. Telecommunications already has had a lively history of mergers, particularly within the wireless segment: Verizon Wireless was created from a merger of Bell Atlantic and Vodafone AirTouch; SBC and BellSouth merged their wireless units to create Cingular Wireless; in early 2004, Cingular Wireless acquired AT&T Wireless for $41 billion, creating the largest U.S. cellular telephone company; and in late 2004 Sprint PCS announced that it would acquire Nextel in the coming year.

Although U.S. cellular carriers have not incurred punishing costs for spectrum licensing comparable to those of their European counterparts, they have had to lobby the Federal Communications Commission (FCC) vigorously to release the bandwidth that the carriers deem necessary to complete the full rollout of 3G. Much of the sought-after 3G bandwidth had previously been reserved for federal agencies like the Department of Defense (DoD). In October 2001, the federal government postponed for three years any plan to auction spectrum used by the DoD. "While the cellular industry had done well in advancing its case for transferring Pentagon spectrum to the industry, for the past year the situation was altered with the attacks on the World Trade Center and the Pentagon."[6] In July 2002, President Bush announced plans to free up 90 MHz of spectrum (45 MHz of which would come from the band used by the DoD) for commercial wireless services. The DoD has until 2008 to relocate its systems in the 1,710–1,755 MHz band to other bands, according to officials, who said that several agencies have been working on ways to satisfy the spectrum needs of both commercial and government parties.[7] In 2004, the FCC was expected to sell spectrum returned to it by NextWave Telecom (which filed for bankruptcy after buying spectrum in the late 1990s). In early 2004, however, FCC Chief of Staff Bryan Tramont noted, "As far as 90 MHz of 3G spectrum, an auction could be held late next year, but it is contingent upon Senate passage of legislation to create a fund to reimburse federal government agencies that relocate to other frequencies."[8] Until the auctions of spectrum, carriers are continuing to engage in costly competition for limited spectrum and to focus on completing the 2.5G rollout, further postponing the rollout dates for 3G.

From 2.5G to 3G

In early 2002, many players in the U.S. cellular industry announced that 2.5G would be widely available within the year and that they were on a migration path to launch 3G. (See figure 10–1.) By the end of that year, however, deployment of 2.5G remained incomplete. The transition had been stymied by delays in equipment availability, heavy capital expenditures, regulatory complications, competition among providers, and declining economic conditions. The U.S. carriers were also influenced by stories of the embattled European 3G deployment, casting a cloud of skepticism over the future of the 3G market in the United States. However, in March 2003, the top six U.S. providers announced that 40–70 percent of their net-

FIGURE 10-1

Migration path of next-generation technologies

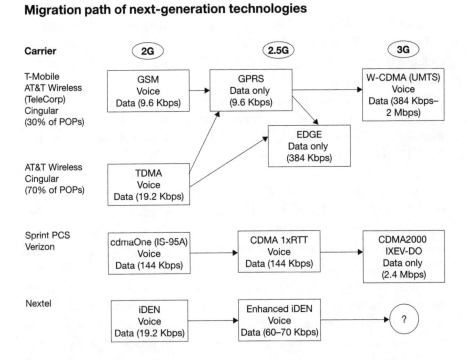

Source: Adapted from SG Cowen, "Wireless Winners Emerge," 2003.

works had been upgraded to 2.5G. Verizon Wireless and Sprint PCS offered CDMA2000 network technology, a 2.5G upgrade hailed as "3G—in essence," offering many features of 3G performance without requiring significant network change. (See table 10-3.) In June 2003, Cingular announced the launch of another pre-3G technology, EDGE, providing 3G's high data-transfer speed of 384 kilobytes per second.[9]

An important motivation for migrating to 3G is to address the capacity constraints of voice services offered on existing 2G networks. Standard & Poor's sees the proliferation of data services in the marketplace as the catalyst for wireless carriers to upgrade their network infrastructures to provide gaming, entertainment, ringtones, event marketing messaging, and location-based services. (*Location-based services* refer to a tracking system that allows the network to find a mobile user's location.)[10] For cellular carriers, the movement toward data services also allows them to build on their backroom infrastructure, provide bundled voice and data services, and retain existing customer relationships. (2.5G is adequate for most light and medium data-dependent applications, such as e-mail and SMS.

TABLE 10-3

Projected 2.5G deployment (as of March 2003)

Carrier	2.5 technology selected	Percent complete	Total upgrade capital required (in $ millions)	Estimated cost per POP (points of presence) (in $)	Actual or estimated completion date
Verizon Wireless	CDMA2000 1xRTT	100%	$1,200	$5.29	June 2003
Cingular	GSM/GPRS	50%	$2,800	$12.90	Q2/Q3 2004
AT&T Wireless	GSM/GPRS	85%	$3,045	$15.00	Q2/Q3 2003
Sprint PCS	CDMA2000 1xRTT	100%	$800	$3.79	2002
T-Mobile	GPRS	100%			
Nextel	Enhanced iDEN	na	na	na	na

Source: Adapted from SG Cowen, 2003, and Forrester IdeaByte, January 20, 2004.

For more demanding applications—even downloading an e-mail attach-ment—broadband transfer rates become highly desirable.)

The Emergence of Wi-Fi

Wi-Fi burst onto the wireless market, as we have seen, just as cellular car-riers were facing growing doubts and extended delays in their deployment of 3G. Rather than wait for the 3G network to be completed, the carriers have opted to incorporate Wi-Fi into their service models to satisfy grow-ing demand for readily-accessible, easy-to-use mobile access to the Inter-net. Many heavy users have already deemed 2G and 2.5G too slow; those people tend to search out Wi-Fi hotspots and hotels that offer in-room broadband. But Wi-Fi in turn presents its own challenges, as a brief sur-vey will illuminate.

Home Networks and Private Networks

Wi-Fi emerged in the 1990s as a grassroots phenomenon: amateurs built home networks using a combination of vendor products and do-it-yourself ingenuity. According to Peter Stanforth, chief technical officer for Mesh-Networks, "Someone with just a little technical know-how could go down to RadioShack and, for a few hundred bucks, could build his own wireless network."[11] A base station with a broadband connection and a Wi-Fi card in each device enables a homeowner to network devices throughout the house and access the Internet without laying cables.

The second-stage deployment of Wi-Fi was private networks within enterprises and organizations like colleges and universities. Such organi-zations often built out existing wired LANs with Wi-Fi, creating WLANs without needing to lay cable. Twenty percent of U.S. businesses were Wi-Fi-enabled in 2002, and large enterprises accounted for three-quarters of the $1.88 billion spent on Wi-Fi equipment that year; some observers forecasted that 95 percent of U.S. businesses would be Wi-Fi-enabled by 2005.[12] Other predictions were more cautious: by mid-2003, only 45 per-cent of U.S. enterprises had implemented wireless.

Wireless is viewed as a strategic technology, with IT managers often presenting a vision of what is possible and business managers determining how best to use the new infrastructure to achieve organizational goals. Enterprises that have deployed WLANs have the perspective that build-ing a secure, reliable, centrally managed wireless infrastructure will save them from the unappealing task of tracking down and eliminating rogue wireless networks, while opening up opportunities for new applications that would be impossible with a decentralized or ad hoc deployment.[13]

Wireless technology is increasingly being utilized in a variety of industries (retail, transportation, financial, education) and functions (manufacturing, purchasing, shipping, and customer service). By 2002, 87 percent of U.S. universities had Wi-Fi access points, and 94 percent are expected to have them by 2005.

Wireless is allowing all members of an organization's value system (suppliers, customers, and partners) increasing access to real-time data, resulting in increased productivity, streamlined processes, and improved communication and problem solving. Applications such as e-mail, SMS, calendar/scheduling, inventory management, and Internet access are the most ubiquitous. Putting a WLAN access point in a cafeteria or conference room can increase the productivity of employees who frequently move around a building or campus and carry a WLAN-equipped laptop or PDA. This also extends to employees with greater mobility, such as the sales force, retail division managers, or construction contractors—anyone who moves around client sites. With a wireless system, a doctor can access records and order tests while still with the patient, thus "... increasing the time spent with patients from 20 percent to 50 to 60 percent."[14] (Table 10-4 gives a sample of enterprise-based wireless applications.) Typically, organizations deploy a WLAN with a specific application in mind, but a hidden benefit is that after the initial phase, the infrastructure is then in place for subsequent applications.

Despite its growing implementation, security issues remain a challenge in the implementation of Wi-Fi strategies. Citing security concerns following deployment of Wi-Fi in ninety of its manufacturing plants, General Motors suspended plans to implement Wi-Fi at its corporate headquarters.[15] On average, companies are fairly evenly split between those that allow remote access to the corporate LAN and those that do not, with larger companies more likely to allow remote access compared to smaller ones. The principal reasons stated for not allowing remote access, whether from home or public locations, were lack of need and security concerns.[16] In 2003, the Wi-Fi Alliance introduced Wi-Fi protected access (WPA), which adds authentication to the existing encryption keys. This means that the WPA key changes on a regular basis instead of being static, making it more difficult for hackers to decode. Additionally, some security concerns are attributable to individual responsibility, including turning on

TABLE 10-4

Enterprise-based wireless applications

Enterprise	Use	Results
UPS (shipping)	As packages are scanned, information is transmitted instantly to the UPS network.	A 35% gain in productivity (after an Implementation cost of $120 million)
Air Canada (mechanics)	A wireless toolkit gives mechanics real-time access to maintenance orders before planes land, allowing them to prepare for incoming service requests.	Positive results from 5-month pilot (after initial $234,000 investment), though its return on investment has yet to be determined.
Dartmouth College	In response to users' request, IT is replacing its legacy network and upgrading its wireless network to bundle voice, data, and video services and deliver them cost-effectively.	Reduced capital and operating costs.
Bechtel (engineering)	Bechtel uses wireless data retrieval via PDAs to accelerate contract negotiations, match expertise, and track time sheets.	Increased productivity and more efficient operations management, saving $25,000 per month in server operations alone
Del Monte (food processing)	All sales force laptops are Wi-Fi-enabled. Del Monte is spending $100,000 to expand its WLAN from 10 access points to an estimated 150, and investigating adoption of VoIP.	The number of employees at headquarters with WLAN-connected computers and handhelds will increase from 20 to approximately 100 for less than half the cost. (Expansion of their existing paging and radio system would have cost over $250,000.)
Southern Wine & Spirits (beverage distribution)	The nation's largest alcoholic-beverage distributor uses a Wi-Fi inventory-tracking system to flag price spikes, adjust orders, and transmit real-time sales and customer data. Wireless automation of sales force (with annual revenue of $4 billion).	Transfers sales force time from paper management to cultivating client relationships. There was an increase in sales volume of 2–3% in the first year.

Sources: CIO magazine, *Broadband Business Report, BusinessWeek,* Earthweb.com, *Network Computing.*

the security feature of the wireless equipment and adhering to password and ID security policies.

Public WISPs and WLANs

Wireless Internet access to hotspots in public spaces is provided by wireless Internet service providers, or WISPs. WISPs range in size from large players with thousands of hotspots to small players with a dozen or so, typically clustered in a single locale. Public networks are of two types: commercial (typically pay-for-service) and community (typically free). Commercial hotspots seek to appeal to business customers, specifically the 27 million "laptop warriors" and "windshield warriors" (car-driving business travelers and truck drivers) willing to pay for access at airports, hotels, conference centers, train stations, truck stops, and the like. The locations of most commercial hotspots are selected to appeal to business travelers eager to access their companies' Intranet from the road. (Owners and operators of cafés, restaurants, laundromats, and hotels also offer Wi-Fi as a customer-service enhancement or direct revenue source.)

Most free public hotspots belong to community-based networks set up by volunteer groups, agencies, individuals, and some municipalities. However, some hotels, restaurants, and retail businesses also offer free networks

TABLE 10-5

Public hotspots in North America

	2001	2002	2003	2004
Airports	64	88	134	154
Hotels	444	825	4,013	8,828
Retail outlets	460	2,678	23,100	36,600
Enterprise guest areas[a]	50	75	520	1,620
Train stations and seaports	na	3	33	149
Community hotspots[b]	2	40	720	3,000
Other		23	160	460
Total	1,020	3,732	28,680	50,811

[a]Businesses that offer Wi-Fi to visiting customers, suppliers, and temporary workers.

[b]Parks, libraries, and other public areas.

Source: Adapted from "Freedom to Connect: Wireless Internet Access Is Popping Up in Unexpected Places," *Rocky Mountain News,* 19 January 2004.

with the hope that providing access will encourage customers to linger and thus purchase more of their product. There are numerous Web sites that list a directory of free hotspots located around the country.

According to Gartner Research, the number of public Wi-Fi hotspots in North America is expected to surge from fewer than thirty thousand in 2003 to almost fifty-one thousand in 2004.[17] (See table 10-5.) Meanwhile the number of U.S. WLAN users—both consumer and business—is predicted to exceed 5.26 million by 2007.

Wi-Fi Aggregators

To sign on to a fee-based hotspot, a user opens a wireless-enabled laptop or PDA and launches a Web browser. The WISP's log-in page appears. The wireless gateway identifies the user, relaxes its firewall rules appropriately, and allows the user appropriate privileges. Since there is no standard technology, a user can have trouble accessing a given WISP's configuration. This challenge is exacerbated by the possibility that a hotspot user may need to sign on and pay a fee for access to various providers as the user moves from airport, to café, to hotel. Aggregators address this issue by bundling hundreds or thousands (and eventually hundreds of thousands) of hotspots—private, public, and free—to provide users easy access with a single log-on and a single bill.

An aggregator's success is dependent on the aggregator's ability to build its network. Aggregators such as Wayport Inc., iPass Inc., and Go-Remote offer a combination of dial-up, wired Ethernet, and Wi-Fi, while Boingo resells only Wi-Fi. An aggregator typically counts access points, not separate venues, in their "number of locations." (For example, a vendor counts each access point within a large hotspot such as an airport rather than the airport hotspot as a single location.)[18] Aggregators provide access to hotspots via deployment of their own access points and roaming agreements (access to WLAN via multiple WISPs). Aggregators can also provide better long-term viability and enhanced security to their customers than the smaller individual access providers. A user who subscribes to an aggregator simply logs in and proceeds; other users enter a credit card number and sign up for a subscription or "pay as you go" session. Table 10-6 lists the largest Wi-Fi aggregators and their affiliations.

One of the earliest and perhaps best-known aggregators, Boingo, utilizes multiple existing networks rather than deploying its own infrastructure. It purchases access from hotspot operators on a wholesale basis,

TABLE 10-6

Independent Wi-Fi aggregators

Provider and number of hotspots	Partnerships
Boingo 8,000 under contract; 3,300 in service in 18 countries, 798 cities in 47 states	Roaming agreements with Wayport, Surf and Sip, NetNearU, Deep Blue Wireless, T-Mobile, and Sprint PCS Commercial access to "Hotspot in a Box" Wholesaler agreement with Telecom Italia
Wayport 600 hotels, 12 major airports, and 75 McDonald's restaurants	Roaming agreements with Verizon Wireless, AT&T Wireless, iPass, GoRemote, Boingo, Sprint PCS, and SBC Communications Technical partnerships with Intel, Sony, Dell, Sharp, and IBM to develop Wi-Fi products Hotels, airports, McDonald's restaurants
Airpath Wireless 1,500	Roaming agreements with BT Openzone, FatPort Corporation, GoRemote, iPass Sprint PCS Nondisclosed contracts with cellular and telco partners
GoRemote 7,800 hotspots in 45 countries and territories, and 1,391 hotel Ethernet locations in more than 27 countries	Wayport, Nortel, WebEx, Cisco, Nokia, Microsoft, Checkpoint, Airpath Wireless, 3Com Partnerships with ISP and telco providers (AOL, Qwest) in the U.S. and worldwide
iPass 10,000 (Wi-Fi and Ethernet broadband)	Cisco and Intel to improve roaming solutions for mobile clients General Motors to provide Wi-Fi service to 20,000 GM employees Verizon

Sources: Company Web sites.

integrates these networks, and sells access to them as a single service. In early 2004, Boingo had a network with access to more than three thousand three hundred hotspots in forty-seven U.S. states and eighteen countries. Customers pay a subscription fee ($21.95 monthly, $7.95 for forty-eight hours) for unlimited access. A user downloads Boingo's software, which allows for a search of available networks and lets the user know when he or she is within range of a high-speed service signal (or where the closest one is).

Wayport focuses on the hospitality industry and provides both wireless and wired access in hotels and airports. In May 2003, Wayport changed its business model from selling access to consumers to a wholesale model whereby it charges the venue to build, set up, and maintain a Wi-Fi hotspot while the venue or a separate service provider sells or gives away the connection.[19] That same year, they signed an agreement with McDonald's to expand its Wi-Fi access service.

However, not every Wi-Fi player has achieved success. There was mixed reaction in May 2004, when Cometa Networks, which was founded in 2002 with investments from Intel, AT&T and IBM, shut down operations two months after AT&T severed ties to the company, citing its disinterest in the Wi-Fi wholesale business model. Some in the industry cited Cometa's insufficient funding, needed to support its original plan for twenty thousand hotspots, as the cause of its failure. Others pointed to the inherent power of the founders and the challenges independents and other aggregators encountered in working with them. As Sky Dayton said in revealing that Boingo had attempted to strike a roaming agreement with Cometa, "Even though their network wasn't much more than a promise, they were acting as if they were already the market leader."[20]

Despite the rapid spread of hotspots, pricing models for Wi-Fi are still evolving. Some believe that free hotspots will make the pay-for-service model of companies like Boingo obsolete; if a user can go to a coffee shop where access is free, paying a monthly fee to a Wi-Fi aggregator is unappealing. Others believe that Wi-Fi access will only become truly ubiquitous, and profitable, when it is clearly worthwhile to pay a fee for easy, fast, secure, and reliable access. For example, many users would clearly be willing to pay for Wi-Fi access at all airports, eliminating the need to manage different hotspot operators at each airport. "[Wi-Fi is] both a threat and an opportunity. If it's free, you lose revenue," says Tom White, vice president of marketing for telephony at Comcast Corporation, "But if there's a way to put together a business model that works, it creates opportunities for new products and services and additional growth."[21]

Wireline Telecoms

Wireline telecoms are seeking to enter the wireless market to address the shift from wireline to wireless voice services (average monthly wireless-usage minutes will soon be five hundred fifty minutes, versus five hundred for land-line usage) in the United States, to pursue a way for existing DSL customers to expand their networks, and to respond to the competition from cable companies offering high-speed Internet access.[22] Wi-Fi is viewed as an appealing option because it allows the landline carriers that are rich in physical infrastructure and expertise in back-office support functions like customer service and billing, to build on these strengths. Wireline telecoms are pursuing a high-bandwidth/low-cost option by bundling Wi-Fi with broadband and ISP services. They are marketing to their existing enterprise voice service customers by offering customized Wi-Fi enterprise network services (e.g., a portal to a hotspot directory). As one commentator puts it, "[Wi-Fi] networks are not necessarily seen as money-makers for telecom firms . . . , but companies would concede key chunks of the market without them."[23]

For example, Verizon Communications announced a $1 million plan in early 2003 to install Wi-Fi hotspots at one thousand of its New York City pay phones. (Six months later, that number was scaled back to five hundred because of the cost and complexity of obtaining electrical service.) Verizon offers Wi-Fi service as a perk to its DSL and dial-up customers, who can log on to the network from a nearby restaurant, automobile, or park bench. In addition to avoiding real-estate obligations, Verizon avoids revenue-sharing or reseller agreements by using its ability to backhaul data on its own infrastructure. Despite this initiative, Verizon president Larry Babbio has commented that "the Wi-Fi industry is so early in its deployment cycle that I am not sure where it's going to wind up."[24]

Other landline carriers are pursuing different Wi-Fi strategies:

- In 2003, SBC Communications announced plans to launch one thousand hotspots in a thirteen-state area within a year and twenty thousand by the end of 2006 through installation of its own access points and roaming agreements. In 2004, SBC entered into agreements to give its FreedomLink Wi-Fi customers access to hotspots in thousands of UPS locations and McDonald's restaurants.

- BellSouth announced in early 2004 a pilot program to build about one hundred Wi-Fi hotspots in Charlotte, North Carolina. The company's existing DSL and dial-up customers will be able to access the service at no charge. Since 2001, BellSouth has been deploying Wi-Fi equipment for some customers' enterprise LANs. "It's an ongoing collaboration," said Joe Lardieri, director of emerging technologies. "Consequently, we have some very happy Wi-Fi customers out there."[25]

- In early 2004, AT&T severed ties with Cometa, and in mid-2004 stated that it will resume a push into wireless once it has sole control of its brand following Cingular's acquisition of AT&T Wireless.

It is clear that the landline carriers must articulate and implement a strategy to move toward being a provider of wireless services and Wi-Fi in particular.

Cellular Carriers Enter Wi-Fi

When it first emerged, cellular carriers did not know what to make of Wi-Fi and continued to concentrate on 2.5 and 3G technologies. Even as analysts speculated that the advent of Wi-Fi posed a potentially devastating threat to 2.5 and 3G services, many cellular carriers dismissed the technology as hype. However, Wi-Fi continued to gain momentum, attracting over $1 billion in venture capital while the cellular carriers pursued the much delayed 2.5G rollout and defiantly defended their 3G plans. But the boldest and most conspicuous move was that of T-Mobile.

T-Mobile: The Preemptive Strategy

In 2002 Deutsche Telecom's T-Mobile—at the time the sixth largest U.S. cellular carrier—became the first to offer Wi-Fi services for a fee. The carrier purchased the bankrupt Wi-Fi firm MobilStar, and subsequently announced a partnership with Starbucks to offer Wi-Fi access at two thousand six hundred Starbucks cafés nationwide, in essence creating a WISP division. (The companies have since extended their partnership to include hotspot access in Starbucks' European cafés.)

The WISP changed its name to T-Mobile HotSpot and established commercial partnerships with others, including Kinko's; Delta, American, and United airlines; and Borders Books & Music stores. With nearly three thousand nine hundred locations by mid-2004, T-Mobile thus became the largest public hotspot operator in the United States.[26] Users sign up for a service plan with T-Mobile, and upon visiting any T-Mobile HotSpot service location, they simply launch their browser, log in, and connect.

T-Mobile selected existing commercial venues as hotspots in keeping with its strategy of popularizing Wi-Fi by making the service recognizable and readily accessible. To provide roaming access beyond T-Mobile hotspot locations, the company also forged strategic alliances with Wi-Fi providers Boingo, Wayport, and iPass. T-Mobile offers plans ranging from an unlimited $39.99 monthly subscription to a $6-per-hour pay-as-you-go plan charged to a credit card; users with an existing T-Mobile cellular account can add Wi-Fi service at a discounted price.

Following T-Mobile's success, other cellular carriers responded and have begun to offer Wi-Fi through limited deployment of their own Wi-Fi access points and by entering into strategic partnerships with independent providers to resell Wi-Fi services. Sprint PCS has agreements with aggregators such as iPass and has a reciprocal roaming agreement with AT&T Wireless covering major U.S. airports as well. (Other vendors have not divulged their specific partnerships as yet.)

Wi-Fi as a Complement to 3G

The question for cellular carriers is *how* to embrace Wi-Fi. The adoption of Wi-Fi as a complementary technology is contingent on addressing service-related barriers, including availability of dual-access technology, reliable nationwide network access, and successful bundling of Wi-Fi with existing service packages, especially for business clients.

Device makers and carriers are addressing the first barrier by developing dual-capacity devices featuring both 3G and Wi-Fi technology:

- Nokia plans to release the Communicator 9500 phone in 2004, which will be capable of connecting to three different technologies: 2.5G/3G, high-speed data connection via EDGE, and WLAN access via Wi-Fi.

- Intel is developing a phone handset equipped with a camera, UMTS (Universal Mobile Telecommunications System) capability, and seamless roaming from GSM (Global System for Mobile Communications) to 3G to Wi-Fi, slated for release in 2005.

- QUALCOMM is developing cell phone chips with Wi-Fi capability.

- Motorola and Nextel are developing a phone with Wi-Fi and iDEN (Integrated Digital Enhanced Network) capabilities.

- Sony Ericsson has developed a Wi-Fi/GSM access card to enable PC users to connect to Wi-Fi via cellular service.

- Sony Ericsson recently announced a dual-mode chipset that combines CDMA2000 with 802.11b, a melding of technologies that lets users bypass the standard cell phone network whenever they're in range of an open Wi-Fi hub.

Meanwhile, a steady drop in the price of Wi-Fi equipment (Wi-Fi cards have dropped in price from $300 to $50; the equipment cost for a commercial hotspot is $2,000, one-fifth of its cost in 2000) is facilitating the legitimization and spread of Wi-Fi. This increase in the number of access points will provide the critical mass the industry needs to achieve widespread adoption, especially by the business customer. However, this depends on aggregators forging agreements that provide widespread availability of services.

As in the traditional cellular voice industry, greater access is achieved through roaming agreements that allow a customer of one mobile phone operator to use the network of a competitor. While some carriers have entered into limited roaming agreements for Wi-Fi service, much is yet to be done. When T-Mobile announced its first roaming agreement (with iPass in 2003), it matched the largest carrier-owned commercial Wi-Fi service in the United States with the world's largest virtual network for enterprise users requiring remote access while traveling. This agreement was a significant step forward in the building of universal coverage. As Joe Sims, general manager of T-Mobile's Wi-Fi business, noted, "We fully expect to make money in the public hotspot business." He noted that the company had learned some important lessons—namely, that the hotspots must be in locations with heavy traffic from business customers and that a profitable Wi-Fi business must build a national network and brand that will give users the ability to log on at a variety of locations using the same service.[27]

AT&T Wireless also views roaming agreements as a critical component in its business strategy. "Through our own properties and roaming agreements, AT&T Wireless offers Wi-Fi access in hundreds of locations around the country to serve the needs of today's mobile professionals," said Jeff Bradley, senior vice president for business data offers at AT&T Wireless. In announcing an agreement with Sprint PCS in 2004, he continued, "This agreement with Sprint will add important new venues and builds on our strategy of expanding Wi-Fi networks as a compliment [*sic*] to our national, wide-area EDGE (Enhanced Data rates for Global Evolution) network."[28]

In addition to offering expanded Wi-Fi access, these carriers are giving consumers the ability to pay for a single plan that covers hot spots in a variety of locations. Additionally, many of the carriers are bundling their cellular and Wi-Fi services to customers for more attractive pricing. However, it remains to be seen if these carriers are creating viable value propositions for Wi-Fi. Though the top players in telecom all offer Wi-Fi services, Wi-Fi's business value is still up in the air. "There isn't any coherent road map to follow," says John Baker, executive director for business and market development at Verizon Communications.[29] The lack of clarity in the business models of carriers is reflected in the simultaneous efforts on the part of telecommunication companies to shape Wi-Fi as a revenue-generating service and as a customer-service enhancement.

In the ongoing competition to sustain growth and retain subscribers, some cellular providers see Wi-Fi as an attractive complementary offering for customers who want high speed and flat-rate data transfer. Other carriers are opting to add Wi-Fi only to preexisting profitable business services. Nextel, for instance, announced in mid-2003 that it would offer a customized Wi-Fi network to its business clients. "This lets a customer leverage existing infrastructure while upgrading to a more flexible Wi-Fi network," explained Ernie Cormier, Nextel's vice president of business solutions.[30]

At present, telecom companies appear to share skepticism about the viability of Wi-Fi as a freestanding service. "Today, the economics don't allow it [Wi-Fi] to be offered in a standalone way. Nobody's willing to put up a complete $100 billion network," says Naveen Dhar, VP for marketing and business development at Mobility Network Systems. Rod Nelson, chief technology officer for AT&T Wireless, concurs: "On its own, it's very difficult for us to see a business case [for Wi-Fi]."[31]

Wi-Fi as a Substitute for 3G

Despite the large carriers' view that Wi-Fi is a complementary technology that adds value to its existing customer base, it remains conceivable that

Wi-Fi and other high-speed solutions will capture most of the wireless enterprise traffic. Demand for mobile data service is likely to mature only when the service is readily available and when it adds real value for the customer. According to the Yankee Group, the 2003 market for wireless data services represents only 10 percent of the addressable market. Among the enterprises seeking the benefits of fast data transfer are content providers such as those in the music industry. The record company EMI, for instance, anticipates that wireless content will generate $1–2 billion in add-on revenues for the $30 billion recorded-music industry.[32]

If handsets and pocket-sized devices ultimately prevail, the usage pattern will preclude mobile data applications like browsing the Internet and watching movies and will favor 3G. However, if the Wi-Fi network succeeds in becoming truly nationwide and virtually ubiquitous, it would establish itself as the readily available technology, and large-screen devices, such as PCs, would take a substantial share of the market for reliable data traffic.

It is worth keeping in mind that users are unlikely to care much which technology they use to access the Internet. The critical factors in their decision are likely to be mobility, speed, coverage, ease of use, and price. "The issue is more about bandwidth than system A vs. system B," observes Nicholas Negroponte of MIT. "If you give me broadband—something over 2 million bits per second, preferably over 5 million—I cannot really use it without devoting my fullest attention (which means my hands and eyes, not just my ears). In so doing, I am probably not walking, certainly not at the wheel of a car. Therefore, if I am stopped and 'attending,' many of the issues that face cell-phone operators aren't present (like hand-off). The problem is different. There really is room to cohabitate."[33]

The role of voice services in this scenario, meanwhile, is still being played out and portends to be a driver in the complement/substitute debate. Wi-Fi's initial focus was data services, and thus the technology was not designed to support voice services. However, by employing Voice over IP (VoIP) technology, a Wi-Fi phone becomes usable, which converts analog voice into compressed digital packets sent via the Internet. Broad support of VoIP solutions from major telephony vendors allows integration into existing networks via a gateway for internal and external communications, giving VoIP-enabled Wi-Fi handsets advanced features like speed dialing, conference calling, forward calling, and push-to-talk.[34] Thus, the movement toward a Wi-Fi/3G phone would allow a user to bypass the standard cell phone network whenever they are in the range of an open Wi-Fi access point or utilize Wi-Fi when their cellular network does not provide coverage. This would also promote Wi-Fi as a substitute for 3G as it would reduce the potential demand for the 3G network.

The cellular carriers are aware that enterprises are evaluating and implementing Wi-Fi not as a separate technology but as a coherent evolution of their technology infrastructure. More than 80 percent of companies are using WLANs for horizontal applications such as e-mail and Internet access, and almost one-third include some sort of telephony component.[35] Research shows that there is a strong interest in Wi-Fi telephony among organizations that plan to deploy a WLAN in 2004, a combination that could siphon corporate revenue away from cell phone carriers toward Wi-Fi providers.[36]

Wi-Fi has carved out a place within the business model of cellular, in that the national cellular carriers have all announced plans to offer Wi-Fi. Although 2.5G thus far has failed to attract a significant market for wireless data transfer, carriers see Wi-Fi as an opportunity to reinvigorate that market by providing data transfer to customers at impressive speed and strikingly lower cost. While 2.5G and 3G offer speeds of 53 Kbps and 128 Kbps to 2 Mbps, respectively, Wi-Fi offers speeds of 11 to 54 Mbps.[37] Third-generation technology promises increased bandwidth and 2 Mbps for fixed applications, but cellular carriers have not been content to wait for 3G deployment. By entering into Wi-Fi partnerships, the national carriers have conceded that their customers would seek out inexpensive Wi-Fi data transfer elsewhere. Adding Wi-Fi service, though, has put 3G at risk since 3G will never be able to match Wi-Fi's speed. Should Wi-Fi surpass 3G in popularity, some carriers may lose out on revenue-sharing wholesale and resell agreements.

As cellular carriers partner with Wi-Fi providers, and as more network is deployed, Wi-Fi will become increasingly attractive and significantly reduce the potential demand for 3G. Users whose data-services needs are met by Wi-Fi will need 3G only for voice services, small-screen applications, and simple data services. This scenario raises a serious question for the cellular carriers: why make the capital investment in a 3G network if they currently have a 2.5G network that is "almost" broadband and if their data-services needs are increasingly being met by Wi-Fi?

Notes

1. Wi-Fi is the brand identity for the 802.11b standard of the Institute of Electrical and Electronics Engineers (IEEE). The 802.11 standards are a group of engineering specifications for wireless local area networks (WLANs). Table 10-7 lists the various specifications and their respective transmission speeds and ranges.

TABLE 10-7

802.11 ranges and transmission rates

Specification	Spectrum	Range	Data transfer rate
802.11a	5 GHz	100 feet	54 Mbps
802.11b	2.4 GHz	300 feet	11 Mbps
802.11g	2.4 GHz	300 feet	54 Mbps

As the technologies overlap, in some arenas the term *Wi-Fi* is extending beyond 802.11b to include all 802.11 specifications. The 802.11b standard, the most ubiquitous of the three, operates in the free and unlicensed spectrum in the 2.4 GHz band that the FCC set aside for low-power systems like cordless phones and microwave ovens. The 802.11a standard exceeds Wi-Fi's speed but uses a different frequency spectrum and has seen only modest implementation. In late 2003, the FCC increased the spectrum allocation, improving service to users by allowing devices to switch between 802.11a and 802.11b, depending on the strength of the signal. The goal was to avoid the possibility that as products with multimode capabilities were rolled out, the spectrum would become more crowded, leading to dropped signals, cross-signal interference, and unhappy customers. "[Spectrum] is like a highway," says Allen Nogee, an analyst with InStat/MDR. "You may not have the cars on it at the time, but you will soon." Deployment of multimode 802.11a+b+g wireless networking solutions, scheduled for 2004, is expected to make discussion of standards obsolete due to seamless connectivity. Meanwhile, standardization ensures that equipment from different manufacturers works together with reasonable certainty. Wireless cards are becoming a standard built-in feature in laptops, PDAs, and other Internet devices, and it is estimated that by 2006, there will be about 99 million Wi-Fi-enabled devices.

2. The term *3G* refers to a specification for the third generation of mobile communications technology. (Analog cellular was the first generation; digital personal communications services, the second.) Third-generation technologies include a variety of interfaces, like CDMA2000, and EDGE.

3. Kenneth Leon, "Telecommunications: Wireless," *Standard & Poor's Industry Survey*, May 27, 2004.

4. Tom Watts and Jonathan Schildkraut, "Wireless 2003: Winners Emerge" (SG Cowen, 2003); and Tom Watts and Jonathan Schildkraut, "Perspectives: AT&T Wireless" (SG Cowen, 2003).

5. IBM Wireless e-Business, "Exploiting the Full Opportunity of 2.5G and 3G Networks" (white paper, October 2001).

6. Jim Lewis, director for technology policy at the Center for Strategic & International Studies in Washington, quoted by Bob Brewin, "Auction of Defense Department Spectrum Delayed Until 2004," CNN, October 10, 2001.

7. Carmen Nobel, "Feds Free Up Wireless Spectrum," *eWeek*, July 23, 2002.

8. "FCC Action Expected Soon in Several Key Proceedings," *Telecommunications Reports*, June 1, 2004.

9. "Cingular Wireless Is First to the Edge," Cingular press release, June 30, 2003.

10. "Telecommunications: Wireless," *Standard & Poor's Industry Survey*, May 27, 2004.

11. "Wi-Fi: A Wild Card in Telecom Restructuring," Knowledge@Wharton, March 26, 2003.

12. Alan Cohen and Bob O'Hara, "802.11i Shores Up Wireless Security," *Network World*, May 26, 2003.

13. Dave Mota, "Wi-Fi All-Stars," *Network Computing*, May 27, 2004.

14. Galen Gruman, "Wireless, Just What the Doctor Ordered," *CIO*, August 1, 2003.

15. Heather Green, Steve Rosenbush, Roger O'Crockett, and Stanley Holmes, "Wi-Fi Means Business: The Up-from-the-Streets Movement Is Catching On in the Corporate World. Will the New Wireless Networks Pay Off?" *BusinessWeek*, April 28, 2003, 86–92.

16. "WLANs Are Hot but Security Is Hotter," Wi-Fi Planet, available at http://www .wi-fiplanet.com/news/article.php/1546161.

17. Roger Fillion, "Freedom to Connect: Wireless Internet Access Is Popping Up in Unexpected Places," *Rocky Mountain News*, January 19, 2004.

18. *Wi-Fi Networking News* found a large discrepancy between the number of sites listed on some vendors' sites and actually unique hotspots. For example, in Seattle, Boingo listed 26 locations, all of which were unique. iPass had 160 entries that represented 149 unique venues. GoRemote, on the other hand, had 35 entries, which represented 7 unique physical locations. More information is available at http://wifinetnews.com/archives/ 003875.html.

19. "Skeptics Question Wi-Fi's Viablity," *eWeek*, June 14, 2004.

20. Dan O'Shea, "Industry Unsurprised by Cometa Shut Down," *TelephonyOnline*, May 19, 2004. Available at http://www.telephonyonline.com.

21. "Wi-Fi: A Wild Card in Telecom's Restructuring," Knowledge@Wharton. March 26, 2003.

22. Berge Ayvazian, "The Yankee Group Predictions for 2003" (Boston: Yankee Group, 2003).

23. Jason Gertzen, "SBC to Establish 20,000 Wi-Fi Hot Spots in 13-State Area," *Knight Ridder/Tribune Business News*, July 23, 2003.

24. "Verizon Scales Back Pay-Phone Wireless Fidelity Plans," *Boston Globe*, November 24, 2003.

25. Kevin Fitchard, "Verizon Nod Gives Wi-Fi a Big Backer," *TelephonyOnline*, December 2, 2003.

26. Scott Thurm and Nick Wingfield, "Nimble Giants: How Titans Swallowed Wi-Fi, Stifling Silicon Valley Uprising," *Wall Street Journal*, August 8, 2003, A1.

27. Matt Richtel, "Wi-Fi Providers Rethinking How to Make Money," *New York Times*, June 7, 2004.

28. Bill Landon, "Sprint and AT&T Wireless Sign Bilateral Airport WiFi Roaming Agreement," *PDA Today*, April 19, 2004.

29. "Wi-Fi: A Wild Card in Telecom's Restructuring," Knowledge@Wharton. March 26, 2003.

30. Denise Pappalardo, "Nextel to Offer WiFi Service," *Network World Fusion*, August 8, 2003.

31. "Wi-Fi: A Wild Card in Telecom's Restructuring," Knowledge@Wharton. March 26, 2003.

32. Bill Menezes, "On the Record, Music Giant EMI Is Tapping Huge Wireless Content Market," *Wireless Week*, May 15, 2003.

33. "Wi-fi Is Like the Internet Itself: MIT's Nicholas Negroponte Says the New Technology Is 'Reenacting the Bottoms-up Process That Surprised People So Much,'" *BusinessWeek Online*, April 28, 2003.

34. John R. Vacca, "Wi-Fi Phones: A Reality?" *Mobile Business Advisor*, July 1, 2004, 1,457.

35. "Enterprise WLAN Adoption Doubles," *Frontline Solutions*, August 27, 2002.

36. Sarah Kim, "Wi-Fi Telephony Answers the Call for WLAN-Enabled Applications," *ZDNet*, November 11, 2003.

37. Junco Yoshida, "Battling Anemia, 3G Searches for Booster Shot," *EBN*, October 10, 2003.

11

Wireless Local Area Networks

Why Integration Is Inevitable

H. T. Kung

I T IS INCREASINGLY EVIDENT that the growth of wireless local area networks (WLANs) based on 802.11x standards like Wi-Fi will soon be massive and widespread. Enterprises and end users are enthusiastically committing resources to WLAN deployment to benefit from the technology. This phenomenon resembles the widespread deployment of private wireline Ethernets in the 1990s.

The rapid deployment of WLANs in homes, offices, and public areas and the relatively inexpensive bandwidth of WLANs are prompting many observers to ask how the emergence of WLANs will affect the telecom industry. Some see WLANs as direct competitors to the telecommunications high-bandwidth third-generation (3G) technologies; others view the two phenomena as complementary.[1] Some perceive WLANs as providing mainly mobile data services, while others expect WLANs to generate a new wave of opportunities in voice services.[2]

This chapter will examine the fundamental reasons why the impact of WLANs on telecommunications will be profound, even though it is too early to predict the specific implications for particular industrial sectors or for the definitions of standards. We will offer an analytic road map, with analysis and application scenarios, of how WLANs could be integrated into telecommunications devices, systems, and services. We view this integration process as only the latest instance of the merging of existing communication and data networks, with WLAN-enabled cellular handsets as a convergence point. Such handsets can be viewed as an initial focal point in the integration of WLAN in telecoms, in the sense that they are certain to bootstrap other integration efforts.

Usage Examples of WLANs in Telecoms

We expect many users to be eager to use cellular handsets for WLAN access. The ability to access WLANs with handsets, when in a WLAN environment, would represent a welcome convenience for those who always carry cellular handsets and regularly use WLANs in their homes and offices via other devices. These users can now use some handsets to download and upload multimedia content and messages, conduct videoconferencing, and play interactive cell phone games over high-bandwidth, inexpensive, always-connected WLAN connections. Today, however, they must tolerate the inconvenience of switching to a PDA, laptop, or desktop with a WLAN interface before they can access a WLAN.

Early versions of dual-mode handsets that support both cellular and WLAN connections are already undergoing market trials.[3] Other models are expected to become available shortly. Consider, for example, the various smartphone handsets currently on the market, which implement PDA-like functionality with cell phone form factors. It will be relatively straightforward to enable these handsets to support WLANs, since many PDAs already have built-in or add-on WLAN interfaces and protocol stacks to run applications such as Web browsing and instant messaging. Indeed, a recent exhibition demonstrated a number of WLAN applications on an existing smartphone handset by using a WLAN card inserted into the SD card slot.[4]

Another possible scenario is the use of WLANs by fixed-wire phone operators to provide local loops and to access Voice over IP (VoIP) services from data links such as DSL/cable lines, which would represent a last-mile alternative for operators and a convenience for their subscribers. These subscribers can now use WLANs to access PBX systems or phone lines with the WLAN-enabled portable phones or the dual-mode cellular phone handsets described earlier. In WLAN-enabled homes and offices, cellular handset users can thus leverage the convenient features of handsets (phone books, caller lists) while consuming higher-quality and possibly also cheaper noncellular phone services. Fixed-wire phone operators may very well bundle these added services with conventional DSL and cable modem offerings.

Integration of WLANs in Telecoms

From a technological perspective, integration means that cellular handsets have the dual capability of using both WLANs and telephone networks. We will call these dual-mode handsets *WLAN-enabled handsets*.

Integration also means that WLANs and cellular networks are able to interoperate at certain network layers. There are two approaches to integration, often called *tightly coupled* and *loosely coupled* internetworking.[5] In the tightly coupled approach, integration is implemented at a network layer below the IP layer. With integration of this kind, the WLAN will appear to the cellular core network as another cellular-access network. As a result, seamless handoff between cellular and WLAN networks can be expected. Further standardization and development efforts are needed, however, to realize this capability, and deployment of tightly coupled internetworking is thus likely to be years away.

The other approach, loose coupling, implements integration at the IP layer. Using IP protocols, the cellular core network can use existing authentication, authorization, and accounting (AAA) systems, such as the home-location register (HLR) or home-subscriber server (HSS), to support WLAN services and applications. That is, a terminal on a WLAN can send and receive AAA messages to and from the operator's AAA gateway over an IP network. Loose coupling is readily implementable using existing protocol standards, and it can already be useful in providing AAA and other services for WLANs. For purposes of this chapter, we will assume that only loose coupling is implemented.

There are also less integrated methods, such as using a GPRS/WLAN PC card in a PC or PDA to allow it to use both General Packet Radio Service (GPRS) and WLAN networks. Hybrid approaches of this kind can be useful in some applications, such as providing both WLAN and dial-up support for travelers. But because these solutions still require users to carry PDAs or PCs, we expect them to have less impact on telecommunications than integrated solutions.

For a more detailed discussion on integration methods, refer to the six coupling scenarios defined by the 3rd Generation Partnership Project (3GPP), each with an increasing level of integration for the interworking.[6]

The Challenges and Opportunities of Integration

Independently Developed WLANs

In loosely coupled integration, the telephone network will integrate its core with independently developed WLANs rather than using traditional access networks designed together with the core. Sometimes the core will even be integrated with WLANs that are independently deployed and managed by other operators. In this case, loosely coupled integration is a matter of integrating *private* networks (WLANs) with *public* networks (phone networks). This degree of integration of heterogeneous networks appears to be unprecedented in the telecommunications industry. Needless to say, it must be feasible not only technically but also as a business proposition.

Public WLANs

The business viability of public WLAN hotspots, such as airports, conference centers, exhibition halls, railway stations, and stores, is subject to considerable debate. These hotspots and the business opportunities they embody have attracted substantial attention from telecommunications operators, but the hotspot business has not proven as profitable as initially expected, except in places like busy airports where there are many business travelers. This pattern is understandable, given that most WLAN deployment so far is concentrated in homes and enterprises where the WLAN interface is available to users via laptops, desktops, or PDAs. Most people who visit public WLAN areas, however, are not carrying laptops or PDAs. We expect that when WLAN-enabled handsets become popular, public WLANs and related roaming, billing, and aggregation services will see greatly increased usage.

WLANs and Voice over IP

By definition, WLANs transport IP packets, and they are thus often linked with VoIP in discussions of their use in telecoms. For some telecommunications operators, VoIP is a distraction in the sense that it diverts revenue from traditional voice services rather than increasing total revenue. The reality, however, is that VoIP-related services are rapidly gaining momentum throughout the world (e.g., the Skype VoIP services), and their momentum cannot be stopped.[7] This is the case fundamentally because it makes economic sense for voice services to share packet-switching data networks, and because such sharing helps promote deployment of new data services. Telecommunications operators ought to, at least in the long term, plan on increasing their revenue from nonvoice services, by promoting data services. WLANs' roots in the data world and existing data applications make them well suited to facilitate new data services and to create revenue in new areas such as broadband content, online games, and multimedia streaming services.

The Capacities of Handsets

Another issue is how well WLAN-enabled handsets with stringent size constraints can make use of the high-bandwidth link offered by WLANs. In recent years, cellular handsets have substantially expanded their capabilities in computing, storage, display, and peripherals. In fact, they have become one of the most powerful and integrated multimedia devices available to consumers. For example, with a gigabyte SD memory card, USB drive, or hard drive, the storage capacity currently available in today's handsets is already large enough to accommodate an entire ninety-minute movie in a compressed video format. With such prodigious storage capacity, handsets will need to use high-bandwidth and inexpensive WLANs for file downloads and uploads.

Figure 11-1 illustrates a scenario in which a handset user downloads a large video file from a remote server over WLAN. Initially, the user accesses a traditional cellular connection. Upon detecting the presence of a WLAN access point (AP), the handset reroutes the connection to the Internet to transfer packets from the server to the AP, and the WLAN to transfer packets from the AP to the handset. The new route will support data transfer at a much higher bandwidth and at a much lower cost to the user. The detection of the AP by the handset can be performed automatically using standard AP-discovery protocols. The rerouting can also be done automatically, without even breaking the connection, using techniques similar to mobile IP.[8]

FIGURE 11-1

Downloading video via handset over WLAN

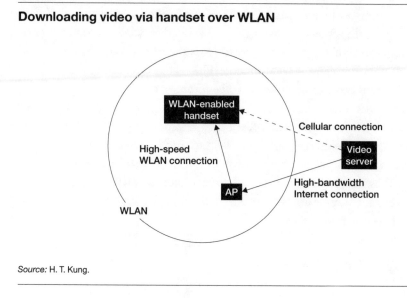

Source: H. T. Kung.

A handset can receive compressed streaming video over WLAN from a video server and simultaneously send it, also over WLAN, to a projector that outputs images on a wall-mounted display, or to an LCD display, for easy viewing. (In a *digital home* scenario, the video server could be a so-called *home media center*, and the display could use a *home media adapter*.) Figure 11-2 depicts this video-streaming scenario. As we shall see, the handset can also decrypt an encrypted video to implement Digital Rights Management (DRM) functions on the fly. As a recent exhibition on applications of WLAN-enabled handsets demonstrated, today's high-end cellular handsets have enough computing power to perform streaming and decryption functions in real time.[9]

Moreover, WLANs can provide high-bandwidth but inexpensive transport to support high-resolution Multimedia Messaging Services (MMS), videophone, and videoconferencing, via handsets. Using WLANs, an MMS recipient can afford to receive "pushed" messages automatically without worrying about the download cost or time, even when such messages are large. As with e-mail receipts, MMS recipients can enjoy the convenience of the automatic receipt of messages.

Consider, too, the use of such handsets in a video-over-IP telephone application. During a telephone session, a user can position the handset's camera to face himself, listen to the other party's voice on the handset's speaker, and watch the other party's image on the handset's display while talking into the handset's microphone. This setup is much simpler and less error-prone than an equivalent setup involving a laptop, desktop, or PDA and all the peripheral devices required for an Internet-based videophone session. With ENUM (standing for "electronic numbering," or "telephone number mapping"), which uses telephone numbers to retrieve domain names, the handset user can have the additional convenience of being able to use the same telephone number for both cellular and IP connections.[10]

As for the power consumption of WLAN-enabled handsets, the applications mentioned earlier are mostly indoor and stationary, and thus have easy access to power supplies. When the WLAN interface is not in use (such as during a traditional cellular call), a handset will turn it off automatically (or the user can do so) to conserve energy. Moreover, we note that when a handset uses a WLAN in a file download or upload, its WLAN interface will need only to be turned on for a relatively short time, due to the WLAN's high bandwidth. Over time, WLAN circuits will improve with respect to power consumption when their applications move beyond laptops and desktops to consumer electronics (such as an MP3

FIGURE 11-2

Streaming video from video server to projector via handset over WLAN

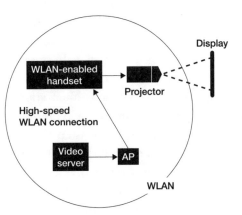

Source: H. T. Kung.

player or a digital camera) with stringent energy efficiency requirements. Indeed, the development of low-power single-chip solutions for WLANs has recently been one of the most active areas in chip design.

Industry Perspectives

Manufacturers are likely to readily appreciate the value of adding WLAN support to handsets. Initially, the market for WLAN-enabled handsets, as for most new products, will be relatively small. Manufacturers of consumer products with rapid innovation cycles will take the lead in the hope of capturing the first-mover advantage—a rationale that motivated some sector leaders to provide WLAN support in PDAs and other consumer electronics.

Hardware development for new WLAN-enabled handsets will leverage chips and circuits already developed for various WLAN products. Software systems, by contrast, may present a greater challenge. In particular, handset manufacturers will need solutions for WLAN protocol stacks. The smartphone vendors that use operating systems with built-in support for such protocol stacks (such as Linux, Symbian, and Windows Mobile) will have an immediate advantage.

Cellular telephone operators, on the other hand, may have trouble seeing why they ought to provide WLAN-related services before such services prove themselves viable in the marketplace. Traditionally, operators rely on cutting-edge industrywide standards in rolling out new generations of technologies and services such as GSM, GPRS, and 3G. In this way, they can share the first-mover risk by moving together. But in the case of WLAN, whose development and deployment are mostly pursued in a grassroots fashion, there is no such coherent and unified cross-industry push. A few visionary operators may break with tradition and aggressively embrace the opportunity of WLANs on their own, but many other telephone operators will probably take a gradual approach to integrating WLAN services. Exactly how the picture will unfold is hard to discern at present. We can be certain, though, that when WLAN-enabled handsets become widely available, operators will step up the pace of integration in order to offer a vast array of new services enabled by these handsets.

A near-term initiative that many telecommunications operators can pursue is the reuse of existing authentication and billing infrastructures by applying them to WLAN services. For example, GSM cellular phones' SIM (subscriber identity module) cards can be used for authentication and charging purposes for both WLAN access and content services that use WLANs for content delivery. Also, a WLAN-enabled handset user will be able to rent or purchase a video and retrieve it over a WLAN utilizing his or her subscription account with a telecommunications operator.

Alternatively, the user can pay via his or her telephone subscription account to download content covered by DRM agreement using a handset with built-in DRM support. For instance, the user may purchase a content key for a piece of MP3 music or an MPEG-4 video using his telephone subscription account, and then use his handset to decrypt otherwise unplayable content. DRM rules could be flexible: for instance, they could specify that content downloaded to the handset can only be uploaded to other devices twice and played a maximum of ten times within the initial six months.

Cellular operators' authentication and billing systems are particularly useful for these applications, since their per-user rather than per-household setup is more suitable to mobile users who may be away from home. The system can truly support a simple-to-use "single-sign-on" mechanism that offers great convenience while providing a reasonable level of security and privacy. In addition to the application service providers, SIM card–based authentication provides a way to track customers' behavior, such as their buying habits, on an individual basis.

ISPs have a long-standing interest in VoIP services—an interest that has recently substantially increased, in part due to VoIP's success in countries like Japan, which has millions of VoIP subscribers. Another explanation for ISPs' growing interest in VoIP is the standardization of new protocols like Session Initiation Protocol (SIP) and ENUM, which facilitate deployment of VoIP services: the SIP protocol provides end-to-end signaling over the IP network, and the ENUM system allows search by telephone number through the Domain Name Service (DNS) for such related information items as name, IP address, e-mail address, fax number, street address, personal interests, and the like.[11] A given ENUM search may not retrieve all of these items, for reasons of privacy protection (but the ability to use a telephone number to retrieve a domain name represents a significant convenience for users). These standards enable VoIP service providers to use heterogeneous systems to provide a variety of new data and voice services.

However, VoIP still faces a formidable obstacle: the inconvenience of having to find a headset, gateway, or computer to use VoIP services. Some recently released USB and Wi-Fi VoIP handsets and embedded VoIP boxes have mitigated the problem somewhat. WLAN-enabled handsets, which support both cellular and WLAN services, will completely eliminate this obstacle.

Fixed-wire phone operators can also benefit from WLAN-enabled handsets. Subscribers often choose to make cellular calls even when a fixed-wire phone is readily available; it has been reported that in the United Kingdom about 30 percent of mobile calls are actually made from the user's home.[12] It is also commonplace to call a person at his or her cellular rather than fixed-wire number to ensure that the person called will retrieve the caller ID from the cellular handset and pick up the call. The use of dual-mode WLAN-enabled handsets in VoIP can thus help offset fixed-wire providers' loss of subscribers and minutes to cellular providers. Furthermore, fixed-wire telephone operators will be able to provide voice services beyond the boundaries of their own local-loop facilities: they can provide VoIP services over DSL, Ethernets, or other data lines, or use WLAN as a local loop.

Cable operators also express interest in providing VoIP services. In Japan, several major VoIP service operators are backed by cable operators. Moreover, some of the cable set-top box's Digital Rights Management functions can migrate to a WLAN-enabled handset with built-in DRM support, as we saw earlier. Incorporating DRM functions in a handset is particularly natural when the handset also acts as a remote controller for a set-top box.

A new generation of service providers, often called "aggregators," is focusing on WLANs. Through franchise arrangements, aggregators combine the services of multiple WLAN operators under a single brand name and also provide roaming support to customers. Thus, aggregators' customers no longer perceive hotspots as islands but as a large, unified wide area network. The franchise can wield its technology and marketing power to set up new hotspots quickly, and can exercise aggregated buying power to negotiate favorable backhaul network fees. As we have mentioned, usage of hotpots will increase greatly when WLAN-enabled handsets become widely available. WLAN aggregators are likely to be major players in telecommunications services within a few years.

Three-in-One WLAN-Enabled Handsets as a Convergence Point

This picture has emerged from our discussion thus far: WLAN-enabled handsets offer the triple functions of a traditional cellular voice phone, an

FIGURES 11-3A AND 3B

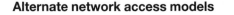

Alternate network access models

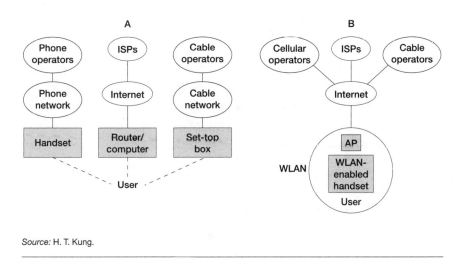

Source: H. T. Kung.

Internet-download-and-multimedia-communications device, and a cable set-top box's DRM capability. These three-in-one handsets thus represent a convergence point for three networks: a phone network, the Internet, and a cable network. Figure 11-3a illustrates the traditional setup, whereby a user uses separate devices and network paths for services on the three networks. With a WLAN-enabled handset, as figure 11-3b shows, a user will be able to reach all three networks at once over WLAN.

Clearly, WLAN-enabled handsets represent a keystone in WLANs' integration into telecoms. With these handsets, operators will be in a stronger position to roll out WLAN-related services.

An Agenda for the Near-Term Future

Accelerating the integration of WLANs into telecommunications providers will require further efforts in several spheres of technology, applications, and regulatory policy.

In handset technology, work in the following areas would be essential in realizing our vision about WLAN-enabled handsets and their use as outlined earlier:

- *WLAN-enabled handsets.* To achieve high performance, these handsets should be *integrated* GSM/WLAN, GPRS/WLAN, or 3G/WLAN handsets, rather than cellular handsets with plug-in WLAN modules. Furthermore, such an integrated handset should allow simultaneous use of both WLAN and GSM/GPRS/3G.

- *Power-efficient WLAN circuits and MAC-layer protocols.* To support VoIP over WLAN, the power consumption for transmitting or receiving should be no more than 200 mW, and that for simply listening should be much lower. This may be achieved with a low bit rate comparable to what is required for VoIP sessions.

- *WLAN resource discovery and control protocols.* WLAN-enabled handsets should be able to discover and control nearby resources, such as projectors and data servers, automatically.

- *WLAN/WLAN and WLAN/cellular handoff protocols.* These handoff protocols can support applications such as VoIP, where connections will need to be maintained when a handset user moves from WLAN to cellular network or another WLAN, and vice versa.

- *Audio and video streaming.* For example, a WLAN-enabled handset can stream audio or video over WLAN to a TV or speaker via a WLAN home media adapter.

- *Latency-sensitive WLAN protocols.* For applications that have stringent quality of service (QoS) requirements, such as VoIP, we will need to minimize or eliminate delay uncertainty introduced by current protocols such as Request To Send/Clear To Send (RTS/CTS), and/or provide priority scheduling.

- *WLAN Virtual Private Networks (VPNs).* Like a laptop/desktop, a WLAN-enabled handset should be able to set a VPN connection to a remote server for authentication and security purposes.

- *New peripheral interfaces such as various sensing devices.* For example, via an interface to a Radio Frequency Identification (RFID) reader, a WLAN-enabled handset can serve as an always-on mobile server that can identify RFID-tagged objects in the nearby area.

We also need to address new opportunities, such as DRM and handset controllers for various Wi-Fi appliances. Perhaps, given the popularity of

Apple's iTunes/iPod online music configuration, we can anticipate another successful business model based on WLAN-enabled DRM handsets. Last but not the least is the need for establishing a certification process that can certify WLAN-enabled handsets and related software.

In the application and services arena, there are multiple directions to pursue. One would address vertical markets in facility security, manufacturing, education, health care, retail, exhibition halls, tourist spots, and warehouse management, spheres in which WLAN-enabled handsets could serve the functions of communications (for instance, walkie-talkies), monitoring and tracking, and personalization in a local environment. These handsets can incorporate RFID readers to further enhance their capability to serve these markets. Such handsets would need to compete with existing solutions based on PDA devices and low-tier Digital Enhanced Cordless Telecommunications (DECT) phone networks or Personal Handy Phone System (PHS) cellular systems. WLAN devices that do not emit strong radio interference will be necessary for environments like factories and hospitals, with electronically sensitive instruments.

A new generation of WLAN-enabled operator-offered services will emerge. These might include SIM-based authentication, charging, and billing for WLAN access and WLAN-related services (single-sign-on); MMS push, interactive cell phone games, and video telephone conferencing over WLAN; and multimedia content-download service using WLAN-enabled DRM handsets. If corresponding versions already exist on cellular phone networks or the Internet, these applications will need to be extended to WLAN environments. For example, it will be possible to port digital TV or some popular interactive online games on the Internet to WLAN-enabled handsets.

Integrating WLAN-enabled VoIP handsets in enterprises and educational institutions should be an immediate goal while fixed-wire phone companies and cable operators are developing public systems capable of using these handsets.[13] These VoIP systems can benefit from new protocols such as SIP and ENUM.

A WLAN-enabled handset will offer enormous versatility as a consumer electronics device. With its built-in speaker, microphone, camera, and recording capabilities, such a handset is a natural monitoring device for a baby's room, a patient-care area, or a building entrance. A WLAN-enabled, handset-based monitoring system can afford an always-on network connection and can transport high-resolution pictures and videos.

With its large storage capacity, a handset will function as portable storage for data and video files, similar to today's USB storage devices. Unlike USB storage, however, a handset can transfer files or stream video over WLAN to servers, projectors, or displays.

A WLAN-enabled handset is also a versatile control device. It can be a remote controller for any home appliance, entertainment device, or gate control with a WLAN interface. Through the attached SIM card, moreover, the handset-based remote controller can support authenticated control functions.

Regulatory initiatives will be necessary to ensure that public unlicensed spectrums for WLAN applications are sufficient and safe. For example, new regulations will be needed to discourage malicious radio interference in a WLAN environment. In the future, technology advances will allow WLANs to operate at speeds of a gigabit per second or more; thus, allocation of additional unlicensed spectrum will be needed to support increased bandwidth and quality of service over WLAN.

Regulation will also need to address the management of telephone numbers. A user of a WLAN-enabled handset could use several telephone numbers on his or her handset (cellular number, VoIP number, home and work fixed-wire phone numbers, and instant messaging number). We will need to develop schemes to allocate these numbers and to encourage their convergence, perhaps through systems like ENUM.[14]

Conclusion

Integrating WLANs into telecommunication systems promises extraordinary benefits for end users. With a WLAN-enabled handset, a cellular phone user will have immediate and convenient access to a multitude of cost-effective broadband WLAN applications and services without having to rely on a PDA or a PC. These handsets will serve as a common access device for the Internet, cable, and phone networks. The single-sign-on and always-on features of WLAN-enabled handsets are certain to inspire new application and business initiatives.

Handset manufacturers, together with ISPs and fixed-wire operators and WLAN aggregators, are expected to be among the first to move toward integration, with WLAN-enabled handsets as an initial focal point. The initial market for WLAN-enabled handsets will probably outstrip the market for PDAs within a few years, given that these next-generation handsets will include a WLAN interface and PDA-like functionality. When such handsets become widespread, other sectors—such as public WLANs—will take off as traditional cellular operators and WLAN aggregators aggressively promote WLAN services. All telecom sectors, including cellular operators, should be prepared to offer services that incorporate WLAN capabilities.

Notes

1. See "3G Is Safe from Wi-Fi," October 20, 2003. Available at http://www.3g.co.uk/PR/Oct2003/5974.htm; and W. Lehr and L. W. McKnight, "Wireless Internet Access: 3G vs. WiFi?" (Cambridge, MA: Center for eBusiness, Massachusetts Institute of Technology, 2002), available at http://ebusiness.mit.edu.

2. B. Strachman, "Voice over WLAN: Will the Market Finally Answer?" InStat/MDR, March 14, 2003, available at http://www.instat.com/.

3. See Brad Smith, "Intel Shows Advanced Smartphone Concept," *MobileMag*, September 22, 2003, available at http://www.mobilemag.com/content/100/340/C2063/; "MiTAC Mio 8380 First Windows Powered Clamshell Smartphone," *MobileMag*, July 21, 2003, available at http://www.mobilemag.com/content/100/340/C1845; "Seamless Switching of WIFI and Cellular for Voice, Data and Real-Time Video Conferencing Services," Calypso Wireless Inc., available at http://www.calypsowireless.com/WP.pdf; and T. Marshall, "DoCoMo Tests 3G/WiFi Dual-Mode Phones," September 12, 2003, available at http://www.telecomtv.com/newComms.php?cd_id=341.

4. The exhibition was the iBakeoff: WLAN-Cellular Network Integration Exhibition, held in Taipei, Taiwan, on January 9, 2004. For a description of the smartphone, see "MiTAC Mio 8380 First Windows Powered Clamshell Smartphone," *MobileMag*, July 21, 2003, available at http://www.mobilemag.com/content/100/340/C1845/, 2003.

5. M. Buddhikot, G. Chandranmenon, S. J. Han, Y. W. Lee, S. Miller, and L. Salgarelli, "Design and Implementation of a WLAN/CDMA2000 Integration Architecture," *IEEE Communications Magazine* 41, no. 11: 90–100.

6. 3GPP TS 22.934, "Feasibility Study to Wireless Local Area (WLAN) Interworking," V1.1.0, 2002.

7. S. Baset and H. Schulzrinne, "An Analysis of the Skype Peer-to-Peer Internet Telephony Protocol," Columbia University Technical Report CUCS-039-04, September 2004, available at http://www1.cs.columbia.edu/~salman/publications/cucs-039-04.pdf.

8. C. Perkins, ed. "IP Mobility Support," *RFC 2002, Internet RFC/STD/FYI/BCP Archives*, available at http://www.faqs.org/rfcs/rfc2002.html.

9. iBakeoff: WLAN-Cellular Network Integration Exhibition, Taipei, Taiwan, January 9, 2004.

10. J. Morris, "Enum: Mapping Telephone Numbers onto the Internet: Potential Benefits with Public Policy Risks," Center for Democracy and Technology, April 2003, available at http://www.cdt.org/standards/enum.

11. D. Sisalem and J. Kuthan, "Understanding SIP," 2002, available at http://www.iptel.org/sip/siptutorial.pdf; and Morris, "Enum."

12. "The Everywhere Phone," BT Group, available at http://www.btplc.com/Innovation/Mobility/everywhere/.

13. V. Lipset, "Dartmouth Intros Wireless VoIP," Wi-Fi Planet, September 26, 2003, available at http://www.wi-fiplanet.com/columns/article.php/3084501.

14. Morris, "Enum."

12

Widespread Adoption of Wireless Enterprise Solutions

Ellen Daley, John Keane, and Ali Towle

I T IS SAFE TO SAY that the market for mobile and wireless enterprise solutions is still in its infancy. In this chapter, we will survey the factors that must converge for the mobile and wireless enterprise market to reach its full potential, and offer our best guess as to how the market will develop over the next five years.

The rate of adoption of emerging technologies—in this case, mobile and wireless—can be explained by the interaction of three interdependent factors:

- *Technical maturity.* The various technologies involved in a successful wireless solution—networks, software, and devices—must reach a critical state of maturity to ensure that effective and reliable solutions can be developed at a reasonable cost.

- *Proven solutions.* A number of well-publicized mobile and wireless solutions need to exist to convince corporate executives that return-on-investment (ROI) opportunities are real.

- *The business climate.* A healthy economy is necessary for companies to fully fund investments in solutions that employ new technologies.

Figure 12-1 illustrates how these three factors interact. Simply stated, advances in one component of the model create further opportunities in the other two, but widespread adoption typically requires the convergence of all three. In other words, the speed of adoption is influenced by the health of the business climate. A healthy business climate means that funds are available for investment in the technology. Investment in the technology, in turn, supports technical innovation and maturation. Technical maturity promotes the development of proven solutions. Proven solutions demonstrate that the technology is viable, stimulating the business climate and encouraging further investment—and the cycle continues.

In the case of mobile and wireless today, technical maturity and proven solutions have been achieved, but a weak business climate has discouraged widespread adoption. To understand more fully the current state of corporate adoption of mobile and wireless technology, let us look more closely at the three components of the Widespread Adoption Model.

FIGURE 12-1

The Widespread Adoption Model

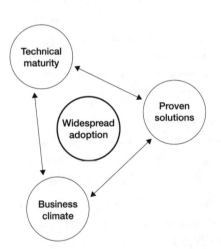

Source: ArcStream Solutions Inc.

Technical Maturity

Enterprises undertaking mobile and wireless initiatives must consider three technical areas: networks, software, and devices.

Wireless Networks

Recent advances in wireless network technology include the progression of coverage, improved data-transmission speed and security, and reduced cost. In our opinion, networks have matured to the point that high-impact solutions are viable across a variety of applications.

More Pervasive Coverage

Wireless wide area networks (WWANs), with the advent of high-speed wireless network technology, like GPRS, 1xRTT, and 1evDO, are offering wireless data at bandwidths rivaling dial-up speeds, and at times close to broadband, in major metropolitan areas. Wireless local area networks (WLANs), like Wi-Fi (Wireless Fidelity), are providing campus-based computing, or "hotspots" of high-speed, high-bandwidth computing, which is quickly replacing traditional wired LAN connectivity.

In locales where WWAN coverage continues to be spotty, particularly in rural areas and within buildings, emerging technologies allow roaming between WWAN and WLAN, enabling users to switch seamlessly to whichever network is available. The other approach to spotty WWAN coverage is to build a hybrid solution, which works in an always-on mode when wireless access is available and in a disconnected mode when access is unavailable. In disconnected mode, information is stored on the device until the user can establish another connection.

It is important to note that wireless spectrum usage beyond WWAN and WLAN is also being leveraged—specifically, by radio frequency identification (RFID) technology, which can actively identify tagged items within a wireless field. RFID is attracting interest from the supply chain side of manufacturing, consumer goods, and retail companies. The main hurdles for RFID include persuading the industry to agree on a common set of standards for interoperability. Cost is still another inhibitor, but, as with all technologies, as manufacturing advances continue, the cost constraint will diminish.

Improved Security

Security concerns, once a key inhibitor to deploying wireless solutions, continue to be mitigated. The recognized 802.11 encryption flaw has been eliminated by an improved protocol, 802.11x, enhanced network layouts, and vendor-specific security measures.[1] Furthermore, proven examples of how to protect data transmission via Virtual Private Networks (VPNs) and other means are easing the alarm about hacking and data vulnerability.

Reduced Cost

The cost of using WWANs continues to drop as carriers compete on price to acquire corporate customers. Meanwhile, setting up a WLAN access point can cost as little as $20. In addition, leveraging hybrid solutions can provide benefits similar to those of pure wireless solutions at lower cost in time and dollars than a sustained WWAN connection.

Software

Mobile middleware and infrastructure software extend the reach of existing enterprise applications. Such software affords seamless integration with back-end systems while providing the capability to synchronize, alert, distribute software, and repurpose content for various device form factors. The entry of large incumbent players in this market has driven down both cost and risk, attesting to the maturity of this portion of the industry.

Vendor Transition and Consolidation

At the tail end of the Internet bubble, pure-play specialized mobile vendors dominated the mobile middleware space. More recently, traditional software infrastructure packages—from the likes of IBM, Sybase Inc., and Oracle—have started offering these same capabilities, often by acquiring one of the pure-play niche vendors (for instance, Sybase bought AvantGo). Furthermore, for mobile and wireless solutions to be operational and scalable, they must be integrated with enterprise-management software, such as Unicenter from Computer Associates and OpenView from HP. Again, modules within these standard software packages now offer mobile and wireless integration and operational support.

Reduced Cost and Risk

Now that incumbent vendors are offering mobility modules, enterprises are no longer obligated to invest separately in mobile and wireless infrastructure. This development cuts associated costs, and also lessens the risk for enterprises interested in testing the mobile and wireless waters.

Devices

The fact that enterprises are increasingly utilizing laptops, tablet computers, and personal digital assistants (PDAs) suggests that today's devices adequately support the specifications of current mobile and wireless implementations. The evolution of these devices will remain exciting as manufacturers continue to innovate to increase capabilities, improve usability, and reduce cost.

Increasing Capabilities

As manufacturing processes improve and technologies advance, the industry continues to increase processor speed and enhance display resolution, battery life, and memory. Furthermore, nearly all new mobile devices are being shipped with built-in connectivity or card support for wireless access (WWAN and WLAN)—a sign of the industry's confidence in wireless.

Advances in converged devices continue to be interesting to watch. Designed to free mobile users from the need to carry both a phone and a personal digital assistant, converged devices are gaining popularity, especially in response to the rollout of faster wireless networks that promise to make Web browsing and wireless data synching more practical. At present, however, converged devices tend to be a bit larger and more expensive than their stand-alone counterparts.

Finally, though the mobile phone is not often used for enterprise data applications, its high market penetration positions it as an attractive potential channel for businesses to better serve their customers, such as with loyalty programs and point-of-sale payment systems. Mobile phones will probably become more attractive as improvements are made in screen resolution, data-entry methods, and the usability of device operating systems.

Improving Usability

Across the industry, there is a less sharp focus on enhancing usability through innovative product design. For example, the BlackBerry, introduced in early 1999, was one of the earliest devices to offer a mini-QWERTY keyboard that could be used to thumb-type messages—an innovation that simplified data entry. Today, many new devices are leveraging the QWERTY keyboard.

Shrinking Cost

As the market has already witnessed, advances in manufacturing and in the technology components themselves will continue to drive down prices. For example, the most expensive component in devices today is, arguably, the screen. Therefore, manufacturing companies are focusing on innovations, such as electronic ink displays, that will provide cheaper screen technology.

Of course, there will never be a "magic bullet" device adequately suited to all uses and users. Although good news for device manufacturers, this fact of life will continue to complicate the device-selection process. For each mobile and wireless initiative, an enterprise will need to consider the work-flow and information needs of end users, the device's data-entry and display capabilities, and its weight and battery life, among other variables, and then select the device best suited to the bulk of the tasks that the end users are expected to perform.

Proven Solutions

Widespread enterprise adoption is contingent on proven examples that can serve as proofs of concept for potential adopters. To demonstrate how enterprises are utilizing and benefiting from mobile and wireless technologies, we offer six case studies drawn from a variety of industries.

Calpine Corporation

> *This project proved the financial benefits of wireless computing.*

> —Scott Schilling, warehouse inventory manager, Calpine Corporation

Calpine Corporation is the largest independent power generator in the United States, with $7 billion in annual sales. As an old-line utility full of acquisitions, Calpine owns eighty-six power plants; many were stocking and managing their own inventories of spare parts. For an electrical generator, spare parts are not just nuts and bolts—some parts, such as pumps and motors, cost in excess of $50,000. On average, Calpine plants were carrying as much as $1 million in duplicate common parts.

"My jaw dropped when I came to Calpine. In retail, for example, inventory control and bar coding are common practice. Utilities are about twenty years behind," remarks Scott Schilling, warehouse inventory manager, with years of experience in honing inventory processes. Schilling knew there was much to be gained by unifying and streamlining parts management across Calpine's multiple plants—namely, improving the company's profit margin by reducing the costs of operations and plant maintenance. But to effectively share parts across plants, Calpine needed reliable up-to-the-minute information on the exact status of each item. Were a plant to go down, Calpine could not afford to fumble around for the necessary part only to discover that it had gone to another plant two days earlier. Schilling saw that Calpine needed a way to track the whereabouts of all parts in real time.

Calpine had recently implemented MRO Software's Maximo as an enterprise asset management (EAM) solution. Maximo provided one view of the inventory across all the plants and the central warehouse, but a number of gaps remained. In order to take full advantage of Maximo, Schilling needed to implement a wireless inventory management solution and initiate a warehouse standardization program. Schilling went looking for a system that would allow Calpine warehouse staff to scan in digital data directly from a part bar code and enter transactional information on the spot that would flow automatically into a centralized data system. After looking at the available options, Schilling chose the mobile inventory management solution from DataSplice Corporation. DataSplice's thin-client solution forms a bridge between enterprise data systems and mobile devices.[2]

For hardware, Calpine chose Intermec 802-11b wireless access points and the Intermec 750 ruggedized Pocket PC handheld device with built-in bar-code reader. "I wanted something indestructible and weatherproof with a large color screen," Schilling explains, "I wanted the guys in the plant to pick it up and use it—to know that it was durable."

Technically, the implementation was rather painless, but physically reorganizing the parts themselves was another story. "There were not a lot of people at the plant level with warehousing experience," Schilling notes. After standards had been developed and implemented to describe and label bins and parts—so the plants could all "talk" to each other—an inventory "tech team" would visit each plant to bar-code label all bin locations, print a label for each inventory item, and move it to its unique bin location. Once the process was complete, after about three weeks, incoming parts were automatically assigned to the appropriate location.

With implementation complete at eleven plants and roughly one additional plant going online per month, Calpine is already seeing the payoff in three areas. At each new plant that goes online, the cost of stocking parts has been reduced by $1 million. In addition, with real-time automated inventory control, Calpine has cut in half the amount of equipment that goes unaccounted for—an additional annual savings of approximately $50,000 per plant. Finally, by eliminating many manual processes (issuing parts-to-work orders, monthly cycle counts, inventory reconciliation, annual physical inventory, returning parts, and locating parts), Schilling calculates that each plant will save 920 labor hours a year, conservatively adding up to another $23,000 in annual savings per plant. Schilling is more than proud of the outcome.

Solution Summary

Calpine's wireless inventory management system addresses the company's real-time inventory data needs in an effort to reduce inventory holding and labor costs across its geographically dispersed warehouse sites. The solution consists of:

- *Network.* Low-cost WLAN from Intermec

- *Software.* DataSplice for Inventory, which simplifies the process of integrating mobile devices with Calpine's enterprise asset management system, Maximo, made by MRO Software

- *Device.* The Intermec 750 ruggedized handheld with built-in barcode reader

Partners HealthCare

Until it matures further, wireless offers Partners some niche utility. Each opportunity is assessed individually by weighing risk versus reward.

—John Glaser, CIO, Partners Healthcare System Inc.

Partners HealthCare runs Massachusetts's biggest hospital group. Formed in 1994 by the merger of Brigham and Women's Hospital and Massachusetts General Hospital, the not-for-profit organization offers primary and specialist care, acute care, and other services. For this health-care organization, Partners' CIO John Glaser asserts, wireless is "two years away from maturity." Wireless is still hard to manage in a health-care environment. Security and the need to build redundancy remains a challenge. But one area where Partners has found the rewards of wireless to outweigh the potential risks is wireless medication administration.

Avoidable medical mistakes happen. The problem is not carelessness, but that highly qualified people are working under stress in a setting characterized by multiple complex processes. A breakdown at any step could compromise patient safety, perhaps in the form of an adverse drug event. At Partners, for every one hundred patients, 5.5 adverse drug events occur. As a result, "some patients are forced to stay another night, some have life-threatening reactions, and, unfortunately, some die," Glaser explains. But of those 5.5 events, at least 28 percent are preventable—hence Partners' investment in wireless medication administration. "The return in this case is not about money, although the average expense per drug error event is $6,000," says Glaser. "The value is a moral one—we're saving lives."

The wireless medication-administration project, known as eMAR, is a charting application used by nurses to document the administration of patients' medication. The eMAR application is integrated with the physician order entry (POE) system and the pharmaceutical system. The process has four basic steps:

1. The physician enters the medication order in the POE system, which also provides some decision support (it notifies the doctor of patient allergies, potential reactions, and the like).

2. The order flows from the POE system to the eMAR system, where the nurse acknowledges receipt of the order.

3. The nurse obtains the medication(s) from the drug-dispensing cabinet.

4. Before administering the medication to the patient, the nurse scans the bar codes on the patient's wristband and on each medication.

Thus, the name and dosage of the patient's medication are verified against active medication orders, alerting the caregiver to possible medication errors. Potential inconsistencies in medications, dosages, and administration times, as well as omissions, are quickly identified and avoided. The automated solution ensures that nurses and doctors administer the right medication to the right patient at the right time, thus minimizing avoidable medication errors.

Partners has been testing the eMAR concept for several years. The original desktop version yielded a low adoption rate among the nursing staff. Then Partners developed eMAR functionality for the PDA. Although the nurses responded favorably to the small portable device, Partners concluded that the PDA was not capable of handling the processing and interface needs of the eMAR application. Finally, in 2003, after evaluating several device lines, Partners found its sweet-spot device in the Fujitsu B series subnotebook with integrated bar-code reader. The solution relies on 802.11b wireless LAN access for full functionality. To avoid potential violations of patient privacy, always an issue for health-care organizations, Partners installed an additional layer of security on the network via Cisco's LEAP authentication protocol.

Solution Summary

Partners' wireless eMAR solution helps eliminate avoidable errors in medication administration. The solution consists of:

- *Network*. Low-cost Wi-Fi and an easy-to-install authentication protocol from Cisco, LEAP

- *Software*. A fully integrated data source developed in-house by Partners IT

- *Device*. The Fujitsu B series subnotebook with built-in bar-code reader

The Pepsi Bottling Group

Our need to be connected on a real-time basis is growing by the day.

—Paul Hamilton, vice president of supply chain, Pepsi Bottling Group

The Pepsi Bottling Group (PBG) is the largest manufacturer, distributor, and seller of Pepsi-Cola beverages, accounting for about 40 percent of PepsiCo's global beverage sales. PBG operates about one hundred plants and delivers its drinks (including Aquafina water, Lipton's Iced Tea, Mountain Dew, Slice, and, of course, Pepsi-Cola) through third-party distributors and directly to stores.

"Every day we send six thousand salespeople out to make a difference both for our business and for the businesses of our retail customers," says Paul Hamilton, vice president of supply chain. "When our sales reps go into a store today, they have only a few minutes of the store manager's time in order to make a sale." Meanwhile, sales reps are accountable for more and more information: a proliferation of SKUs, a complex pricing scheme, unique customer agreements and promotions, and lists of authorized products that can vary from store to store, even within a chain. To maximize their selling capability, the PBG sales force needed an efficient system with which to quickly track information on individual SKUs, promotions, and account specifics.

PBG armed its sales force with Symbol PDT 8000 Pocket PCs and a customized version of Eleven Technology Inc.'s sales application, SMART-Selling software. The Pocket PCs tie into the back office via 802.11b wireless connectivity, if available, or a dial-up line. The new software promotes sales in two ways. First, it provides information about a customer and identifies selling opportunities in the account. Second, it gives sales reps their monthly priorities. These two elements provide the sales team with the overall guidance and account-specific information needed to drive revenue at every opportunity.

"Our current application today replaces our paper-based system of the past. Our new application is much more sophisticated," Hamilton says. "We're going to be providing our retail partners with critical pieces of information to improve their business. We feel quite confident that the tools we're developing will deliver accurate, timely information on a consistent basis day in and day out, order by order."

The impact of PBG's new selling solution is expected to have a measurable impact in several spheres:

- Increased sales through reduced out-of-stocks as a result of better demand forecasting.

- Improved product management and the reduction of costs associated with invoice disputes. The application prevents reps from selling unauthorized products to a particular account.

- Increased store compliance with trade promotions, resulting in increased consumer demand. The application reminds reps of current agreements, affording closer management.

- Improved rep productivity attributable to less time spent on low-value work, such as jotting notes, calculating order quantities, and manually counting inventory.

"Our sales representatives today must address a number of issues when visiting each of our customers. Their ability to provide the right information to that retail customer, at the precise moment it is required, is of utmost value to us," says Hamilton. "Specifically, we want reps to be able to deliver selling materials which help drive the category, and information to help eliminate out-of-stock product inside the store. This application has allowed us to do both, and both of those better than we'd ever expected to do."

Solution Summary

Pepsi Bottling Group's mobile sales solution arms its sales force with a portable tool to quickly call up account-specific information. The tool also allows reps to more accurately forecast account demand, allowing for more precise ordering, and reducing costly out-of-stocks. The solution consists of:

- *Network.* Hybrid functionality—low-cost WLAN coverage, when available, or mobile synchronization via dial-up when WLAN is not available

- *Software.* A customized version of Eleven Technology's SMART-Selling software, designed specifically for mobile devices

- *Device.* Symbol PDT 8000 Pocket PC with built-in bar-code reader

Pitney Bowes

There is no question this was a business-driven project. The advances of wireless devices and software just furthered our expectations.

—Ralph Nichols, service program manager, Pitney Bowes

From simple postage meters to complicated computer-based mailing systems, Pitney Bowes has been a global leader in mail-processing services for over eighty years. For large-volume mailers, such as financial institutions, retailers, direct marketers and utilities, round-the-clock support from Pitney Bowes' Document Messaging Technology (DMT) division is mission critical.

"We had reached a point within the company where the servicing of products and customers was dramatically different than our traditional profiles." Ralph Nichols, DMT's service program manager, explains,

"Our products had evolved. Many were now computer-based. And, in the DMT division, we had 120 clients with on-site service."

The on-site service model is akin to customer relationship management: Pitney Bowes employees not only maintain products, but also train client companies' employees and help the customer resolve issues. "Our proprietary service-management system, ACESS, which had been designed for traditional dispatch, break-fix service, had no capability for this new type of service model," Nichols says. To make matters worse, ACESS was not fully integrated with the inventory-management system, so field technicians had no means of looking into inventory and supply. The system was unable to correlate stocked inventory with actual need for a part, which often resulted in expensive and unnecessary rush orders.

DMT's goal for the project was clear: an enterprisewide, customer-focused application that would be available around the clock. The system would provide a simple and direct way for service technicians to input and retrieve real-time information and to link inventory consumption to service activities and products.

As part of a corporate reengineering effort to become more customer-focused, Pitney Bowes had decided to standardize on Siebel Systems' customer relationship management (CRM) system, including Siebel Field Service v7.04 for service management. The DMT division extended the Siebel Field Service solution wirelessly to on-site service technicians via Antenna Software's A3 for Siebel.

After considerable field-testing, Pitney Bowes chose the BlackBerry 957 device on the Cingular Wireless Mobitex network. Although Pitney Bowes technicians had carried handheld devices in the past (Motorola KDTs and, more recently, RIM 850s), they were not easy to use for data input. "The BlackBerry 957 is a real breakthrough device," Nichols says. "The battery life is light years ahead of other devices, some of which do not last as long as a typical ten-hour workday. In addition, they are lightweight and durable, and because of the thumbwheel and menu-driven interface, they can be used with only one hand."

By April 2003 all 625 on-site service technicians, across 120 sites, had been deployed. Nichols singles out inventory reduction and labor savings as the areas that will realize the greatest benefits. "With our enhanced knowledge of parts usage, we expect to reduce inventory levels at least 15 percent in the first year," he says. "This results in a significant hard-dollar expense reduction." Pitney Bowes also anticipates a 90 percent decrease in the number of emergency and rush orders, which will eliminate expensive freight costs and lost productivity when people interrupt normal work to handle emergency requests.

On the labor front, Pitney Bowes expects to be able to measure and improve how technicians spend their time. Because the application and device are so easy to use for input and retrieval of data, technicians can easily record their daily service activities. This information will provide service managers and support personnel with a real-time view of service operations and shed light on high-performing and problematic products and employees. When problems come to light, Pitney Bowes can determine why they are occurring or recurring. Do the employees or customers require more training? Is there a defect in a part shipment from a certain supplier? "Now we have real-time business intelligence that ties part consumption and labor utilization to every module of every product, which affects overall product and service quality," Ralph Nichols says. "These have a direct impact on customer satisfaction."

Solution Summary

Pitney Bowes' wireless field-service solution provides a real-time view of service operations, affording better control of inventory management and product performance, and thus improving service quality and customer satisfaction. The solution consists of:

- *Network.* WWAN— Mobitex from Cingular Wireless

- *Software.* Antenna Software's A3 for Siebel Systems, a specially designed mobile extension of Siebel Systems' Field Service solution

- *Device.* The BlackBerry 957

Cubist Pharmaceuticals Inc.

Mobile computing gives us the ability to expedite the delivery of information from our field representatives and better educate our customers. With the expected enhancements on the horizon, it can be done in real time, giving us a competitive advantage within our industry.

—Gregory Stea, executive director of sales, Cubist Pharmaceuticals Inc.

Cubist Pharmaceuticals Inc. ("Cubist"), headquartered in Lexington, Massachusetts, is a leader in the research, development, and commercialization of novel antimicrobial drugs, which combat serious and life-threatening infections. Prior to FDA approval of its first commercial drug, CUBICIN (daptomycin for injection), indicated for the treatment of complicated skin and skin structure infections caused by susceptible strains of certain Gram-positive microorganisms, the company needed a sales application to support the sales account managers who would sell CUBICIN.

This system would need to interface with data from a number of disparate systems and provide both a "hospitalcentric" view of accounts for the sales organization and a "contactcentric" view of information for the marketing organization. In addition, the data model and user interface had to be designed for ultimate flexibility so that new drugs could be tracked by the system as they were developed. Most importantly, the system had to provide a comprehensive mobile and office-based interface. The application would be used both in a disconnected (offline) mode by mobile users when conducting hospital visits, and by office-based staff, who would access the same application on desktops or laptops, when needed.

After a diligent review of the traditional sales force automation (SFA) packages on the market, Cubist concluded that a custom application was its best option. "The SFA software products could not adequately accommodate our hospital-based sales model. The majority of packaged products are geared to the community sales-model, where the focus is on the contact management of individual physicians," said Kelly Schmitz, Cubist's director of IT.

To build the solution needed, Cubist engaged the systems integration firm ArcStream Solutions Inc. ArcStream Solutions worked with Cubist to implement an account management system to run as both a mobile and a desktop application through a Web interface. Cubist selected Tablet PCs as the mobile device, due to the ample screen size. Because the sales account managers work in the field, the mobile system was designed to operate in a totally wireless mode if wireless connectivity is available. If not, the mobile application can operate in a disconnected mode, using a database synchronization process to upload and download information when Internet connectivity becomes available. Synchronization of the Tablet PC on a regular basis affords access to current information, updated alerts, and application improvements.

Cubist's custom account management system improves the effectiveness of the hospital sales account managers in the field. Account managers, if armed with current information at their fingertips, can accurately and proactively identify and manage their accounts and action plans. In addition, being able to capture data during a hospital visit, rather than transcribing handwritten notes after the fact, increases the accuracy of visit logs and records. Meanwhile, for sales management, the account management system affords the ability to accurately analyze the sales of CUBICIN and other drugs, allowing for greater adaptability of sales plans and territory management. And because the database is shared by sales and marketing, all account notes, information, formulary status information, and literature requests are documented for review—improving communication between the sales and marketing departments and improving the quality of each and every customer interaction.

Summary Solution

To summarize, the Cubist account management system addresses the hospital-based sales model. In addition, the mobile, Tablet PC access increases the efficiency of the account managers in the field and improves communication between the sales and marketing organizations. The solution was made possible by the availability of:

- *Network.* Hybrid functionality—WWAN or WLAN coverage when available, or mobile synchronization via a dial-up when WWAN or WLAN is not available

- *Software.* A custom application designed by Cubist and developed by ArcStream Solutions

- *Device.* Tablet PC

ExxonMobil

We're not trying to push Speedpass from an RFID technology-and-standards perspective. We're trying to push Speedpass as the standard brand for mobile payments.

—Joe Giordano, vice president, business and product development, Speedpass

ExxonMobil engages in oil and gas exploration, production, supply, transportation, and marketing around the world. It also owns Speedpass, a wireless payment system. And even if you are not an ExxonMobil gas customer, you will soon become a Speedpass user if you eat at McDonald's or buy groceries at Stop & Shop. At least Joe Giordano, vice president, business and product development, hopes so.

Nine years ago Giordano created Speedpass, the wireless payment system launched by what was then Mobil Oil Corporation. A project that began as a means to improve customer satisfaction has potentially become the future of wireless payment systems. "At the time, 1993–1994, there was big momentum at Mobil to differentiate the brand by offering 'faster, friendlier service,' " recalls Giordano. "I was part of the 'faster' team. We were generating idea after idea on how to make the process of buying gas quicker." This focus, coupled with a trip to Dallas, where Giordano encountered an RFID toll pass similar to EZ Pass or Fast Lane, was the genesis of Speedpass.

Speedpass is a small wand-shaped device containing a Texas Instruments radio frequency transponder. A customer simply waves the wand in front of a sensor pad at the point of purchase, and the charge is automatically registered on his or her credit card. ExxonMobil has implemented Speedpass at 8,100 service stations (more than half) in the United States, 1,250 in Canada, and 80 in Singapore.

"In the early 1990s, people were being asked to master a number of new technologies. We were just trying to make life simpler," Giordano says. On average, Speedpass users shorten a typical three-and-a-half minute transaction by thirty seconds. The secondary benefits include stronger loyalty and higher spending—Speedpass holders average one more visit per month. This increased revenue has justified station owners' typical $15,000 investment. "Sales per store increased, and customer satisfaction is extremely high. So, on any measure that we can think of, Speedpass has exceeded our expectations," Giordano says.

Meanwhile, Speedpass is transitioning from a gas-purchasing device into a cash payment alternative. Speedpass has become the leader in RFID payment systems, but a central problem persists: RFID payment systems are proprietary and based on different standards. If consumers must have a separate key chain for each place they shop, the convenience of RFID payment will be undermined; but Giordano understands this. "The value of Speedpass is not in the exclusivity of the technology," he says. "It is in the relationships with our 8 million users. In a world without standards, we will likely expand to accommodate a reasonable set of technology providers."

In the meantime, the Speedpass venture is extending its lead in mobile commerce by charging other companies, like McDonald's, for the right to let their customers use Speedpass in the form of either a one-time charge or a small transaction fee. ExxonMobil is banking on the classic network effect: the more consumers sign up for Speedpass, the more attractive Speedpass becomes to retailers. "We're developing relationships with lots of retailers, and we want to be their customer identification and payment system," Giordano says. Giordano views Speedpass as enabling customer relationship management programs in a much more cost-effective way than is practical today. "Besides a very efficient way to handle cash payments, Speedpass provides retailers with a way to learn about their customers, as well as define targeted service offerings and rewards." Speedpass enables ExxonMobile to gain great insight into its customers by capturing information about the time, location, and nature of each purchase using Speedpass.

Today, the 8 million Speedpasses in circulation can also be used at 440 McDonald's in the Chicago area and at 4 Stop & Shops in Massachusetts. Meanwhile, intra-Speedpass promotions (for instance, with every $20 gas purchase, get $5 off at McDonald's) are on the horizon. In five years, Giordano hopes that the Speedpass program will have at least 30 million members.

Solution Summary

ExxonMobil's RFID initiative to improve customer satisfaction and loyalty via faster service has become the paradigm of wireless payment systems. The Speedpass phenomenon demonstrates that wireless technologies have the potential to impact customer populations in ways that transcend the cell phone and PDA. The solution consists of:

- *Network.* Localized RFID

- *Software.* Proprietary customer relationship management software

- *Device.* Key fob (RFID transponder)

The Business Climate

As these case studies demonstrate, mobile and wireless technologies have achieved a reasonable level of maturity and can demonstrate return on investment. However, initiatives to date are still largely confined to progressive companies testing the waters with relatively small projects. When an improved economic climate stimulates greater investment in mobile and wireless, generating larger projects that champion the technologies' viability, widespread adoption will follow.

Corporate spending on technology has slowed significantly since the year 2000. During economically conservative times, corporations typically cut back spending on initiatives that depend on emerging technologies, which are perceived as relatively risky investments with unpredictable returns on investment. Use of mobile and wireless technologies is being delayed by economic conditions.

A prolonged investment freeze can stall technical innovation and slow the natural advancement and maturation of these technologies. The situation is a classic Catch-22: corporations do not invest in emerging mobile and wireless technologies because they appear immature and risky, and this lack of investment in turn hobbles the maturation process and limits the number of proven successes. Until the business climate improves enough to encourage large-scale corporate investment, widespread adoption will continue to lag behind expectations. So what does the future hold?

The Future of Mobile and Wireless

When will mobile and wireless be embraced by others besides early-adopter enterprises and executives? A range of scenarios could play out over the next five years. We will end this chapter with a set of predictions about the future of mobile and wireless use within corporate enterprises.

Networks

- *Significantly improved data coverage.* WWAN data coverage will be extended to secondary markets and along some major interstates. Meanwhile, WLAN hotspots will be deployed in several retail and corporate businesses, extending roaming capabilities between WLAN hotspots and WWANs. Carriers will see a moderate increase in revenue from adoptions, which will serve to fund further network upgrades.

- *Advanced RFID technology.* In the specialized area of RFID, organizations will rally to resolve standards and security concerns. The costs of RFID tags will continue to decrease, resulting in utilization of RFID in the supply chains and warehouse management systems of several industries. For lower-priced items, RFID tags will be deployed at the palette and case level (e.g., grocery products); for higher-priced items, such as consumer electronics, RFID tags will be deployed at the individual product level. Commercial and governmental mandates (such as by Wal-Mart, Department of Defense, and the Food and Drug Administration) will drive significant advances in multiple areas of RFID technology.

- *Improved security.* Security will cease to be a major worry as the 802.11x WLAN fix lives up to its promise. Virtual private networks will continue to improve, offering even more robust functionality. With their security worries well addressed, companies will integrate wireless solutions more pervasively with their most critical data and systems. These solutions' increasingly compelling returns on investment will fuel further interest and investment in wireless solutions.

- *Reduced cost.* Carriers' desire to penetrate the enterprise market will promote competitive pricing, primarily for WWAN data. The industry will continue to see more carriers and start-ups moving into WLAN deployments to augment their networks.

Software

- *Vendor consolidation.* The large application and infrastructure software providers will continue to purchase and develop key technologies to ensure that their offerings completely address mobile and wireless requirements. Within five years there will be very few pure-play mobile and wireless software vendors, due to acquisition and competition from these large vendors. For enterprises, the result will be a narrowing of choice (and lessening of confusion) during product selection.

- *Reduced cost and risk.* As trusted incumbent software providers offer mobile and wireless extensions, the cost and risk of mobile and wireless solutions will decrease significantly. Since there will be fewer software products, each will have been deployed much more frequently. Their track records will produce significantly more feedback and economic return with which to create an even more capable product offering.

Devices

- *Increased capabilities.* Devices will continue to boast longer battery life, more memory, and faster processors. Meanwhile, integrated network capability will become a given for phones and other devices, including laptops, easing competition for access to wireless networks. Finally, the penetration rate for mobile phones with data capabilities will increase. Some enterprises will use these data-ready phones as an additional communication channel with their customers—offering opt-in services, loyalty programs, discounts and promotions.

- *Improved usability.* Device usability will advance tremendously, particularly in the area of data-input options. Voice recognition technologies will continue to develop but will not be used significantly within the five-year time frame.

- *Reduced cost.* The cost of devices will continue to fall, due to high demand and advances in manufacturing.

Proven Solutions and the Business Climate

More and more enterprises, across a range of industries, will deploy solutions with clearly stated business value. As proven successes reach a threshold level and attract more media attention over the next two years, other enterprises will feel comfortable with mobile and wireless solutions and more will invest.

Recent indicators point to a moderately improving business climate. If companies increase their investments in mobile and wireless solutions, the Widespread Adoption Model (see figure 12-1) predicts advancing technical maturity, more proven solutions, and, accordingly, increased wireless adoption.

We are confident that the mobile and wireless industry will grow at a heightened rate as soon as the three components of the Widespread Adoption Model converge. Although predictions of exponential wireless adoption made in the late 1990s have not been fulfilled to date and may never reach the levels originally predicted, widespread adoption will be imminent as soon as the business climate picks up.

Acknowledgments

Without the generous contributions of the following people, the writing of this chapter would not have been possible. The authors would like to thank Scott Schilling of Calpine Corporation, John Glaser and Steve Flammini of Partners Healthcare, Nate Quigley of Eleven Technology, Paul Hamilton of Pepsi Bottling Group, Karen Davis-Farage and Terri White of Antenna Software, Ralph Nichols of Pitney Bowes, Gregory Stea and Kelly Schmitz of Cubist Pharmaceuticals, and Joe Giordano of ExxonMobil.

Notes

1. The 802.11 encryption flaw resulted in off-the-shelf approaches to breaking into seemingly secure wireless networks.

2. *Thin-client* refers to a small-footprint application that does not store significant data on the client side; rather, it uses a network to request and receive data in the thin-client application. A typical thin-client application is a Web browser.

Policy and the Broadband Future

13

The Inevitability
of Broadband

Reed E. Hundt

I F IN THE TWENTIETH CENTURY technology permitted America to
dominate in war and grow rich in peace, thus far in this century it has
let us down, at least in the latter respect. Since 2000 the information, communications, and technology (ICT) sector of the economy—comprising
everything from computer chips to telephone service—has grown very little. What's more, the future appears, in the words of the poet Robert
Lowell, "frizzled, stale and small." The *Harvard Business Review* declares
that ICT is a mere commodity of no strategic value, and that firms should
not focus on investing in new technologies.[1] Great inventors like Bill Joy
speculate that consumers might have purchased all the technology they
want, and great business leaders like Larry Ellison proclaim that the
golden age of ICT is behind us.

Of course, ICT growth could never have sustained the torrid pace of the
bubble years (1997–2000). But few expected that mounting job losses, flat
revenue, and falling stock prices would be the next new things. At risk are far
more than the sheer animal spirits that drive technology growth cycles. Because of the dependence of the American economy on technological growth,
a dispirited ICT sector threatens both the quality of American life and national competitiveness. In this anxious time, the country reasonably turns to
the government, and even to the often-obscure Federal Communications

Commission (FCC), for policy prescriptions that will bring about a revival of ICT growth.

The FCC laid out its broadband policy in February 2003. Cable and telephony companies will invest in the hardware and software necessary to alter their respective fiber-coaxial cable and copper networks in order to provide broadband. These two industries will compete like nineteenth-century railroads racing across the continent. Meanwhile, the FCC will welcome wireless broadband access technologies, such as Wi-Fi or 802.11, and perhaps electric utility lines may provide broadband access too.

Many argue that this policy suffices. After all, while growth is flagging in most parts of the ICT sector, broadband Internet access is the fastest-growing communications service ever. As of year-end 2003, about 23 million households were subscribing to either the cable company's or the telephone company's offer of fast data transmission—at rates of up to 1 megabit per second, or about ten to twenty times the speed of narrowband access over a telephone line. (Neither wireless broadband nor electric-line broadband is widely available.) Broadband access prices at first exceeded $40 a month, but the telephone companies have reduced monthly fees to $30 and even lower in some markets, and as a result the telephone companies are catching up to cable's early lead in residential customer acquisition.

Yet just as the great railroad boom ended in bankruptcy for most firms, the FCC's current policy creates unnecessarily high costs and high risks for both telephone and cable firms as they contemplate extending broadband both in scope and in scale, which means offering much faster rates of access to many more homes. As a result, both types of firms are discouraged from investing in truly big broadband—what might be called the "10/100 × 100 vision," or speeds of 10–100 megabits per second for each of 100 million households. What is needed is a national universal service program to promote a physical link—probably involving both wireless and fiber media—enabling data rates of 10–100 megabits per second, with voluminous capacity for numerous service providers, to every home. In order to implement such a policy, the country needs a detailed plan to preserve the economic viability of existing telephony and cable firms for years to come. (Let academics insist that such an injection of practicality is unwelcome; this essay is about how to achieve results.) In this way, the FCC can stimulate economic growth, help create new jobs, and ensure efficient communications services from the perspectives of both investors and users.

FCC Broadband Policy's Failure to Stimulate the Communications Sector

In response to the post-2000 collapse of equity values for telecommunications firms, the FCC has encouraged consolidation in a number of markets, including broadcast TV and radio, cable, and mobile communications. In the broadband market, its current policy is also explicitly proconcentration, notably in its reversal of rules permitting rival broadband firms to lease and share some of the facilities of telephony firms. In general, consolidation—in the absence of new entrants or newly discovered markets—will eventually lead to higher prices, reduced output, and diminished scale for the entire market sector. This consolidation policy should, however, enhance both scale and returns for the survivors. In broadband, the policy already appears to be contributing to a two-firm race for market share, as telephony and cable jointly convert to broadband the 60 million households that had previously subscribed to narrowband Internet access.

A consolidation policy, however, tends to inflate the equity values of surviving firms at the expense of a whole sector's growth. If the FCC favors this approach, it may be emulating Andrew Mellon, Herbert Hoover's secretary of the treasury, whose response to the great crash of October 1929 was to seek liquidation of virtually everything.[2] Hoover wanted some new economic stimulus, but the federal government's powers were few and its appropriations scant. Hoover tried to persuade the private sector and state and local governments to spend money. As history records, his efforts failed.

His successor, Franklin Roosevelt, favored a policy not unlike Mellon's. In many sectors, such as communications, he supported industry coordination and even monopoly in order to reduce capacity. To this end, he created the FCC in 1934 and charged it with regulating the long-distance monopoly to guarantee its economic viability, rather than increasing economic growth.

Roosevelt's policy also failed. Only the spending necessitated by the Second World War restored economic growth to the American economy. Most economists now believe, with the benefit of hindsight and the teachings of John Maynard Keynes, that the right response to economic downturn is to increase spending so as to soak up unused capacity—in short, to prime the pump. And if the government needs to borrow for this purpose, then let it borrow. The Bush administration is following Keynes in incurring a record federal deficit, while pushing through large tax cuts on the premise that those who have extra money will spend it—perhaps even on broadband access!

As was the case in the Great Depression, the fundamental problem of the ICT sector is too much capacity. The telephone companies' capacity to carry voice is underused because cellular networks carry the traffic instead. Every household that subscribes to broadband simultaneously increases unused capacity by abandoning second lines that used to be connected to computers for narrowband Internet access. Cable companies pass 100 percent of homes, but cannot increase subscribership much beyond 65 percent, because satellites now offer competing video packages. We have five or six cellular carriers (subject to a pending merger), but few use efficient percentages of all their networks. More than a dozen long-haul data networks link cities, though two or three would suffice for existing traffic and even for projected future traffic for a decade to come. Manufacturing plants that make the components and systems of networks are underutilized; software firms have more engineers and programmers than they need, or have laid off skilled employees in the absence of demand. And if both telephone and cable firms—not to mention wireless entrants—build broadband networks past the same households, by definition at least half the capacity will be unused.

The results of this overcapacity have included bankruptcies at record levels, suppressed stock market values leading to a negative wealth effect, and reductions in workforces—all bad news for this sector of the economy. Overarching this unhappy picture is a continuing trend to invent ways to make more capacity for less cost. Such *technological deflation* makes it harder and harder for firms to generate profits unless they have substantial market power.

This situation is not an easy one for a regulatory agency, much less for the industry itself. The two large categories of demand are business investment in ICT, which Congress aspires to stimulate with tax breaks and military spending, and consumer demand for communications, which the FCC hopes to stimulate with its broadband (and wireless) policies. At the same time, we can understand why the FCC would hope that consolidation will eliminate (that is, liquidate) capacity. Indeed, in many markets, such as cellular service and various forms of chips (particularly application-specific integrated circuits), some consolidation could well produce more efficient scale without affecting competition or innovation except in positive directions.

Can overcapacity and disinvestment in many markets be offset by new capacity-creating investment in broadband? Perhaps it is not unreasonable to hope that new investment will increase revenue for vendors to broadband service providers, that broadband subscribers will generate meaningful new revenues for the sector, and that other service providers (such as sellers of software, e-commerce, and other content applications) will use broadband connections to create new demand over broadband connections.

But at least three problems may remain unsolved by the FCC's broadband policy. First, while telephony and cable are expanding the scope of their existing networks so as to offer broadband, they are not necessarily in a position to build truly big broadband, with speeds of 10–100 megabits per second to the user. Second, although their investments should make them more efficient, the emerging broadband market will not necessarily produce overall growth in the communications sector. Indeed, paradoxically, the two-firm broadband policy may lead to further contraction. Finally, the current policy is directed at not much more than half the country, ignoring potential demand from at least 50 million homes and the social benefits that would flow from linking all to a new medium of communications.

The FCC's broadband policy sets in motion a new high-stakes contest. It has an imperial quality, as if the government were summoning two large and well-trained gladiators into the ring of converging broadband solutions. But will the ICT sector benefit from a bread-and-circuses battle between telephony and cable? Perhaps the right goal is economic stimulus resting on an expandable, multimode physical platform that will sustain technological evolution while providing viable economic futures for both telephony and cable firms.

Under current policy, telephony is supposed to alter its circuit-switched, copper-based access network so as to offer broadband, while cable allocates to broadband some of the capacity of its fiber-coaxial cable network now used to deliver video. Almost everyone agrees that neither telephony nor cable is optimally designed for broadband (a function of when their networks were built, as opposed to a strategic choice), but expansion of their scope is possible. The Bells in particular appear to face the greater challenge: they need to install glass fiber and optoelectronics in their network (enhancing throughput, measured by bits per second) in order to offer broadband to more customers and also to reduce the expense of operating their current networks. Indeed, telephony has already begun to procure the piece parts for passive optical networks that will be designed to target likely subscribers.

Both telephony and cable firms may be diluting current earnings by competing on price in the broadband market. Moreover, because their starting points are different in technological, economic, and (somewhat) regulatory terms, their investments do not produce identical offers. Telephony's broadband network allows for high-speed Internet access and voice services; cable's broadband network offers high-speed access and video but (subject to the development of voice-over-Internet protocols) not voice.

Telephony firms can be expected to enter video warily, since the investment would be large and the competitive battle very bruising to the returns of all participants. Cable should be similarly cautious about entering voice, again because the investment would be significant and the competition could be a fight to a winner-takes-all result.

Many technologists inside and outside the telephony and cable industries discuss the possibility of a single fiber-based network for delivering voice, video, and data. This configuration is referred to as "the triple play," and, as in baseball, it signifies that one side is out. Any economically viable firm that produced such a triple play could reasonably be expected to dominate communications, technology, and even media markets. Currently, access networks are responsible for about 40 percent of the value obtained from all video, voice, and data markets. That 40 percent translates into, very roughly, $150 billion in revenue per year. A triple-play provider could own that whole market, making it one of the largest firms in the world, measured by market capital. By contrast, Microsoft earns only about $40 billion in revenue a year, notwithstanding its market power over a key link in the PC value chain.

Neither telephony nor cable is perfectly situated to build a big-broadband, or triple-play, network. Cable could probably build such networks more cheaply than telephony can. A number of start-ups—WIN, WOW, Knology Inc., RCN Corporation—did try to build triple-play businesses during the boom years. The technical difficulties are many, and the capital demands substantial. But the fundamental problem was that the cost per home passed exceeded $1,000, and with cable and telephone firms enjoying dominant market shares of at least two of the three elements of the triple play, the new entrant was unlikely to earn an attractive return. The outcome was thus a function of history, not of optimal engineering design. In the absence of existing cable or telephone firms, private firms would undoubtedly build fiber to many homes in America, if not all 100 million homes that constitute the total vision of big broadband, and thereby achieve at least the 10–100 megabit per second offer. Meanwhile, the financial bust so shrank investor willingness to make large network investments that even firms as well capitalized as the Bells appear unlikely to build truly big broadband networks to all homes in this decade. Instead, they will make very significant investments in passive optical networks to perhaps as many as 20 or 30 million homes.

Moreover, a very good reason for cable or telephone firms not to escalate competition into a battle to be the triple-play provider is that losing the battle might be fatal. After all, one lesson of the 1996 Telecom Act is that competition has losers. In the 1990s many observers assumed that interexchange carriers (IXCs), such as AT&T and MCI, and local telephony companies would compete to offer voice and other services when Congress and regulators ended the separation between these markets. What happened, with greater speed than anyone publicly predicted, was that the local telephone companies became vastly bigger in terms of enterprise value and the IXCs shrank to shadows of their former selves. The latter live on mainly as the primary providers of data services to business customers, and even that largely because local telephone companies are only now entering that market.

The two-firm broadband market may seek what economists call a *Nash equilibrium*.[3] That is, neither firm will adopt a fight-to-the-death strategy, and hence neither will undertake to build a big-broadband triple-play network. Investors may well encourage such an outcome. If so, each firm may focus on economies of scale and scope in its existing markets—including today's little broadband, to perhaps as much as half the country—and not on the more speculative future services that big broadband might enable, nor on extending any broadband offer to the remaining half of the country. This somewhat stagnant outcome is what the FCC should think about how to avoid.

Telephony may deliver voice more efficiently over an enhanced network, based in larger part on passive optical networks. The Bells will need fewer employees and will be able to generate greater returns on equity. Moreover, they will be in a position to offer voice, Internet access, and wireless to customers, lowering operating expense by consolidating marketing and customer care. Cable can obtain similar results by bundling video and high-speed access. These efficiency gains should increase returns for both types of firms, and generate potential productivity gains for other sectors of the economy that use communications services as an input. However, such efficiencies may not translate into material economic stimulus for the ICT sector as a whole.

The ICT sector today is characterized by technological change that creates consumer benefit without promoting economic growth for the sector. Examples include the browser war that produced free browsers for all, and many generations of microprocessor enhancement accompanied by continual declines in price per unit of performance. Today's broadband rollout is directly cannibalizing the narrowband Internet market: virtually every new broadband customer at $30 a month (and falling) drops a narrowband subscription at perhaps $20 a month. The same customer also tends to drop a second $20 telephone line that had been dedicated to narrowband access. And some new cable broadband customers may drop the multichannel digital cable option. Of course, it already goes almost unremarked that bundling long distance into cellular and local voice has effectively cut total long-distance revenue by a large percentage.

No one should suggest that the FCC block efficiencies that promote consumer welfare. However, deflation and consolidation do not make for a Keynesian approach to the sickly ICT economy. Again, some individual firms may end up as winners in a declining sector. Moreover, value may well be transferred over time from one segment of ICT to another, just as software and services have in the aggregate tended to capture value in ICT. However, notwithstanding the profitability of a few winners, and the sectoral trends, in the short term everyone would benefit if the sector's pump were primed by someone and something that produced aggregate revenue growth. This is not the focus of the FCC's broadband policy.

Furthermore, the FCC's broadband policy seeks growth from, at most, about half the country. About 60 percent of U.S. households subscribe to narrowband Internet access. To date, virtually all broadband subscribers previously belonged to this group. At prices above $20, about 40–50 million of the 60 million narrowband households have indicated a willingness to pay for broadband. Thus, the FCC's broadband policy effectively seeks growth from only half of the country's 100 million households. By contrast, the wireless policies of the 1990s have generated economic growth from virtually all segments of economy. Indeed, penetration may well exceed 100 percent, as many consumers acquire more than one wireless communication device.

Service-Level Competition, Innovation, and Growth versus Infrastructure Redundancy

Ever since the federal government sued to break up AT&T in 1974, Democratic and Republican administrations, Congress, and regulatory agencies have pursued the goal of competitive communications markets by means of laws, orders, rulemakings, lawsuits, international negotiations, and bully-pulpit proselytizing. Policy makers have consistently embraced competition in communications services and products as a means to pursue economic growth (because monopolies constrain output), innovation (because in networked industries, monopolies deter innovation), efficiency (because competition reduces rent-taking and pushes prices down to long-run incremental cost), productivity gains (because efficient communications make other firms more productive), welfare gains (because competition transfers value from firms to customers), and social benefits (because more widespread networks create nonquantifiable social gains for all participants).

In the 1990s, the competition policy of the FCC in fact helped open up monopolized communications markets to competition. This policy applied to cable (satellite was invited to compete), local phone (new entrants were invited to lease facilities from the Bells), long-distance voice (the dominance of AT&T and MCI was challenged by the Bells), wireless (auctions drew four to five new players into competition with the duopoly crafted by the policies of the 1980s), and narrowband Internet access (new entrants were permitted to use the Bell network at very low cost). Counterexamples were created by Congressional actions overriding the FCC, notably laws opening the door to consolidation of broadcast radio, a multibillion-dollar gift of spectrum to broadcast TV stations ostensibly for their exclusive development of digital over-the-air TV, and a prohibition on the creation of low-power FM radio stations. For the most part, however, the procompetition policy prevailed.

Competition and technological innovation produced radical drops in retail service prices and new service-level innovation. Elasticity effects and the appeal of new services together produced record-breaking economic growth. Even as the stock markets rose and fell to record degrees, the information economy grew continuously from the early 1990s until the early 2000s. Ten years ago about 60 percent of U.S. homes were connected to about twenty-five cable channels; today, 85 percent of homes are receiving an average of eighty-five channels from cable and satellite providers. In the same period 25 million cell phone subscribers became more than 125 million. Ten years ago the Internet was an academic hobby; today more than 60 percent of homes are online. The Web has grown to more than 10 billion pages. More than 80 percent of all classrooms—from elementary school to graduate school—have Internet access.

In many service categories, prices dropped radically. Newly competitive markets have passed on cost reductions to consumers: from 1995 to 2000, frame-relay prices dropped 12 percent a year; SONET, 30 percent a year; wireless voice, 19 percent a year; and long-distance voice, 6 percent.[4] End users responded to lower prices by buying a greater volume of services. Telecommunications-services revenue increased from $175 billion to $320 billion between 1995 and 2002. Overall, telecommunications-services revenue (encompassing wire, wireless, and Internet) has more than doubled in ten years, and accounts for more than twice as large a share of the GDP as it did a decade ago. In short, in the 1990s it was the single best driver of growth in the economy.

All along, the focus of competition policy has been how to encourage growth in retail services while acknowledging the significance in the value chain of its most critical link: the *access network*. Also called "the last mile" or "local loop," the access network is the portion of a wire or wireless network that connects individual end users in buildings, homes, or mobile locations to the aggregation points where their traffic is combined with others' and their requests for connection are routed (in packet-data networks like the Internet) or switched (in circuit-based networks like the telephone system) to the desired destinations, whether Web servers or other end users. The access medium may be a wireless hop from a handheld device to a base station's antenna, or copper-wire telephone line from a bedside table to a telephone pole to a central office, or the cable connection from the set-top box on the TV to the same telephone pole to what the cable company calls its hub, where the video pictures are received from a satellite feed.

The core problem of access networks from the perspective of government is threefold: (1) how to ensure innovation toward the most efficient network solution (defining efficiency as throughput per dollar), (2) how to ensure enough return on investment for the access-network provider to continue to innovate (return must equal or exceed the cost of capital), and (3) how to obtain efficient pricing through deregulated competition or, if necessary, uncostly regulation of oligopolistic markets (defining efficiency as a market in which marginal revenue equals marginal cost). More simply, government policy has been to facilitate service-level competition by obtaining efficient investment and efficient pricing from the access proprietor. Broadband is only the latest access technology; what is new is that the FCC no longer adheres to this policy goal.

Historically, the encouragement of multiple proprietors of access networks has been a key element of FCC policy. In the 1990s, Congress and the FCC created a six- or seven-firm wireless market through spectrum auctions. Local telephony for businesses became a multifirm market when Congress and the FCC obligated incumbent firms to lease their local loops to rivals, which built switches and other facilities to cobble together access alternatives. In cable data access, the Federal Trade Commission tried to create a multifirm market by obliging AOL Time Warner to carry at least three other Internet access providers on its network. These policies created multiple service offerings for wireless narrowband Internet access, and the early stages of little-broadband (cable-modem) Internet access.

However, FCC policy over the years has not insisted on the construction of parallel, unconnected physical infrastructures, which appears to be the goal of today's broadband policy. Instead, under both Republican and Democratic administrations, the FCC respected the efficiency and possible inevitability of natural monopoly in the market of physical fixed-wire links to households. Therefore, the FCC favored, in effect, shared use of local-loop bottlenecks. The goal, after all, was not redundant local access but competition and growth in the services market that used the access medium.

The results of past policy were spectacularly successful for services growth. In addition, massive capital was poured into other facilities that connect to the physical links of local access, such as switches, data centers, long-haul networks, and other data management systems. Innovation has thrived in these market segments, and in general the conversion from circuit-switched to packet-based technologies has proceeded rapidly. The more physical capacity in the access network, the faster and more innovative will be investment in the hardware and software of other parts of the end-to-end network. In the 1990s, expectations of increasing capacity in the access network helped drive such investment. Revenue soared for software and hardware vendors at both the component and the system level.

Meanwhile, incumbent telephony and cable firms responded by upgrading access networks. This virtuous cycle was interrupted by the stock-market crash. Now both service-provider revenue growth and innovation in other aspects of the overall network appear to have slowed.

We are in a new era of cost cutting and risk-averse investment. That alone is not totally regrettable: firms should be pressured by cyclical change to become more efficient. However, the new FCC broadband policy does not appear likely to stimulate in a timely way a new virtuous cycle of revenue growth, innovative investment, new services, and more revenue growth. Indeed, service-level competition and innovation do not appear to be the chief goals of the FCC. The danger is an ICT version of a liquidity trap, if capital expenditure declines as a percentage of industry revenue, and aggregate revenue also falls.[5]

In fairness, the current FCC does see wireless (or even the electric grid) as a third and potentially disruptive entrant into the broadband access market, the role that wireless played in voice markets in the 1990s. Wireless broadband might be the mode of transmission that stimulates innovation in access as well as creation of new retail services. It is possible, even, that wireless will deprive the last mile or local loop of significant competitive advantage, and thus restrict the capability of any last-mile owner to extract rents from that asset. To these ends, however, the FCC could do more to encourage wireless innovation. The FCC could auction a large swath of spectrum to anyone who promises to make it available to manufacturers of wireless communication devices, under any set of rules that mitigates interference and prescribes clear guidelines for device behavior. This spectrum would resemble a private park and could be used as experimental proving grounds for wireless broadband solutions. The desired outcome would be a wireless access link that provides an effective big-bandwidth alternative to fiber at a much lower cost. Furthermore, the FCC should allow any secondary use of any spectrum that does not impose material cost on any existing user of spectrum. The FCC should also create major new allocations of unlicensed spectrum. Finally, any wireless service provider should be guaranteed interconnection at fair forward-looking prices to all other broadband providers. Each of these steps would enhance opportunities for wireless solutions to challenge existing access providers.

FCC policies promoting wireless could also be used to encourage other configurations of the triple play that would include wireless. One perpetual merit of a policy of promoting competition is that future creativity in technology or marketing is often vastly more intriguing and valuable than any current speculation. In the interest of promoting multiple variations of double, triple, or quadruple plays, the FCC should see to it that the wireless industry does not consolidate into structures that preclude combinations with other industries, and that wireless innovation is encouraged as described earlier.

It must be admitted that breakthrough wireless-access technologies could significantly deflate access revenues (just as wireless voice helped drive down long-distance prices in the 1990s). Again, the problem of demand stimulus emerges. Wireless technologies would presumably stimulate demand for new software and hardware, but would they in general raise or lower telecom-sector revenues? This may be an unanswerable question, but should it go unasked? And should we not try to mitigate the downside risks? As a highly placed government official was quoted as saying in July 2003, "I personally don't think anybody is safe. I don't believe any company currently in communications is so well-structured and tied down that they are guaranteed to be here 15 years from now."[6] Although we should welcome innovations that produce efficiency, the potential destruction of firms vital to our economy and society deserves serious attention from government. Happily, we have at hand an ideal way to stimulate new revenue growth: it is, in a phrase, a new universal-service policy for big broadband.

Universal Service to Promote Revenue Growth and Innovation

Under current policy, government is in effect deciding to exclude millions of households from the emerging broadband network for the reason that retail prices for broadband access will plainly exceed some people's willingness to pay. In any market, some are unwilling or unable to pay for goods and services. Governments intervene in some such markets: bus service is offered for those without private cars; public education is available for those who do not purchase private education. In all such interventions, responsible government must calculate the cost and benefit of the intervention.

In networks the benefits of interventions are both social and economic. There is social value in enabling even those who cannot pay to be on the network. There is also an economic value to all other subscribers in adding more participants to the networked community, though that value is external to the value appreciated by a single user. Creating the social value and internalizing the economic value to others is the twin rationale for what is usually called universal service. (Exemplifying the continuing failure in policy debates to name things accurately, the term *universal service* does not apply to everyone and all services. For many years it has been used to refer to federal and state policies pertaining to users in high-cost, less dense, often rural areas and, for the most part, only voice service.)

The current FCC has no meaningful universal-service policy for broadband. Yet its broadband policy is likely to undercut the universal-service policy for voice. As the FCC knows, when voice becomes a data application provided over a broadband connection, telephone companies will lose voice revenue. But if the FCC mulcts broadband customers for contributions to underwrite universal service for the traditional voice network, the bizarre and unfortunate result will be that the new network subsidizes the perpetuation of the old network. In what way would this make sense? The nation would thus end up with a smaller (in scale and scope) new broadband network without allaying the decline in revenue and utilization of the old voice network. Alternatively, without contribution from broadband customers to circuit-switched customers, those left behind in the circuit-switched market will make higher and higher contributions to universal service. This implicit tax on circuit-switched traffic unfairly penalizes the proprietors of that network—the telephone companies—and unfairly advantages those who offer data services, whether through wireless, coaxial cable, or other technical solutions. Moreover, those who do not use computers will bear the increasing cost of supporting universal voice service: social equity is not promoted by that allocation of burden. For reasons of both efficiency in networks and fairness in contribution to social goals, the current scheme must be changed or simply abandoned.

Indeed, we may wish good riddance to the current horrid universal-service scheme for voice, which is a sin against fairness and logic. It taxes the poor in cities to pay for the well-off in suburban areas. It charges businesses too much and charges many residential customers less than they are willing to pay. It is inefficiently collected and poorly disbursed. And it pays for a copper network and voice service when efficiency demands fast access to the Internet. Indeed, the only merit of the universal-service system is that it is so complicated that it might as well be secret, and thus does not arouse much righteous indignation except in academic circles.

By contrast, a policy aimed at enabling all Americans to use a computer on the Web can generate economic and social benefits, as well as providing a significant stimulus to the economy. As matters stand now, U.S. Internet penetration rates have been stuck at around 60 percent for some time. Some attribute the standstill to the difficulty of using computers and managing keyboards; perhaps voice-activated computers or the emergence of laptops as communications devices (called Wi-Fi networks) will lead to higher penetration rates. But it is reasonable to speculate that if noncomputer users could obtain access to truly big broadband at home, it would persuade nonusers to buy a computer to take advantage of the Internet, as well as the video and telephone service they already buy. We might then witness a reduction in the 25 percent of Americans who still have no experience of the Net. We might see a rise in the penetration rate among people of color and those whose native language is not English, both groups among whom Internet penetration is relatively low. We might even see a rise in general happiness; surveys show that those on the Net are statistically more likely to be happy than those off-Net!

If as many Americans were online as watch satellite and cable television—about 85 percent of homes—many social benefits could be distributed and many social needs served by online communication. Political associations could be created more readily, thus increasing participation in democracy. Health care and education could be provided more efficiently to target populations that are otherwise costly to reach, such as shut-ins, workers, and those geographically distant from medical centers and schools.

From an economic perspective, each potential subscriber derives value from joining the network. Furthermore, each new subscriber increases value—external to the business relationship that the subscriber enters into when joining the network—for everyone else on the network. (To simplify, the new subscriber pays for the ability to contact existing subscribers, but existing subscribers gain the additional benefit of contacting the new participant. That additional benefit is external, or not captured by any given subscriber's payment.) A government may reasonably try to realize for all citizens the external benefits of network size, just as in helping to pay for a transcontinental railroad, a government may consider the future benefits of attracting new wealth-generating immigrants to the West.

From a political perspective, even without economic or philosophical justification for universal network access, it is very likely that rural America will get subsidies for communication, given the political power our federal system disproportionately allocates to relatively underpopulated states. The question is not whether to help rural America. The real question is how to structure an access program in order to stimulate economic growth, avoid wasting assets, and obtain an efficient network.

It is worth noting here that the FCC has required every television set to have a digital over-the-air tuner, even though when the order goes into effect, fewer than 10 percent of Americans will be watching over-the-air TV. We have approximately two televisions per home; the tuner will cost about $200 per TV. By designating the $400 from each home for big-broadband access instead of over-the-air digital TV, we might have enough subsidies to mete out to users in such volume that virtually all households could pay for broadband. Alternatively, or by way of a supplemental source of money, government could retrieve the tens of billions of dollars' worth of spectrum it granted to broadcasters for free (to send signals to the tuners that 90 percent of homes will not be using). The point of this tangent is not to dwell on the failures of past government policy but to indicate that money can be spent: the debate concerns the target. And perhaps universal broadband is a worthier national policy than universal over-the-air TV.

The political winds have so shifted that many industries now benefit from government-generated stimulus. Beneficiaries include housing, pharmaceuticals, airlines, steel, dividend-paying firms, and others. Indeed, ICT may be the only sector left that money has yet to be thrown at!

Suppose the FCC chose to connect all Americans to big-broadband service by duplicating a universal-service success story: the E-Rate program. This program provides funds to help schools pay for Internet access, which they buy from private firms. Internet access has increased from under 10 percent of classrooms in the mid-1990s to nearly 90 percent now. Unlike virtually every other communications service, E-Rate penetration rates are about the same in poor areas as in rich ones. The schools must contribute some monies themselves, and they are free to choose their access providers in the marketplace.

Applying these principles to big broadband, the FCC could first define what service was to be made universally available and affordable. To create a new medium, the service should offer access to a link capable of delivering at least 10 megabits per second. This level of physical access would create a platform for a host of new services and applications, most of which cannot be readily predicted. (Few would have guessed, for instance, that Japan's leading wireless carrier would earn revenue by offering different ringtones on cell phones for the sake of variety.) We do know that at 10 megabits per second, real-time video would be added to text and maybe voice, in effect creating a new medium (just as television did not so much complement as subsume radio).

At least three possible implementation models are worth consideration; others might emerge from a robust discussion. First, government could grant every taxpayer a tax credit (like the earned-income tax credit) assignable to any firm that provided the requisite broadband access. Cable, telephony, and any other entrants, such as wireless, would compete for the credit. It would be annually assignable, keeping competition vibrant.

As we have seen, approximately 40 million households are willing to pay the current market price for at least little broadband (1 megabit per second), in most places about $30 a month. In order to convert most of the remaining 60 million households, which do not frequently use a computer, the credit might need to be as much as $10 to $20 a month. For the sake of encouraging widespread construction of big-broadband networks, the credit could be assigned to every household regardless of income. In rural areas, where distances create larger costs, the credit would have to be larger. In the aggregate, at $15 a month per 100 million households, the total credit would cost about $18 billion a year. If instead the credit were targeted at households with lower incomes and in less dense areas, its cost could be reduced substantially. In any event, the credit could be phased out when the capital investment for the networks was recouped.

The broadband provider could charge whatever the market would bear, but to win the credit, it would have to win over the customer. Providers would thus be encouraged to experiment with differentiated services to persuade customers to subscribe. One household might subscribe if broadband were bundled with cable; another might prefer a combination of wireless and broadband; a third might select a long-distance voice and broadband bundle. Marketers would invent many other techniques to win the customer and the accompanying credit. Some might even give away broadband to very low-income customers just to win the credit. Such techniques should be encouraged: the goal would be to get everyone online.

By comparison, the E-Rate alone disburses about $4 billion a year to provide Internet access in 2 million classrooms. To obtain big-broadband access for 100 million homes in return for tax credits at only about four times that level hardly seems disproportionate in terms of cost and benefit.

A second proposal is for state utility commissions to designate one (or more than one) preferred big-broadband provider. This firm would be obligated to provide a physical link of at least 10 megabits per second to every household in a designated geographic area. Any technically qualified solution would be acceptable, so both wireless and wire-based alternatives could compete for the state designation. Fiber-based solutions would probably win in many markets, but the limiting factor would not be the physical medium but the large-scale capacity and reliability required by the terms of the bid. The state would guarantee the designated provider a return on the cost of its investment in the physical link.

The preferred broadband firm would then auction its physical capacity to service providers, each of which would be obliged to attach to the link its own electronic equipment and any other hardware or software necessary to deliver data access. It is reasonable to assume that the local providers of telephony, cable, and wireless could pay at auction at least $10 a month per home passed. Thus, the link provider would collect a minimum of $120 a year per home passed, and possibly much more, depending on the number of firms seeking access to the physical medium. This solution, however, would be inimical to the interests of cable and telephone firms in markets where they provide broadband access; perhaps it would suit only markets where they do not.

A third proposal is for government to encourage cable and telephony to merge their local-access networks, thus relieving each of them of substantial costs. They would keep their services separate and competitive, however, and would agree to expand the capacity of their access networks to 10 megabits per second. This model resembles an exemption from antitrust laws passed by Congress to permit competing local newspapers to share printing facilities in order to achieve economies of scale while continuing to compete in the content business.

These proposals are intended to start conversation, not to advocate a program. Any of them—and better ones that might be advanced—would probably provide much more economic stimulus to the networking industry than the private spending currently proposed, and would generate innovation and competition in the service layer of future big-broadband networks. These proposals are goal-oriented: the goal is to tie the nation together via the new medium of broadband and to use that medium as a platform for innovation in services. These proposals can also pose less risk and create more predictability for the ICT industry as a whole than the current FCC plan. Moreover, as big-broadband networks reach every household, we could reasonably expect to phase out the current voice subsidy system. The resulting savings alone would go a long way toward paying for these proposals.

The Key Goal: To Promote Economic Growth

Few countries have two parallel networks like those that have tempted U.S. regulators into endorsing two-firm broadband competition without in any way encouraging big-broadband build-out. In other countries, governments tend to view the access link as a natural monopoly. Those governments also worry that their economies are not sufficiently vibrant to attract capital even to a two-firm competition, given the high fixed costs in the broadband market. As a result, most foreign regulators tend to favor the creation of a single national provider of broadband physical links. They are willing to subsidize that provider in the interests of expanding the capacity per home and the number of homes passed by the provider. Then they compel the provider to sell the physical link's capacity to competing retail service vendors. Finally, they are likely to compel vendors to carry communication to each other (sometimes called interconnection) in order to discourage a leading service provider from eliminating its rivals, because it has to share the value of its subscriber base with those rivals. This scenario very roughly describes South Korean policy, for example.

The United States has often gone its own way, to its own benefit, in communications policy. When Europe mandated a single cellular transmission standard (GSM, where G literally and aspirationally stood for *global*), America opened the door to standards competition that permitted QUALCOMM's CDMA business to develop here at home and to win foreign markets, especially in Asia. But in broadband it is far from clear that the United States' unusual approach is the wisest. If the FCC were to adopt policies promoting big broadband to all households, we could better ensure our competitiveness with other national economies and bring our ICT policies into line with the Bush administration's Keynesian approach to tax policy.

At the very end of the twentieth century, narrowband Internet access became the fastest-growing communications service in history. America did not conquer the Internet because the Web was foreordained to be in English. Indeed, the Web protocols were invented in Geneva. We dominated cyberspace because in the last half of the 1990s thousands of firms sold narrowband access for the lowest prices in the world to a huge installed base of PCs that borrowed copper phone lines for no extra charge. Presto: 60 million online homes. Narrowband access used a natural monopoly as its key link, but the telephone companies were not permitted to seek advantages in service markets by selling access discriminatorily.

Narrowband Internet created the platform—the widespread interconnected Web experience—that in turn served as the petri dish for the growth of dot-coms. Entrepreneurs experimented with selling everything from pet supplies to cars to airplane tickets on and through the Web. Many such efforts failed, principally because delivery of tangible objects takes place not in cyberspace but in the three-dimensional world, where movement costs money. But predictions of e-commerce growth have come true, more or less. The Dow Jones Internet Index rose 82 percent in 2003, and eBay's 2003 revenue was $2.17 billion, an increase of 78 percent over the previous year. Yahoo!'s market cap was more than $15 billion in 2003—not nearly what it was during the boom, but still a prodigious number. According to Tom Eisenmann of Harvard Business School, the aggregate capital contributed to dot-com companies that relied on narrowband Internet access has earned at least an internal rate of return of about 9 percent.[7] Many Internet companies failed, but their losses were more than offset by the valuation gains of successful dot-coms like Yahoo! and eBay.

Now future growth is uncertain, and the cornucopia of new services may not be refilling. When the labor leader Samuel Gompers was asked to explain his policies, he replied: "More." More demand is the right answer for communications markets: more demand for existing services, new services, new connectivity, and new ideas. With more demand, new investment will follow in due course. By contrast, promoting investment in the absence of perceived demand either will not work or will work less well than new demand.

In summary, what are the best ways to promote demand? First, do not pursue a policy that could cause serious economic harm to cable and/or telephony firms while discouraging construction of the physical links that big-broadband services require. Second, stimulate growth through an efficient universal-service policy that will produce economic and social benefits. A decade ago John Malone, perhaps the single most important builder of American cable networks, predicted that three inventions—the microprocessor, digitization, and fiber optics—would revolutionize the media and communications industries and drive their convergence into a single market. Malone foresaw a five-hundred-channel universe. And in late 1993, to capture the value of this triple technological revolution, he sought to merge his cable company, TCI, with the phone company Bell Atlantic. The two firms jointly promised to build an "information highway" carrying all voice and all video channels to at least 40 percent of all homes in the United States. To support this big pipe, the two huge companies would raise the capital necessary to build fiber networks to homes. The merger plans collapsed in 1994.

Malone's dreamy vision of providing access plus all services deserves to be revived, though not in the form he proposed a decade ago. Since the Bell Atlantic–TCI merger was proposed, the Internet has arrived. Malone did not foresee Berners-Lee's great gift to the world of the Web protocols. He did not predict that the great content cornucopia would consist not of his ballyhooed five hundred channels but of the more than 10 billion pages on the Web. (Of course, many more hours are devoted to watching video channels than to reading Web pages; the North American ratio is roughly 10 to 1.)

Yet Malone was right that the access network is key to innovation and growth in ICT. Even with the availability of some broadband, the access bottleneck will be exasperating for years to come. Current microprocessors are capable of displaying in fractions of seconds movies or videoconferences that fiber can carry at the speed of light from anywhere in the world. Meanwhile, 100 million people sit at the screens of these information-hungry computers waiting impatiently for still pictures and words to resolve themselves slowly into recognizable form. Rather than waiting hours to download a film, the consumer drives to Blockbuster for a rental. So we have a problem of complementary products: no shoestrings, plenty of shoes; no access network, plenty of services that would like to move across that network. We have skimpy connection and plenty of computing potential that yearns for the big-broadband connection.

Perhaps a single triumphant triple-play-selling network embodying John Malone's failed merger would solve the problem of access by generating abundant capacity—if not for all, at least for many households. But is that the direction of current policy? The risk of a negative answer is very great.

Many chapters of regulatory history counsel against government policies that promote specific technologies. However, a high-capacity physical link is not so much a technology solution as a platform for innovation and a basis for service-level competition. It should serve not as a barrier to innovation but as a door to a future of technology discovery. And because our ICT sector is ailing, it should give us the short-term remedy of demand stimulus. We need that more than a burst of value-destroying deployment of little-broadband service to a portion of our consumer base.

Notes

1. Nicholas Carr, "IT Doesn't Matter," *Harvard Business Review*, May 1, 2003.

2. Herbert Hoover, *The Memoirs of Herbert Hoover: The Great Depression, 1929–1941* (New York: Macmillan, 1952), 30.

3. A *Nash equilibrium* is a set of strategies in a noncooperative game such that no player would be better off changing strategies unless all the players did so.

4. SONET stands for *synchronous optical network*, a technology that allows different types of formats to transmit on a single line.

5. A *liquidity trap* can arise when expected returns on investment are low. Investment falls and cash holdings rise, and businesses then continue to hold cash because they expect spending and investment to remain low.

6. Chris Baker, "FCC Chief Says Tech Is Wild Card," *Washington Times*, July 8, 2003, available at http://www.washtimes.com/business/20030707-101146-5642r.htm.

7. See Thomas Eisenmann, "Valuation Bubbles and Broadband Deployment," in *The Bandwidth Explosion*, eds. Robert D. Austin and Stephen P. Bradley (Boston: Harvard Business School Press, 2005).

14

Protecting Telecommunications Infrastructure from Malicious Threats

Jeffrey Hunker

B ROADBAND TELECOMMUNICATIONS is emerging as the control plane for the modern economy. Information previously captured in physical form—including sensitive business data and, increasingly, data on which the national security/emergency preparedness (NS/EP) functions of government depend—is now digitized and transported on broadband infrastructure. Protecting and ensuring the reliability of broadband telecommunications and information infrastructures is thus a high priority for both business and government. Worry is not misplaced. Telecommunications infrastructure has failed in a number of spectacular ways in recent years:

- AT&T's long-distance network went down in early 1990 when a minor failure caused a switch to execute flawed software. The failure cascaded across the system, causing other switches to fail in turn.[1]

- The failure of a telecommunications satellite in 1998 cut off service to nearly 90 percent of pagers in the United States. Many banking

and financial services were interrupted, as was communication between doctors and emergency workers.[2]

- Internet and cell phone service was degraded when a train accident
  in Baltimore in 2001 severed fiber-optic cables used to exchange
  data among Internet service providers (ISPs). Service suffered as far
  away as Africa.[3]

- The September 11, 2001, attack on the World Trade Center caused
  telecommunications outages in lower Manhattan. Destruction of
  Verizon's central office cut off service to providers who leased cable
  capacity from Verizon.[4]

- Internet worms and viruses have destroyed end-user files and congested Internet Protocol (IP) networks at a cost estimated in billions of dollars.[5]

Not all of these failures were intentional, and service was usually restored
within hours (only the September 11 attack resulted in a far longer outage). But the point is clear: telecommunications service can be disrupted.
As the complexity and reach of the broadband infrastructure grow, so does
the need to ensure its reliability and availability in the face of accidents
and malicious threats.

The national security implications of protecting telecommunications
infrastructure were first recognized before 1914.[6] Our current vigilance
about malicious threats, however, is a product of the last ten or fifteen
years. President Clinton signed a directive in 1998 acknowledging national
security threats to the nation's critical infrastructures and ordering a plan
to protect them from attack.[7] The directive and subsequent policies focused on cyber-based systems, and the Clinton and Bush administrations
have launched a series of initiatives to protect U.S. interests, including
telecommunications, from cyber attack and other forms of attack. An *Economist* special report estimates the worldwide cost of viral attacks in 2001 at
over $13 billion, and notes that 40 percent of the large businesses and gov-
ernment agencies it surveyed had suffered information systems intrusions.
Business spending on information technology security in the United States
is forecast to grow from $6 billion in 2001 to $13 billion in 2005.[8]

The telecommunications infrastructure is riddled with security vulnerabilities. The reason is straightforward: only a rudimentary "infra-

Critical Infrastructures: Some Definitions

Critical infrastructures are systems essential to the smooth functioning of the U.S. economy, government, and society—the telecommunications, electric power, water, transportation, and energy sectors. Sometimes the definition is broadened to include sectors like food supply.[9] *Critical infrastructures protection* ensures the reliability and performance of these systems.

There is not a clear boundary between information systems (encompassing all computers and information systems) and telecommunications infrastructure. This chapter will use an inclusive definition of *telecommunications infrastructure* encompassing all systems and activities that support the exchange of electronic, voice, and image data via any media, including end-user devices and handheld wireless devices. This broad definition captures the increasingly seamless integration of information-based functionality with communications connectivity.

Cyber security encompasses the totality of information and computational systems, including communication between those systems.[10] *Cyber security* and *telecommunications infrastructure protection* are essentially synonyms.

---

structure" exists for managing risk in the broadband infrastructure. Key questions about infrastructure protection remain unanswered:

- What telecommunications assets are we trying to protect, and from whom?

- How is security measured? What are the costs and benefits of adopting a standard measure?

- What levels of security are sufficient? Could what individuals and firms consider appropriate differ from what the national interest requires?

- Who is responsible, and who pays, for securing the infrastructure?

These questions are not principally technical in nature. The fundamental challenge is balancing cost and risk. Achieving a balance involves technological choices, but it also involves policy choices and managerial decisions.

In the broadband world, these choices must be made across globally distributed networks of providers and users, and choice-making structures—legal, managerial, economic, and regulatory—are lacking. Whether and how mechanisms are created to foster trade-offs between benefit and risk will determine how security considerations shape the evolution of broadband.

What Is the Telecommunications Infrastructure?

The telecommunications infrastructure is in rapid transformation from distinct circuit-switched networks—narrowband public telephone networks and IP-based packet-data networks like the Internet—to an interconnected network that provides multiple services.[11] Today's telecommunications infrastructure consists of *converged networks* of circuit-switched networks interoperating with broadband packet-based IP networks.[12] Two trends are noteworthy. First, proprietary switching and communications protocols are transitioning to open-systems protocols. Second, circuit-switched services are giving way to Internet package-switched services.[13] Over time, converging networks will evolve into a Next-Generation Network based on advanced IP network architecture. In the meantime, telecommunications infrastructure consists of a complex set of interconnecting voice- and IP-based networks. The interconnections between these networks are poorly understood.[14]

Points of Vulnerability

The broadband network is vulnerable to both physical and cyber-based threats.[15]

Vulnerabilities of the Entire Telecommunications Infrastructure

A number of vulnerabilities exist, both at individual points and in signaling-and-control systems.

Single Points of Vulnerability

Communications nodes—the telco hotels and central switching offices where communications cables and hardware converge—are subject to physical disruption.[16] Fixed telephone networks are highly centralized; a few hundred switches handle the entire country's long-distance traffic.[17]

IP networks may be particularly susceptible to single-point-of-failure vulnerabilities. A handful of networks carry much of the global Internet traffic.[18] ISPs exchange backbone traffic at network access points or private peering points. The locations of the few international gateways to other continents are not secret.[19]

High-capacity fiber-optic trunk lines carry multiple-provider traffic economically, but if cut (say, where they cross a bridge), they can disrupt parts of the network. At the local level, first-mile links are a point of particular vulnerability.

Signaling-and-Control Systems

Signaling-and-control systems that direct network traffic are increasingly vulnerable to cyber attack as convergence integrates previously separate systems. Authentication (verification of the identity of parties granted access) between systems is particularly weak.[20]

The public telephone network is controlled by a signaling network that is "out of band" (carried on different paths than message traffic) and not accessible to outsiders. However, an attacker could manipulate the network with insider help or by breaking into the phone company's private network.[21] Phone networks rely increasingly on IP-based online administrative functions; remote access to these functions makes systems and databases more susceptible to manipulation.[22] The telephone network is also vulnerable to physical and, to some extent, logical attacks. An accidental fiber-optic cut in New Jersey in 1982 shut down much of the East Coast's telephone system, including air-traffic control.

Vulnerabilities of IP Networks

IP networks are less mature, less well understood, and less secure than circuit-switched telephony. In addition to sharing some of the telephone network's vulnerabilities, IP networks have unique vulnerabilities.[23]

Internet Protocols

The most widely used Internet protocols, notably Version 4 (IPv4), have multiple security flaws. That is, the network architecture itself creates vulnerabilities. Because the source of packets cannot be reliably authenticated, a malicious attacker can mask his or her (or its—attacks are increasingly automated) location on the network. Sniffing (eavesdropping on messages), spoofing (faking message origin), message altering, and message interception are all possible.[24] Newer protocols like IPv6 partially correct these shortcomings, but their adoption has been slow. A number of nations, including the United States, have made rapid replacement of IPv4 a national goal.

Internet Routers, a Key Component of IP-Network Infrastructure

Internet routers direct the flow of traffic. Because routing protocols are executed "in band" with the communications they control (i.e., message content and network control information are part of the same stream of data), such messages are accessible online; if communications links are disrupted, so are routing and control messages.

Routers are rarely well secured, configured, or monitored.[25] If one router is compromised, "trusted" relationships could be used to disrupt other routers. The Border Gateway Protocol (BGP), used at borders between networks, allows networks with different protocols to connect with each other. BGP provides inadequate message authentication and is susceptible to attack. False routing information could cut off portions of the network.[26]

Domain Name Servers

Domain name servers (DNS) provide routing directions (the addresses to which packets are sent). Thirteen domain name servers maintain the core directories of Internet addresses. There has been at least one cyber attack on DNS servers.

Virus, Worm, and Malware Attacks

Virus, worm, and malware attacks have caused massive congestion on the Internet and destroyed files on end-user devices. (Worms differ from viruses in that a user need not open a file attachment for a worm to propagate.) A cascading failure could occur if infected servers corrupted their neighbors. This sort of failure has occurred on other types of routing/ switching systems. We have yet to see sustained network degradation from viruses, worms, and malware, but without protective measures, damaging attacks are virtually inevitable.

Congestion

Congestion initiated by distributed denial of service (DDoS) attacks floods IP networks with packets. In DDoS attacks, malicious attackers commandeer "zombie" computers to bombard targeted systems with packets, flooding the target and cutting it off from the network.

Other Major Sources of Vulnerabilities

Operating systems, software, and wireless networks are also vulnerable.

Improper Systems Configuration

End-user systems typically require effort to configure. Many operating systems are shipped with their security features turned off, so action is required to turn them on. Software updates and security "patches" require installation. Improper execution of such activities, which is all too common, constitutes a major vulnerability.[27] The core problem is a combination of inadequate training, a shortage of systems administrators familiar with adequate security procedures, and our growing reliance on key information and communication systems.

Software Bugs, Errors, and Design Choices

Software remains a handcrafted product whose complexity creates vulnerabilities. Much of the software that runs IT networks is too complex to be thoroughly tested, and user companies rarely know how it will interact with other tools and technologies.[28]

Wireless Networks and Protocols

Security protocols have been incorporated into 802.11x standards, but wireless networks and protocols are less secure than wireline systems. "Hotspots," points where people access wireless computer networks, remain security holes, and cellular traffic is susceptible to interception.[29]

How Vulnerable Is the Telecommunications Infrastructure?

Disagreement prevails about the security implications of migration to packet-based communications. Some authorities have expressed alarm that the open environment of packet networks invites access, manipulation, and theft of information transmitted via the public telephone network. Others argue that the system will become resistant to attack because data can be dynamically rerouted around disabled nodes.[30] The latter assessment is comforting but probably misleading because more and more sophisticated threats continue to emerge.

How Alarmed Should We Be?

September 11 revealed that the United States is not immune to hostile attacks from unconventional sources. Public records do not distinguish serious attacks from minor incidents, but the trend is clear: attacks that affect the performance of the telecommunications system are increasing. (See figure 14-1.)

Other than the World Trade Center bombing, there have been few if any physical attacks on network infrastructure. The sophistication of cyber attacks has, however, decidedly increased. To date, there are three classes of cyber attack. The classic threat is attempts to penetrate or "hack" into systems—computers, routers, and switches, and the SCADA (supervisory control and data analysis) systems that control industrial operations. We lack good data on the number of computer systems that have been penetrated; many institutions choose not to report attacks, and insiders probably account for much of malicious behavior.[31] However, the public record reveals a number of system penetrations; the 1998 "Solar Sunrise" penetration of Defense Department computer systems was feared to be a foreign action but turned out to be the work of two American teenagers. Only a few penetrations have affected the infrastructure itself, and then only with limited effect; one hacker disabled a telecommunications switch affecting the operations of a Massachusetts airport. More notable is accidental disabling of the telephone infrastructure. The Galaxy I communications satellite stopped functioning in May 1998, disabling phone, pager, and ATM services. A cut fiber-optic cable caused much of the East Coast to lose telecommunications, including the air-traffic control system. A 2003 fiber-line cut disrupted service for sixty thousand customers in Washington state. (See figure 14-2.)

Summer 2003 witnessed several powerful virus attacks. The virus SoBigF launched e-mails using the address lists of infected machines; at its peak it was the source of one in every sixteen e-mails on the Net. To date, viral attacks have remained merely a serious nuisance, but attacks against telecommunications infrastructure—such as viruses targeting router operations—are plausible.

A third class of threat, DDoS attacks against high-profile Internet-based businesses, generated attention in February 2000 when the stock-market valuations of the attacked companies declined precipitously—they recovered quickly—and President Clinton convened the first-ever cyber-security summit with industry. Viral and DDoS attacks can be combined:

FIGURE 14-1

Malicious acts, growing potential, and incidence

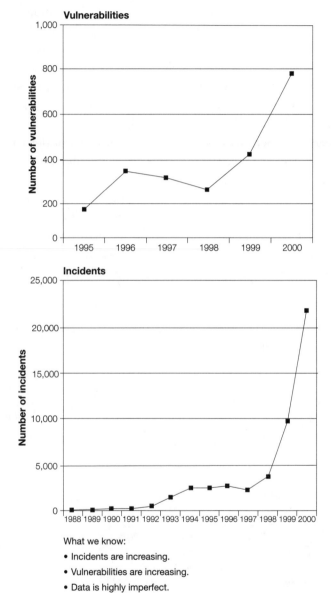

What we know:

- Incidents are increasing.
- Vulnerabilities are increasing.
- Data is highly imperfect.
- Cyber will be a theater of operations between nations.
- Cyber crime is increasing exponentially.

Source: Jeffrey Hunker.

The Blaster virus, active on the Internet shortly before SoBigF, was designed to launch a DDoS attack against a Microsoft site, but the attack was averted.

Cyber crime has increased in frequency and sophistication, but so far it apparently tends to involve use of the Internet to perpetrate crimes like fraud, extortion, and theft of information rather than attacks on the infrastructure itself. A terrorist threat against the telecommunications infrastructure has not yet materialized. Are security concerns therefore overstated?

No—for two reasons. First, the range of potential perpetrators and motivations is broad. The taxonomy of threats in figure 14-3 illustrates their breadth. Cyber as a field of conflict is now part of the military lexicon, and several nations apparently have offensive cyber capabilities (those most frequently mentioned are the United States, Russia, China, Israel, and France). And there is precedent: the KGB planned physical attacks on the U.S. telecommunications infrastructure in the 1960s and 1970s.[32]

Second, dependence on broadband infrastructure will shortly reach a point at which security—that is, reliability—is an absolute requirement. Like electricity, broadband supports an expanding universe of applica-

FIGURE 14-2

Attack sophistication and tools

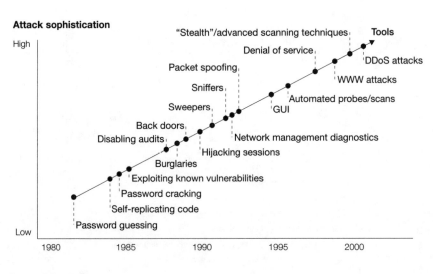

Source: Jeffrey Hunker.

FIGURE 14-3

Taxonomy of threat

	Target	
Aim	National security	Economic/social fabric
To destroy information or disable infrastructure	Attacks on critical infrastructure National security information Warfare Terrorism	Vandalism (hacking, cracking) Crime (extortion, etc.)
To retrieve information	Espionage	Privacy violations Digital rights management Intellectual property rights Economic espionage Crime (extortion, etc.)

Source: Jeffrey Hunker.

tions. Right now, the broadband world cannot ensure dependability or security: even without malicious attack, the average downtime of an Internet router is approximately one hundred times that of a telephone-network switch. Security considerations will thus increasingly shape the future of broadband.

Protecting the Telecommunications Infrastructure

The 1964 Cuban Missile Crisis revealed the government's need for enhanced telecommunications resources, leading to the creation of special systems that prioritize NS/EP communications on the public telephone network. The National Communications Center (NCC), created in 1984 and supported by the Defense Department, provides real-time operational coordination of the public telephone network in times of crisis.

The advent of the Internet, wireless, and broadband, and the dependence of the electricity, transportation, and energy industries on telecommunications, have stimulated reevaluation of federal policies to protect the telecommunications infrastructure. Federal policies emphasize voluntary cooperation between business and government, but they have a strong regulatory component. The policies of the Clinton and Bush administrations embody three principles: (1) the telecommunications infrastructure is the

FIGURE 14-4

Key elements of U.S. policy on telecommunications infrastructure protections

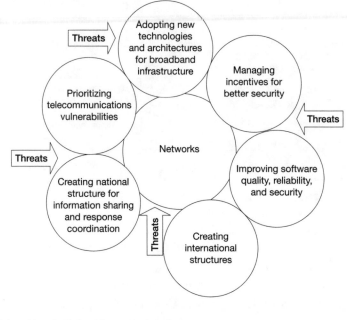

Source: Adapted from the National Communications Center.

foundation for other critical infrastructures; (2) national security requires operational coordination with the private sector; and (3) voluntary cooperation is preferable to regulation. These principles in turn give rise to the six key elements of national policy, shown in figure 14-4.

Creating New Public-Private National Structures

The Department of Homeland Security has established Information Sharing and Analysis Centers (ISACs) to enable critical sectors to share information and collaborate to protect the economy. At least in theory, the ISACs will coordinate with each other and with federal response assets, notably within the Department of Homeland Security.[33]

The goal is to adapt the NCC model of business-government operational coordination to other sectors, creating a national system—the Cyber

Lessons Learned from Y2K

The initiative to handle the year 2000 (or Y2K) bug—software failures due to date-field miscoding—offers lessons applicable to telecommunications security, particularly the need for private-sector response. Important lessons from the Y2K effort include:

- *Leadership and education are essential.* As Y2K czar, John Koskinen spent almost three years educating and organizing businesses to head off Y2K-related software failures. Koskinen had previously been deputy director of the Office of Management and Budget.

- *Incentives are essential.* Incentives can be both carrots and sticks. The Securities and Exchange Commission required member firms to inform investors how they were preparing for Y2K-related problems, thus mandating attention to the issue. Federal legislation exempted from Freedom of Information Act requirements (public disclosure) any Y2K-related information that businesses shared with government.

- *Operational coordination between business and government is essential.* An operations center—the Information Coordination Center (ICC)—coordinated the actions of federal agencies, state and local governments, and business. Voluntary agreements with businesses and business associations provided assets and coordinated federal and private responses. For over a month preceding and following the millennium, the ICC was continually operated by a public-private staff.

The Y2K experience demonstrates that, with massive effort, voluntary business-government partnerships to address security threats can be made to work.

Warning and Information Network (CWIN)—to assess, protect against, and respond to threats against cyber systems (see figure 14-5). At least in principle, ISACs now cover telecommunications, financial services, transportation, electric power grids, and the nondefense portions of the federal government (national security agencies have their own system). ISACs are voluntary and vary greatly in form and function. Those closest to being

FIGURE 14-5

Government-industry response system: the Cyber Warning and Information Network (CWIN) response

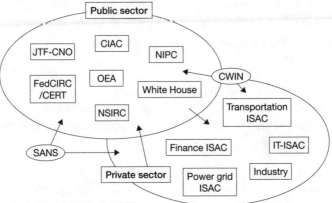

CIAC: Computer Incident Advisory Capability

FedCIRC/CERT: Federal Computer Incident Response Center and Federal Computer Emergency Response Team

JTF-CNO: U.S. Space Command's Joint Task Force-Computer Network Operations Unit

NIPC: National Infrastructure Protection Center

NSIRC: National Security Incident Response Center

OEA: Office of Energy Assurance

SANS: The SANS (SysAdmin, Audit, Network, Security) Institute, a cooperative research and education organization

Source: Adapted from Cyber Warning and Information Network (CWIN).

truly operational are telecommunications (the NCC), electric power, and financial services.

Multiple obstacles impede effective functioning of this system. Businesses are loath to share network-security information with government or competitors. No templates exist to specify what information is of greatest value or how it is to be shared. The NCC has effectively coordinated telephone-system response, but it is unclear whether this model can scale up to cover the broadband infrastructure.

Prioritizing Telecommunications Vulnerabilities

Nationwide vulnerability assessments help prioritize vulnerabilities and threats. In the broadband world, however, vulnerability assessments are tricky. The threat spectrum is poorly understood and continuously changing, and the most obvious threats, like viruses, may not be the most serious.

FIGURE 14-6

Interdependencies among infrastructures

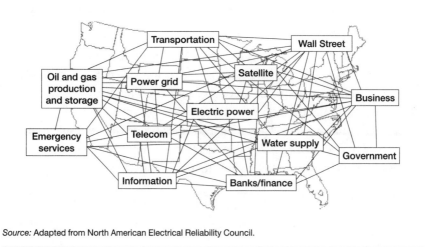

Source: Adapted from North American Electrical Reliability Council.

An even more difficult challenge is understanding the interdependencies between telecommunications and other infrastructures. Methodologies for analyzing infrastructure interdependencies are still immature. Predicting how a telecommunications breakdown will affect the performance and behavior of, say, the electric power grid or a pipeline system is difficult at best. Figure 14-6 is a simplified version of a map of interdependencies produced by an initiative based at Sandia and Los Alamos National Laboratories. Specific infrastructures have their own models and simulation tools, but tools to simulate and analyze interdependent infrastructures in a manner that addresses protection, mitigation, response, and recovery needs, do not exist.

Adopting New Technologies and Architectures for Broadband Infrastructure

Federal policy is promoting (though not mandating) specific changes in network architecture:

- *A shift from IPv4 to IPv6.* IPv6 has improved security features. Several other countries are moving to fully implement IPv6: Japan has committed to do so by 2005; China and the European Union are considering expedited systemwide adoption.[34] Whether and how these initiatives will succeed is an open question.

- *More secure BGP and domain-name system protocols.* Attacks that exploit vulnerabilities in either of these protocols could cause widespread network disruptions.

- *Improved Internet routing protocols.* Such protocols would reduce
  the impact of DDoS attacks.

Fundamental changes in architecture have been discussed. In 2001 the
U.S. government solicited design proposals for Govnet, a separate and
highly secure packet-switched network. Govnet would carry government
communications and might link with private-sector infrastructure providers.
The project appears not to have advanced since proposals were solicited.

The Cyber Security Research and Development Agenda, the product
of a 2002 analysis conducted by the Institute for Information Infrastructure Protection, identified a set of issues important to the security of the
information infrastructure that are either unfunded or underfunded by
private and government-sponsored research initiatives (see the list of topics in the accompanying box).[35]

Managing Incentives for Better Security

"People buy a hunk of shining technology, wipe their brow, and say,
'Great. I've taken care of it,'" says Peter Horst of TruSecure Corporation,
"when they might have been better off saving money and doing something simple in terms of policy and process." Companies must not ignore
human-based security measures like password guidelines. It is crucial too
that accountability for a security failure fall to those responsible for ensuring security in the first place. "Insecurity is often due to perverse incentives, rather than the lack of suitable technical protection mechanisms,"
says Ross Anderson of Cambridge University's Computer Laboratory.[36]

Managerial responsibility for security used to be taken for granted.
Now that broadband infrastructure is in highly distributed hands, incentives must motivate very dissimilar owners and operators. Both public-
and private-sector initiatives are trying to direct the attention of senior
management to broadband security:

- *Awareness and education.* The federal government's bully pulpit is
  a powerful force, as is the participation of federal agencies in standards bodies and industry gatherings. Lack of trained security

Security Issues for Information Infrastructure

Research topics identified by the Institute for Information Infrastructure Protection are as follows:

- *Enterprise security management.* Security mechanisms need to be integrated into a coherent capability for managing access to and use of business information infrastructure.

- *Trust among distributed autonomous parties.* Methods are needed for different entities to establish relationships across networks dynamically and without recourse to a central authority.

- *Discovery and analysis of security properties and vulnerabilities.* The security properties and behavior of large-scale systems are frequently difficult or impossible to predict from the performance of their components.

- *Secure system and network response and recovery.* Issues of scale, coordination across administrative and policy domains, and coordination of diverse systems are arising as the infrastructure grows in size and complexity.

- *Traceback, identification, and forensics.* Enterprises' abilities to detect and respond to attacks internally, including tracing, identifying, and determining the source and nature of any attack, need to be strengthened.

- *Wireless security.* Security must become a fundamental component of wireless networks. Solutions developed for wired networks may be applicable to wireless applications.

- *Metrics and models.* A need exists for data and defined metrics to express the costs, benefits, and impacts of security controls.

- *Law, policy, and economic issues.* Security decisions are made in a context of poorly understood economic factors, laws, regulations, and government policies.

professionals is often cited as a reason for continued infrastructure vulnerabilities. Thus, federal investment is now targeted at educational programs, such as the recently created Scholarship for Service program, which supports students in approved network-security programs in exchange for a period of federal service.

- *Federal standards and procurement.* Historically, telecommunications and cyber-security concerns have been a federal priority only for defense-related agencies. The White House Office of Management and Budget now vigorously monitors federal agencies' compliance with information security programs, in concert with vigorous congressional oversight of agencies' telecommunications security. Federal standards for information systems security now have teeth. Defense Department procurements for telecommunications and information systems must meet security standards, and the Federal Information Management Act imposes standards on other federal agencies' systems and procurement. Federal security standards for procurement have been tried before, unsuccessfully. In a sense, the new standards represent an experiment to gauge how effectively federal procurement can affect private-sector markets.

- *Regulation.* Voluntary private-sector participation is the putative goal of federal policy, but the financial-services and health-care sectors (which jointly account for over one-quarter of the U.S. economy) are under regulatory mandate for telecommunications security. The Health Insurance Portability and Accountability Act (HIPAA) is creating a unified data infrastructure for health-care providers. The Department of Health and Human Services has adopted technical standards for cyber security in implementing the act. The 1999 Financial Services Modernization Act requires customer-record privacy; banking regulators are interpreting this mandate to impose a specified level of telecommunications and in-formation systems security on financial-service providers.

- *Best practices.* The FCC's Network Reliability and Interoperability Council has developed a code of best practices whose wide accep-tance would improve network security. Standards and best practices are important elements in "shared risk" situations—Underwriters Laboratories is a good example—and certain standards are maturing. British Standard 7799 has been internationally adopted as ISO 17799, and standards like COBIT and FISCAM are widely used.

- *Insurance and risk management.* Because many insurers exclude telecommunications-related losses from business-interruption insurance, a market is emerging for cyber-security insurance, led by companies like Chubb Corporation, AIG, and Marsh Inc.

Improving Software Quality, Reliability, and Security

Many known flaws in operating systems remain unpatched. Systems operators may be too busy or may lack training; the affected systems may be too critical to risk a faulty patch. It is essential, however, to patch software vulnerabilities immediately when they are discovered. Ironically, most security breaches exploit well-known vulnerabilities for which fixes are available. Work is under way to create a less haphazard way for users and software providers to collaborate when vulnerabilities are discovered. Common test beds, to test patches in different software configurations, are also in the works. The Defense Department is experimenting with automating the patch process.

In the longer term, protecting the telecommunications infrastructure will require software with fewer defects, and systems architectures with inherently improved security. A significant amount of R&D is exploring ways of producing defect-free software.

Creating International Structures

Telecommunications infrastructure protection is not an exclusively domestic agenda. Backbone telecommunications providers already share standards developed by the International Telecommunications Union (ITU). In other areas, international cooperation ranges from excellent to rudimentary. Criminal penalties and procedures, information-sharing structures, standards, and best practices vary markedly from country to country. And as the broadband infrastructure expands, so does the number of providers. Efforts are afoot to encourage other nations to adopt the Council on Europe's Convention on Cybercrime or its equivalent, and the

Organization for Economic Co-Operation and Development telecommunications and information systems security guidelines.

Will a Risk-Management Infrastructure Emerge?

Business is investing resources to protect the telecommunications infrastructure from malicious attack; R&D is seeking solutions to fundamental security problems; network vulnerabilities are being identified and fixed; and public-private systems are evolving. Even so, security remains an add-on in the broadband infrastructure. No widely accepted liability standards or other risk-management techniques serve to focus senior management's attention on telecommunications security. As long as this is the case, security will remain a secondary consideration in the private sector.

The fundamental question is when an *infrastructure of telecommunications-infrastructure risk management* will begin to mature. A boutique-size market for cyber-security insurance is emerging. The legal community is showing interest in applying tort law (legal liability) to network disruptions. Vulnerability assessments are becoming more commonplace. Federal engagement in codifying effective standards is encouraging. But an efficient risk-management infrastructure calls for several issues to be resolved.

How Is Security Measured? Determining Costs and Benefits

Quantifiable measures are lacking of the risks to users from deliberate attack or system unreliability. Assertions abound about the extent, frequency, and impact of network attacks, but the accompanying statistics are mostly "mythical numbers" that have won credence only through continual repetition.[37]

For enterprises to make economically efficient choices about how much risk to accept, and for governments and societies to make choices about investment in reliability, we need to quantify risks. To create a risk profile, we must be able to (1) measure losses and (2) determine the likelihood of an attack or a destabilizing event. Quantification of risk to a network requires data sets that either do not exist or are unavailable to the research community (e.g., because of companies' reluctance to share information about vulnerabilities or attacks). Nor do databases exist, except in proprietary settings, to create risk-shifting and risk-mitigation strategies. The situation is reminiscent of automobile insurance a century ago—an intellectual framework exists for measuring risk and developing risk-mitigating measures, but actuarial databases to support underwriting are lacking.[38]

Who Decides and Who Pays? The Need for Governance

The reliability and security of broadband infrastructures depend on their underlying architecture. Internet2 and the proposed Govnet are initiatives designed to alter the architecture of cyber systems. Both illustrate an essential point: building reliability and security into the broadband telecommunications infrastructure is fundamentally a question of governance. The issues are: Who pays? And who decides when and how to migrate to a new architecture?

For packet-switched networks, the question is daunting. There are around fourteen thousand autonomous systems on the Internet.[39] A bewildering array of voluntary standards organizations oversees these networks.[40] In traditional telecommunications, close coordination among providers prevails as a legacy of the hegemony of AT&T: in packet-based systems, no one is operationally responsible; operational governance is a matter of loose collaboration.

The Internet Engineering Task Force (IETF) is an open international community of network designers, operators, vendors, and researchers that oversees technical standards on the Internet. Organized relatively informally into working groups like security, routing, and transport, the IETF has created many communications protocols that power the Internet.[41] But some observers are convinced that Internet security and reliability would be promoted by restructuring the IETF. Since 1992, after acknowledging its organizational and productivity problems, the organization has been seeking ways to bring network standards to market sooner. (It can take more than five years to finalize specifications.)[42]

It is also far from clear that choices about Internet architecture and protocols—and the underlying decision processes—are even close to socially and economically optimal. How do we impose a system of governance on global infrastructures that anticipates externalities (effects on others) and future design issues without undermining positive social externalities like innovation? Exploration of these questions has been limited because answering them requires expertise in technology, decision science, economics, and other fields. Few researchers have the cross-disciplinary knowledge to integrate these perspectives creatively.

Developing Efficient Incentive Structures

Networks are shared systems. One user's actions have potential impacts on other users, and new protocols may affect users differently. The challenge for policy makers is to create incentives that motivate collective action by highly diverse users and operators to promote security. Creating such incentives requires contemplating how risk can be shifted or managed among network participants, and how risk is perceived and measured.

Inadequate regard for security imposes risk on others that they may not know about and might not accept voluntarily. There are many possible ways to address this issue. Technological options might help make risks more visible. Legal mechanisms could transform involuntary risk into voluntary risk. For example:

- Should the target of a DDoS attack be able to sue the unwitting owners/operators of computers used as launch sites for the attack?

- Should there be a standard minimum level of security that all system operators must maintain or else incur economic or legal penalties?

- If a virus damages a user's computer, who should be held responsible: the system owner/operator or the ISP? What standard of care should each adhere to in order to protect the network?

The legal system and public policy could establish rules that assign responsibility to those who can most efficiently reduce the risk, which is the underlying principle of risk management.

Comprehensive cyber security requires that everyone act in a secure manner. This kind of collective-action problem pervades society, and many approaches exist: (1) market forces, (2) regulation, (3) tort liability and contracts, (4) voluntary standards and best practices, (5) insurance, (6) public disclosure, (7) reputation (e.g., bond ratings), and (8) procurement. Deciding which is best, and who will decide, will have tremendous implications for evolution of the Internet.[43]

Market Forces

Because of externalities, market forces are unlikely to function as a compelling incentive for security in open networks. The benefits of security are shared, but its costs accrue to individual users. The free-rider problem is substantial: everyone hopes that everyone else is investing in security. Thus, a different model seems required if incentives are to operate meaningfully.

Regulation

Regulatory approaches are widely dismissed as politically unfeasible or rigid and slow. As we have seen, though, both financial services and health care operate under vigorous regulatory cyber-security standards. The extent of allocative inefficiencies and the impact of imperfect information in these regulatory environments remain to be determined.

Tort Liability and Contracts

It is not yet clear whether the U.S. tort-liability system will become a central component of the incentive structure. It seems unlikely that tort liability will play a large role, because its rules are least satisfactory when losses are purely financial, massive, and caused by an insolvent bad actor. Contracts between parties to maintain network security, on the other hand, are likely to become a primary element of the network-security infrastructure. Particularly in proprietary networks, contracts are an efficient way to ensure a common security threshold.[44]

Voluntary Standards and Best Practices

Despite many efforts, there exists no widely accepted and technically specific set of either standards or best practices for network security for the Internet. BS 7799 has been adopted by the ISO, but this standard is process-based rather than identifying minimum systems-configuration requirements.[45]

Insurance

The fundamental challenge for cyber-security insurance is developing quantitative measures of risk and creating data sets to predict risk levels. As has been noted, these do not currently exist.

Public Disclosure

The Securities and Exchange Commission's requirement that firms describe their readiness for Y2K-related risks is an instructive model: it effectively focused the attention of auditors, insurers, investors, boards, and senior management on such risks.

Reputation and Ratings

Financial ratings (like those of Standard and Poor's and Moody's) are effective instruments for making known a firm's financial soundness. The National Security Agency's Orange Book and its successors are similar efforts to rate the security of devices and systems.[46] These efforts have had limited success and almost no impact on the commercial market.

Procurement

Large-scale procurements by governments and the private sector are a potentially useful element in a cyber-security incentive system if made subject to common standards. Procurement standards can be used in a number of ways. They could specify, for example, that vendors ensure a certain level of organizational cyber security or invest in specified levels of systems redundancy.

People Matter: Adopting an Integrated Perspective

Infrastructures are not merely the sum of their physical and electronic components. Because they rely on people, risk perception, risk measurement, and communication with the public are important for security and reliability. A truly integrated perspective on infrastructure reliability requires an interdisciplinary approach—in fact, it requires an unprecedented integration of engineering with the social and behavioral sciences. As the National Academy of Sciences' 2002 report, *Making the Nation Safe: The Role of Science and Technology in Countering Terrorism*, notes, "The interface between technology and human behavior is an important subject for investigation. The research agenda should be broad-based, including topics such as decision making that affects the use of detection and prevention technologies; the ways in which deployment of technologies can complement or conflict with the values of privacy and civil liberty; and factors that influence the trustworthiness of individuals in a position to compromise or thwart security."[47]

Conclusion

Protecting the telecommunications infrastructure from malicious threats is a critical agenda. Security issues should therefore be a factor in shaping the evolution of the broadband network. But despite growing business investment and federal engagement, security remains an afterthought in most of the broadband infrastructure. Change will require an infrastructure of security risk management across the broadband network. Such an infrastructure is well entrenched among public telephone network providers. The question is whether a legal, managerial, and standards-based structure will develop across the much broader, and more complex, broadband infrastructure.

Notes

1. Institute for Security Technology Studies (ISTS), *Information and Telecommunications Sector Vulnerabilities and Threats* (Hanover, NH: Dartmouth College, 2003), available at http://www.ists.dartmouth.edu/library/analysis/itsv.pdf.

2. ISTS, *Vulnerabilities and Threats*, 27.

3. William H. Cheswick, Steve Bellovin, and Aviel Rubin, *Firewalls and Internet Security* (Boston: Addison-Wesley, 2003), 28.

4. Cheswick, Bellovin, and Rubin, *Firewalls*, 27.

5. "A Step-by-Step Migration Scenario from PSTN to NGN" (Alcatel technical paper, January 3, 2002), 6, available at http://www.bitpipe.com/detail/RES/1017857272_648.html.

6. Terrence K. Kelly, "Transformation and Homeland Security: Dual Challenges for the U.S. Army" (paper presented at the Commonwealth Institute Project on Defense Alternatives for the RAND Corporation, July 2003).

7. Tom Standage, "A Survey of Digital Security," *Economist*, October 24, 2002.

8. A survey carried out by the Meta Group in August 2002 found that fewer than one-quarter of firms surveyed had increased spending on information technology, but almost three-quarters had increased their budgets for information security technology. Overall, information security remains a small budget item, which has been compared unfavorably with the amount spent on coffee. But spending on communications security is rising, both in absolute terms and as a percentage of firms' information technologies budgets (Standage, "Survey of Digital Security").

9. President's Commission on Critical Infrastructure Protection, *Critical Foundations: Protecting America's Infrastructures* (Washington, DC, 1997), available at http://www.tsa.gov/interweb/assetlibrary/Infrastructure.pdf.

10. *National Plan for Information Systems Protection, Version 1.0: An Invitation to a Dialogue* (Washington, DC: the White House, 2000).

11. *Vulnerabilities and Threats*, 9.

12. National Security Telecommunications Advisory Committee (NSTAC), *Convergence Task Force Report*, 6, available at http://www.ncs.gov/nstac/Convergence Report-Final.htm.

13. National Security Telecommunications Advisory Committee, *The NSTAC's Response to the National Plan*, 6, available at http://www.ncs.gov/nstac/NationalPlanReport-Final.htm.

14. ISTS, *Vulnerabilities and Threats*, 9–10, 14.

15. This section draws heavily on ISTS, *Vulnerabilities and Threats*.

16. ISTS, *Vulnerabilities and Threats*, 14.

17. Computer Science and Telecommunications Board, National Research Council, *Trust in Cyberspace* (Washington, DC: National Academy Press, 1999).

18. ISTS, *Vulnerabilities and Threats*, 16.

19. Ibid., 21.

20. Ibid., 23.

21. Ibid., 22.

22. Ibid., 23.

23. Ibid., 25.

24. Ibid., 23.

25. Ibid., 3.

26. ISTS, *Vulnerabilities and Threats*, 35–36; NSTAC, *Network Security/Vulnerability Assessments Task Force Report*, March 2003.

27. *The National Strategy to Secure Cyberspace* (Washington, DC: the White House, February 2003), 33.

28. ISTS, *Vulnerabilities and Threats*, 27.

29. Ibid., 23.

30. NSTAC, *Convergence Task Force Report*, 2; ISTS, *Vulnerabilities and Threats*, 3, 17–18, 27, 30.

31. It is frequently said that insiders account for 80 percent of all computer attacks. The author has been unable to find documentation of this claim and believes it to be one of those "mythical statistics" that gain credibility by dint of frequent repetition.

32. Christopher Andrew and Vasili Mitrokhin, *The Sword and the Shield: The Metrokhin Archive and the Secret History of the KGB* (New York: Basic Books, 1999), chap. 10.

33. IT-ISAC is a forum for sharing information about, and effective solutions for, network vulnerabilities and threats. See https://www.it-isac.org/.

34. *National Strategy to Secure Cyberspace*, 30.

35. Institute for Information Infrastructure Protection, "Cyber Security Research and Development Agenda" (Hanover, NH: Dartmouth College, January 2003).

36. "The Weakest Link," *Economist*, October 24, 2002.

37. Professor Ashish Arora, Carnegie Mellon University, conversation with author.

38. Professor Mark Grady, George Mason University, conversation with author.

39. ISTS, *Vulnerabilities and Threats*, 15.

40. For instance, the Internet Engineering Task Force (IETF), the Internet Assigned Numbers Authority, the Internet Corporation for Assigned Names and Numbers, the Internet Society, the North American Network Operators' Group, the ITU Telecommunication Standardization Sector, and the International Packet Communications Consortium. NSTAC, *Convergence Task Force Report*, 9.

41. See http://www.ietf.org.

42. Carolyn Duffy Marsan, "IETF's Quest to Be Quicker Moves Slowly," *Network World Fusion*, November 17, 2003, available at http://www.nwfusion.com/news/2003/1117ietf.html.

43. Professor Mark Grady, conversation with author.

44. Lee Zeichner, LefINet, Bethesda, Maryland, conversation with author.

45. The International Organization for Standardization (ISO) is the source of more than one thousand four hundred international standards, such as ISO 9000 and ISO 14000. ISO is a network of national standards institutes in 148 countries working in partnership with international organizations, governments, industry, business, and consumer representatives. See http://www.iso.org.

46. The Rainbow Series is a six-foot-tall stack of variously colored books on evaluating "trusted computer systems" according to the National Security Agency. Portions of the Rainbow Series have been superseded by the Common Criteria Evaluation and Validation Scheme (CCEVS). See http://niap.nist.gov/cc-scheme/index.html.

47. National Academy of Sciences, *Making the Nation Safe: The Role of Science and Technology in Countering Terrorism* (Washington, DC: National Academy of Sciences, 2002).

15

Open Spectrum

The Great Wireless Hope

Kevin Werbach

Almost everything you think you know about spectrum is wrong. For nearly a century, radio-frequency spectrum has been treated as a scarce resource that the government must parcel out through exclusive licenses. Spectrum licensing has brought us radio, television, cellular telephones, and vital public safety services, but the assumptions underlying the licensing model of spectrum management no longer hold.

Today's digital technologies are smart enough to distinguish between signals, allowing users to share the airwaves without exclusive licensing. Instead of treating spectrum as a scarce resource, we could make it available to all as a commons, an approach known as *open spectrum*. Open spectrum would allow for more efficient and creative use of the airwaves. It could foster competition and innovative services, reduce prices, create new business opportunities, and bring our communications policies in line with our democratic ideals.

Despite its radical implications, open spectrum can coexist with traditional exclusive licensing. Two mechanisms facilitate spectrum sharing: unlicensed parks and underlay. The first employs allocated frequency bands, but no user is given an exclusive right to transmit. Very limited sets of frequencies have already been designated for unlicensed consumer devices, such as cordless phones and wireless local area networks, but more is needed to unleash the full potential of spectrum sharing. The second approach allows unlicensed users to coexist in licensed bands by making their signals invisible and not intruding on those of other users. Which approach turns out to be preferable will depend on how technology and markets develop. Both should be encouraged. The risks are minimal and the potential benefits extraordinary.

If the U.S. government wants to put in place the most proinnovation, proinvestment, deregulatory, and democratic spectrum-policy regime, it should do everything possible to promote open spectrum. Specifically, Congress and the Federal Communications Commission (FCC) should take four steps:

- Establish rules to foster more effective cooperation among unlicensed users.

- Set aside more spectrum for unlicensed uses.

- Abolish restrictions on nonintrusive underlay techniques across licensed bands.

- Promote experimentation and research in unlicensed wireless technology.

Existing unlicensed bands offer a glimpse of the possibilities of open spectrum. A handful of frequencies are left open for anyone to transmit within technical parameters such as power limits.[1] Unlicensed bands are congested and devoid of interference protection. Indeed, the most widely used, at 2.4 GHz, is so crammed with microwave ovens, cordless telephones, and baby monitors that it is known as "the junk band." Yet it is the site of the most explosive phenomenon in the wireless world: Wi-Fi.

Wi-Fi (IEEE 802.11) is a protocol for unlicensed wireless local area networks, which offer high-speed data connections within a few hundred feet of an access point. A market that did not exist five years ago now generates over $2 billion annually and continues to expand despite a technology recession. There are thousands of public access points in the United States, and hundreds of thousands more in homes and businesses. Several million laptops are equipped with Wi-Fi cards, and most laptop vendors are building Wi-Fi into their newer models. Venture-backed start-ups are springing up to improve Wi-Fi technology and apply it to new markets, such as residential broadband access.

But Wi-Fi represents only a fraction of open spectrum's potential. If the U.S. government pursued full realization of open spectrum, it would achieve several vitally important policy goals while shifting away from heavy-handed regulation toward a free-market environment in which innovation and service quality matter more than government-granted privileges. Open spectrum is rooted in well-established engineering techniques and mainstream economics, and its viability has been proven in mass-market implementations involving millions of users.

The Battle over Spectrum Policy

For all its benefits, open spectrum represents a challenge to traditional ways of thinking. Licensed users fear that open-spectrum techniques will generate interference that harms their businesses or important public services. Incumbents will seek to preserve the inflated values of their government-issued licenses. Some economists who advocate turning spectrum into private property have been unwilling to acknowledge that open spectrum is even more market-based than the approach they favor. These and other groups argue for actions that would hamstring open spectrum. The concerns they raise are legitimate, but their worries are unfounded. Spectrum policy is full of mistaken assumptions that have guided decision making for too long:

1. *Wireless spectrum is scarce.* Spectrum appears scarce because our current regulatory regime puts strict limitations on its use. If multiple users were allowed to share frequency bands dynamically, and to cooperate to improve efficiency, spectrum could be as abundant as air in the sky or water in the oceans.

2. *Auctions are the best mechanism to put spectrum into the marketplace.* Conventional wisdom holds that auctions are the only efficient mechanism for spectrum assignment because they leverage market forces. Auctions have benefits, but they force service providers to pay high up-front costs and grant what amounts to a monopoly over certain frequencies. Allowing companies to compete through innovation while sharing the spectrum as a common resource is in many cases a superior approach.

3. *Massive capital investment is needed to exploit the spectrum.* Licensed service providers, such as cellular telephone operators and television

broadcasters, must build out expensive distribution networks before
they can deliver services to customers. Often they must also pay for
the spectrum itself in auctions. These huge capital expenditures
must be recovered through service fees. In an unlicensed environment, access to the airwaves is free, and the most significant expense—
intelligent radios—is borne directly by end users.

4. *The future of wireless lies in third-generation (3G) systems.* Although
   3G represents a useful advance in cellular technology, spectrum
   and build-out costs for 3G will be enormous. Many wireless data
   services could be more efficiently delivered through unlicensed
   short-range technologies, reserving wide-area 3G service for situations in which those alternatives are unavailable.

5. *Wireless technologies are not viable solutions to the last-mile bottleneck.*
   The last mile poses special challenges for wireless systems. These
   hurdles may be overcome through unlicensed systems that use
   long-range communications, wideband underlay, or meshed architectures. Given that cable and telephone wires into the home are
   controlled by dominant incumbents, and that extending fiber to
   every home would be enormously costly, open spectrum represents the best hope for a facilities-based broadband alternative.

Thinking Differently About Wireless

First, let's explain in detail what we mean by the term *open spectrum*.

Open Spectrum Defined

Most wireless frequency bands are licensed, which means that the government grants an entity the exclusive right to transmit on a particular frequency.[2] Transmission in the band by any other party is prohibited as
"harmful interference." This regime is considered necessary because the
alternative would be a "tragedy of the commons": a chaotic cacophony in
which no one could communicate reliably.[3] The tragedy-of-the-commons
idea resonates with our intuitions. After all, too many sheep grazing in a
meadow use up all the grass. Too many cars on a highway cause traffic
jams and collisions. Why should spectrum be different?

But spectrum *is* different. It is different because it is nonphysical, and
because new technologies make it practical to avoid the tragedy of the

commons. These technologies allow more than one user to occupy the same range of frequencies at the same time, obviating the need for exclusive licensing.[4]

Open spectrum is an umbrella term for such approaches.[5] As used here, the concept encompasses established unlicensed wireless technologies like Wi-Fi. But the existence of Wi-Fi does not obviate the need for further action to facilitate open spectrum. Wi-Fi was designed for short-range data communication within the limitations of current spectrum rules. It therefore requires wired "backhaul" connections to the public Internet. Moreover, existing unlicensed bands and technical standards are not optimized for efficient spectrum sharing. Enlightened policies will allow the emergence of self-contained open-spectrum systems that can handle a range of services and environments. A true open-spectrum environment would foster the same degree of openness, flexibility, and scalability for communication that the Internet provides for applications and content.

There are two ways to implement open-spectrum technologies. The first is to designate specific bands for unlicensed devices, with rules to foster coexistence among users. This approach allowed Wi-Fi to flourish in the 2.4 GHz and 5 GHz bands. The second mechanism is to "underlay" unlicensed technologies within existing bands without disturbing licensed uses. This approach, epitomized by the ultrawideband (UWB) technology that the FCC authorized in 2002, effectively manufactures new capacity by increasing spectrum efficiency. Underlay is achieved by using an extremely weak signal or by employing agile radios able to identify and avoid competing transmissions.[6]

Underlay approaches will eventually be more significant because they can work across the entire spectrum rather than requiring designated parks. If underlay is successful enough, we may not need licensed bands at all someday. But the important point today is to facilitate both unlicensed bands and underlay in keeping with technological capabilities and market demand. Enabling such development calls for four steps: eliminating hindrances codified in existing rules, creating more unlicensed bands, establishing rules to facilitate new forms of underlay, and funding research into next-generation technologies.

The Ocean Analogy

We are accustomed to thinking of the radio spectrum as a scarce physical entity, like land. Charts illustrating the partitioning of the spectrum, and auctions of geographically defined rights to slices of the airwaves, reinforce the notion of the physicality of spectrum. This is a mirage. There are only signals, transmitters, and receivers. What we call "spectrum" is simply a convenient way to describe the electromagnetic carrying capacity for the signals. Moreover, the spectrum is far less congested than we imagine. Run a spectrum analyzer across usable radio frequencies and mostly you will hear silence. Even in bands licensed for popular applications like cellular telephones and broadcast television, most frequencies are unused most of the time.[7] This is so because spectrum allocations assume dumb devices with rudimentary ability to distinguish among signals, thus requiring wide bands with large separation.

With today's technology, the best metaphor for wireless is not land but oceans.[8] The oceans are huge relative to the volume of shipping traffic, and pilots maneuver to avoid collisions. (Ships "look and listen" before setting course.) General rules define shipping lanes, and a combination of laws and etiquette define how boats should behave toward one another. A regulatory regime to parcel out the oceans to facilitate safe shipping would be over-kill.[9] It would sharply curtail the number of boats that could use the seas simultaneously, raising prices in the process. The same thing is true of spectrum. Allowing users to share spectrum, subject to rules that ensure they do so efficiently, would be far more effective than turning over more spectrum to private owners.

The Crowded-Room Analogy

If the idea that many users can coexist in the same spectrum sounds counterintuitive, another analogy might help. Wireless communication in the radio-frequency spectrum is fundamentally similar to wireless communication in the acoustic spectrum, or speech. Imagine a group of people in a room. Everyone can converse simultaneously, even with music playing in the background, as long as people speak at normal volume. If someone starts yelling, other speakers will have to speak louder in order to be heard. Eventually, people in one part of the room will be unable to communicate, and each additional person who starts yelling will further reduce the total number of conversations. We could call this a tragedy of the commons. We could enact laws giving certain individuals the right to speak during a defined period, ensuring that they can shout without interference. But that would be an unnecessary solution with negative consequences.

Recall the original scenario. What allows multiple simultaneous conversations is that the speakers are modulating their voice levels, and the listeners are able to distinguish one conversation from another. It's the intelligence at both ends of the conversation, not the integrity of the signal, that allows for efficient communication. The same thing is true in the radio frequencies. Intelligent reception devices can distinguish among more simultaneous transmissions than can simple ones. The more sophisticated and agile the system, the more the overall carrying capacity of the spectrum increases.

One might protest that the crowed-room analogy breaks down if people want to communicate across a room. But in fact many such conversations can occur simultaneously, and careful listeners can pick out individual speakers. Now imagine that the people in the room could pass messages on paper. By cooperating to relay communications, they could significantly increase the number of intelligible conversations, especially over long distances. Relaying and other cooperative techniques can serve the same function in the wireless world.[10]

As this analogy suggests, the term *interference* is problematic. Radio waves at the relevant frequencies do not bounce off one another; they pass through each other cleanly, like intersecting ripples from two stones thrown into a pond.[11] Overlapping signals simply make it harder for a receiver to distinguish one from another. "Interference" is thus contingent on real-world factors. Again, this should not be surprising. If two television sets sit next to one another, and the picture is sharp on one but fuzzy on the other, the difference is that one has a better tuner. Do we register interference when it shows up on one set or both? Should the least well-designed set define the requirements for all? What if a hypothetical set with certain characteristics *might* experience a degraded picture in that location? Under current spectrum policy, such hypothetical interference prevents frequency sharing.

The rules we adopt will influence behavior. If interference is defined with reference to a dumb receiver, vendors will save money by making receivers as dumb as possible. If there is no guarantee of spectrum exclusivity, on the other hand, manufacturers will have the opposite incentive: they will build devices robust enough to handle a variety of situations, bounded by the technical rules for use of the spectrum band. Those who build transmitters or deliver services over the spectrum will respond to similar incentives. The point is not that the least restrictive environment is always best. It is that our current system assumes, without justification, that an exclusive licensing regime is the only viable answer.

Technologies of Wireless Freedom

There are three main techniques for magnifying the efficiency of wireless devices in a shared environment: spread spectrum, cooperative networking, and software-defined radio.

Spread Spectrum

In a spread-spectrum system, wireless communications are digitized and chopped up into pieces that are spread across a range of frequencies.[12] The receiver pieces the message together at the other end. Because a given frequency carries a tiny part of each communication, it is only occupied for a tiny slice of time. If another message is occupying that slot, only that portion of the signal must be resent. Invented in the 1940s, spread spectrum has been used for military and other applications that require robustness and resistance to jamming and eavesdropping. (Only the receiver knows how the signal is spread across the range of frequencies.) Today many mobile phone services use spread spectrum to improve efficiency within licensed bands, but the technique is more powerful when used for underlay or in unlicensed bands.

Cooperative Networking

The capacity of a wireless system is influenced by its architecture. A broadcast television network allows for many receivers but only one transmitter. By contrast, cellular telephone systems use a hub-and-spoke architecture of cells and towers to allow people to both place and receive calls. But hub-and-spoke architecture is not the best we can do. If the end-user devices were to cooperate with one another by relaying the signals of other users, the system could be more efficient.[13] With cooperation, adding users increases supply as well as demand. One form of cooperative network is *meshed architecture*, whereby every transmitter also serves as a relay. A user need only communicate with one other user, rather than with a central tower, to send a signal anywhere on the network. Some cooperative networks can be deployed *ad hoc*, meaning that any new nodes automatically become part of the network.

Software-Defined Radio

Every radio can be tuned to pick up a certain range of frequencies, and the tuning is traditionally fixed in the radio hardware. Thus, the same radio can't pick up both FM radio and mobile phone transmissions, or both 2.4 GHz and 5 GHz wireless LAN signals. Software-defined radios, by contrast, can tune dynamically over a wider range of frequencies. They can also receive or transmit different kinds of wireless transmissions automatically. A so-called agile radio can adapt to the local environment and seek out open frequencies.[14] Even in licensed bands, most of the spectrum is empty most of the time. Agile radios can take advantage of that empty space, moving out of the way when another transmission appears.

All these techniques are the subject of academic research and corporate R&D. Even so, licensed spectrum has been the dominant paradigm for so long that there is still a lot we don't know about how radios work. We do know that many of our intuitions are wrong. Research shows that factors we would expect to reduce the capacity of a system—such as adding more transmitters, creating more paths for signals to travel, and putting receivers in motion—can actually increase capacity.[15] This is so because the more data about the surrounding environment a smart receiver possesses, the better it does at distinguishing the desired signal. The commercial viability of any system using these techniques will depend on business conditions. This is one reason that government policies should promote both designated unlicensed bands and underlay approaches in licensed bands.

The Myth of Scarcity

We still regulate the radio spectrum based on the technology of the 1920s. Spectrum licensing arose in the 1920s because primitive radio receivers were unable to distinguish well between different transmissions. Thus, the only way for multiple users to share the spectrum was to divide it up. In 1912, the failure of nearby ships to respond to the *Titanic*'s distress calls had prompted calls for regulation. By licensing spectrum to broadcasters, and imposing wide separations between bands, the government ensured that receivers could distinguish signals.

The exclusive-licensing model was almost certainly the right approach when it was developed, and it has been in place for so long that we take it for granted. But our approach to spectrum is an anomaly: we shrug at intense government regulation of communications over the airwaves that would be unconstitutional in other media. After all, wireless communication is speech. Under the First Amendment, the government faces a high burden in justifying any law that defines who may communicate and who may not. Yet Congress and the FCC routinely determine who may broadcast on certain frequencies, and regularly shut down "pirate" radio broadcasters and others who flout the rules.

The rationale for limiting speech over the airwaves is that the alternative is chaos. Spectrum is scarce—so the argument goes—so the number of speakers must be restricted, or no one's message will be intelligible in the cacophony of interfering voices.[16] As we have seen, though, that scarcity is not an immutable property of a physical resource. It's a historically and technologically contingent judgment.

Much has changed technologically since the 1920s. And, indeed, there has been a corresponding shift in the government's approach to spectrum assignment. Auctions have replaced outright grants, competitive hearings, and lotteries as the tool of choice. Beginning with Ronald Coase's seminal 1959 article, "The Federal Communications Commission," economists have argued persuasively that competitive bidding is the most efficient way to assign scarce licenses among competing users.[17] Starting with the personal communications service (PCS) auctions of 1994, the FCC has raised over $30 billion for the U.S. Treasury and delivered substantial new spectrum to the marketplace.

Most debate about spectrum policy today involves variations of the auction concept. Some parties advocate secondary markets or moving from licenses to fee-simple ownership, while others propose combining auctions with annual lease fees after the initial license period.[18] These debates, intense as they are, remain within the confines of the exclusive-licensing paradigm. If we decide to license wireless frequencies, there are important questions about how best to do so. But why take licensing for granted?

A Spectrum Commons

Capacity-magnifying techniques like spread spectrum, cooperative networking, and software-defined radio make it possible to view spectrum as something other than a physical resource that must be allocated through licensing. Portions of the radio spectrum could be treated as a commons.

A commons, like the air we breathe and the language we speak, is a shared, renewable resource. It is open to all. It is not necessarily completely free or inexhaustible, but if users follow commonsense rules to prevent depletion, the commons can *seem* limitless. A commons is entirely compatible with competitive capitalism. The key is that the marketplace exists among users of the commons; the commons itself cannot be bought or sold. We have no trouble accepting the automobile and trucking industries, which depend on public highways that are free to use and maintained by government. And we accept that anyone can drive on a highway, but that everyone has to observe speed limits and other safety rules. Public roads even coexist with private toll roads, but we don't conclude that privatizing all roads would improve the quality of transportation in the United States.

A spectrum commons works just like the highways. Government defines the scope of the common resource and establishes rules to facilitate efficient use. In the case of spectrum, that means setting aside unlicensed frequencies, adopting rules to facilitate new "underlay commons," setting power limits and other technical standards, and responding to breakdowns.

The beauty of a spectrum commons is that it creates the right incentives. Exclusive licensing and propertization create spectrum monopolies, which seek to maximize the rents they can collect. Forcing licensees to buy spectrum at auction ensures that it goes to those who value it most highly, but it also forces the winner to recoup its up-front investment, biasing the way it uses the spectrum. In a commons environment, by contrast, companies can respond to marketplace demands by tailoring new services, since the costs of entry are minimal.

Open Spectrum in the Real World

The rapid growth of the Wi-Fi market has led to real-world acceptance of the open-spectrum concept.

The Wi-Fi Explosion

Arguments about the benefits of open spectrum have in the past been largely theoretical. Techniques like spread spectrum have been employed primarily in licensed bands and military applications. Academic research has demonstrated the benefits of a spectrum commons, but without mass-market commercial examples, few were convinced the idea could fly in the real world.

Real-world validation arrived in the form of Wi-Fi and related wireless technologies.[19] The 802.11b standard, the first to take off commercially, operates in the 2.4 GHz band and delivers data speeds up to 11 megabits per second. The 802.11a standard operates in the 5 GHz band and offers connections up to 54 megabits per second.[20]

The Institute of Electrical and Electronics Engineers (IEEE) issued the final 802.11b standard in 1999. The first mass-market implementation, Apple's AirPort technology, went on the market that year. Since then, the market has grown rapidly, with wireless cards now standard equipment in laptops. Vendors like Cisco, D-Link, NETGEAR, and Proxim Corporation are doing brisk business selling access points for home networks. On the enterprise side, more than 1 million access points are now in use in over 700,000 companies, according to the Yankee Group, a technology research and consulting firm.[21] Another research firm, Cahners In-Stat Group, foresees the Wi-Fi hardware market generating over $5 billion in 2005, excluding service revenues.[22]

Lessons of Wi-Fi

Wi-Fi is an existence proof for the validity of the open-spectrum argument, and the success of Wi-Fi demonstrates that spectrum sharing works in the real world. Without heavy-handed control by government or by service providers, an entire industry has emerged in an already crowded unlicensed band without any protection against interference from other users. That industry has developed, furthermore, with no legal protections against competing uses. Despite repeated warnings of a "meltdown," only isolated anecdotal cases of congestion among Wi-Fi users have been reported. Companies like Intel and Microsoft are devoting substantial resources to these technologies, which they would be unlikely to do if they were seriously concerned about a tragedy of the commons.

Moreover, wireless LAN technology is evolving and diversifying rapidly. Vendors are beginning to deliver hybrid 802.11a/b chipsets, and devices that add software intelligence to Wi-Fi are coming on the market. Based as it is on improvements in hardware, innovation in the Wi-Fi world is conforming to the computer-industry curve of Moore's Law.[23] Like personal computers (but unlike most telecommunications services), Wi-Fi devices become cheaper and more sophisticated every year. They are standards-based components sold in a competitive market at volumes that allow for economies of scale. These new devices become part of the network as soon as users install them. Capital investment is thus spread among users, rather than shouldered up front by a network operator. By contrast, 3G services can only be deployed after service providers build expensive network infrastructure and proprietary hardware.

Limitations of Wi-Fi devices are being addressed through market forces. For example, first-generation Wi-Fi equipment has a weak built-in security mechanism. For users concerned about security, third parties and hardware vendors developed supplemental security solutions integrated with standards-based Wi-Fi deployments. Meanwhile, an enhanced security standard, 802.1x, was recently ratified by the IEEE.

One key to the success of Wi-Fi is that it uses a different business model than traditional telecommunications and broadband services. Because the network grows incrementally with every new access point and device, there is no need for incentives to convince a monopoly service provider to build out expensive infrastructure. No one needs to predict what the killer applications will be, because users will find them on their own. The operator within a licensed service must invest in delivering services in the hope that customers will pay enough to recoup that investment. With Wi-Fi, services grow bottom-up through market forces.

There are many things Wi-Fi cannot do. For example, as a short-range LAN technology, it cannot provide universal coverage over a large area, nor is it designed for mobile scenarios such as connecting from a car. For these applications, Wi-Fi coexists gracefully with licensed services. Vendors like Nokia are building equipment that supports both Wi-Fi and licensed wide-area cellular services, allowing users to switch automatically to the best network for their immediate needs. And licensed mobile operators are beginning to enter the Wi-Fi hotspot business.

Open Spectrum and the Last-Mile Bottleneck

Unlicensed technologies could play an important role in residential broadband adoption. Today, incumbent cable and local telephone companies dominate the residential broadband market with cable modem and digital subscriber line (DSL) services. These companies control the two primary wires into homes. To deploy high-speed services, they must upgrade their networks, which requires significant investment. Most incumbent service providers now charge $45–$50 per month for broadband connections, and impose such limitations on their services as highly asymmetric bandwidth, prohibitions on home servers and virtual private network connections, and limits on streaming video usage.

The operators claim that these restrictions make their broadband offerings economically viable, though equivalent services in other countries are priced significantly lower. Subscribership is increasing, and new technologies are reducing the costs of broadband infrastructure, but many companies have raised their prices as competition dried up.

The fundamental problem in the residential broadband market is the same as in wireless: service providers must build expensive networks and define the services for which they think users will pay, then charge high rates to recover their costs. Most cable modem and DSL providers market their services as providing faster Web surfing than does dial-up access. Many end users don't find this compelling, especially at $50 per month. Unlike the open Wi-Fi market, there is no incentive for innovators to roll out new service offerings or better technology, because everything must go through the network owner.

Standard Wi-Fi technology provides only short-range connections, to a range of approximately three hundred feet, insufficient for most residential broadband deployments. For broadband to be delivered to a home, the home must connect to a high-speed Internet trunk, which can be shared among many customers. Thus, having a fast Wi-Fi connection in a house does not substitute for DSL or a cable modem, because the wired connection is still necessary to reach the public Internet. Nevertheless, there are several ways that unlicensed wireless devices could deliver last-mile broadband service. Companies like Tropos Networks, MeshNetworks, and SkyPilot have created systems that use meshed architecture: rather than connecting to a central hub, each device can send information to every other device within range. As we saw earlier, information can be routed through the network via many different paths, depending on capacity, line of sight, and other characteristics. The mesh approach circumvents shortcomings that hobbled earlier fixed-wireless systems in the last mile.

Other companies, such as Alvarion and Motorola, have created proprietary technologies on top of Wi-Fi radios to allow significantly increased range in traditional point-to-multipoint deployments. Operating in the unlicensed 5 GHz band, Motorola claims that its Canopy technology can serve up to one thousand two hundred subscribers from a single access point at a range of up to two miles. Unlicensed wireless connections could also serve as "tails" at the end of existing phone, cable, or fiber infrastructure in residential neighborhoods.

All these configurations have limitations. A mesh, for example, tends to introduce delay (latency) when traffic makes multiple hops. Metropolitan-area connections may not match the subscriber density of shorter-range

Wi-Fi links. And as with any wireless service, connection quality depends on physical geography and the local spectral environment. As a result, it is unlikely that unlicensed technologies will account for the majority of broadband connections in the foreseeable future. Even with a small share of the market, however, wireless last-mile systems would foster competition and innovation. Wired broadband providers would have to improve their offerings or lower costs to compete.

Demand Pull

Even if they are not used as the primary connection method, unlicensed wireless technologies will influence the broadband market. Wi-Fi access points are being widely deployed for home networking: users install these devices to share broadband connections among several computers, share peripherals such as printers, or give themselves untethered Internet access anywhere in the house. Digital consumer electronics devices are beginning to incorporate Wi-Fi connections as well. For example, Moxi Digital (which recently merged with Digeo Inc., a company funded by Microsoft cofounder Paul Allen) incorporates an 802.11a transmitter in its personal media center, making it possible to stream high-quality audio-video among TVs and stereos throughout a house. Intel is spearheading a standards effort to allow Wi-Fi to interoperate with FireWire (IEEE 1394), a wired standard popular for digital media applications.

As home networks and related devices proliferate, they will create a "pull" for broadband applications. Wi-Fi hardware is becoming cheap enough for hardware manufacturers to include it without greatly affecting device prices. As users buy laptops and electronics hardware with built-in high-speed wireless connections, they will find new uses, such as sending music files from a computer to a stereo system or sharing downloaded pictures. Many of these applications will benefit from broadband connections into the home. Wireless devices will therefore stimulate broadband demand even if the last-mile connection is wired.

Policy Recommendations

Open spectrum is not inevitable. Technologies now available or in development will pave the way for a more open and efficient wireless environment, but without the right policy framework, those technologies may not see the light of day. Wi-Fi cannot simply evolve into the full realization of open spectrum. If the United States wants to enjoy the benefits of open spectrum, we must facilitate it.

First, Do No Harm

Despite its promise, open spectrum profoundly threatens the status quo. It represents potential competition for existing services, wireless and wired. It also runs counter to prevailing assumptions about which policies are market-based. Unless policy makers have a clear understanding of open spectrum's implications, they could prevent it—deliberately or inadvertently—from reaching its potential. The FCC and Congress must take care that threats from incumbent industries do not undermine the potential of unlicensed technologies.

Requests for Regulatory Protection

SIRIUS Satellite Radio filed a petition with the FCC in 2002 seeking restrictions on Wi-Fi based on trumped-up alarm about interference with its adjacent licensed satellite transmissions. Though SIRIUS had not yet even launched its service and the potential for interference was minimal, it wanted restrictions and new device requirements imposed on the Wi-Fi industry. The SIRIUS petition was withdrawn in response to serious objections, but it suggests how licensed users could seek to hamstring unlicensed alternatives. Wireless operators may rely on similar tactics and legal maneuvers to prevent unlicensed services from encroaching on their markets.

Spectrum "Propertization"

If the FCC were to give spectrum licensees full ownership rights, the availability of spectrum for unlicensed uses would shrink significantly. Companies that pay for control over frequencies need to recoup their investments and will want to exclude competing users. Even if spectrum owners collected tolls from unlicensed use, the transaction costs would be substantial. Worst of all, propertization is a one-way street. Once spectrum becomes private property, converting some of it to unlicensed "parks" or eliminating restrictions on band sharing could require costly eminent-domain proceedings. Giving spectrum licensees greater flexibility or opportunities to engage in secondary-market transactions may make sense, but further propertization would have very negative consequences.

Backhaul Discrimination

Unlicensed wireless data devices must at some point connect to the public Internet. For point-to-multipoint systems like Wi-Fi, a local access point connects to a wired data connection such as a T1 line to deliver traffic to the Internet. Bringing data from local access points to a central high-speed link is known as *backhaul*. Backhaul typically employs the wire of local telephone companies, which are not typically subject to competitive pricing pressure. Moreover, if telephone companies come to view unlicensed wireless as a threat, they may seek to prevent wireless services from connecting to their networks. An advantage of meshed networks and systems that combine short-range unlicensed "tails" with long-range unlicensed "backbones" is that they cut down on the need for wired backhaul connections. Until such alternatives are widely available, the FCC should police anticompetitive behavior and reject rule changes that would allow telephone companies to discriminate in the provision of wireless backhaul.

Affirmative Steps

Meanwhile, policy makers should take steps to facilitate open spectrum. Most existing unlicensed wireless services, including Wi-Fi, operate in the 2.4 GHz and 5 GHz bands. These bands are relatively narrow, at high frequencies that limit their propagation, and they are subject to many competing uses. Though unlicensed devices can coexist in apparently crowded spectrum, their ability to do so is not absolute. Moreover, Wi-Fi's software protocols lack the adaptive and cooperative characteristics of truly scalable unlicensed networks. Current FCC rules have done a reasonable job of setting conditions that allow for innovation and market growth, but a four-step government program is needed to make open spectrum a reality:

- Promulgate rules to foster more effective cooperation among unlicensed users.

- Set aside more spectrum for unlicensed uses.

- Abolish restrictions on nonintrusive underlay techniques across licensed bands.

- Promote experimentation and research in unlicensed wireless technology.

All four elements are important. Wi-Fi, other unlicensed technologies in designated bands, and underlay are all part of the answer. Furthermore, the mix will change over time: existing unlicensed bands are delivering value today, but the long-term winners will be new approaches designed for open spectrum. The only way market forces can find the best solutions is to give alternative approaches a chance. By announcing a comprehensive open-spectrum agenda, the U.S. government would embolden investors and technologists to devote resources to making open spectrum a reality.

Fostering Effective Cooperation

The first step is to enhance existing unlicensed bands, which were not designed with open spectrum in mind. The FCC should work with the private sector and the technical community to identify minimal requirements to facilitate efficient spectrum sharing. One near-term outcome could be service rules for the 5 GHz band to foster growth of wireless data networking applications. Such rules should not predetermine technology or applications, but could mandate, for example, devices capable of two-way packet-switched communications. The FCC should also identify obstacles in its existing rules, such as outmoded prohibitions on repeaters, whose elimination would promote spectrum sharing.

In the future, as it establishes new unlicensed bands and eliminates underlay restrictions, the FCC could define more "rules of the road," either as requirements or as advisory best practices. For example, companies could be encouraged to build devices that modulate output based on actual conditions and/or that repeat traffic for other users, enabling meshed architectures.

Rules should be defined in consultation with industry representatives and technical experts to ensure that they do not over- or underspecify standards. Accommodations should be made for uses of spectrum other than data networking, including scientific activities like radio astronomy. Different rules could apply to particular bands or techniques. Whatever decisions are made will need to be reviewed periodically as conditions evolve.

Expanding Unlicensed Spectrum

Improving existing unlicensed bands is not enough. Most are so narrow and congested that their utility for open spectrum is limited, and the high frequency of the most prominent bands limits signal propagation. Lower-frequency spectrum that penetrates weather, tree cover, and walls would facilitate services like last-mile broadband connectivity. The FCC should identify additional spectrum bands that can be designated as unlicensed "parks," with a focus on frequencies below 2 GHz where propagation is best. The FCC will need to consult with other agencies like the Department of Defense, the Federal Aviation Administration, and the Department of Commerce; with technical and scientific organizations like the National Academy of Sciences and the IEEE; and with the private sector. Furthermore, the U.S. government should work through the World Radio Conference and other international forums to create global unlicensed bands wherever possible.

There are many possible sources for additional unlicensed spectrum. The 5 GHz unlicensed band could be expanded relatively easily, a move that would also help bring the U.S. allocation in line with that of other countries. Because of its limited propagation capabilities, however, 5 GHz should not be seen as a long-term solution. Creating unlicensed spectrum parks elsewhere would require relocation or other accommodations of existing users, a process that the commission has not hesitated to pursue in the past.

Removing Constraints on Underlay

The FCC's 2002 approval of ultrawideband was a major step forward. The commission rejected overblown predictions of interference, relying on technical data and prudent restrictions on UWB deployment, but its initial rules put overly severe limits on where and how UWB can be used. If fears of interference prove ungrounded, the FCC should loosen its restrictions without delay.

The FCC should look at other ways to facilitate underlay of unlicensed communications in existing spectrum bands. Underlay can be achieved via either weak signals or agile receivers. As technology advances, the FCC could consider a rule allowing underlay in certain bands, provided that devices check the local environment before transmitting and vacate a frequency within a certain number of milliseconds if a licensed service appears there. Underlay could also be used as a transition mechanism in bands with few incumbents. Those incumbents could be allowed to remain in the band without current guarantees against interference.

Driving Technology Development and Adoption

The government should also find new ways to encourage development and deployment of unlicensed devices, such as liberalizing rules for experimental licenses, funding research, and using its procurement power to drive adoption of Wi-Fi or other technologies. The Defense Advanced Research Projects Agency (DARPA) of the Department of Defense has a distinguished history of supporting cutting-edge research in data networking, including the packet-switching technology that led to the Internet. Because of their military applications, DARPA has long funded research into meshed wireless networking, ultrawideband, and software-defined radio. These efforts should be perpetuated, and smooth transfer of the resulting technologies to civilian applications should be a high priority.

The FCC and other agencies should review their rules to eliminate restrictions on unlicensed devices in existing programs. For example, the FCC does not allow schools and libraries subsidies for unlicensed networking devices because they do not constitute a communications "service." Government should not try to pick winners among competitors in the marketplace; it should work in tandem with the private sector to ensure that innovative technologies reach their potential. Alongside these specific steps, the FCC and Congress should maintain their efforts to foster investment and competition in communications. Open spectrum will flourish in a growing market.

A Near-Term Opportunity in 700 MHz

The forthcoming revival of analog television spectrum will provide an opportunity to put some of these policies into practice. Congress has directed the FCC to auction the 700 MHz spectrum now occupied by broadcast channels 60–69. (The auction has been delayed several times.) Because of its propagation characteristics, the 700 MHz spectrum could make an excellent unlicensed wireless park, a scenario that could not be contemplated when plans were first drawn up for revival of that spectrum. Congress should designate some or all of the 700 MHz spectrum for unlicensed devices. The FCC could allow, as a transitional mechanism, only underlay uses that do not intrude on incumbent licensees.

Conclusion

We are laboring under a faulty set of assumptions about spectrum. We take it for granted that companies must pay for exclusive rights to spectrum, and that they must invest in significant infrastructure build-out to deliver services. We also take for granted pervasive regulation of how spectrum is used, which would be intolerable in any other medium so closely linked to speech. We assume that market forces, if they are allowed into the wireless world at all, must be restricted to choices among monopolists rather than allowed to foster free competition. Open-spectrum technologies force us to rethink our assumptions about wireless communication. Making more efficient use of the spectrum we have can effectively eliminate the capacity constraints that currently limit wireless voice and data services. By opening up space for innovation, more efficient use of spectrum could foster new applications and services. It could provide an alternative pipe into the home for broadband connectivity. And it could allow many more speakers access to the public resource of the airwaves.

Today we stand at a crucial point. Inaction or harmful restrictions on new technologies could fritter away the extraordinary opportunity that spectrum offers. We should listen to what the market and technology are telling us. Computers have made wireless devices vastly smarter; it is time for our policies to become smarter as well. Promoting open spectrum is the most democratic, deregulatory, proinvestment, and innovation-friendly move the U.S. government could make.

Notes

1. The most prominent unlicensed bands are in the 900 MHz range, the 2.4 GHz range, and the 5 GHz range.

2. Some bands are licensed for shared use, meaning that more than one entity is permitted to transmit. Other users are still prohibited from using the spectrum.

3. The "tragedy of the commons" is the tendency to overuse a scarce public resource, such as a shared field for grazing sheep. Biologist Garrett Hardin popularized the phrase in a classic 1968 essay. Garrett Hardin, "The Tragedy of the Commons," *Science* 162 (1968): 1,243–1,248.

4. See, for example, Kevin Werbach, "Open Spectrum: The Paradise of the Commons," *Release 1.0*, 19, no. 10 (November 2001): 1–26, available from the author or at http://www.release1-0.com. Also see Yochai Benkler, "Open Spectrum Policy: Building the Commons in Physical Infrastructure" (paper presented at "Saving the Information Commons," a conference of the New America Foundation, May 10, 2002), available from http://www.newamerica.net/Download_Docs/pdfs/Doc_File_122_1.pdf; and Yochai Benkler, "Overcoming Agoraphobia: Building the Commons of the Digitally Networked Environment," *Harvard Journal of Law and Technology* 11 (1998): 287, available from http://www.law.nyu.edu/benklery/agoraphobia.pdf.

5. The term is far from ideal. *Open* is a notoriously vague term in the computer world, and unlicensed wireless systems do not necessarily resemble open-source software or open technical standards. The word *spectrum* evokes an image of discrete frequency bands, precisely what open spectrum seeks to overcome. Nevertheless, because *open spectrum* is the most widely used term for the phenomenon we are describing, we employ it here.

6. Underlay is similar in some ways to low-power radio stations that can broadcast without harming high-power commercial stations in the same band. However, open-spectrum underlay is even less likely to have any noticeable effect on licensed users because it uses intelligent devices and modulation techniques.

7. Among the sixty-seven channels reserved nationwide for broadcast television, an average of only thirteen channels per population-weighted market are actually in use. The remaining "white space" is set aside to ensure that antiquated analog receivers can distinguish among the channels.

8. Futurist George Gilder made a similar analogy—"You can no more lease electromagnetic waves than you can lease ocean waves"—in a pioneering series of "Telecosm" articles in the early 1990s. See George Gilder, "Auctioning the Airways," *Forbes ASAP*, April 11, 1994, 99–110. See also Rich Karlgaard, "2002 Hangs on These," *Forbes*, January 21, 2002, 31.

9. The key is the relative lack of scarcity. Some ocean resources have become scarce: certain fish stocks, for example, have been depleted by overfishing. In those cases, economic and regulatory mechanisms make sense to allocate the scarce resource. With spectrum, we are far from this kind of scarcity.

10. Technologist David Reed calls this phenomenon "cooperation gain." See David P. Reed, "Comments for FCC Spectrum Policy Task Force on Spectrum Policy," in Federal Communications Commission docket no. ET 02-135 (July 23, 2002), available at http://www.reed.com/OpenSpectrum/FCC02-135Reed.html.

11. I have borrowed this analogy from David Reed.

12. This chapter uses the term *spread spectrum* in a general sense. An even broader term is *wideband*, applicable to any method that employs a wide channel.

13. See Reed, "Comments." For a description of one scalable architecture, see Tim Shepard, "Decentralized Channel Management in Scalable Multihop Spread-Spectrum Packet Radio Networks" (PhD diss., Massachusetts Institute of Technology, 1995), available at http://www.lcs.mit.edu/publications/pubs/pdf/MIT-LCS-TR-670.pdf.

14. Some commercial wireless systems today incorporate a degree of frequency agility, but truly agile radios are still at the research and development stage.

15. See Reed, "Comments," 13–18.

16. See *Red Lion Broadcasting Co., Inc. v. Federal Communications Commission*, 395 U.S. 367 (1969).

17. Ronald Coase, "The Federal Communications Commission," *Journal of Law and Economics* 2, no. 1 (1959): 17–35.

18. See "Comments of 37 Concerned Economists," Federal Communications Commission docket no. WT 02-230 (February 7, 2001). See Thomas Hazlett, "The Wireless Craze, the Unlimited Bandwidth Myth, the Spectrum Auction Faux Pas, and the Punchline to Ronald Coase's 'Big Joke': An Essay on Airwave Allocation Policy," *AEI Brookings Joint Center for Regulatory Studies Working Paper* 01-02 (January 2001); Arthur De Vany, "A Property System for Market Allocation of the Electromagnetic Spectrum: A Legal-Economic-Engineering Study," *Stanford Law Review* 21 (1969): 1,499; and Jora Minasian, "Property Rights in Radiation: An Alternative Approach to Radio Frequency Allocation," *Journal of Law and Economics* 18 (1975): 221. See "Reply Comments of New America Foundation, et al.," Federal Communications Commission docket no. ET 02-135 (July 22, 2002).

19. The Wireless Ethernet Compatibility Alliance (WECA) originally used the term *Wi-Fi* to designate 802.11b, and *WiFi5* for the higher-speed 802.11a standard. To avoid customer confusion, the group has changed its policy and will now issue the Wi-Fi compatibility mark to devices using both standards.

20. These are theoretical peak speeds. Under real-world conditions, 802.11b delivers several megabits per second, and 802.11a delivers several tens of megabits. By comparison,

wireline broadband connections over cable or copper phone lines (DSL) typically deliver data speeds of 1 megabit per second or less.

21. See Stephen Lawson, "Wireless LAN Use Growing Fast," *InfoWorld*, August 1, 2002, available at http://archive.infoworld.com/articles/hn/xml/02/08/01/020801hnwlangrowth.xml.

22. See "Wi-Fi: It's Fast, It's Here—and It Works," *BusinessWeek Online*, April 1, 2002.

23. Moore's Law, named for Intel's co-founder Gordon Moore, posits that micro-processor performance doubles roughly every 18 months. It has held true for more than thirty years.

16

The Balkanization of the Broadband Internet

Jonathan Zittrain

M OST OF THE CHAPTERS in this book about the broadband world focus on the broadband part of the pairing. They examine much-anticipated high-bandwidth broadband opportunities such as videoconferencing, telemedicine, interactive television, ubiquitous Web cameras, and distributed supercomputing. Broadband obstacles appear, at first glance, to reside in the economic and political dynamics of such matters as last-mile fiber deployment, wireless spectrum allocation and protocols, and the wisdom of preserving government-compelled cross-subsidizations in the long-distance and local-loop U.S. telephone markets. The policy end of these views of broadband opportunities and barriers is simply to make bandwidth available as cheaply and ubiquitously as possible. The hope is that what consumers pay today for monthly Internet dial-up access can, in the future, bring them a network pipe that will enable the dream applications of the broadband world.

World is the overlooked component of this vision—a vision that anticipates that broadband service is a fixed product. The assumption is that however it's deployed, broadband Internet will be a simple commodity, differentiated at most by tiers of service reflecting ever-faster available speeds: more money might buy a consumer greater guaranteed bandwidth. Three likely differentiators of service—geography, network topology, and application-specific reach—are rarely mentioned but vitally important. I discuss these differentiators and their worrisome implications in this chapter.

Bandwidth is indeed getting thicker, cheaper, and ever-more-saturating, just as the standard broadband-deployment model anticipates. But multiple factors are at work alongside this trend that will impede the realization of the broadband world even as the technical means to achieve it mature. Though the future may offer plentiful network access, the network itself will be subdivided into cantons crossable only under certain circumstances: if one's broadband drop is in the right location, with a respectable reputation; if one is accessing a network destination that itself has been approved by a number of entities in a position to block it; and perhaps if one is conveying data only from applications that themselves meet with network approval.

This chapter will look at three types of barriers that are turning the Internetworked world into a patchwork crisscrossed by multiple types of boundaries. If these barriers and the underlying reasons for their proliferation are not addressed, broadband will end up merely providing extra lanes to the hackneyed metaphor of the information superhighway, one open to fewer and fewer forms of transportation and then to only some drivers, carrying only certain approved cargo.

Geographic Barriers Defined by Legal Jurisdiction

Each human denizen of cyberspace is, of course, in a particular physical location. So long as it's not a boat adrift in the midst of the open ocean (a prospect given its due later in this chapter), that location is under the sway of at least one sovereign—a national government—and of regional and municipal authorities. These sovereigns have historically only fitfully insisted that the inhabitants of their respective territories adhere to some particular standard of Internet behavior, which has contributed to a sense of Internet anarchy. Such forbearance can be attributed to a number of factors.

First, the places where Internet usage has become commonplace are roughly those whose sovereigns are least worried about its direct effects. Western democracies may not see the Net as an undifferentiated good, but the fundamental idea of connecting people together, and enabling them to access and exchange unprecedented amounts of information and "content," is firmly in keeping with those countries' cultures and political ideologies. Countries like Cuba, Iran, and North Korea—charier of a populace informed by multiple sources of information—have banned Internet use altogether or severely restricted who can use it. These controls may have made it less imperative to try to control the behavior of the few who have been accorded access.

Second, the regulatory apparatus of participating countries' governments—Western or otherwise—have had little to do with the inception and growth of the Internet. By the time college students and dial-up consumers gained widespread access to the Internet in 1994—when the introduction of the Web browser and its associated protocols made content easy to access and use—the Net was a fait accompli. A phenomenon that had been quietly funded and nurtured by grant-making arms of government—specifically the U.S. National Science Foundation and the Department of Defense—was simply not on regulators' radar.

Third, the architecture of the Internet did not lend itself to simple and obvious regulatory intervention. The network's protocols were designed by informal teams of engineers from hundreds of universities and private companies, meeting over the network and in person to figure out what the network should look like and to whom to delegate tasks for making it so. There was no stable, easily controlled "Manhattan Project" team that could be given new marching orders or even financial incentives to alter their plans in keeping with regulatory preferences. By comparison, when U.S. nationwide phone companies upgraded their networks from analog to digital in the early 1990s, law-enforcement interests worried about losing the long-standing technical ability to conduct wiretaps. Digital networks could be far more difficult—even impossible—to tap with legacy equipment, and the ensuing debate about whose job it was to ensure wiretappability ended with the passage of CALEA, the federal Communications Assistance for Law Enforcement Act of 1994.[1] CALEA required telecommunications carriers to ensure the feasibility of digital wiretapping, and committed the government to pay the reasonable costs of designing and implementing such access. The Internet model has traditionally had no telephone company counterpart, and in the absence of an easily reached set of firms that could be ordered to make Internet architecture amenable to regulation of individual users, local governments may have simply thrown up their hands.

The first two of these dampeners on regulation have lost force as the Internet has matured—indeed, they are a hallmark of its maturation. No longer an experimental playground for computer scientists, the Internet invites regulation, both because of what its many mainstream users can see and create—such as threatening or subversive speech, pornography, crime-facilitating materials, and spam—and because of what they can engage in or become victims of—such as gambling, hacking, and consumer fraud. Some of these activities can be more objectionable to the liberal governments that funded the Net than they are to the repressive regimes that are more slowly permitting it a foothold.

Still, attenuation of the third factor—the technical difficulty in regulating the medium and molding its evolution—has been elusive. Even if governments now have a motive to regulate Internet behavior—and if in the service of such a motive they wish for a ready means to identify troublemaking Internet users—the problem remains that the "broadband world's" inherently global scope transcends local regulatory reach. Even when its substantive goals are widely shared, it can be difficult for one country to dovetail its enforcement objectives with another's. And because the Net's perceived ills vary from one jurisdiction to the next, concerted action for such goals as spam control, suppression of certain forms of political speech, or abolition of gambling through international agreement seems hopeless. If countries try to regulate alone, conventional wisdom holds that targets of Internet regulation can simply shift their activities to the most geographically hospitable jurisdiction while continuing to interact with Internet users worldwide.

This is why the most intriguing themes in ongoing jurisdictional and governance debates point toward a reassertion of effective local governmental control over the Internet usage of people within each locality's territorial boundaries. Such control is being asserted in two ways.

Local Control Enabled by the Source of Content: The "Check-a-Box" Solution

The French courts recently heard a case brought against Yahoo! for permitting online auctions—auctions available to everyone on the Internet—that displayed Nazi memorabilia in claimed contravention of French law. France asserted its right to demand that Yahoo! cease offering certain kinds of auctions, but only after the court chartered a three-expert panel to assess the extent to which Yahoo! could implement such a ban without having to apply it to residents of other countries.[2] The panel concluded that Yahoo! could determine with reasonable accuracy which customers were accessing its auctions from France and therefore could apply the strictures of French law to French customers without preventing, say, Americans from browsing auctions of Nazi material. Firms have sprung up to offer just such geographic pinpointing. Though far from perfect, they can sort most users geographically, and force those who wish to mask their geo-identities to undertake some burden and inconvenience if they want to appear as if they are in a location different from their real one.[3]

The search engine Google, which offers country- and language-specific variants, obeys the informal requests of German officials to eliminate potentially illegal sites from the German-language site google.de.[4] So far Germany does not appear to have additionally asked Google to eliminate such sites from those accessible to Germany-based visitors to the main google.com English-language site, but the notion of country-specific information tailoring has stuck—and German visitors to google.com are, as best Google can manage, redirected automatically to google.de.

Geolocation by online service providers is likely to become easier and more accurate over time. Global Positioning System and other locational triangulation chips are becoming cheaper and thus finding their way into laptops and cellular phones, and commercial opportunities are growing for Internet vendors to offer services on the basis of geography. Soon one might be able to step off a plane, open a laptop or handheld personal digital assistant, and find an ad for a local restaurant displayed on the first sponsored Web site one visits. To the extent that geolocation is possible, the notion of an undifferentiated "broadband world" begins to give way to one with country-based boundaries.

Wholly apart from the commercial opportunities that Web vendors may embrace from geolocation, countries can point to these new digital boundaries to require Web sites and other Internet services to ensure that content entering their physical territories is designed to hew to their laws—or simply not be sent at all. Purveyors of information under this scheme can no longer object that one country's content controls will force them to subject all Internet users to a single country's laws, because they can no longer credibly claim that Internet participation entails all-or-nothing exposure to the Net's masses. Content and service providers are left with less searing objections to the administrative burden of tailoring information for multiple jurisdictions—just as opponents of nationwide collection of state sales taxes in the United States point to the difficulties of mastering each state's sales-tax collection and remittance rules.

Many old-school Netizens, eager to maintain a global Internet unsusceptible to government control, were furious at their technologically savvy brethren for adverting to the possibility of geolocation in the Yahoo! France case. Their outrage led to partial repudiation of the court's decision by at least two members of the panel that enabled it, Internet pioneers Ben Laurie and Vint Cerf. Laurie apologized outright, and Cerf observed after the decision that "if every jurisdiction in the world insisted on some form of filtering for its particular geographic territory, the World Wide Web would stop functioning."[5] This is an overstatement, in the sense that sources of content on the Web are perfectly able to tailor their information delivery on the basis of whatever demographic they can solicit or discern from those who surf their sites. But it is completely accurate if one regards "World Wide" as an affirmative ideological value for the Internet, not just a technical description of its historically undifferentiated reach.

One can imagine a framework for Internet publishers—whether large Web site operators or individual home page designers or message board posters—where, before information goes public, the author or publisher can indicate where in the world the information is to be exposed. One could check "United States" as a whole, or select specific states. One could check or uncheck Zimbabwe, or Australia, or the European Union. Such technological flexibility, combined with countries' demands that content be filtered to hew to local laws, might induce risk-averse providers to distribute their content only where legal risk is deemed low, or where potential profit is thought to exceed such risk.[6] Users in "unchecked" countries eager for information would then be effectively denied access to it by faraway content providers anticipating the actions of zealous local governments seeking to expand local regulation into the formerly unfettered Internet space. Worse, overcautious or indifferent Internet content providers could omit "unimportant" countries from the list of locales able to view their offerings, reinforcing a digital divide even when such countries are not explicitly seeking active control over Internet content. The gleam of the World Wide Web would indeed be dulled if it became simply another window into traditional content for many surfers and an opaque window for others.

Such a scenario is not inevitable. Countries worried about being left off information providers' check box lists could pass safe-harbor legislation providing immunity as an enticement to remain on check box lists of digital destinations. Or they might index their pertinent laws to those of a country unlikely to be omitted from such lists. The call for uniform substantive law suitable for a broadband world might be strengthened as countries seek to be bunched together in the minds of content providers. Indeed, we might see the emergence of model codes to which individual countries could subscribe.

Local Control Enabled by the Destination of Content: The Pennsylvania Solution

Even with growing technical abilities to filter the information one places on the Internet according to viewers' locations, information providers may balk at abiding by foreign governments' demands. Rather than writing off, say, Saudi Arabia as an Internet destination for fear of legal liability, an on-line newspaper might continue to make itself available there—calculating that there is little Saudi Arabia can do unless the newspaper has in-country assets or other countries are willing to enforce unpopular Saudi judgments. The same reasoning may occur to individual message posters or bloggers who want to protest China's actions in Tibet, or fly-by-night pornographers and spammers who maintain no obvious central office or staff sensitive to international legal compliance regimes.

This may explain why some governments, rather than pressuring the sources of content elsewhere, are focusing on controlling Internet service providers closer to home in an attempt to localize Web surfers' online experience. Indeed, Saudi Arabia and China have both adopted comprehensive schemes whereby Internet destinations deemed to violate local law or convention are made unavailable to resident surfers.

In Saudi Arabia, all Internet traffic is routed through a proxy server at the government's Internet Services Unit (ISU), whose staff maintains a list of sites to be filtered. The Internet Services Unit acts on filtering criteria promulgated by the state and on specific filtering requests from individual state agencies. General descriptions of the criteria are available on the ISU's Web site.[7] Thousands of sites are blocked, including anonymizers and translators that might serve as easy alternative launching pads to otherwise-blocked sites.[8]

In China, thousands of routers around the country are apparently configured to simply refuse to carry packets going to or from Internet points of presence that have earned a bad reputation with the authorities. Increasingly subtle forms of filtering are also evident, such as temporarily denying access to Google to users who run searches for sensitive keywords, like the name of China's president Jiang Zemin.[9] Private companies that offer

Internet access in China have long done so only after agreeing to apply whatever filtering measures are requested by the state.

Such filtering is far from foolproof, but it can drastically increase the burden of getting desired information—especially when the absence of information is subtle, such as a missing entry on a list of search results. Peer-to-peer networks can seek to frustrate official filtering by implementing censorship-resistant technologies that mask the origination of data while replicating it across hundreds of sources.[10] But particularly when the use of such technologies can itself be monitored, and participating users can be punished in a distinctly nonvirtual way, the resources that a state can put into Internet filtering can tip the cat-and-mouse game consistently in favor of the cat.

It is no surprise that judicially isolated countries whose censorship agendas are unpopular on the international stage would turn to solutions they can apply close to home to create an Internet in keeping with local custom. But such practices are starting to take root in other settings as well. In the United States, Pennsylvania law allows the state attorney general to call a Web page to the attention of a local judge. If the judge finds it probable that child pornography is displayed on that page, the attorney general can demand that any Internet service provider with Pennsylvania customers make sure the page is not visible to those customers. There is so far only one documented instance of the Pennsylvania attorney general invoking the formal process to demand action by a local ISP; typically, the attorney general has made dozens of "informal" requests to ISPs, which have been fulfilled.[11] The threat of legal action alone can make a system of informal notifications—and corresponding blocks—sufficient.

The Pennsylvania law represents one half of a clear tension in American thinking about localizing the Internet. On the one hand, Rep. Christopher Cox of California has introduced into Congress the Global Internet Freedom Act, which would make it explicit U.S. policy to maintain the Internet as a source of information that repressive governments do not want their subjects to see.[12] Cox sees the Internet as a precious conduit for the worldwide export of democratic ideas, and contemplates subsidizing technologies to circumvent local attempts at Internet censorship. Such technologies, of course, could be used to evade the efforts that Pennsylvania—and now other U.S. states and Western countries—are undertaking to bring the Internet into line with their respective laws.

This tension is also demonstrated by a service offered by the U.S. government, through its Voice of America (VOA), to Iranian Internet users to assist them in circumventing Iranian Internet filtering.[13] The service—meant to allow Iranian users to see sites blocked within Iran—itself attempts to block access to pornographic Web sites.

Topological Barriers Defined by Network Reputation

Imposing geographic barriers upon the Internet would transform a network originally intended by its designers to be indifferent to physical borders and distances. But those who designed the network—and their heirs, who manage and run its backbones and other components today—consciously built in the prospect of another sort of barrier: a topological one.

A network has a topology, analytically independent from its physical shape. The Internet developed as a way of rigging together existing networks; it was and is a network of networks. The essential "secret sauce" of the Net is a set of open protocols that allow data to navigate this network of networks seamlessly—as if each exchange of data from point to point were conducted over a dedicated line drawn straight from source to destination rather than a series of ad hoc connections from one node to the next. These protocols enable locally connected nodes to pass data in short network hops, each step a little closer to the data's destination. Any given node is owned or managed by some entity—now, usually a private Internet service provider. These ISPs route traffic to and from their own customers within their own networks; more importantly, they convey customer traffic addressed to the rest of the Internet to other ISPs, with whom they may have transit or peering arrangements. *Transit* arrangements essentially allow an ISP to have its own larger ISP—and the larger ISP takes responsibility for trying to get the smaller ISP's customers' bits to and from the right destinations. *Peering*, an arrangement among similarly sized ISPs, is in its purest form a simple handshake: I'll route your bits headed my way if you'll route my bits headed your way. In some peering arrangements, a given ISP will agree to route other ISPs' through-traffic, even if the ultimate destination is not technically within its own customer base.

The minutiae of routing agreements are pertinent here because the scheme by which Internet routing takes place presumes a structured numeric labeling of every Internet address—structured because such addresses are clumped by ISPs. The nature of labeling and clumping enables network operators to program their routers to recognize the responsibilities they owe to data at their own borders: Do they route it onward no matter what? Do they only route it if intended for their own customers? Do they ignore it entirely? Such distributed routing is self-consciously simple, while central to network functioning. But within it lie the seeds of far more sophisticated routing—a "smart" routing based on more discerning judgments about the source of the data, its destination, and possibly the nature of the data itself.

Why would an ISP or network carrier start making such judgments and then act upon them? The reasons range from practical to mercenary to ideological.

Network-Defensive Topological Barriers

The rise of network abuse—denial-of-service attacks, false routing information, massive volumes of spam—has occasioned a need for network administrators to identify abusers and block their network access. This can be a particularly difficult task, partly because network abusers often work from multiple points of entry, notably the hijacked machines of otherwise perfectly legitimate users. More serious difficulty arises because the Internet is so distributed. Unless the particular subnetwork that hosts a given abuser takes quick action—and abusers often choose their host networks precisely because they are slow to react—other networks must notice the activity, label it, choose to act against it, and then reprogram their respective routers to ignore data coming from (and perhaps destined for) the abuser. Network operators must then decide how long to continue shunning an abuser—sometimes an innocent user whose virus-infected computer was hijacked by a hacker and who has now cleaned it legitimately wishes access restored—typically without being able to communicate with anyone at the shunned network address. In a case of "dynamic" address assignment, a hacker may release a targeted address back to an ISP's pool, at which point it is reassigned to an unsuspecting legitimate user—one who has no easy way to understand why some parts of the Net may be inaccessible, or whom to talk to about it, since as far as the user's own ISP is concerned and can detect, access is unhindered.

Fiascos of this kind are persistent and annoying distractions from ISPs' larger mission of routing packets and building out their customer bases. Yet an ISP ignores such issues at its peril, both because its own users will find their broadband experience greatly diminished by others' network abuse, or because if its own users engage in network abuse, the ISP will find itself shunned by others. As the Internet matures, it is likely that ISPs will invent more formal and systematic ways of communicating with each other to pool information about network troublemakers. ISPs that refuse to join such a pool may find their own packets assigned second-class status by pool members, fostering a new digital divide even as the physical layers necessary for broadband are steadfastly rolled out. At such a point, shopping for an ISP would no longer be a simple matter of assessing price, bandwidth, reliability, and customer service; it would also involve understanding the network's reputation with other networks. This scenario would favor larger, more established networks over smaller ones, and at its extreme might encourage wealthy Internet customers to purchase multiple Net connections from different vendors—so that if a path is blocked on one network it might be tried on a different route. (The much-heralded ability of packets to "route around" blockage is little help here, since such rerouting requires the cooperation of nearby routers; the shunning described here would not be easily circumvented by such automatic rerouting.)

Mercenary Topological Barriers

Simple peering and transit arrangements persist among ISPs. If someone as aggressive as Bill Gates ran a large Tier-1 ISP (defined as an ISP that connects primarily to other Tier-1 ISPs), would he or she do anything differently from the average ISP owner? Quite possibly. From its inception, the Internet has lacked the ability to guarantee a certain amount of bandwidth from point A to point Z. Such *quality of service*, as it is called, is difficult precisely because of hop-to-hop routing from one entity to another, with the expectation only of "best efforts" to move packets toward their destinations. An absence of guaranteed bandwidth can hobble deployment of network-intensive applications like video and even audio over broadband.

Companies like Akamai have sprung up to "forward position" Internet content at key points within the Net's topology, both spreading out demand for the same content across a patchwork of way stations (each with identical offerings), and matching a particular consumer's demand for content with the way station topologically nearest to that consumer. Whom should Akamai charge for its services? Is it the consumer through its ISP proxy, since nearer content means better throughput, or is it the supplier of content, since an ability to reach consumers worldwide without network interruption makes the supplier's content more valuable? The answer can be either, both, or something in between, and by all accounts Akamai makes different deals with different ISPs, hoping at the very least to call it even with a consumer's ISP for the "forward hosting" of content within that ISP's core network.

ISPs themselves are in a position to create and drive such deals more aggressively. Some may even wish to string together special arrangements with network partners to ensure quality of service for a larger chunk of the network. ISPs that were not parties to the deal would still have connectivity, but "best efforts" could decline to good efforts or even "some effort" or simply "effort." Cisco, the leading manufacturer of Internet routers, touts such "smart" features in its latest line of hardware.[14] The prospect of strategic behavior by ISPs has been raised before: Mark Lemley and Larry Lessig did so in a filing before the FCC, objecting to a merger of major ISPs on the grounds that cable-television providers, in their roles as ISPs, might block or slow down Internet video packets from sources that had refused to appear on the providers' non-Internet standard cable TV head-ends.[15] There is no evidence of such strategic behavior yet. But the industry has yet to find its Bill Gates, and the regulatory framework that might proscribe such behavior is genuinely uncertain.

The growing broadband world is marked by a number of fault lines, many corresponding to the borders of the myriad individual networks that the Internet comprises. So far, the centripetal force of continuing mutual compatibility has prevented these fault lines from becoming anything more than irrelevant municipal-like boundaries crossed in a packet's journeys. But they persist, and any number of strategic rationales could cause them to matter greatly.

Ideological Topological Barriers

The tools that ISPs have developed to identify and deal with network abuse could be conscripted to apply to users whose behavior is disfavored or legally sanctioned by a government—but who are not, in the narrow sense, abusing the network itself. ISPs have worked to avoid legal responsibility for the misbehavior of their own customers—or for the misbehavior of *other* ISPs' customers since they merely carry such customers' packets. They wish to act as they choose with respect to network abusers, and similarly hope to have little outside pressure in dealing with non-network-implicating abuse. Yet ISPs could find themselves asked to take action to enforce a given sovereign's laws. For example, the U.S. Digital Millennium Copyright Act of 1998 grants ISPs a substantial "safe harbor" against claims of contributory copyright infringement, since they merely carry packets, but the safe harbor applies only if the ISP "has adopted and reasonably implemented . . . a policy that provides for the termination in appropriate circumstances of subscribers and account holders of the service provider's system or network who are repeat infringers."[16] Conceivably, then, U.S. network providers could be asked by aggrieved private parties to terminate at least their own abusive subscribers' access—a direct topological barrier—and could refuse only at risk of infringement.[17]

ISPs themselves have, perhaps to their dismay, invited such regulation as they have tinkered with tools and procedures to combat expanding (and ever-more-expansively defined) network abuse. One example is an informally coordinated effort to fight spam—not simply because huge volumes of spam can disrupt a network, but because spam in any volume is considered abhorrent. Services like the Mail Abuse Prevention System (MAPS) use somewhat subjective judgments to create and maintain lists of spammers and those who abet them; ISPs can elect to filter incoming mail against the MAPS list.[18] Alternatively, ISPs could simply shun all traffic at the packet level—whether e-mail or not—from a disliked site.

This scenario is a private form of the "Pennsylvania solution" described earlier, here conceived and implemented by private parties rather than governments, and for reasons that go well beyond a fight against spam. Private barriers can be found at companies that wish to restrict what their employees can see and do on the Internet to attempt greater worker efficiency or to avoid a perceived threat of hostile workplace environment lawsuits. Such barriers can also be found where schools and libraries implement Web content filtering, either in accord with their own values or to protect government subsidies conditioned on filtering, occasioned by such laws as the U.S. Children's Internet Protection Act.[19] Filters can also be used by parents who want to restrict their kids' online activities on home PCs, attempting to restrict access to a broad range of content, whether pornography, tobacco advertising, or hate speech. (In the latter category lies the Anti-Defamation League's "Hate-Filter," a joint project with a commercial filtering company, targeted for parents who want to restrict access to neo-Nazi and other racist sites.)

Such ideological restrictions have been passionately embraced by a comparatively small corps of parents, schools, and libraries. Where these restrictions are in use, the ideological rationales of their implementers make it difficult for others to simply buy a way around the barrier in question, whether as a consumer of information or as its banned supplier. Should "open wireless networks" come to pass—networks in which consumers' wireless computers also serve as routers, eliminating ISPs entirely from the exchange of network traffic in a densely populated area—we might see consumers applying ideological litmus tests to those who seek to participate in their network: people might be willing to route friends' traffic but not that of strangers, or perhaps only traffic from certified dog lovers or gun owners or Democrats. To the extent that network connectivity is a favor or a loose exchange rather than a cash-and-carry deal under a contract, ideological effects might flourish precisely to the extent that it is possible to discriminate among users and ask that they certify themselves as members of one group or nonmembers of another.

Systemic Barriers Defined by an Endpoint Application's Reputation

Geographic barriers are intended to reinforce a state's control over users within its borders. Topological barriers are intended to reinforce a network operator's control over its network. A third type of barrier ignores the physical or logical distribution of a network's members and focuses instead on the *type* of traffic a network carries.

The Internet's framers intended an hourglass design, with a simple set of narrow protocols in the middle, anchored by Internet Protocol, resting on a large collection of physical carriers at the bottom and innumerable applications on the top. Such a design kept the network simple. Indifferent to the physical media on which it is dependent and of the nature of the data it is passing, the network need not care whether the data consisted of chunks of e-mail, instant messages, Web pages, Webcams, or Kazaa music files. This so-called *end-to-end architecture* enabled the Internet of today: a flexible metanetwork capable of subsuming existing networks. End-to-end is a technical rule of thumb, suggesting that features that might be tempting to install in the middle could more beneficially be located at the ends and handled by individual applications.[20]

End-to-end is also lately a political rallying cry—voiced with growing frequency as worries surface about "the end of end-to-end" for nontechnical reasons. Publishers alarmed about the unauthorized spread of intellectual property realize that, if properly encouraged, network intermediaries could try to choke off illicit traffic while permitting legitimate traffic to pass.

For example, different Internet applications, such as Web services, e-mail, and Kazaa, typically use different "ports." A given port can be allowed or disallowed by any ISP along the data's path; an ISP that blocks an application port is functionally blocking use of the application itself. Some in the Internet technical community have considered *selective port blocking* by ISPs as a way of combating the spread of viruses where end users have proved unable or unwilling to take appropriate countermeasures along their "edge" of the network. A recent paper titled "Internet Service Providers: The Little Man's Firewall?" broaches the idea of blocking slightly inward from the edge, and the author seems aware how heretical his ideas might seem to his peers since it violates the end-to-end rule.[21] His suggestion is thus tentative and limited.

The mainstream music and video industries may have no such qualms about calling for systemic blocks and controls in the heart of the network. Of course, such moves breed countermoves, and applications unpopular with publishers (or by ISPs conscripted to help them out) can work to disguise their data and port assignments to resemble more innocuous network activities. But this cat-and-mouse game imposes costs on the participants—particularly the mice—and mainstream publishers are eager to play it while they work to establish fully licensed music and video Internet distribution services.

The ability to throttle traffic on an application-by-application basis presents the emerging broadband world with a thorny issue. More important, though, is the thought that the default rule of the network engineers' hourglass could be inverted: ISPs might be induced to offer Internet connectivity only for approved and certified applications. Approval and certification of applications could entail any number of government-mandated or industry-managed hurdles, motivated in the first instance by a desire to stanch the flow of pirated copyrighted material. We can see a version of this scenario already on some corporate and hotel networks. Whether for security purposes or to funnel users to particular activities and Web sites, Internet access can be limited to a highly circumscribed set of tasks. The Tivos of today and the PCs of tomorrow might connect to networks only for previously approved purposes. Existing applications run by large players would be grandfathered in; unheard-of killer apps written by two people in a garage could no longer simply be set loose for anyone to try, as the Gnutella file-sharing service once was.

Such systemic barriers are deeply offensive to the values of Internet designers, and they represent a drastic transformation of today's Net from an engine of innovation to little more than interactive cable television.

ISPs have some reason to fight this transformation (after all, they benefit whenever people have new reasons to use the Net) and plenty of reason to embrace it (after all, many belong to corporate structures with an interest in copyright protection, all of which would benefit if publishers trusted the online environment enough to use it as a primary delivery vehicle for their content). The managed network counterparts to the unmanaged Internet—cell phone networks, cable-TV networks, satellite systems—are both less inspired in their range of uses and far more enticing to publishers as vehicles for reaching their markets precisely because of their consumer limitations. As ISPs compete with these managed networks, adding a bit of "management" to the Net's chaos could prove an appealing prospect.

Conclusion

Is there any way for enthusiasts about a broadband world—those who assumed that the *world* part of the equation would take care of itself if the *broadband* were physically brought to the four corners of the world—to ensure continued global reach for the Net, speaking both geographically and in terms of its baseline principles of nondiscrimination among users and uses?

Perhaps. ISPs ought to think carefully about where they stand on an open Internet. No ISP is fond of a principle that could constrain future business models, including those that depend on network discrimination. But now that ISPs are beginning to deploy in developing countries, they ought to consider conditioning service on a "bill of rights" for Internet users intended to head off government intervention. In cases where governments can choose among competing ISPs—or license only those that meet certain requirements—ISPs may have little leverage when it comes to insisting on an open Internet. In other cases, the ISPs may hold the cards; the citizens of a developing country may want more from the legacy Internet than the rest of the Internet expects to gain from their participation. That asymmetry—itself a form of discrimination, real or merely perceived—might enable outside ISPs to use their monopoly status to insist on nondiscriminatory principles in Internet deployment. In-country ISPs are often so mistrustful of one another that they refuse to peer directly; thus packets from one house to another in Ghana might traverse the Atlantic twice on an elliptical trip—illustrative of the power that outside ISPs wield when internal ones fail to cooperate.[22]

Internet users, builders, and content suppliers face a choice about the Internet's future: will the broadband world be open to all, and will Internet access be a commodity whose future can be shaped by anyone who knows how to program, or will access and ability depend not just on gaining a carrier signal but also on being the "right" person doing the "right" things with it?

If anything, it is surprising that routing has remained so dumb for so long—that the grace period during which the Internet has developed unencumbered has been more than a fleeting honeymoon once the power of the Net was appreciated by mainstream governments and private firms. That grace period has now ended, and what will come next is entirely up for grabs.

Notes

1. See 47 U.S.C. §§ 1001-1021.

2. See County Court of Paris [France], Interim Court Order (November 20, 2000), *La Ligue Contre le Racisme et l'Antisemitisme et L'Union des Etudiants Juifs de France v. Yahoo!, Inc. et Yahoo France* (containing the opinions of the consultants Ben Laurie, François Wallon, and Vinton Cerf), available in English at http://www.cdt.org/speech/international/001120yahoofrance.pdf.

3. See, for example, Quova Inc.'s GeoPoint, described at http://www.quova.com/shtml/technology/tech_geopoint.shtml.

4. See Jonathan Zittrain and Benjamin Edelman, "Localized Google Search Result Exclusions: Statement of Issues and Call for Data," October 2002, available at http://cyber.law.harvard.edu/filtering/google/.

5. See Mark Ward, "Experts Question Yahoo Auction Ruling," BBC News, November 29, 2000, available at http://news.bbc.co.uk/1/hi/sci/tech/1046548.stm.

6. For an insightful discussion of this concern, and an exploration of the theories whereby a country could choose to enforce another's judgment even if it would never endorse such a judgment rendered locally, see Molly S. Van Houweling, "Enforcement of Foreign Judgments, the First Amendment and Internet Speech: Notes for the Next *Yahoo! v. LICRA* (Special Feature: Cyberage Conflicts Law), *Michigan Journal of International Law* 24, no. 3 (2003): 697–717.

7. See the Internet Services Unit's explanation of its content-filtering practices, available at http://www.isu.net.sa/saudi-internet/content-filtering.htm.

8. See Jonathan Zittrain and Benjamin Edelman, "Documentation of Internet Filtering in Saudi Arabia," December 2002, available at http://cyber.law.harvard.edu/filtering/saudiarabia/.

9. See Jonathan Zittrain and Benjamin Edelman, "Empirical Analysis of Internet Filtering in China," March 2003, available at http://cyber.law.harvard.edu/filtering/china/.

10. For one example of such a system designed specifically for anticensorship (rather than anticopyright enforcement) purposes, see "Publius Censorship Resistant Publishing System," available at http://cs1.cs.nyu.edu/waldman/publius.html.

11. See "Order of Court of Common Pleas of Montgomery County, Pennsylvania, in the Matter of the Application of D. Michael Fisher, Attorney General of the Commonwealth

of Pennsylvania, for an Order Requiring an Internet Service Provider to Remove or Disable Access to Child Pornography," (July 2002) (no. Misc 689), September 17, 2002.

12. See http://policy.house.gov/assets/ACF876.pdf.

13. For an account of the VOA service, see http://www.theregister.co.uk/content/55/32567.html.

14. See "Controlling Your Network: A Must for Cable Operators," available at http://www.cptech.org/ecom/openaccess/cisco1.html.

15. See "Written Ex Parte of Professor Mark A. Lemley and Professor Lawrence Lessig, in the Matter of Application for Consent to the Transfer of Control of Licenses MediaOne Group, Inc. to AT&T Corp.," Federal Communications Commission, 1999, CS docket no. 99–251, available at http://cyber.law.harvard.edu/works/lessig/cable/fcc/fcc.html.

16. See 17 U.S.C. § 512(a) and 17 U.S.C. § 512(i).

17. See *Harlan Ellison v. Stephen Robertson, et al.*, 189 F. Supp.2d 1051, 2002 U.S. Dist. Lexis 4166, Civ. No. 00-04321 (FMC) (C. Dist. Cal., March 12, 2002), interpreting 512(i) to require AOL to have a policy of termination of repeat infringers, but stopping short of demanding that it actually cut off such alleged infringers; the case is currently on appeal.

18. See http://www.mail-abuse.org.

19. See http://www.ala.org/ala/washoff/WOissues/civilliberties/washcipa/cipatext.pdf.

20. See J. H. Saltzer, D. P. Reed, and D. D. Clark, "End-to-End Arguments in System Design" (paper presented at the Second International Conference on Distributed Computing Systems, April 1981), 509–512, available at http://web.mit.edu/Saltzer/www/publications/endtoend/endtoend.mss.

21. See Johannes Ulrich, "Internet Service Providers: The Little Man's Firewall?" available at http://www.sans.org/rr/special/isp_blocking.php.

22. For more detail on the Internet Exchange Point (IXP) problem, see Ethan Zuckerman and Andrew McLaughlin, "Interconnection in Developing Countries (or 'The Missing Links')," available at http://cyber.law.harvard.edu/bold/devel03/modules/modIC.html.

Index

About the Authors

Jeremy Allaire

Jeremy Allaire is Technologist in Residence at General Catalyst Partners, where he focuses on identifying new investment opportunities in the areas of software infrastructure, enterprise software applications, and Internet technology. He also works with the firm's existing early-stage portfolio companies on product development and go-to-market strategies. Prior to joining General Catalyst, Mr. Allaire was chief technology officer of Macromedia following its merger with Allaire Corporation, a company he helped found. The Allaire Corporation pioneered the Internet Application Server and development tools market with industry-leading products such as ColdFusion, JRun, and HomeSite.

Mr. Allaire is a regular author and analyst of Internet technologies. In addition to remaining involved with Macromedia as a Founder Emeritus, he is a board member of the Massachusetts Interactive Media Coalition (MIMC) and privately held Applied Messaging.

Scott D. Anthony

Scott D. Anthony is a partner at Innosight, a consulting firm founded by Harvard Business School professor Clayton M. Christensen to help companies improve their ability to create innovation-driven growth. He has worked with companies in industries such as telecommunications, consumer products, medical devices, software, primary materials, petrochemicals, and communications equipment. Mr. Anthony serves as the editor of *Strategy & Innovation*, a bimonthly newsletter published by Innosight and Harvard Business School Publishing. Prior to joining Innosight, he was a senior researcher at HBS, where he coauthored (with Clay Christensen) a book entitled *Seeing What's Next: Using the Theories of Innovation to Predict Industry Change*. Scott received a BA in economics, summa cum laude, from Dartmouth College and an MBA with high distinction from Harvard Business School, where he was a Baker Scholar.

Robert D. Austin

Robert D. Austin is an associate professor at the Harvard Business School, where he teaches courses in Technology and Operations Management and chairs an executive program for chief information officers. His research focuses on information technology management and more generally on management of knowledge-intensive activities. He has written on these subjects in four books—*Creating Business Advantage in the Information Age, Corporate Information Strategy and Management* (both coauthored with Lynda Applegate and Warren McFarlan), *Measuring and Managing Performance in Organizations,* and *Artful Making: What Managers Need to Know About How Artists Work* (coauthored with Lee Devin)—as well as in academic and trade journals. Before arriving at HBS and during one recent leave from HBS, Professor Austin was a manager for multinational firms in the automotive and software industries.

Stephen P. Bradley

Stephen P. Bradley is the William Ziegler Professor of Business Administration at the Harvard Business School, where he teaches Competitive and Corporate Strategy in the Advanced Management Program, and is the faculty chair of the Executive Program in Competition and Strategy. In the past, he has served as the Senior Associate Dean for Faculty Development, Chairman of the Program for Management Development, Chairman of the Competition and Strategy Unit, Chairman of the Managerial Economics Unit, Course Head for Managerial Economics, and Associate Director of Research.

Professor Bradley's research interests center on the impact of technology on industry structure and competitive strategy. He has published a number of articles and books that deal with the convergence of information technology and telecommunications, including *Sense and Respond: Capturing the Value in the Network Era* (with Richard Nolan), *Globalization, Technology, and Competition* (with Jerry Hausman and Richard Nolan), and *Future Competition in Telecommunications* (with Jerry Hausman). He serves as a member of the board of directors of CIENA Corporation, Ameriss Corporation, and the Risk Management Foundation, Inc.

Clayton M. Christensen

Clayton M. Christensen is the Robert and Jane Cizik Professor of Business Administration at the Harvard Business School, with a joint appointment in Technology and Operations Management and General Management. His research and teaching interests center on the management issues related to the development and commercialization of technological and business model innovation.

Prior to HBS, Professor Christensen served as chairman and president of Ceramics Process Systems Corporation (CPS), a firm that he cofounded with several MIT professors in 1984. From 1979 to 1984 he worked as a consultant and project manager with the Boston Consulting Group. In 1982 he was named a White House Fellow, and served through 1983 as assistant to U.S. Transportation Secretaries Drew Lewis and Elizabeth Dole.

Professor Christensen is the author of the bestselling books *The Innovator's Dilemma: When New Technologies Cause Great Firms to Fail* which received the 1997 Global Business Book Award, *The Innovator's Solution,* and *Seeing What's Next.* Christensen's writings have been featured in a variety of publications and have won a number of awards, such as the Best

Dissertation Award from The Institute of Management Sciences for his doctoral thesis; the Production and Operations Management Society's 1991 William Abernathy Award; the Newcomen Society's award for the best paper in business history in 1993; and the 1995 and 2001 McKinsey Awards for articles published in the Harvard Business Review.

Eric K. Clemons

Eric K. Clemons is Professor of Operations and Information Management at the Wharton School of the University of Pennsylvania, where he is head of the Information, Strategy, and Economics Area. His current research involves the changes to competitive strategy, marketing, product design, and distribution resulting from the increased availability of information. He focuses on outsourcing, risk management, intellectual property rights, and channel strategies in financial services, travel, and consumer packaged goods.

He is currently a member of the editorial board of the *Journal of Management Information Systems* and the *International Journal of Electronic Commerce*.

Ellen Daley

Ellen Daley is Vice President, Client Solutions, for ArcStream Solutions Inc., where she is responsible for understanding key technology trends across devices and networks, and how these technologies can be effectively applied to deliver high-value solutions for ArcStream's clients. She works with clients to identify areas where mobile and wireless technologies can provide true business benefit to them. Prior to joining ArcStream, Ellen was a manager for Deloitte Consulting's Telecommunications practice, where she was involved in preparing 3G bid documents for several international governments.

Ms. Daley holds a bachelor's degree in physics from the Rochester Institute of Technology and a master's degree in communication engineering from George Mason University.

Thomas R. Eisenmann

Thomas R. Eisenmann is an associate professor in the Entrepreneurial Management Unit and Class of 1961 Fellow at the Harvard Business School. His current research explores management challenges in businesses that build and leverage digital networks. Professor Eisenmann teaches Managing Networked Businesses in Harvard's MBA elective curriculum. He is the editor of *Internet Business Models: Text and Cases*.

Previously, Professor Eisenmann spent eleven years as a management consultant at McKinsey & Company. As the cohead of McKinsey's Media and Entertainment Practice during the early 1990s, he directed teams addressing a broad range of strategic, organizational, and operational issues for clients engaged in network broadcasting; cable programming; newspaper, magazine, and book publishing; and motion picture production.

He is a member of the editorial board of the *International Journal on Media Management* and serves on the advisory boards of many Internet start-ups.

Virginia A. Fuller

Virginia A. Fuller is a research associate with the Technology and Operations Management Group at the Harvard Business School. Her research interests focus primarily on the application of information technology in developing countries, as well as the implementation of IT in more traditional contexts. She is currently developing case-based material for the new Information Technology Management module in Harvard's MBA curriculum. Her research studies draw from a number of international contexts, including China, the Philippines, South Africa, and India. Ms. Fuller graduated cum laude from Wellesley College.

Bin Gu

Bin Gu is an assistant professor in Management Science and Information Systems at the University of Texas at Austin. He received his PhD in Operations and Information Management from the Wharton School of the University of Pennsylvania. His research interests include information economics, management of digital business, strategic use of online information, and information-based business strategies. Dr. Gu's recent publications have appeared in the *Journal of Management Information Systems* and the *Journal of Financial Services Research*.

Ted Hanss

Ted Hanss is the Director for Enabling Technologies at the University of Michigan Medical School, leading efforts to apply innovative and emerging information and communication technologies in teaching and learning, research, and clinical service. From 1997 to 2004, while on loan from the University of Michigan, Ted was the Director of Applications Development for Internet2. He coordinated activities across the Internet2 membership aimed at building and deploying the next generation of network-based applications in support of research and education. Previously at Michigan, Ted served for several years as a senior manager in the University of Michigan's Information Technology Division. Among other responsibilities, he was Director of the Center for Information Technology Integration, a computer science research and development lab focusing on distributed systems. Ted Hanss has a BS in biology from Boston College and an MBA from the University of Michigan.

Reed E. Hundt

Reed Hundt is currently a consultant to communications firms with McKinsey & Company. He is on the board of various companies. He served four years as Chairman of the Federal Communications Commission (FCC), from 1993 to 1997. He is a graduate of Yale Law School and Yale College. He is the author of *You Say You Want a Revolution: A Story of Information Age Politics* (Yale University Press: 2000).

Jeffrey Hunker

Jeffrey Hunker is Professor of Technology and Public Policy at the H. John Heinz III School of Public Policy and Management. From 1996 to 2000 he was Senior Director for Critical Infrastructure, National Security Council, under the Clinton administration. In this capacity, he developed the first-ever national strategy for cyber security and protecting critical information, Internet, and computer systems. In 2000, he produced the Presidential National Plan for Information Systems Protection, Version 1.0, which coordinated the efforts of twenty-one federal agencies and leading private-sector companies in the high-tech, telecommunications, financial services, transportation, energy, and defense sectors. He also developed the President's 2000 Cyber-Security Summit with Internet leaders, as well as launched the Partnership for Critical Infrastructure Security, a national organization with over 130 *Fortune* 500 companies as members.

John Keane

John Keane is founder and CEO of ArcStream Solutions Inc., a privately held business and technology consulting firm that helps companies improve their sales effectiveness and achieve operating efficiencies through better integration of sales, service, and supply chain disciplines.

Prior to founding ArcStream, he worked at Keane Inc., for twelve years, supporting the company's revenue growth from $60 million to $1.1 billion. Mr. Keane was copresident from 1997 to 2000; and from 1994 to 1996, he had responsibility for Keane's Canadian and northeastern United States operations. He joined Keane's executive committee in 1995 and the company's board of directors in 1998.

Mr. Keane is a graduate of Harvard College and Harvard Business School.

H. T. Kung

H. T. Kung is William H. Gates Professor of Computer Sciences and Electrical Engineering at Harvard University. Since 1999, he has cochaired a joint PhD program with the Harvard Business School on information, technology, and management.

Professor Kung's research and writings focus on computer and telecommunications systems and their application in business. Prior to joining Harvard in 1992, he taught at Carnegie Mellon and led research projects on high-performance computer and network systems. His professional honors include Member of the National Academy of Engineering, Member of the Academia Sinica (in Taiwan), and recipient of the Inventor of the Year Award by the Pittsburgh Intellectual Property Law Association in 1991.

Panos Markopoulos

Panos Markopoulos studied computer engineering at the University of Patras, Greece, and obtained his PhD in computer and information science from the University of Pennsylvania in 2004. His dissertation concentrated on how classic models from the economics of spatial differentiation literature behave when consumers are uncertain about the exact product locations. He is currently a lecturer at the Wharton School.

Takeshi Natsuno

Takeshi Natsuno is the Managing Director of i-mode Strategy at NTT DoCoMo, where he is responsible for the strategic direction and implementation of i-mode, the world's largest wireless Internet service. He is acknowledged as one of the founders of i-mode, and was selected as one of the twenty-five most influential e-business leaders worldwide by *BusinessWeek* in 2001. Mr. Natsuno is the author of *i-mode Strategy* and *i-mode Wireless Ecosystem*.

Prior to joining NTT DoCoMo, Mr. Natsuno was an executive vice president at a venture company focused on Internet technologies investment, and worked in real estate development within the Japanese energy industry. He earned an MBA from the Wharton School of the University of Pennsylvania.

Dr. Stagg Newman

Dr. Stagg Newman is Senior Telecommunications Practice Expert at McKinsey & Company, where he provides technology and regulatory advice and strategic analysis to client teams and clients across the firm's global telecommunications practice.

Prior to joining McKinsey, Dr. Newman served as Chief Technologist at the Federal Communications Commission, where he advised the commissioners and senior staffers on strategic technology issues. Much of his work centered on the FCC's market opening initiatives for advanced telecommunications capabilities. This work included developing policy that encouraged competition in broadband access among cable companies, incumbent telephone companies, new entrant telephone companies, and broadband wireless companies.

From 1994 to 1997 Dr. Newman was Vice President, Network Technology and Architecture, Applied Research, at Bellcore, where he led the optical networking, wireless, and network access research program.

Rick Spitler

Rick Spitler is a managing director with the New York strategy consultancy Novantas. Mr. Spitler has broad experience in service industry strategy development, particularly in issues involving technology innovation and impact on corporate strategies. He has served clients in North America, Latin America, Asia, and Europe, and across the spectrum of financial services and information industries. His recent presentations and speeches focus on new customercentric business models, and reflect his client work in shaping corporate strategies around end-customer values. Mr. Spitler is a recognized expert on elasticity-based pricing and the effect of pricing strategies on customer behavior. His work on technology's impact on the evolution of the industry has formed the basis for speaking engagements, publications, and joint research activities.

Ali Towle

Ali Towle is Director of Marketing for ArcStream Solutions Inc. In this capacity she leads the company's market research efforts and manages the company's integrated marketing programs. Ms. Towle has written numerous articles regarding mobile and wireless technology for publications such as *Mass High Tech* and *Health Data Management*.

Ms. Towle's ten-year marketing career also includes positions at Fidelity Investments and the National Basketball Association. She holds an MBA from MIT's Sloan School of Management and a BA from Columbia College at Columbia University.

David M. Upton

David M. Upton is the Albert J. Weatherhead III Professor of Business Administration at Harvard Business School. He is currently course head for the required first-year MBA course in Technology and Operations Management, and has taught second-year elective courses in Operations Strategy and Operations Improvement and Information Technology. He is faculty chair of Harvard's executive course on Operations Strategy and Improvement, and has taught the operations course in the Advanced Management Program for senior managers as well as the China-based Managing Global Opportunities. More recently, he has joined the faculty, teaching Delivering Information Services, a course for senior information systems managers.

His current research project involves operations from around the world, and focuses on the application of information technology in operations, primarily on business-to-business applications of the Internet. He has written articles in numerous journals, most recently in *Management Science, Harvard Business Review, California Management Review* and the *Journal of Manufacturing Systems*. His books include *Strategic Operations: Building Competitive Advantage Through Operating Capabilities* and *Designing, Managing and Improving Operations*.

Dr. Douglas Van Houweling

Dr. Douglas Van Houweling, President and CEO of Internet2, is also a professor in the School of Information at the University of Michigan. He served as a member of the National Academies Panel on the Impact of IT on the Future of the Research University, and continues to serve as a member of the Forum on IT and Research Universities. He is the recipient of the EDUCAUSE 2002 Excellence in Leadership Award, and currently serves on the boards of Merit Network, Altarum, Cyber-state.org, Syntel, and Adaptec.

Dr. Van Houweling was Chairman of the Board of MERIT Inc., a Michigan statewide computing network, when the National Science Foundation awarded it responsibility for operation and management of the NSFNET national backbone in partnership with IBM, MCI, and the Michigan Strategic Fund in 1987. He was also Chairman of the Board of Advanced Network and Services Corporation, a not-for-profit organization that implemented and operated the world's largest Internet backbone network from 1991 until 1995.

Dr. Van Houweling previously served as the Vice Provost for Information and Technology at the University of Michigan, where he was responsible for the University's strategic direction in the information technology arena.

Kevin Werbach

Kevin Werbach is Assistant Professor of Legal Studies at the Wharton School, University of Pennsylvania. He is also the founder of the Supernova Group, a technology analysis and consulting firm, and organizer of Supernova, a leading executive technology conference.

Mr. Werbach is the former editor of *Release 1.0*, a publication that explores trends related to the Internet, communications, and computing. He also coorganized Esther Dyson's exclusive PC Forum conference for four years. His writing has appeared in *Harvard Business Review, Fortune, Wired, Slate*, the *Industry Standard, Harvard Law Review, Red Herring*, and *Business 2.0*. Mr. Werbach is also a speaker and commentator in the media, including CNN, CNBC, NPR, ABC News, *USA Today*, the *New York Times*, the *Wall Street Journal*, and the *Washington Post*.

Mr. Werbach is a fellow of the Global Institute for Communications in Japan, and serves as an advisor to several emerging technology and venture capital firms.

Jonathan Zittrain

Jonathan Zittrain is the Jack N. and Lillian R. Berkman Assistant Professor for Entrepreneurial Legal Studies, and Cofounder and Faculty Codirector, Berkman Center for Internet & Society at Harvard Law School. His research includes the technologies and politics of control of Internet architecture and protocols, the influence of private intermediaries upon online behavior, and the future of open-source software. He has a strong interest in creative, useful, and unobtrusive ways to deploy technology in the classroom. His writings on these subjects have appeared in diverse publications, including scholarly journals and the *New York Times, World Economic Forum Worldlink*, the *Boston Globe, Forbes*, and *CIO*.

Professor Zittrain became the chief forum administrator for the CompuServe Information Service in 1985 and was a regular editorial columnist for *Computer Shopper* from 1986 to 1990. He has also worked for the U.S. Department of State and served on the staff of the U.S. Senate Select Committee on Intelligence. He is a faculty fellow of the World Economic Forum.